For David
in anticipation of
future conversations!
very best wishes, Kristen Brustad

THE SYNTAX OF SPOKEN ARABIC

A Comparative Study of Moroccan, Egyptian, Syrian, and Kuwaiti Dialects

Kristen E. Brustad

Georgetown University Press
Washington, D.C.

D1598371

Georgetown University Press, Washington, D.C.
© 2000 by Georgetown University Press. All rights reserved.
Printed in the United States of America.

10 9 8 7 6 5 4 3 2 1 2000

This volume is printed on acid-free offset book paper.

The Semitic Translator font used toprint this work is available from Linguist's Software, Inc., P.O. Box 580, Edmonds, WA 98020-0580; telephone 206-775-1130.

The manuscript was prepared with Nisus Writer software, developed by Nisus Software, Inc., P.O. Box 1300, Solana Beach, CA 92075.

Geoffrey Khan's "Hierarchies of Individuation" (Table 1-1) first appeared in his article "Object Markers and Agreement Pronouns in Semitic Languages," published in the *Bulletin of the School of Oriental and African Studies* 47 (1984): 470; permission to reprint it here was kindly given by Oxford University Press.

Library of Congress Cataloging-in-Publication Data

Brustad, Kristen.
The syntax of spoken Arabic: a comparative study of Moroccan, Egyptian, Syrian, and Kuwaiti dialects / Kristen E. Brustad
p. cm.
Includes bibliographical references and index.
ISBN 0-87840-789-8 (pbk : alk. paper)
1. Arabic language--Dialects--Syntax. 2. Arabic language--Dialects--Grammar. I. Title.

PJ6723 .B78 2000
492.7'5--dc21

00-029360

To the memory of all Arabs who have died
as a result of the Gulf War
1990-

Acknowledgments

This book represents a substantial reworking of the doctoral dissertation I presented to the Department of Near Eastern Languages and Civilizations of Harvard University in 1991. After spending 1991-1996 working on other projects, I began the process of revision in the summer of 1996, supported in part by a semester teaching leave in 1997 and two summer research grants in 1997 and 1999 from Emory University. I am grateful to the Department of Middle Eastern Studies at Emory for providing a very supportive academic home, to John Samples, Gail Grella, and Deborah Weiner of Georgetown University Press for their patient support of this project, and to two anonymous readers who provided valuable feedback on the draft manuscript. I am indebted to the friends and colleagues who have contributed so much to this work over the years, reading, discussing, advising, and especially correcting, and I take full responsibility for the remaining errors.

The original research upon which this study is based was supported by a Fulbright-Hays Doctoral Dissertation Research grant for travel to Germany, Morocco, Egypt, Syria, and Kuwait in 1988-89, and greatly facilitated by the Commissions for Educational and Cultural Exchange in Morocco and Egypt, and the United States Information Service offices in Syria and Kuwait. In Kuwait, Dr. Kazem Behbehani, director of the Research Department of the University of Kuwait, arranged affiliation and living quarters at the University, and Mr. Ali al-Rumi, director of the Kuwaiti Folklore Center, put his resources and staff at my disposal. In Germany, Professor Otto Jastrow took time to meet with me and offer the wisdom of his experience in fieldwork methodology.

Field research would not have been possible without the generosity and warm hospitality of which Arab culture is deservedly proud. I will always be grateful to the many people who opened their doors and their lives to me during my fieldwork, taking time to give interviews and facilitate contacts with others: in Morocco, the Jebaris, Sidi Belkziz, Said Hamzaoui and his family, and Sarah Chayes and her friends; in Egypt, Zeinab Ibrahim and her family, Zeinab Taha and her family, and Lisa White and Muhammad al-Qawasmi; in Syria, Wajd and Samar and their friends, the Rabbats, and Dr. Jim Nesby; and in Kuwait, ʿAli al-Rayyis, and especially Mariam al-ʿAgrouga and her family.

Four people deserve special thanks for suffering through the original dissertation above and beyond the call of duty. Hulya Canbakal spent many late nights on campus keeping me company and feeding me. Michael Cooperson's reading and comments helped me sharpen vague ideas, and reassured me that I had something to say. John Eisele suffered through illegible rough drafts in record time, while somehow teaching me how to present linguistic arguments. Most importantly, my advisor, Professor Wolfhart Heinrichs, had the confidence in me to approve the project, the patience to wait while I struggled to produce, and the beneficence to extend unwavering support.

I have been privileged to study and work with many of the best people in the field. My teachers and mentors at the American University in Cairo and Harvard University managed to give me a first-rate education despite less-than-full cooperation on my part at times, and my colleagues at the Middlebury College School of Arabic 1983-1987 and 1991-1998 not only created the cross-dialectal language experience that inspired this work, but also gave freely of their time and insights.

Irrepayable debt is due: John Swanson, who set me on the academic path in the first place with a big push; my RRAALL cohorts, constant sources of inspiration, moral support, and references; Abbas el-Tonsi, who first taught me to pay attention to nuances of language structure and meaning; Ahmed Jebari, who taught me Moroccan without *teaching*–the mark of a truly gifted teacher; Nuha Khoury and Nasser Rabbat, who accepted me as a speaker of Levantine Arabic long before I (more or less) became one; Ahmed Jebari, Nadia El-Cheikh, Mohammad Abd al-Karim Taha, and Driss Cherkaoui, who out of friendship spent hours on end helping me puzzle through analysis problems and rough spots on some very poor quality tapes with the kind of dedication to the task that cannot be hired at any price; my parents, who let me get on a plane to Cairo twenty years ago; Danny Al-Batal, who graciously accepted apologies for missed dinners, trips to the park, soccer and basketball games; and Mahmoud, for all of the above, and then some.

Table of Contents

TABLES

Figures

Notes on Transcription and Glosses

Since the object of this study is the syntactic structure of the language, the transcription is more phonemic than phonetic. Hence epenthetic vowels are not marked, and short, unstressed vowels are often transcribed as schwas. Arabic /wa/ (/u/, /wə/, /wi/) *and* is usually transcribed here as /w/. Non-phonemic emphatic notation (such as /ṛ/) is omitted; emphatic /ḷ/ is marked only in the word /aḷḷāh/ *God*. When citing examples from other works, I have adapted the original notation to the system used here. The quality of /a/ and /ā/ varies a great deal across regions; this variation is not reflected in the transcription, except for deflection of final /a/ to /e/ in Syrian. Initial glottal stop /ʾ/ is marked where clearly pronounced. I have added the often silent /h/ of Syrian feminine pronoun /ha/ within brackets for morphological clarity.

Final vowel length is rarely phonemic in Arabic, and final vowels are transcribed without length except in three cases: (a) following Cowell (1964), on negating particles /mā/ and /lā/, to distinguish them from nominalizer /ma/ and conditional /la/; (b) on /fī/ *there is*, in which the length of /ī/ is phonemic (contrasting with /fi/ *in*); and (c) in cases in which the affixing of an object pronoun to a verb ending in a vowel is realized as the lengthening of that vowel (e.g., /šāfu/ *they saw* followed by /u/ *him* becomes /šāfū/ *they saw him*).

Vowel length in Moroccan is rarely phonemic. Harrell notes that vowels are either "short, unstable" or "relatively long, stable" (1962:10); he does not mark vowel length, but rather vowel quality. Caubet (1993), on the other hand, marks vowel length. Following the suggestion of an anonymous reader of the manuscript, and with the help of Dr. Driss Cherkaoui, I have marked approximate vowel length here. Moroccan labialized consonants are transcribed with superscript ^{w}, as in: x^{w}, b^{w}, and m^{w} (on labialization in Moroccan, see Harrell 1962:9-10).

In the following chart, alternate forms separated by a slash represent regional or register variants. A bar underneath a letter signals an interdental sound, a dot indicates a velarized (emphatic) sound. Symbols /č/ and /j/ represent affricates, /š/ and /ž/ fricatives, /ʾ/ is the glottal stop, and /ḥ/ and /ʿ/ indicate voiceless and voiced pharyngal fricatives.

Standard Arabic	Dialect transcription M	E	S	K	Phonemic transliteration M	E	S	K
ء	ء/أ	ء/أ	ء/أ	ء/أ	ʾ	ʾ	ʾ	ʾ
ب	ب	ب	ب	ب	b	b	b	b
ت	ت	ت	ت	ت	t	t	t	t
ث	ت	ت/ث	ت/ث	ث	t	t/s	t/s	ṯ
ج	ج	ج	ج	ج/ي	ž	g	ž/j	y/j
ح	ح	ح	ح	ح	ḥ	ḥ	ḥ	ḥ
خ	خ	خ	خ	خ	x	x	x	x
د	د	د	د	د	d	d	d	d
ذ	د	د/ذ	د/ذ	ذ	d	d/z	d/z	ḏ
ر	ر	ر	ر	ر	r	r	r	r
ز	ز	ز	ز	ز	z	z	z	z
س	س	س	س	س	s	s	s	s
ش	ش	ش	ش	ش	š	š	š	š
ص	ص	ص	ص	ص	ṣ	ṣ	ṣ	ṣ
ض	ض	ض	ض	ض	ḍ	ḍ	ḍ	ḏ̣
ط	ط	ط	ط	ط	ṭ	ṭ	ṭ	ṭ
ظ	ظ	ظ	ظ	ظ	ḍ/ẓ	ḍ/ẓ	ḍ/ẓ	ḏ̣
ع	ع	ع	ع	ع	ʿ	ʿ	ʿ	ʿ
غ	غ	غ	غ	غ	ġ	ġ	ġ	ġ
ف	ف	ف	ف	ف	f	f	f	f
ق	گ/ق	ق	ق	ق/گ/ج	q/g	q/ʾ	q/ʾ	q/g/j
ك	ك	ك	ك	ك/چ	k	k	k	k/č
ل	ل	ل	ل	ل	l	l	l	l
م	م	م	م	م	m	m	m	m
ن	ن	ن	ن	ن	n	n	n	n
هـ	هـ	هـ	هـ	هـ	h	h	h	h
و	و	و	و	و	w	w	w	w
ي	ي	ي	ي	ي	y	y	y	y

Vowels:

ا	ا	ا	ا	ا	ā	ā	ā	ā
و	و	و	و	و	ū	ū	ū	ū
ـيـ	ـيـ	ـيـ	ـيـ	ـيـ	ī	ī	ī	ī
ـَ	ـَ	ـَ	ـَ	ـَ	a	a	a	a
ـِ	ـِ	ـِ	ـِ	ـِ	i	i	i	i
ـُ	ـُ	ـُ	ـُ	ـُ	u	u	u	u
ـَو					ū	ō	ō	ō
ـَيـ					ī	ē	ē	ē
[schwa]					ə	ə	ə	ə

Abbreviations and Symbols

comp	sentence complementizer
f	feminine
fut	future
gen	genitive exponent
imper	imperative
imperf	imperfective
indic	indicative
m	masculine
nom	nominalizer
neg	negative particle
obj	object marker
p	plural
perf	perfective
prog	progressive
rel	relative pronoun
ques	interrogative particle

3	third person
*	judged ungrammatical by informants
---	indicates alternation of speakers within texts

Data Tag Abbreviations

CA	Classical Arabic
E	Egyptian
G	Gulf Arabic
J	Jordanian
K	Kuwaiti
L	Lebanese
M	Moroccan
N	Najdi
P	Palestinian
S	Syrian

Numbers (M1, K2, etc.) refer to speaker codes (see Appendix 1).

Arabic Script

The use of the Arabic script in transcribing the data is meant to serve two purposes: (a) to make the material accessible to Arabic speakers not trained in or comfortable with reading phonetic script, and (b) to highlight the close relationship among the varieties and registers of Arabic by rendering transparent the correspondence between spoken and formal registers and varieties. Hence I have adhered closely to conventions of formal Arabic orthography, which do not necessarily reflect the phonetic or phonemic values of the utterances. Short vowels are marked only as necessary as a pronunciation aid.

In cases of regular phonetic/phonemic shifts, such as /q/ to /ʾ/ in the urban dialects of Egypt and the Levant, formal orthography has been maintained. In other cases, multiple reflexes of a single phoneme coexist within a single dialect (e.g., /t/ and /s/ for standard (ث) in Egyptian and Syrian). Moroccan pronunciation of /q/ varies regionally and lexically. Kuwaiti reflexes of /q/ as /g/ and /j/, /k/ as /k/ and /č/, and /j/ as /j/ and /y/ appear to be in a state of flux. In these cases, the Arabic symbols used reflect phonetic realization. I have borrowed letters for the sounds /g/ (گ) and /č/ (چ) from the Persian script.

Morphological Glosses

Due to spatial constraints and the length of many of the examples, the morphological translation does not line up vertically with transcribed Arabic. However, care has been taken to correlate the two transcription layers so that each Arabic word or phrase corresponds to a morphological grouping linked by hyphens, and an exact one-to-one correspondence has been maintained. Morphological glosses for texts over four lines in length have been omitted except where necessary to show grammatical structure. Glosses I have added to examples cited from other works are in brackets [].

Morphemic boundaries have not been marked except for the definite article (/il-/), because rules for pronouncing /il-/ when prefixed to certain consonants can sometimes make its presence opaque. Indirect objects with preposition /li-/ are transcribed as suffixed to the verb phrase when pronounced as part of the verb phrase (as indicated by stress patterns). Where gender and agreement are not relevant to the discussion, *he* and *she* refer to human gender, *it* to non-human singular entities. Where gender or number agreement is at issue, I have used morphological notation *3ms* or *3fs*. Non-finite subordinate verbs are translated as non-finite: *he-go* rather than *he-goes*. (Kuwaiti does not make this distinction.) In dialects that use the pair of negative enclitics /mā - š/, *neg* has been marked only once. Following the convention of Arabists, verbs cited out of context are given in dictionary form, third person masculine perfective, and translated as infinitives.

Introduction

Dialectology has been an important part of linguistic research for over one hundred years.[1] During this time, it has developed schools and methods from quantitative to sociolinguistic, and explored theoretical questions on the mechanisms of language change and the nature of linguistic variability. Studies involving Arabic dialects have contributed to sociolinguistic gender theory (e.g., Haeri 1996), code-switching and formal syntax (e.g., Eid 1983, 1991, 1996), and general linguistic theory (e.g., Ferguson's [1959b] seminal article "Diglossia," which generated an entire field of linguistic inquiry).

Arabists are fortunate to count among their ranks such energetic dialectologists as Behnstedt, Fischer, Jastrow, and Woidich, whose extensive studies of Egypt, Mesopotamia, Syria, and Yemen (among others), have exponentially increased our phonological, morphological, and lexical knowledge of many areas. However, the picture remains far from complete. In addition to vast geographic and social territory that has yet to be canvassed, little attention has been paid to comparative syntactic data, and even a comparative morphological study is lacking (though enough published material for such a study exists). It is true that the large geographic area and range of variation among Arabic dialects render comparative studies difficult. But Arabic dialectology has much to offer linguistic theory precisely for those reasons. The wealth of information that may be collected and studied over such a large area, a good amount of historical evidence that can be brought to bear, as well as increasingly detailed studies on social history, all make Arabic a powerful case for testing, proving, and even generating theory.

Arabic dialectology can also contribute to our understanding of formal Arabic.[2] Mitchell and El-Hassan claim that modality, mood and

---

[1]For an historical overview of the field, see Walters (1988).

[2]Arabists use a number of terms to describe the language they study. *Classical Arabic* and *Old Arabic* refer to early historical periods, Classical to the formal, standardized variety and Old Arabic to non-standard registers (see e.g. Fischer 1995). (By "standardized" I mean following a set of largely prescriptive rules.) *Middle Arabic* refers to non-standard registers that begin to emerge early in medieval texts (see Blau 1965, 1966-67; Hopkins 1984). *Modern Standard Arabic* refers to the modern standardized register, and *dialects* to

aspect must be studied in "the mother-tongue end of the stylistic spectrum of conversation" (1994:2). I would argue that the study of all syntactic forms should take place there, since subconscious syntactic processing is formed through the acquisition of the native tongue, and for Arabic speakers, this tongue is their dialect.

An unfortunate recent trend in certain areas of Arabic linguistics has been the continual narrowing of the scope of analysis. During the Arabic Linguistics Symposium at Emory University in 1997, one presenter disclaimed the validity of his analysis for any Moroccan dialects other than "his own." While sociolinguistic questions demand a narrow focus and detailed observation, the field is equally in need of structural and comparative studies based on a broad spectrum of data.

Previous Studies in Arabic Dialect Syntax

The four dialect regions included in the present study are among the best-documented with both grammars and published texts. Of these, the best analyses of structure, and those that pay most attention to semantics and pragmatics, are Cowell's *Reference Grammar of Syrian Arabic* (1964) and Harrell's *Short Reference Grammar of Moroccan Arabic* (1962), both of which are mainly descriptive in approach, yet attempt to discover semantic and pragmatic explanations of syntactic structures. Each has many important observations about the dialect it treats. Caubet's (1993) detailed grammar of Moroccan, with particular attention to Fez and the surrounding region, is particularly welcome addition. Caubet takes a functional approach to the syntax of Moroccan, parallel in many ways to the approach used here. Her analyses, as well as inclusion of the texts from which she drew her examples, make her study a valuable contribution to the field.

Egypt is also well-represented in the literature. The teaching grammars of Mitchell (1956) and el-Tonsi (1982) provide information on the speech of the Cairo, and Khalafallah (1969) treats the Arabic spoken in Upper Egypt. Behnstedt and Woidich's (1985, 1988, 1994)

spoken varieties and registers. *Educated Spoken Arabic* refers to a formal register of spoken Arabic that combines both spoken and formal features. I take these labels to represent points along a linguistic continuum of varieties (e.g., dialects and historical periods) and registers (from formal or written to informal or spoken), terms I will use here.

multi-volume study of Egyptian Arabic offers an excellent range of text data covering almost all of Egypt, and focusing on rural dialects. Woidich has published extensively on Egyptian (1968, 1975, 1980a,b), and Eisele (1988, 1990a,b), Eid (1983), and others have contributed studies on particular aspects of syntax.

The Syrian area is rich in dialect variation, much of which is well-documented in work of Behnstedt (1989, 1990), Cantineau (1946), Cowell (1964), Grotzfeld (1965), and Lewin (1966). Less is available on the rural dialects of the northwestern and coastal regions, but Feghali's (1928) study of the syntax of Lebanese includes interesting data taken from rural speech.

While descriptions of the Gulf dialects as a group are continually expanding, the pool of data remains small, and few recorded texts from this region have been published. Qafisheh (1975) and Holes (1990) provide a good deal of information on Gulf Arabic, but contain no texts, and Holes' grammar follows the form of a reply to general cross-linguistic questionnaire rather than a study of problems particular to Arabic. Al-Maʿtūq's (1986) study of the dialect of the Kuwaiti ʿAjmān tribe is based on data including poetry and proverbs, rendering it less than ideal for syntactic study, and al-Najjar's (1984) dissertation on aspect in Kuwaiti is based on composed sentences.

Although Ingham's (1994) study of Najdi Arabic falls outside the geographic bounds of this study, three factors have motivated attention to his work here: first, the Kuwaiti dialect is Najdi in origin (the ruling elite of Kuwait migrated from the Najd over two hundred years ago; ʾAbū Ḥākima 1984:22). Second, his study fills a number of gaps left by previously published grammars, particularly in the realm of syntax. Information provided by Ingham for Najdi has been an important supplement to the rather scarce data available on Kuwaiti syntax. Finally, Ingham's analyses of certain aspects of nominal and verbal syntax have been quite helpful in formulating some of the cross-dialect analyses offered here.

Previous comparative studies of syntactic aspects of spoken Arabic have focused on discrete aspects of the language, and in some cases the analysis remains highly dependent on Classical Arabic structure (e.g., Rosenhouse 1978). Two studies use published data to provide a comparison of one particular construction in every recorded Arabic dialect: Harning (1980) compares genitive constructions and the genitive construct (Arabic /iḍāfa/), and Retsö (1983) compares passive verb morphology. Mitchell and El-Hassan's (1994) study of mood and aspect in the educated spoken Arabic of Egypt and the Levant provides a wealth of data on the verbal system across several registers of Arabic.

Much of the work on the syntax of individual dialects takes as its theoretical framework generative grammar, based largely on artificially generated sentences devoid of context.[3] This approach has not been adopted here, for reasons explained below.

Scope and Aims of the Present Study

Following dialectology in general, Arabic dialect studies have focused on and recorded in some detail the phonological, morphological, and lexical characteristics of individual dialects across most of the Arab world, thus laying the groundwork for comparative studies on those levels. Also following the trends of dialectology in general, syntax has received considerably less attention than phonology and the lexicon. I have chosen to focus on syntax precisely because it remains one of the least-studied areas of spoken Arabic.

Mitchell and El-Hassan, directors of the Leeds project on *Educated Spoken Arabic in Egypt and the Levant*, note that "[r]egional differences are lexical (and phonological) before they are grammatical" (1994:2). The present study bears out that observation to a great extent, even on a broader (though more shallow) scale. Nevertheless, such regional differences can potentially provide insight into the synchronic range of variation in spoken Arabic and point to areas of possible diachronic developments.

Anecdotal evidence lends some support to the view that syntax constitutes a more stable facet of language than either phonology or the lexicon. At the University of Damascus, I met a fourth-year student from an ʿAlawite region near Lattakia living in Damascus to attend school. This speaker easily adjusted her phonology and lexicon to

---

[3]Examples include Ennaji (1985), and many articles in the series *Perspectives on Arabic Linguistics* (John Benjamins Publishing Co., 1990-), which publishes papers from the annual Symposia on Arabic Linguistics in the United States.

Damascene norms, substituting /ʾ/ for her native /q/, for example, but on two occasions, I noticed her use of a particular syntactic construction not usually heard in Damascene speech: a syntactically embedded perfective verb. In the first example cited below, the speaker employs perfective /rəḥət/ *I went* rather than the expected (according to urban norms) non-finite, unmarked imperfective form /rūḥ/ *I go*. In the second, she uses perfective /kammalt/ *I finished* in place of the unmarked imperfective /kammilha/ *I finish it*. Both sentences contain Damascene /ʾ/ rather than ʿAlawite /q/ on /ʾalb/ *heart* and /ʾidirt/ *I was able.*

S1 صار «ريمي»، ما عاد إلي قلب رحت
ṣār "rīmi," mā ʿād ʾili ʾalb rəḥət
became-it "Rimi" neg remained to-me heart went-I
"Rimi" came on, and I no longer had the heart to go [out]

S1 ما قدرت كمّلتها
mā ʾidirt kammalt[h]a
not was-able-I finished-I-it
I wasn't able to finish it

What is important about this example is that it demonstrates the relative ease with which she accomplished phonological and lexical substitution, as opposed to the more difficult syntactic substitution. The speaker has substituted /ʾ/ for /q/, and the verb /ʾidir/ *to be able to* for her native /fī-/ *to be able to* (lit., *to be "in" someone to [do something]*), but has failed to make the corresponding syntactic modification involving shifting from using the perfective with /fī-/ to the unmarked imperfective required by /ʾidir/. If it is true that syntactic change tends to proceed more slowly than phonological and lexical change, then evidence of syntactic variation in the dialects may provide an additional perspective for diachronic studies.

This project aims to compare the syntax of geographically diverse varieties of spoken Arabic. Time constraints limited the scope to four dialect regions, and Morocco, Egypt, Syria, and Kuwait, were chosen as representative of four distinct dialect groups.[4] The study takes as a

---

[4]Fischer and Jastrow's *Handbuch der arabischen Dialekte* (1980) outlines the major groupings of Arabic dialects according to phonological and morphological features.

second goal contributing to the theoretical base of Arabic linguistics through the application of functional approaches to syntax. Pragmatics, discourse analysis, and functional typology all yield important theoretical tools that have yet to be exploited in the study of Arabic dialects. At the same time, this study aims to bring a more nuanced description of spoken Arabic syntax to typologists who have, for the most part, had to rely on grammars of formal Arabic and the impressions of native speakers for information. For example, in his cross-linguistic study on tense, Comrie assumes that the dialects agree with Modern Standard as against Classical Arabic, citing personal communication with an Egyptian colleague and his own work on Maltese for dialects (1985:63). Finally, as a perpetual student of Arabic, I hope to provide fellow students with a description of the structure of spoken Arabic that will aid them in acquiring fluency in the language as well as the ability to move from dialect to dialect.

This book is thus addressed to Arabists, students of Arabic, and general linguists. With the goal of rendering the analysis accessible to all these audiences, I have attempted to keep technical vocabulary to a minimum. A basic knowledge of either Arabic or linguistics has been assumed; where the syntax of spoken Arabic differs significantly from that of the formal register, references have also been provided to the grammars of Wright (1898), which, over one hundred years after publication, remains one of the most comprehensive descriptions of Classical Arabic available in English, and to Cantarino's (1975) syntax of modern formal Arabic.

Approaches to the Study of Syntax

The primary objective of this study is to compare and contrast syntactic features in Moroccan, Egyptian, Syrian, and Kuwaiti Arabic. The question implicitly asked by such a study, to what extent does the syntax of these dialects differ, is not easily answered, for it depends not only on what one is looking for, or the particular features being compared, but also on how one goes about looking for it, that is, the kind of linguistic analysis applied. In the course of examining the data corpus, the need arose for an analytic framework capable of explaining the kinds of language variation found in spoken Arabic. Thus it became necessary to expand the primary goal of the study to include the outline such a framework.

The two main methodological approaches to the study of syntax contrast in methodology and approach. Formal syntax concerns itself solely with language form, and seeks to construct a universal grammar hard-wired into the human brain. The various schools of functional syntax, on the other hand, accord attention to language meaning. I have chosen a functional framework, combining typological, discourse-based, and pragmatic approaches. These approaches seek principles and strategies of information packaging that appear to be common to human language in general or to a large number of language families across the globe. Discourse and pragmatic studies also provide the tools necessary to address questions of the meanings underlying language variation.

One of the assumptions underlying this study is that syntactic variation is not random or "free," but that it occurs according to semantic, pragmatic, or sociolinguistic principles, and that the search for these principles constitutes an important goal of syntactic description. The documentation of linguistic variation is necessary for obvious reasons, but an equally important goal is to explain the variation in meaning as well, to the extent possible. It follows from the assumption of the non-randomness of variation that the speaker has some degree of control over the structures she or he uses. Accordingly, I attempt here to identify the syntactic areas in which the speaker faces choices of "information packaging." In choosing one form over another, speakers present information in a certain way for a particular reason. In exploring these choices, I have found it helpful to include consideration of data that at first appear to be performance errors, mistakes or "slips of the tongue" on the part of the speaker. Formal approaches to syntax dismiss them as human imperfection, mere imperfect renderings of the (implied) perfect system. In some cases, however, these errors open a window to underlying pragmatic choices the speaker is making.

Why should a study of spoken Arabic syntax involve pragmatics? Givón claims that "there are reasons to believe that every language has a wide range of discourse registers, from the loose-informal-pragmatic to the tight-formal-syntactic" (1979a:210). Givón labels the two extremes of this continuum the pragmatic mode and the syntactic mode. (Givón does not formulate this view in terms of a continuum; in fact, he uses the word "dichotomy" [1979a:98], but his "range of discourse registers" reflects an underlying structural continuum.) Grammars of formal Arabic provide information on Givón's "tight-formal-syntactic" end of the spectrum; here I investigate the opposite end. Since spoken Arabic corresponds to the loose-informal-pragmatic end of the spectrum, it follows that pragmatic principles may be better equipped to explain the kind of variation found in the dialects.

One problem with the view that the grammar of a language consists of sets of rules is that a speaker's grammar is never complete, but always evolving. Rules of grammar can never be exhaustively documented, because they vary over time and in different sociolinguistic contexts. Therefore, it is important to explore the kinds of pragmatic principles that account for the existence and use of variant syntactic forms. Harris' (1984) study of Irish English syntax lends further support to the choice of functional approach. Harris has shown that non-standard language varieties cannot always be analyzed successfully as surface structure variants of an underlying grammar, and that "account may have to be taken not only of possible syntactic constraints at the level of clause structure, but also of much wider semantic, discourse and ultimately pragmatic considerations" (Harris 1984: 316).[5]

Much cross-linguistic work in the area of functional approaches to grammar (e.g., Hopper and Thompson 1980, Li 1977, Li and Thompson 1976, 1981, Timberlake 1977, and Wald 1983), and many of the concepts developed by these linguists, are quite applicable to the study of spoken Arabic. In searching for a way to efficiently describe and explain the syntactic variation of Arabic as it is used by native speakers, the methodology that I have adopted is simply to synthesize those concepts that are able to most efficiently account for the actual data.

I also assume, following Palmer, that "even at the formal level, grammaticalisation is a matter of degree, of 'more or less' rather than

[5]Harris' analysis of Irish equivalents to Standard English perfect verbs concludes that Irish English uses five forms to cover the semantic range of the one Standard English form, and proposes four semantic categories that detail the specific differences.

'yes or no'" (1986:4-5). What I understand him to mean is that syntax often involves soft choices rather than hard rules; that is, the speaker's own internal grammar is not structured entirely in categories, but includes continua as well, and this grammar allows him or her a great degree of control in how he or she presents information to his or her interlocutor. While sociolinguistic studies have for years recognized the centrality of speaker control to the use of language, this point of view has received less attention in syntactic studies of spoken Arabic (Belnap 1991 being one notable exception). Holes (1983) and Haeri (1996) show that the speaker controls phonological variables in a communicative way; this view of speaker control can and should be extended to the syntactic level as well.

Pragmatic principles of information packaging are more or less available to the speakers in the same way that formal rules are. The sociolinguistic model for communicative competence in code switching can be used to describe speakers' competence in syntactic form-switching according to a pragmatic competence. In code-switching, speakers negotiate their identities and relationships to the social contexts of speech events. In choosing among syntactic variants, speakers negotiate the mapping of a linguistic system of representation onto the real world, in which things are rarely black and white.

This approach also provides a useful model for linguistic change on the syntactic level, since the reinterpretation of the pragmatics of choice may be responsible for change in the choice of form. Grammaticalization studies have shown that diachronic syntactic change can take place through shift in pragmatic meaning (Traugott and König 1991). For diachronic reconstruction, tracing change in function is as important as tracing change in form.

This view find itself at odds with formal approaches to syntax. In their introduction to generative syntax, Green and Morgan stress that

> [t]he essence of ... *formal syntax* ... is that principles of syntax have to do just with matters of linguistic form, and are independent (in the mind, hence also in the correct theory) of matters of meaning or communicative function (1996:5).

Formal syntax lacks the tools to address the kinds of questions asked here, questions about the variation in meaning and function that I assume to underlie variation in form. Moreover, the highly specialized technical terminology of formal syntax renders it difficult for the lay reader to understand. The vast differences that separate the aims of generative syntax from the aims of this study preclude reference to generative and post-generative syntactic theory here.

While this presentation assumes a basic knowledge of Arabic structure on the part of non-linguist readers, formal Arabic syntax is not taken as framework for analysis for several reasons. First, most grammars of formal Arabic do not provide an appropriate model for a functional study of the syntax of spoken Arabic, because they focus on the desinential inflection system.[6] Second, the goal here is to describe the syntactic patterns found in the dialects without reference to a prescriptive norm. A number of Arabists have assumed that the dialects have descended from or developed out of Classical Arabic (e.g., Blau 1965, 1966-67, Blanc 1970, Harning 1980), but I agree with Fischer (1995) that the modern dialects represent descendents of older dialects. It follows from this assumption that any attempt to reconstruct a history of spoken Arabic should begin with as thorough as possible a description of the present. Occasional reference is made to Classical Arabic syntax only to point out previously unnoted points of comparison with spoken Arabic.

Shortcomings of this Approach

Among the problems of balancing cross-linguistic theory with a description of Arabic is that attempting to give the two somewhat equal weight has led to the inevitable result that neither area is satisfactorily addressed. This study may with fairness be accused of downplaying the range of syntactic variety in spoken Arabic. The attempt to create a framework for a comparative functional study has imposed a somewhat greater degree of attention to shared patterns than to individual cases of variation. In seeking solutions to certain syntactic problems, I have at times taken the liberty of using evidence from one or two dialects to generalize to all dialects, and then sought supporting evidence in the

---

[6]But see Moutaouakil (1989) for a functional analysis of modern formal Arabic.

others where possible. While I have tried to avoid the trap of theory dictating results, it has been helpful to propose some generalizations where they seem warranted.

The practical goal of this study is to present a comparative overview that accounts for a range of actual data, even if that overview emerges at the expense of a more detailed inventory of forms. Here economy takes precedence over exhaustive description, in the hope that a "lowest common denominator" framework can be established within which to explore, in future research, a more detailed inventory. This approach differs from that of studies of particular dialects or regions, which aim to document and describe the complete range data found. Perhaps a combination of approaches will lead us eventually to the best possible analyses.

The quality, quantity, and range of data presented here falls far short of ideal for proving the analyses proposed. Only as this study progressed did certain gaps in the data become clear, and temporal and spatial constraints have ended the search at this point. In a number of instances, the analyses are qualified with calls for further research and more contextualized data.

The arguments presented here tend, at times, to be somewhat circular: in certain cases, analyses are proposed and then used to support each other. Many of them cannot be proved at this point. However, most of them find precedence in hypotheses generated and substantiated by typological and cross-linguistic analyses. In other cases they represent guesses, presented here as hypotheses with a plea for further testing and revision–or discarding. If they prove to be wrong, then they will have contributed in their own way to our understanding of Arabic.

Shortcomings notwithstanding, I hope that the present study can provide a basis for further work, both in expanding the scope of the picture with more data from more dialects, and in providing a theoretical framework within which to ask more sophisticated and detailed questions.

Finally, it is necessary to stress that this study includes, but does not *represent*, varieties of Arabic spoken with the borders of four geopolitical entities. Obviously, no linguistic map would match these boundaries, and terms such as "Moroccan dialect" and Syrian dialect" do not in any sense reflect an actual linguistic situation. As Penny argues,[7] the term dialect implies discontinuity, a sharp or sudden transition in features that does not reflect the gradual, continuous nature of linguistic variation. The word "dialect" appears here merely as a convenient label for a heterogeneous group of varieties of Arabic.

The Data

This study is data-driven: the collection and examination of the basic corpus of data preceded decisions on theoretical approach. I began by taking notes on features and structures that emerged as unexpected, contrasting across dialects, or in need of description, and then I went in search of theory that seemed to describe or explain the phenomena that caught my attention.

The analyses offered herein are based on data collected from three sources: (a) tape-recorded data I collected from informants in Morocco, Syria, Kuwait, and Egypt; (b) commercial tape recordings of plays and interviews from these countries; and (c) published texts and studies. I have sought and used elicited data only as a last resort, in the final stages of documentation. Circumstances have imposed several limitations on the study. The data I collected are scattered at best, and do not fully represent any of these dialect regions. I had only three months of fieldwork in each country, scarcely time to carry out extensive interviewing. The quantity of my Egyptian and Kuwaiti data ended up being rather less than that of Moroccan and Syrian data. While informant data includes a range of sociolinguistic backgrounds (see Appendix 1), the amount of data collected from speakers with at least a high-school education outweighs that collected from lesser- or uneducated ones. The study reflects a marked urban bias, and few rural and no bedouin dialects are represented.

The body of data I collected consists of recordings and field notes I wrote down while observing spontaneous conversations. The recordings consist of both semi-formal interviews and free conversations; topic choice was left to circumstance. Whenever possible, I left the

---

[7]Ralph Penny, Queen Mary and Westfield College, University of London, public lecture "What is the History of the Spanish Language a History of?," Emory University, Atlanta, April 20, 1999.

interviewing and conversing to native speakers, with the aim of minimizing interference from my non-native speech patterns, especially in Morocco and Kuwait. Many of the Moroccan interviews and conversations were recorded with the help of Ahmed Jebari, and the folktales from a rural region near Meknas were collected through the auspices of an American friend who had lived in the community for over a year and spoke the local dialect fluently. Much of my Kuwaiti data comes from two long formal interviews conducted by Kuwaiti folklorist Mariam al-ʿAgrouga, to which I was merely an observer. Appendix 2 contains excerpts from representative texts from each region.

When I have needed additional information or assistance in puzzling out pragmatics, I have used Lebanese, Gulf, and Najdi grammars and data as supplements to the grammars of the dialects examined here. Justification for including information from these neighboring regions is three-fold. First, national boundaries do not represent linguistic ones, and shifts in speech patterns take place gradually. Second, the supplementary material I have used comes from dialects or communities closely related to those under study here: Lebanon and Syria have only recently been separated politically, and Kuwaitis originally came from the Najd. Third, the point of limiting the study to these particular dialect areas was simply that I could not hope to examine all features in all dialects at this point. During later stages of this project, personal circumstances have given me full-time access to a linguistically sophisticated Beiruti informant; where I have sought his judgements I refer to Lebanese rather than Syrian.

Contents of the Study

Reference grammars are available for all the dialects investigated here; thus, this book is not meant to be a description or inventory of the grammar(s) of these dialects. It also falls short of a complete inventory of syntactic structures, and it does not claim to include the full range of variation within each dialect region. The syntactic features for this study have been chosen either for their theoretical or comparative interest, or because the data I have collected is not satisfactorily documented or explained by the existing grammars.

The ten chapters that comprise this study fall into three broad categories: nominal syntax, verbal syntax, and sentence typology.

Nominal Syntax

Nominal syntax in Arabic presents a number of features of interest to Arabists, language typologists, discourse analysts, and dialectologists. These features include definiteness, relativization, demonstratives, number agreement, and genitive and possessive constructions. Spoken and written registers of Arabic all share basic morphological and syntactic properties: the definite article /-l/, the obligatory agreement of the noun and modifying adjectives in definiteness, the construct or /iḍāfa/, also called the genitive construct, and relative clause structure. Most forms of spoken Arabic share the relative pronoun /illi/ and a number agreement system that allows feminine singular verb and adjective agreement with plural nouns, and each dialect has one or more genitive exponents that coexist with the genitive construct. It seems that the dialects share the same basic properties of nominal syntax. However, each of these syntactic structures has a particular question or questions associated with it, due to the fact that previous analyses cannot account for certain data, and because the tendency to rely on morphological markers to describe syntactic behavior results in an incomplete picture, especially of spoken Arabic. It is argued here that, in order to satisfactorily explain the problematic data, account must be taken of the pragmatic and discourse roles that nouns play. The picture that emerges within this kind of framework supports the hypothesis that the native speaker's internalized grammar consists not only of rules and categories but also of principles and continua that the speaker utilizes to express subtleties of meaning.

The first four chapters of the book explore various aspects of nominal syntax. Chapter 1 examines the various definite and indefinite articles that modify nouns, and shows that the traditional treatment of articles as either definite or indefinite cannot satisfactorily account for their meaning and distribution in the dialects. As an alternative, a continuum of definiteness and a hierarchy of individuation are adopted to account for the use of articles across dialects. Chapter 2 uses the hierarchy of individuation to account for certain patterns of number agreement of plural nouns in the dialects, and look briefly at the pragmatics of possessive constructions, contrasting the construct (/iḍāfa/) and the functions of the genitive exponents or possessive adjectives that express the periphrastic genitive (/dyāl/, /bitāʿ/, /tabaʿ/, and /māl/). Chapter 3 explores the structures and strategies of relativization across the four dialect areas. Finally, Chapter 4 examines syntactic and discourse roles of commonly occurring demonstrative articles and pronouns.

Verbal Syntax

Any discussion of the verbal system of a language must take into account a number of morphosyntactic categories and semantic properties that most human languages share, such as tense, aspect, and mood. However, these categories overlap and interact in ways that are not yet fully understood, and differ in their realization in each language so widely that they defy universal definition and description. Mood and aspect are used in different senses and are grammaticalized in some cases and lexicalized in others, and tense, a morphological category, intersects with time reference without overlapping entirely. Moreover, aspect, mood and time reference are all features that operate at the sentence level as well as the verb phrase level, interacting with each other and with other sentential elements such as objects and adverbs, as well as the speech context.

The meanings of the verbal forms in Arabic, whether Classical or modern, formal or spoken, have long been the subject of debate among Arabists and linguists.[8] The questions most frequently addressed include: (1) Do the Arabic perfective and imperfective verb forms represent aspectual or temporal forms? and (2) What is the temporal and/or aspectual nature of the participle? Previous scholarship on tense and aspect in Arabic has been summarized by Eisele, who classifies the literature in two camps: (1) the 'aspectualists,' who claim that the perfective and imperfective are aspectual in nature and not temporal, and (2) the 'tense-aspectualists,' who contend (often vaguely) that these verb forms combine both temporal and aspectual natures (1988:8-36).

---

[8]Participants in the tense-aspect debate include Comrie (1976, 1985), Kurylowicz (1973), McCarus (1976), Fleisch (1974), and especially Eisele (1988), who reviews this scholarship in detail.

Eisele cites a lack of attention paid by aspectualists to the role of tense in the dialects; other literature tends to dismiss the role of aspect in the verbal system of spoken Arabic (e.g., Comrie 1985:63). However, both views seem to be based largely on intuition, since no comparative studies have yet been undertaken. While most previous studies are concerned with the theoretical meanings of verb forms at the sentence level, the focus here is on the use of verb forms in larger discourse contexts taken from natural data.

Studies of tense and aspect in Arabic have received so many different definitions and treatments that it is difficult to find consensus even on terminology. While I have tried to avoid adding to the confusion, it has been necessary to use terminology that reflects the analysis proposed here, even when that terminology differs from that of other studies. In analyzing the verb system, I have substituted *perfective* and *imperfective* for the traditional terms *perfect* and *imperfect*, because I use the term *perfect* to refer to an aspect that I argue is expressed by the participle.

Chapters 5 through 8 treat various aspects of verbal syntax. It is here that the four dialects show at once the greatest similarity and the greatest variation. Chapter 5 presents an overview of verb categories, with particular attention to pseudo-verbs and other types of verbs whose syntactic behavior and function set them apart from "typical" verbs. Chapter 6 deals with the aspectual nature of the morphological forms of the Arabic verb, joining the chorus of voices that agree with Mitchell and El-Hassan, among others, that "Arabic has two tenses, which refer only tenuously to temporal distinctions" (1994:13). Here evidence is presented that aspect plays a greater role than time reference in determining the choice of verb form used, particularly in narrative contexts. I also argue for the aspectual, atemporal nature of the participle, and that participles function in the same manner across all four dialect regions. Chapter 7 explores the nature of tense and time reference in spoken Arabic as seen in data from the four dialects, and points to the importance of "relative tense" to time reference in spoken Arabic. A group of verbs called "temporal verbs" is examined here as well. Temporal verbs form a functionally distinct group in that their main role is to set the temporal frame of reference for the event or proposition, and they also share certain syntactic behavior patterns across dialects.

Chapter 8 contrasts the morphological mood markers of the dialects, and examines the interaction of mood and aspect in conditional sentences.

Sentence Typology

The last two chapters explore aspects of sentence-level syntax and the information packaging strategies that appear to govern negation and word order. Chapter 9 examines patterns of negation across dialects, with particular attention to the pragmatics of negative sentences. The dialects are shown to share three main negating strategies, as well as a "negative copula." Negation is unusual among the syntactic structures examined here in that it provides the only case of a single syntactic isogloss separating geographic regions. Hence negation provides evidence of contact and borrowing in a way few other syntactic features do. Chapter 10 discusses word-order typology in the dialects. The order of the constituent parts of a clause or sentence is one of the most basic components of syntax, and has been a major concern of linguists regardless of their methodological frameworks. The goal of some approaches is to formulate grammar rules in terms of changes in word order, a practice which is best suited to languages that have a fairly fixed word order, such as English, in which "many syntactic processes can be described in terms of changes in linear order" (Comrie 1981:219). However, such an approach is less suited to languages with more flexible order, such as Arabic. A number of previous studies of spoken Arabic have concluded that the order of sentence elements is "variable."[9] The word order of main sentence constituents plays little part in syntactic processes in Arabic; minimally constrained in Classical Arabic, it retains the same flexibility in the modern dialects. Chapter 10 analyzes word order patterns according to theories of information structure, and demonstrate some of the ways in which pragmatic considerations influence the variable order of sentential elements that is characteristic of all forms of Arabic.

---

[9]See e.g. Grand'Henry (1976:85) and Rosenhouse (1984:49). Caubet's (1993) Moroccan grammar provides a welcome exception to this trend, offering a detailed functional analysis of word order variation in Moroccan.

1 The Definiteness Continuum

1.0 Introduction

It is increasingly recognized that, in natural language, many grammatical features such as definiteness, number and animacy interact with each other, and behave more like continua than like strictly delimited categories (Comrie 1981, Givón 1979a, Croft 1990). In Arabic, nouns are said to be either definite or indefinite, but this dichotomy imperfectly represents the real world, in which entities can be more or less definite and specific. Natural language data from spoken Arabic in all four dialect areas contain entities that are neither wholly definite nor wholly indefinite, but rather lie somewhere in between, in an area that may be called 'indefinite-specific.' In this chapter, I will argue that speakers of Arabic exercise a degree of control in manipulating the rules of syntax to try to approximate these shades of meaning. This control allows speakers the flexibility they need to more closely describe the continuum of definiteness that the natural world presents.

1.1 Definite and Indefinite Markers

Definiteness in Arabic seems, at first glance, to be quite straightforward. Prescriptive and descriptive grammars alike describe the system of definiteness and indefiniteness as dichotomous: nouns are either definite or indefinite, and proper nouns are definite whether or not they are marked by the definite article. Nouns can be made definite with the addition of the definite article /(i)l-/, or by the specification of a noun by the addition of another substantive to it to form a possessive construct (/iḍāfa/). In all of the dialects examined here, the definite article is /(i)l-/ or a phonetically determined variant. The following examples demonstrate:

	Indefinite Nouns	Definite Nouns
M	جاهم ضيف	ف الدار
	žāhum ḍīf	f əd-dār
	came-he-to-them guest	in the-house
	A guest visited them	*in the house*

E فستان يجنّن
fustān yigannin
dress it-make-crazy
a stunning dress

في البيت
fi l-bēt
in the-house
in the house

S تاخدي شقفة؟
tāxdi ša'fe?
you-take piece
Will you take a piece?

فات ع المطعم
fāt ʿa l-maṭʿam
went-he into the-restaurant
He went into the restaurant.

K خوش مكان
xōš makān
good place
a good place

ع البحر
ʿa l-baḥər
on the-sea
on the beach

In addition to the definite article, several of these dialects make use of other articles. Moroccan and Syrian employ the particle /ši/ *some,* and all four dialects permit limited use of the article /wāḥid/ (Moroccan /wāḥəd l-/) *one* (f /waḥda/).

In Moroccan, Harrell (1962) notes two "indefinite" articles: a "concretizing" article /wāḥəd l-/ *one*, and a "potential" article /ši/ *some* (1962:147, 189). Examples of these articles from my data include:

M1 كاين واحد الحاجة
kāyn wāḥəd l-ḥāža
there-is one thing
there is something

M10 كيبقى كيقول شي كلمة قبيحة
kaybqa kayqūl ši kəlma qbīḥa
indic-he-keeps indic-he-says some word ugly
he keeps saying a/some bad word

Syrian Arabic shares with Moroccan the article /ši/, although Cowell classifies Syrian /ši/ as a partitive noun rather than an article (1964:467). Syrian speakers also use /wāḥid/ (f /waḥde/ (Grotzfeld 1965:76), primarily with human nouns. Examples of both /ši/ and /wāḥid/ from my data include:

S2 لازم نعمل له شي مقدّمة
lāzim niʿmil-lu ši muqaddime
must we-make for-him some introduction
We must give him some sort of preparation

S2 فيه واحد بدوي فات ع المطعم
fī wāḥid badwi fāt ʿa l-maṭʿam
there-is one bedouin went-he into the-restaurant
There was a [certain] bedouin who went into the restaurant

Egyptian Arabic allows the use of /wāḥid/ with human nouns only (example from Woidich 1980b:32-3; translation mine):

E كان فيه واحد حطّاب
kān fī wāḥid ḥiṭṭāb
was-it there-is one wood-gatherer
There was a [certain] wood-gatherer

Holes notes the use of /wāḥid/ in Gulf Arabic preceding a noun to mean *a certain* (1990:114). My Kuwaiti data contain several examples in which /wāḥid/ modifies human nouns, including:

K3 راحت حگ واحد مطوّع
rāḥat ḥagg wāḥid mṭawwaʿ
went-she to one religious-man
She went to a learned religious man

While the grammars of these dialects vary widely in their treatment of /šī/ and /wāḥid/, the recurrence of these articles across dialects invites comparative study of them. What is the motivation for marking nouns in these ways? What pragmatic role(s) do they play? Harrell's descriptive names, "concretizing" and "potential," allude to the fact that /wāḥəd l-/ and /ši/ fulfill particular discourse functions, which may now be further specified and defined in light of developments in discourse theory in the years since Harrell wrote.

The traditional definite/indefinite dichotomy does not leave room to account for the function of these articles. Why do the dialects need "indefinite" articles such as /ši/ and /wāḥid/ if the unmodified noun is also indefinite? The contexts of the sentences cited above show that the "indefinite" articles /ši/ and /wāḥid/ are in fact not wholly indefinite. Why are they used in some cases and not in others? Why does /wāḥid/ modify only human nouns? Answers to these questions may be found in typological and pragmatic approaches to syntax.

1.2 Definiteness, Indefiniteness, and Specification

Chafe gives a good description of 'definite' status: "I think you know and can identify the thing I have in mind" (1976:39). In other words, in order for a nominal phrase to assume definite status in discourse, it must meet one of several conditions: (a) it must have been *previously mentioned* in the discourse; or (b) it must be a member of a *universal* set of entities, such as the sun, that can be assumed to be known and identifiable without further specification, or (c) the speaker must have good reason to think that the entity is *retrievable* by the listener through knowledge shared by the interlocutors (Chafe 1976). Pragmatically, a definite noun usually represents *given* information, or information that has already been established in the discourse or can be assumed by the speaker to be present or active in the mind of his or her interlocutor. An indefinite noun, then, does not meet any of the above conditions, and represents an unknown, irretrievable entity.

However, not all indefinite nouns are created equal. Medieval Arab grammarians called the grammatical specification of nouns /taxṣīṣ/ *specifying*. Wright notes that /taxṣīṣ/ includes modification of an indefinite noun by adjectival phrases and annexation (1898ii:198). A Lebanese encyclopedia on Arabic grammar defines it thus:

> التخصيص هو تقليل الاشتراك الحاصل في النكرات، ويكون بالوصف أو الإضافة، نحو: «إنّه رجلُ علمٍ»، فإضافة «رجل» إلى «علم» خفّفت من تنكيره، لأنه إذا قلنا «إنه رجل» كان شائعاً، أمّا إذا قلنا «إنّه رجل علمٍ» فإنّنا نكون قد أزلنا عنه بعض الشيوع.
>
> Specification is the lessening of the commonality that occurs in indefinite entities, and [this] may occur through modification or the genitive (/iḍāfa/), such as: *He is a man of learning*, as the addition of 'man' to 'learning' has lessened the indefiniteness of [the former], because if we say, *He is a man*, [the statement] is general, but if we say, *He is a man of learning*, we will have eliminated from it some of that generality (al-Tūnjī and al-ʾAsmar 1993:156).

The principle of partial specification of nouns is thus not new to the description of Arabic. Nor is it new to language typology. Croft calls it referentiality, and formalizes this definiteness hierarchy (1990:116):

Hierarchy of definiteness
- definite
- referential indefinite
- nonreferential indefinite

Croft's term *referential indefinite* describes al-Tūnjī and al-Asmar's phrase *a man of learning*, and his *nonreferential indefinite* describes their nonspecific noun *a man*.

Khan's work on Semitic provides a good model to use in the analysis of nominal syntax in spoken Arabic. Khan (1984) has adapted the work of Chafe (1976), Timberlake (1977), Hopper and Thompson (1980), and others to show that one or more of the features listed in Table 1-1 may operate to attract object marking and agreement pronouns in Semitic, such that the more individuated the noun, the greater the tendency of these markers to occur. He groups these qualities together under a rubric he calls individuation or salience, which he illustrates as follows (1984:470):

Table 1-1: Khan's Hierarchies of Individuation

Individuated/Salient	Non-individuated/Non-salient	
1. Definite	>	Indefinite
2. Non-reflexive	>	Reflexive component
3. Specific	>	Generic
4. Concrete	>	Abstract
5. Qualified	>	Unqualified
6. Proper	>	Common
7. 1st person > 2nd > 3rd > Human	>	Inanimate
8. Textually prominent	>	Incidental

The notion of individuation provides great explanatory power for the syntactic behavior of nouns in spoken Arabic. However, I will modify Khan's framework slightly to include those features that most influence the syntactic behavior of nouns in spoken Arabic. Reflexivity, while relevant to the individuation of nouns, is often expressed in Arabic through verb morphology. And since abstract nouns in Arabic normally take the definite article, concreteness appears to have less central a role than specification and qualification in the syntactic marking of nouns. Parallel to Khan's textual prominence is physical prominence: nouns tend to be marked as more salient when they are present in the immediate environment (see further 4.2). Three other modifications are inspired by and adapted from the work of Cowell and Janda.

First, I will add to the list the feature quantification. Cowell contrasts agreement patterns of nouns denoting "collectivity or generality" with those denoting "heterogeneity or particularity" (1964:423). Belnap's study of number agreement in Cairene Arabic lends further support to this analysis (1991:68-72). Quantification involving numbers ten and lower also appears to have some relevance to the marking of new discourse topics (see 1.5).

Cowell also contrasts concepts of identification and classification, which play a role in the expression of possessive constructions. Identificatory annexion refers to the assigning of an entity to a specific possessor, while classificatory annexion assigns an entity to a set or group (1964:458). This notion of a proper identification contrasted to a generic one parallels Khan's hierarchy of specificity vs. genericness, and Khan's terms specific and generic are defined here to include Cowell's insight.

Finally, I will add to Khan's animacy hierarchy the concept of agency, defined here as the degree to which an individual or entity has the ability to act independently. Agency may be viewed as a kind of sociolinguistic parallel to textual prominence. The concept finds precedence in the work of linguists who have argued for the role of social status and power in language variation and change, among them Janda, who argues for the centrality of a feature she calls "virility" to salience in Slavic languages, which helps explain both synchronic patterns and diachronic changes in Slavic case and number agreement.[1] While virility represents an appealing concept in the age of feminist theory, the concept of agency applies more generally. Factors that contribute to agency include animacy and social status; thus for humans,

[1]Laura A. Janda, UNC Chapel Hill, public lecture at Emory University, 10/16/1997, "Virility in Slavic: A Conspiracy of Factors Over Time and Space;" see also Janda 1999.

gender and age play a role as well. Children have less agency than adults, animals have less agency than humans, and inanimate objects are unlikely to be perceived as having agency at all. I will argue here and in Chapter 2 that agency provides a possible explanation for certain patterns of definite marking and agreement in some dialects.

The major objection to hierarchies of individuation or salience lies in their vagueness. The features that comprise such hierarchies need detailed investigation and definition involving a large corpus of naturally occurring data. Pending such a study, attention will focus here on those features which seem to have the greatest relevance to or explanatory power for the syntax of spoken Arabic. The list in Table 1-2, revised from Khan's (Table 1-1), includes syntactic, semantic, pragmatic, and sociolinguistic features, covering a range of levels that interact in the production of language. These features appear to play a role in pushing a noun toward higher or lower individuation, affecting the speaker's choice of syntactic marking of nouns in spoken Arabic when a choice of marking presents itself.

Table 1-2: Features Affecting Individuation

1. Agency: includes humanness/animacy, social status or power, perhaps gender and age groups as well.
2. Definiteness: syntactic marking or semantic status (e.g., proper nouns).
3. Specificity vs. genericness: the extent to which a speaker has a specific entity in mind.
4. Textual or physical prominence: the extent to which a noun plays a role important to the discourse, or is physically present and prominent.
5. Qualification: modification of a noun with adjectives and other descriptives.
6. Quantification vs. collectivity: the extent to which a noun is specifically quantified, especially with numbers from 2-10.

Taken as a group, it is clear that these features affect the syntactic behavior of nouns, but in a way that is not (yet) possible to describe formally. It is more convenient to formalize them using a continuum, which has the additional advantage of privileging speaker control in determining the marking of a given noun. In Figure 1, the features on the right tend to reflect (or, from the speaker's point of view, attract) higher individuation or salience, the ones on the left, less:

Figure 1: The Individuation Continuum

Unindividuated:	Partly individuated	Individuated:
- agency/animacy		+ agency/animacy
- definite		+ definite
- specific		+ specific
- prominence		+ prominence
- qualified		+ qualified
+ collectivity		+ quantified 2-10

The importance of this continuum lies less in predicting the marking on the noun itself than in explaining the syntactic behavior of the noun in the larger sentential context, as I will show. In other words, the higher the individuation of a noun in the mind of the speaker, the more that noun will attract certain kinds of syntactic marking.

1.3 Definiteness and Individuation

The correspondence between individuation and definiteness in Arabic is not direct, because syntactic rules also affect definite marking. For example, abstract and generic nouns in Arabic are marked with the definite article. Thus an unspecified noun referring to any member of the class may be marked with /(i)l-/, while a specified human noun may not be marked definite. In the following introduction to a joke, the unnamed but somewhat specified bedouin is marked indefinite with the indefinite article /wāḥid/, while the generic restaurant and waiter are both marked definite.[2]

S2 فيه واحد بدوي فات ع المطعم. قال له للگارسون، انطيني بوظة
fī wāḥid badwi, fāt ʿa l-maṭʿam. qāl-lu la-l-garsōn, inṭīni būẓa
there-is one-ms bedouin-ms, entered-he into the restaurant. said-he to-him to-the-waiter, give-me ice-cream
There's this bedouin who went into a restaurant. He said to the waiter, give me ice cream.

Grammar views definiteness as a dichotomy: nouns are either definite or not. But the real world that a speaker knows and desires to represent is far from black and white: some nouns may be somewhat defined or specified but not entirely, either from the point of view of

[2]The joke is cited in full, and its nominal markings further discussed, in 1.5.

the speaker or in the assumptions the speaker makes about the listener's knowledge. Definiteness is a grammatical category in which the speaker has a degree of control, and speakers of Arabic need to represent a range of undefined, partially defined, and fully defined entities. Definite and indefinite represent the black and white ends of a definiteness continuum, while the grey area of partially defined or specified entities falls in between. I will call this range indefinite-specific, after Wald (1983).[3] It includes nouns that are syntactically indefinite, but carry a degree of specific reference that may be reflected in a number of possible syntactic constructions. In other words, an indefinite noun that carries a degree of individuation or specificity may attract a degree of definite or specifying syntactic marking. Or, as described from a different perspective, a speaker may be influenced by these features to mark a noun in a certain way. The rest of the chapter will explore the use of definite and indefinite markers in the dialects, and show how spoken Arabic uses various combinations of syntactic markings to indicate a range of indefinite-specific status.

1.4 Indefinite-Specific Marking

The semantic range from highly individuated (e.g. definite, specific, or animate) nouns to non-individuated (e.g. indefinite, non-specific, or inanimate) nouns includes varying degrees of definiteness and specificity. The more specific the reference of the noun, the greater the probability that the noun will be syntactically marked with some kind of article or specifying construction. This section will examine two kinds of indefinite-specific marking, the article /ši/ in Moroccan and Syrian, and the indefinite suffix /-in/, found in some Gulf regions.

1.4.1 Indefinite-Specific Article /ši/

Both Syrian and Moroccan speakers often identify a noun in the indefinite-specific range with the referential indefinite article /ši/ *some (kind of)*. In the following sentence, /ši/ lends a degree of specificity to the noun /muqaddime/ *introduction*.

---

[3]Wald uses the term 'indefinite specific' to explain the use of *this* in spoken English in sentences such as *I saw this guy ...*

S2 لازم نعمل له شي مقدمة لحتّى ما ينصدم
lāzim naʿmil-lu ši muqaddime la-ḥatta mā yinṣidim
necessary we-make-for-him some introduction so-that neg he-be-shocked
We must arrange some kind of preparation for him so that he won't be shocked

Analogous Moroccan examples include the following /ši kəlma qbīḥa/ *some nasty word*, /ši masāʾil qbīḥa/ *some nasty things*, and /ši nās ḍīfān/ *some guests*:

M10 كيبقى يقول شي كلمة قبيحة، كيقول شي مسائل قبيحة
kaybqa yqūl ši kəlma qbīḥa, kayqūl ši masāʾil qbīḥa
indic-he-keeps he-say some word ugly, indic-he-says some things ugly
He keeps saying some nasty word, he says some nasty things

M2 وانا عندي شي ناس ضيفان
w āna ʿndi ši nās ḍīfān
and I at-me some people guests
While I had some guests

Here, as in the Syrian example, the article /ši/ indicates the partial specificity of the nouns it modifies. It is worth noting that all of the nouns in the Moroccan examples are modified, reflecting the relevance of qualification to the individuation of a noun. The Moroccan data thus provide evidence of correspondence among qualification, specificity, and syntactic marking on nouns. All these examples demonstrate that speakers use /ši/ to indicate that they have a particular type of entity in mind.

1.4.2 Nunation as Indefinite-Specific Marking

In formal Arabic, nunation or /tanwīn/ refers to the endings /-un/, /-an/, and /-in/ that function as indefinite case markers on nouns and adjectives. Nunation thus represents part of the case-marking system of formal Arabic. However, spoken Arabic has no case-marking system. In a number of dialects, nunation in the form of /-an/ (/tanwīn fatḥa/) occurs in certain fixed adverbial expressions, such as /ʾabadan/ *ever, at all*, and /dāyman/ *always*. Adverbial /-an/ is of higher productivity in the educated registers of spoken Arabic.

Another type of nunation, usually realized as /-in/ and occurring on indefinite nouns in a number of bedouin dialects, especially in their poetic register, are considered to be vestiges of the case-marking system of formal Arabic. Yet this suffix provides no case information. Holes mentions "the vestige of" a suffix /-in/, found in "the speech of some less educated Gulf speakers, and in dialect poetry," which marks indefinite nouns only when occurring in "Noun + Attributive Adjective" phrases (1990:115). In his study of Najdi Arabic, Ingham includes the indefinite marker /-in/ as part of noun phrase structure (1994:47):[4]

indefinite	bēt	'house' or 'a house'
indefinite (marked)	bēt-in	'a (particular) house'
definite	al-bēt	'the house'
possessed	bēt-i/-ik	'my/your house etc.'

This schema suggests that /-in/ functions as an indefinite-specific marker, and Ingham's description of the usage patterns of this ending further confirms this analysis (1994: 49; IND = indefinite):

> (i) where a nominal follows another nominal as in *bēt-in kibīr* (house-IND large) 'a large house;' (ii) where a modifying prepositional phrase follows a nominal as in *wāḥd-in min ar-rabuʿ* (one-IND from the group) 'one of the group' (i.e. one of my friends) ... (iii) where a noun is followed by a modifying clause as in *kalmit-in gāl-ō-hā-li* (word-IND said-they-it-to-me) 'a word which they said to me.'

Nunation in Najdi Arabic occurs on indefinite nouns modified by an adjective or relative clause, in other words, on *specified* indefinite nouns. The fact that this ending occurs on indefinite nouns that are modified in some way is significant, for it indicates that such a noun is not purely indefinite, but has a degree of specificity. Urban Kuwaiti seems to have lost the ending except in highly formalized contexts such as poetry; most published material on this phenomenon does not distinguish between poetic use of /-in/,which belongs to a special artistic register, and examples taken from naturally-occurring speech. Al-Maʿtūq's study of the tribal dialect of the ʿAjmān in Kuwait reports

---

[4]It occurs on plural nouns as well: /mgaddm-īn-in/ *submitted-p-indef* (Ingham 1994:167).

similar use of /-in/, but her examples too are taken largely from proverbs and poetry, rather than extemporaneous speech (1986:190-91).

This function of nunation appears to be quite old. Evidence for the use of nunation with /-an/ as an indefinite-specific marker may be found in early Spanish Arabic texts. Corriente reports that this kind of nunation has "the function of linking constituents," these constituents being an indefinite noun with a following adjective or relative clause (1977:121-2). Corriente's examples clearly show contexts in which an indefinite noun is qualified or partly specified, resulting in an indefinite-specific noun phrase marked with /-an/. These phrases include (121-2):

kalban abyaḍ
a white dog

ʿala qalban kāfir
with an unfaithful heart

bi-xāṭiran yattaqad miṯl al-nār
with a mind as bright as fire

Shumaker's (1981) study of the indefinite suffix /-an/ in Galland's fourteenth or fifteenth century manuscript of *Alf Layla wa Layla* (*The Thousand and One Nights*, ed. Mahdi 1984) establishes patterns of /-an/ as a syntactic marker of textually prominent entities that appear to correspond to indefinite-specific patterns. Her conclusions suggest that /-an/ functions in the text as a type of indefinite-specific article. Examples from the text support this analysis; in the following passages, indefinite nouns that are specified with adjectival or relative phrases end in /-an/. From the "Story of the Porter and the Three Girls" (Arabic text from Mahdi 1984i:126; transcription and translation mine):

اد وقفت عليه امرأةً ملتفه في ايزار موصلي مشعر بحرير ...

[id waqafat ʿalayhi imraʾat-**an** multaffa fī ʾīzār muṣilī mušaʿʿar bi-ḥarīr ...

when stood-she over-him woman-**an** wrapped in shawl Mosuli fringed with-silk]

When suddenly there stood before him a woman wrapped in a Mosuli shawl fringed with silk

The suffix /-an/ on /imraʾat-an/ *woman* is marked in the Arabic text, and the noun is partly specified by the following phrase. Another part of the story contains an instance of nunation marking an indefinite noun modified by a relative clause (Mahdi 1984i:138):

فقال جعفر يا امير المومنين، هولاي ناساً قد دخل فيهم السكر ولا يعلمون من نحن

[fa-qāl jaʿfar yā ʾamīr al-mūminīn, hawlāy nās-**an** qad daxala fīhim as-sukr wa lā yaʿlamūn man naḥnu

so-said-he Jaʿfar, O Caliph, those are people-**an** perf entered-it in-them the-drunkenness and neg they-know who we]

Jaʿfar said, Caliph, those are people in whom drunkenness has set, and they do not know who we are

It may be argued that these examples belong to an artistic register and do not necessarily reflect everyday speech. At the very least, though, these texts provide evidence for the indefinite-specific function of nunation as part of some register of Arabic in the medieval period.

Evidence thus exists supporting the use of /tanwīn/ as an indefinite-specific marker in a number of geographic locations from an early period, and surviving until today in parts of the Peninsula, perhaps also in Levantine /ḥadan/ *someone, anyone*, which may be a reflex of this indefinite-specific nunation.

Egyptian dialects do not appear to have any articles that specify or individuate an indefinite noun. In order to express the notion of specificity when referring to an indefinite noun, Egyptian speakers commonly employ the adverb /kida/ *thus, so* as a modifier:

E2 شفت حاجة كدا ...

šuft ḥāga kida

saw-I thing like-this

I saw something ... or *I saw this thing ...*

In addition, Egyptians use several nouns that function in similar fashion, that is, to lend certain kinds of specificity to an indefinite noun, and thus can be identified as specialized indefinite-specific markers, since they have more specialized meanings than does /ši/. The meanings of these articles involve plurality or intensification: /ʾiši/ *some* or *a bunch of*, in a series, *something* in certain idiomatic phrases, and /ḥittit/ *what a ...!* (Badawi and Hinds 1986:25,190). Clearly, /ʾiši/ is related to /ši/. Badawi and Hinds give three contexts for this article; the first is of interest here (1986:25):

E عنده مما جميعه اشي جبنة واشي زيتون واشي سردين ...
ʿandu mimma gamīʿu ʾiši gibna w-ʾiši zatūn wi-ʾiši sardīn ...
[at-him of-what all-it ʾiši cheese and-ʾiši olives and-ʾiši sardines]
he has something of everything-cheese, olives, sardines ...

In such cases, /ʾiši/ intensifies the following noun, and in doing so specifies it; however, /ʾiši/ is not regularly used to specify indefinite nouns, but only in contexts where quantity or variety is stressed.

Other intensifiers are more commonly used in Egypt, among them /ḥittit/, literally a *piece of*. While this particle is mainly understood as an intensifier expressing astonishment or admiration, part of its function is specification:

E3 لقينا فار قدّ كدا هو، حتة فار قدّ كدا هو
laʾēna fār ʾadd kida-hō, ḥittit fār kida-hō
found-we mouse size like-this, piece-of mouse like this
We found a mouse this big, what a mouse this big!

1.5 Definiteness and First Mention: New Topic

On the continuum of definiteness, near the indefinite-specific range, there appears to be an area reserved for the first mention in discourse of 'textually prominent' entities (one of Khan's features, see Table 1-1). The first mention of a nominal entity in discourse may be indefinite, indefinite-specific, or, in some cases (and in Moroccan in particular), definite in marking. Not all first-mention nouns are of equal importance to the discourse; some nouns play a more prominent role than others. Discourse analysts distinguish between figure and ground, or central and marginal entities (and events) in discourse respectively (Hopper and Thompson 1980). An entity that plays an important role in a text is likely to be marked in a way that reflects that status, whereas an entity that is part of the background is less likely to be so marked.

In the following joke, the specified and textually prominent figure *bedouin* is marked with an 'indefinite' article /wāḥid/, while the inanimate, unspecified, even generic nouns /l-maṭʿam/ *restaurant* and /l-garsōn/ *waiter* are marked with the definite article, and inanimate /būẓa/ *ice cream* has no article in its first occurrence:

S2 فيه واحد بدوي فات ع المطعم. قال له للگارسون، انطيني بوظة. جاب له صحن بوظة صار ياكله بالخبز. بلّش الگارسون يتضحّك عليه. قال له البدوي علويش تتضحّك؟ على طبيخك المسگّع؟!
fī wāḥid badwi fāt ʿa l-maṭʿam. qāl-lu la-l-garsōn, inṭīni būẓa. žāb-lu ṣaḥn būẓa ṣār yāklu bi-l-xəbəz. ballaš ig-garsōn yitḍaḥḥak ʿalēh. qāl-lu l-badawi ʿalwēš titḍaḥḥak? ʿalā ṭabīxak l-msaggaʿ ?!
there-is one-ms bedouin-ms entered-he into the restaurant. said-he to-him to-the-waiter, give-me ice-cream. brought-he to-him plate of-ice-cream began-he he-eat-it with-the-bread. he-started the-waiter he-laughs at-him. said-he-to-him the-bedouin on-what you-laugh? at cooking-your the-cold?!
There's this bedouin who went into a restaurant. He said to the waiter, give me ice cream. He brought him a plate of ice cream, he began to eat it with bread. The waiter started laughing at him. He said, what are you laughing at? Your ice-cold cooking?!

The speaker telling this joke introduces its subject, /badwi/ *(a) bedouin*, with the indefinite /wāḥid/ *one*, for two reasons: first, because the bedouin's existence is previously unknown, and second, because he plays a key role in the joke and therefore specific referentiality must be established. On the other hand, /il-maṭʿam/ *the restaurant* and /il-garsōn/ *the waiter* are marked definite at their first mention, the former due to its generic status and the latter because any restaurant may be presumed to have a waiter working in it. Were the speaker to have said /fāt ʿa maṭʿam/ *he went into a restaurant*, it might imply that the restaurant had some importance to the story, in which case further specification would be expected. In contrast, *ice cream*, which also has some textual prominence, is less individuated because it is inanimate, and so its first mention is indefinite but not marked with an indefinite-specific article.

These 'textually prominent' entities fall in the indefinite-specific range, but represent a special case within it. Such entities may be called "new topics," making the article /wāḥid/ a "new topic" article.[5]

Evidence from Syrian suggests that /wāḥid/ modifies only human nouns. Egyptian data exhibit a similar pattern, with the usage of /wāḥid/

[5]I have adapted the term 'new topic' from Wald (1983).

also syntactically restricted to human nouns:

E2 كان فيه واحدة ستّ ...
kān fī waḥda sitt
was-it there-is one woman
There was a/this woman ...

In this Kuwaiti example (repeated from 1.1.1 above), /wāḥid/ also modifies a human noun, /mṭawwaʿ/ *learned religious man.*

K3 راحت حگ واحد مطوّع
rāḥat ḥagg wāḥid mṭawwaʿ
went-she to one religious-man
She went to a learned religious man

Evidence thus suggests that "new topic" status as marked syntactically by the article /wāḥid/ is restricted in Egyptian, Syrian, and Kuwaiti dialects to textually prominent, highly individuated, and specifically human, nouns.

In contrast to the restricted use of /wāḥid/ in the other dialects, the Moroccan article /wāḥəd l-/ is not restricted to human or even animate nouns, but extends to inanimates as well:

M10 كاين واحد النوع آخر د الحوت ...
kāyn wāḥəd n-nūʿ āxur d l-ḥūt
there-is-ms one the-kind other gen the-fish
There's this other kind of fish ...

In Moroccan, /waḥəd/ is obligatorily followed by the definite article /l-/: /wāḥəd l-/, and it is used with a much broader range of entities, not only human but also inanimate entities if they are textually prominent. The following Moroccan passage introduces two characters in similar fashion, and a third differently (all marked in boldface):

M11 حاجيت لك، هادا **واحد الراجل** ما عندوش الولاد، عنده غير **المرا** ومرته عمّرها ما ولدت. ناضت ولدت **واحد البنت**
ḥāžīt-lk, hāda **wāḥəd ər-rāžl** mā ʿəndūš l-wlād, ʿəndu ġīr **l-mra** w martu ʿammrha mā wəldat. nāḍət wəldat **wāḥəd l-bənt**
told-story-I-to-you, this **one man** neg-at-him the-children, at-him only **the-wife** and wife-his life-her neg bore-children-she. arose-she bore-she **one girl**

> *I tell you a story, this is* ***a man*** *who doesn't have children. He has only* ***the wife****, and his wife never bore children. Then she had* ***a daughter****.*

This story opens with the introduction of a main character identified by the article /wāḥəd l-/ *a*. The next characters introduced are /l-wlād/ *children*, marked definite because of their high animacy, except that their existence is negated, and so they do not constitute a topic. *The wife* /l-mra/ is not marked as a new topic, however, presumably because her existence may be inferred, as most men are married, and she thus constitutes a retrievable entity that does not need to be singled out for introduction. The next topic introduced is /l-bənt/ *girl*, marked with /wāḥəd l-/ as a new topic and important to the story. The function of /wāḥəd l-/ as a new topic marker is substantiated by the fact that the man and the girl are the only two characters who reappear in the story.

Two entities are introduced in the next passage. The first, /wəld l-malik/ *[a] king's son* is human, and also has an important role to play in the story, and so the speaker takes care to establish textual prominence for him by marking the phrase with /wāḥəd/. The second identity, /šəržəm/ *window* is neither animate nor topical, and thus is not marked by the new-topic article.

M11 نـاض آللاّ واحـد ولـد الملك – وراه عنـدها شـرجـم ف حال هكا. طلّت م الشرجم

> nāḍ a-lalla **waḥəd wəld l-malik** -- w-rah ʿəndha **šəržəm** f-ḥāl hākʷa. ṭəllat m š-šəržəm
> arose-he O lady **one son of-the-king** -- and see-now at-her **window** like like-this. leaned-out-she from the-window
> *So, my lady,* ***this prince*** *up and -- She had* ***a window*** *like that. She leaned out of the window*

In the third passage, the repetition of /mra xʷra/ *another wife* with the addition of the 'new-topic' article /wāḥəd l-/ may be due to the necessity of marking this second wife as a significant character in the story. After omitting the article in her first mention of the woman, the speaker may have subconsciously felt that the character needed more of an introduction:

M11 ناض اتجوّج مرا خرى اتجوّج واحد المرا خرى

nāḍ tžəwwež mra xʷra tžəwwež wāḥəd l-mra xʷra

arose-he married-he woman other married-he one the-woman other

He up and married another woman, married this other woman

Further evidence that /wāḥid/ functions as a new topic marker lies in the use of /ši/ without /wāḥəd/ in both Moroccan and Syrian. While partially individuated, textually prominent persons may be introduced with /ši wāḥ(i)d/ *someone*, speakers of both dialects can use /ši/ to mean *someone* when the reference is non-individuated, non-specific, not textually prominent, and of low social status. An example from Caubet's Moroccan texts (1993ii:7):

M شي كيكمي السبسي، شي كيبدّل جوانات، شي ...

ši kayəkmi əs-səbsi, ši kaybəddəl žwānāt, ši ...

some indic-he-smokes the-hashish-pipe, some indic-he-exchanges joints, some ...

Someone is smoking the hashish pipe, someone is exchanging joints, someone ...

From my Syrian data:

S2 ... إلاّ يعني عالم اسوأ منها بكتير كتير يعني شي إلن ماضي كتير مشرشح منشان يقبلوا ياخدوا يعني ها البنت

... ʾilla yaʿni ʿālam ʾaswaʾ min[h]a bə-ktīr ktīr yaʿni še ʾilon māḍi ktīr mšaršaḥ minšān yiqbalu yāxdu yaʿni ha l-binət

... except that-is world worse than-her by-a-lot a-lot that-is thing to-them past alot sordid in-order-to they-accept they-take that-is this the-girl

... except for people who are much worse than her, that is, people who have a very sordid past, to accept to marry the girl

The marking of an indefinite noun with the new-topic article /wāḥid (l-)/ appears to be motivated by the high degree of textual prominence played by that noun. The derivation of the article itself, /wāḥid/ *one*, further supports the notion that quantification, individuation, and textual prominence are all related to each other as well as to the syntactic marking of nouns.

1.6 Definite Marking in Moroccan[6]

Moroccan speech in particular is characterized by the occurrence of unexpectedly "definite" nouns that fulfill none of the conditions specified by Chafe (see 1.2). First-mention nouns are normally indefinite in Arabic, as in most languages that mark definiteness. But in the following passage (repeated from above), even though *children* is semantically indefinite, since the man in question has none, and his wife is introduced for the first time, both /l-wlād/ *the children* and /l-mra/ *the wife* both have definite marking in this passage:

M11 حاجيت لك، هادا واحد الراجل ماعندوش الولاد، عندُه غير المرا
ḥāžīt-lk, hāda wāḥəd ər-rāžəl maʿandūš l-wlād, ʿandu ġi[r] l-mra
told-I-to-you this one the-man neg at-him the-children, at-him only the-wife
I'll tell you a story, this is a man who has no children. He has only a wife

The next passage contains the first mention of /bīt/ *room* in the story; therefore, it would be expected to be indefinite. On the other hand, the noun /bīt/ has highly individuated reference in this case, which 'attracts' the definite article here.

M11 باها ملك سلطان وناض دار لها البيت ديالها بوحدها
bb^{w}āha malik səlṭān w nāḍ dār-lha l-bīt dyālha b^{w-}uḥdha
father-hers king sultan and arose-he made-he for-her the-suite gen-hers by-herself
Her father [was] a king, a sultan, and he up and made her a suite of her own

Similarly, /l-wəld/ *the son* in the following refers to a nonexistent child. The importance and (future) agency of the desired son attract definite marking to a noun that should otherwise be indefinite:

M11 ما عندهاش الولد. ناض گال لها انا خصني الولد
mā ʿndhāš l-wəld. nāḍ gāl-lha ʾana xəṣṣni l-wəld
neg-at-her the-son arose-he said-he to-her I needed-for-me the-son
She didn't have [a] son. He up and told her, I need [a] son

---

[6]See Caubet (1983) for a more detailed, formalized approach to definiteness in Moroccan Arabic.

There is no previous mention of /tūr/ *bull* in the passage from which the next example is taken, nor does it appear to have specific or generic reference, and yet it is marked definite. In this case, either animacy has influenced the 'indefiniteness' of the noun and pushed it towards the definite end of the continuum, or the speaker assumes that a slaughtered bull is an expected and retrievable part of celebrating a son's birth:

M11 دبح التور، عرض على الناس
dbəḥ t-tūr, ʿraḍ ʿla n-nās
slaughtered-he the-bull, invited-he the-people
He slaughtered a bull, invited people

Finally, even though the reference of /l-ḥūt/ *fish* in the following sentence is semantically indefinite, generic, and nonspecific, it carries definite marking. What attracts definite marking here may be the textual importance of *fish* to the passage on the depressed fishing economy of Larache from which this sentence is taken:

M10 ماشي تشوف بعينك تقول راه كاين الحوت
maši tšūf b-ʿīnk tqūl rāh kāyn l-ḥūt
fut you-see with-eye-your you-say see-here there-is the-fish
You'll see with your own eyes and say there are fish

The examples just cited may be contrasted to the following passage, in which an indefinite noun does occur. Here true indefinite nouns are not marked with the so-called "indefinite" articles: /blād/ *a place* is without marking, due to its indefinite, unspecific, and inanimate status in the story; in other words, it is not individuated.

M11 والنهار اللي ولدت امّك هربوا عليها خلّوها بالكرش وخواوا بلاد وعمّروا بلاد
w-n-nhār lli wəldat mm^{w}k hərbu ʿlīha xəllāwha b-l-kərš w xwāw blād w ʿamməru blād
and-day that bore-she mother-your deserted-they on-her left-they-her with-the-belly and emptied-they place and settled-they place
The day that your mother gave birth they deserted her. They left her pregnant and moved to another town.

Of the four dialects, Moroccan speech is clearly the most influenced by the specificity and animacy factors, both of which may trigger the use of definite marking. In the following, all animate nouns are marked with either the definite article or a possessive pronoun, even though not all are semantically definite and specific:

M11 عندك سبعة د خواتاتك، وتجوج باك على امّك على الولد، باش تولد الولد

ʿəndk səbʿa d xwātātk w tžuwwž bb^{w}āk ʿla mm^{w}k ʿla l-wəld, bāš təwləd l-wəld

at-you seven gen sisters-your and married-he father-your on mother-your for the-son in-order-to she-bear the-son

You have seven sisters, and your father took a second wife for [a] son, for her to bear [a] son

Kuwaiti speech contains instances of this phenomenon as well. In these examples, /waladha/ *her son* has specific reference, at least in the mind of the speaker, as does /l-ʾahal/ *the people* in the second.

K3 عندها ولدها ضابط

ʿindha waladha ḏ̣ābiṭ

at-her son-her officer

She has [a] son, an officer

K4 هاذا شغلكم انتو يا الاهل

hāḏa šuġulkum ʾintu ya l-ʾahal

this business-your-p you-p O-the-people

This is your doing, people

The difference between specific and non-specific reference is demonstrated by the following passage. The woman in this passage replies twice to the slave's question, saying at first /wlədt bənt/ *I had a girl*, and the second time, /wlədt l-wəld/, literally *I had the son.*

M11 مشى داك العبد عندها، گال لها گال لك سيدي شنو ولدت؟ گات له ولدت بنت. گال لها گولي لي شنو ولدت، راه إيلا ولدت البنت غ ندبحك وندبحها. تا شافته زايد لها بالموس گات له هدا، ولدت الولد

mša dāk l-ʿəbd ʿəndha, gāl-lha gāl-lik sīdi šnu wlədti? gā[l]t-lu wlədt bənt. gāl-lha gūli-li šnu wlədti rāh ʾila wlədti l-bənt ġa-ndəbḥk w ndbəḥha. ta šāft-u zāyd-lha b-l-mūs, gā[l]t-lu hda, wlədt l-wəld

> went-he that-one the-slave at-her said-he to-her said-he-to-you master-my what bore-you? said-she to-him bore-I girl. said-he-to-her tell-me what bore-you see-here if bore-she the girl will-I-slay-you and I-slay-her. until saw-she-him coming at-her with-the-knife, said-she-to-him calm-down, bore-I the son
> *The slave went to her, said to her, 'My master says, what did you bear?' She told him, 'I had a girl.' He told her, 'Tell me what you had--if you had a girl, I will slay you and slay her.' Until she saw him coming at her with the knife. She told him, 'Calm down, I had a son.'*

The discrepancy in marking between the indefinite *girl* and definite *son* may be attributable to the social importance of the male child, giving him a higher degree of individuation. In any case, it is clear that these features operate as semantic continua, leaving a fair degree of control to the speaker.

Another feature that seems to attract definite marking to Moroccan nouns is that of inalienable possession. Diem (1986) investigates the concepts of alienability and inalienability in Semitic, and suggests that this broad distinction is useful in determining the grammaticality of sentences containing pseudo-verbs /ʿand/ and /li-/, both meaning *to have*, in spoken Arabic. These concepts are indeed important, and in fact they are more broadly applicable than Diem suggests, especially to Moroccan. Diem cites two contrasting examples from a Fez informant, the one on the right judged to be grammatical, and the one on the left ungrammatical (1986:278):

M	* عنده بّا مشهور	M	عنده دار كبيرة
	* ʿndu bba mšhūr		ʿndu dār kbīra
	* Er hat einen berühmten Vater		Er hat ein grosses Haus
	[He has a famous father]		*[He has a big house]*

The ungrammaticality of the second example, Diem claims, is due to the inalienable nature of *father*. A more precise explanation is that this inalienable nature interferes not with the construction *to have*, but with the reference of the noun itself: /bba/ *father* is interpreted by my informants as *my father*:

M1 عيّطت على بّا
ʿəyyəṭṭ ʿla bba
called-I on father
I called my father (elicited)

When pushed to make some sense out of Diem's "ungrammatical" example, my Moroccan informants came up with the interpretation *He thinks my father is famous.* Moreover, they found the following sentence acceptable:

M1 عنده بّاه مشهور
ʿndu bbāh mšhūr
at-him father-his famous
He has a famous father or *His father is famous*

The concept of inalienability applies to /bba/ *father* as a noun, regardless of its syntactic position, in that a father cannot be indefinite or "unassigned." The word /bba/ may not be interpreted as *a father* but only as *my father*. An unusual "double' genitive construction cited by Harning shows a similar pattern (1980:132):

M باباها د يمّا
bābāhā de-yimma
father-her gen Mother
der Vater meiner Mutter [my mother's father]

Here, too, the double marking of the possession seems to be motivated by the need to mark the noun /bābā/ *father* as definite.

Similarly, my Moroccan informants have difficulty producing an indefinite form of the word /xa-/ *brother*. In the next passage, the speaker marks /xāy/ *my brother* and /ʿammi/ *my uncle* for possession, resulting in definite noun phrases, even though the sentence clearly indicates that she has neither a brother nor an uncle:

M9 ما عندي خاي ما عندي عمّي ما عندي تا شي واحد ماش ينوب عليّ
mā ʿndi xāy mā ʿndi ʿammi mā ʿndi ta ši waḥəd māš ynūb ʿliyya
neg at-me brother-my neg at-me uncle-my neg at-me even any one will act-on-behalf of-me
I don't have a brother, I don't have an uncle, I don't have anyone who would act on my behalf

Moroccan speakers thus consistently avoid using terms for male relatives in the indefinite. Diem's concept of inalienability, applied to the individuation continuum, explains this pattern. In turn, it is worth noting that these persons have a high degree of agency, which also may operate to attract specific, definite marking. The individuation hierarchy explains why certain kinds of nouns cannot remain "unassigned" or unspecified. The higher the individuation of a given noun or noun phrase, the more likely it is to receive definite syntactic marking. In the case of Moroccan, certain nouns with high animacy indicating close familial relations seem to take definite marking even in contexts low in definiteness.

The continuum of individuation also explains another feature particular to Moroccan speech. In most varieties of Arabic, both members of a definite noun-adjective phrase must agree in definiteness, such that both will carry the definite article, as the following Egyptian and Syrian examples show:

E1 التايير الموف
it-tayēr il-mōv
the-outfit the-mauve
the mauve outfit

S2 المجتمع السوري
il-mužtamaʿ s-sūri
the-society the-Syrian
Syrian society

However, my Moroccan data include examples of asymmetrically definite constructions such as the following:

M10 ... كيتباعوا ف الحانوت عصري
... kaytbāʿu f l-ḥānūt ʿaṣri
... indic-they-are-sold in-the-store modern
... *they are sold in a modern store*

The phrase /l-ḥānūt ʿaṣri/ *a/the modern store* consists of a definite noun (/l-ḥānūt/) modified by an indefinite adjective (/ʿaṣri/), a construction not permitted under the syntactic rules of Arabic. If it were an isolated occurrence, it could be dismissed as a performance error; however, several such examples occur in my data. Moreover, Harrell notes the occurrence of asymmetrically definite noun-adjective phrases in Moroccan, and notes that the adjective tends to remain unmarked unless the reference is quite specific (1962:166). In fact, specificity may not be the only factor involved. The following example contains a noun-adjective phrase in which the noun is specified, but the adjective is indefinite:

M1 عندها دوقها خاص

ʿəndha dūqha xāṣṣ

at-her taste-her special

She has her own taste or *She has a special taste of her own*

The asymmetric definiteness of the phrase /dūqha xāṣṣ/ *her own special taste* may be explained by the low animacy and high abstractness of the noun /dūq/ *taste*, rendering the noun relatively low in individuation, and attracting the indefinite form of the adjective. A Moroccan informant confirms that the adjective is marked definite only in highly individuated contexts, such as the following:

M3 عندها الدار المخيّرة في الشارع

ʿəndha d-dār l-mxayyəra f š-šārəʿ

at-her the-house the-choice in the-street

She has the best house on the street (elicited)

These Moroccan examples show that indefinite marking can interact with definite marking when the noun in question is not highly individuated. The reverse can also happen: at times definite marking can interact with indefinite to give higher specificity or individuation to an otherwise indefinite noun. Chapter 3 will show that this latter phenomenon occurs as well in relative clause structures in all four dialects.

1.7 Summary

The data cited in this chapter show clearly the inadequacy of traditional categories of definite and indefinite, and suggest that definite and indefinite marking represent two ends of a continuum of definiteness, which includes an indefinite-specific range that may be expressed syntactically by one of several strategies.

The articles /ši/ and /wāḥid/ do not mark true indefinite nouns, but rather nouns that lie somewhere between definite and indefinite, in an indefinite-specific range. This range is represented in the syntax of all four dialects, in Moroccan and Syrian by the article /ši/, in all four dialects by the article /wāḥid (l-)/, which functions as a "new-topic" article, and in Syrian, Egyptian and Kuwaiti by the interaction of the semantics with other definite and indefinite markers, such as the use of definite relative pronouns with morphologically indefinite nouns.[7]

The geographical distribution of indefinite articles in Moroccan and Syrian, both of which share /ši/, the related Egyptian article /ʾiši/, and the apparent indefinite-specific function of the suffix /-in/ in the Arabian Peninsula–even though it is disappearing in urban dialects–are facts that invite further diachronic research. The fact that Moroccan and Syrian dialects share the article /ši/ and Tunisian and Iraqi share a similar article /fard/ suggests that these articles have fulfilled this function for a very long time. Likewise, evidence that nunation plays a role as specifying marker in Andalusian texts, a medieval *Thousand and One Nights* manuscript, and the bedouin dialects of the Gulf, suggests that this function has long been part of spoken Arabic. The absence in Egyptian and urban Kuwaiti of an indefinite-specific article suggests that these dialects may have undergone a linguistic levelling process which reduced the number of syntactic markers of definiteness and specificity.

Overall, Moroccan and Syrian dialects show greater richness and variation in nominal syntactic marking, leading to speculation of a degree of cross-dialect hierarchy in which Moroccan shows highest definite and indefinite-specific marking, while Egyptian shows the least. The fact that Cairene Arabic falls on the lower end of the spectrum of dialects in the range of specifying articles is paralleled also by its relative paucity of demonstrative forms, as Chapter 4 will show.

---

[7]Other dialects appear to have indefinite-specific articles as well: Tunisian and Iraqi appear to share a specifying article /fard/ *one* (see Marçais 1977 for a description of Tunisian and Erwin 1963 for Iraqi).

2 Number, Agreement, and Possession

2.0 Introduction

This chapter examines patterns of plural number agreement and genitive (possessive) modification of nouns in the four dialect regions. Each of these structures has two possible syntactic manifestations in spoken Arabic: plural nouns may be modified with either plural or feminine singular forms, and possessive relationships may be expressed using either the construct (/iḍāfa/)[1] or a periphrastic genitive with a genitive particle or exponent. Patterns of feminine singular agreement with plural nouns occur in all four dialects, and are difficult, if not impossible, to explain in purely formal terms. I will argue that the continuum of individuation (1.2) helps explain the choice of one agreement form over another. Harning's (1980) study of genitive constructions in spoken Arabic proposes certain "stylistic" motivations for the choice of the periphrastic genitive over the construct; her conclusions are reexamined here within the framework of individuation.

Chapter 1 proposed that speakers use definite and indefinite markings to indicate the degree of individuation of a noun such that the higher the degree of individuation of the noun, the more likely the speaker to assign to it a specifying or definite article. The following features were shown to affect the individuation of nouns (repeated from section 1.2):

1. Agency/Animacy
2. Definiteness
3. Specificity
4. Textual prominence
5. Qualification or modification
6. Quantification

These features also play a role in the syntactic realization of agreement phenomena and genitive/possessive constructions in the dialects.

---

[1]The construct consists of two consecutive nouns, the second of which "possesses" (literally or figuratively) the first. In general, the construct in spoken Arabic follows the same rules that govern it in formal Arabic, except that the former has no case markings.

The discussion of number agreement begins with a brief overview of the dual in spoken Arabic. While the dual in formal Arabic constitutes more a morphological than a syntactic category, its counterpart in spoken Arabic carries syntactic implications and is of comparative interest.

2.1 The Dual

Two major articles by Blanc and Ferguson stress that the dual is not a productive category in spoken Arabic.[2] While the dual suffix /-ēn/ (Moroccan /-ayn/) is productive in many areas as a nominal ending, no dual adjectival or verbal markings exist. Ferguson (1959b) identifies the absence of dual agreement as one case of grammatical consistency among the dialects which is not found in Classical Arabic. He finds that the dual is least productive in Moroccan and South Arabian dialects, and most productive in the Syro-Mesopotamian area.

Blanc's (1970) seminal study of the dual in spoken Arabic concludes that Arabic dialects share a two-part dual system, comprised of dual and pseudo-dual. Blanc distinguishes regular, productive duals from a non-productive, frozen pseudo-dual category consisting mainly of words referring to paired parts of the body (e.g., Syrian /ʾižrēn/ *legs*). These pseudo-duals function semantically and syntactically as plurals, and in a number of dialects, no alternate plural forms for such words exist. Blanc concludes that the dual is not a concord category in spoken Arabic; rather dual nouns function syntactically like other enumerated nouns, and generally take plural agreement.[3]

2.1.1 Non-specific Dual

Cowell's Syrian grammar claims that the dual is "used to specify exactly **two** of whatever the noun base designates" (1964:367, emphasis

[2]By contrast, the dual in formal Arabic carries full inflection in nouns, adjectives, relative and demonstrative pronouns, and verb conjugations.

[3]Exceptions noted by Blanc for Syrian and Moroccan, in which dual nouns can be modified by feminine adjectives or verbs, may be explained using the individuation hierarchy. All examples cited contain temporal nouns, such as *day*, *month*, or *year*. These nouns consistently occur in syntactic constructions low in individuation, such as non-resumptive relative clauses (see 3.4) Sections 2.2 and 2.3 show that feminine or collective agreement is consistent with speaker's perceptions of such nouns as not highly individuated.

in original). This assertion is refuted by examples from various dialects in which the dual represents a small but inexact quantity, translatable as *a couple of* or *several*. Expressions such as /yomēn/ *a couple of days* or *several days* and /kiləmtēn/ (Egyptian /kilmitēn/) *a couple of words* or *a few words* are common in both Syria and Egypt. Feghali confirms that the dual in Lebanese usually expresses "une quantité indéterminée" (1928:141).

This dual clearly falls in the non-specific range in the Syrian region, where it is often modified by the indefinite-specific article /ši/:

L من بيروت لطرابلس، بدها شي ساعتين سواقة
min bayrūt la-ṭrāblus, bədha ši sāʿtēn swāʾa
from Beirut to-Tripoli, wants-she ši hours-2 driving
From Beirut to Tripoli it's about a two-hour drive

In the central dialects, then, one function of the dual suffix /-ēn/ is to indicate a non-specific paucal plural, *a couple of* or *several*. Moroccans, on the other hand, use the periphrastic dual, rather than the dual suffix /-ayn/, for such expressions. A Moroccan informant gives two possibilities for *a couple of steps*, meaning *a short distance* (both elicited):

M3	جوج خلفات	جوج د الخطوات
	žūž xəlfāt	žūž d əl-xəṭwāt
	two steps	two gen the-steps

Of all four dialects, Moroccan has the most restricted use of dual suffixes. Section 2.1.2 will discuss several features of the Moroccan dual that set it apart from the dual as used in other dialects.

2.1.2 Dual in Moroccan

Moroccan distinguishes phonetically between dual forms such as /ʿāmayn/ *two years* and what are in other dialects pseudo-duals, namely parts of the body, which in Moroccan take the suffix /-in/: as in /yəddīn/ *hands* and /rəjlīn/ *legs* (Harrell 1962:105, Blanc 1970:48). In Moroccan speech, the suffix /-ayn/ (also pronounced as /-āyn/) is restricted to a finite set of nouns involving a few numerals, physical measures, time, and money, such as /ʿāmayn/ *two years*, /ʾalfayn/ *two thousand*, and /yumayn/ *two days* (see Harrell 1962:100-1; see also Lerchundi 1900 for a similar, century-old description of northern Moroccan). These forms are frozen, containing an unusual /ay/ diphthong that occurs only in certain contexts in Moroccan (Harrell 1962:14); hence the normal Moroccan reflex of the diphthong /ay/ is /ī/ (rather than /ē/ as found in other dialects), as in /bīt/ *room* for /bayt/ (or /bēt/). Educated Moroccan informants reject forms such as /ktābayn/ as not Moroccan. The Moroccan /-ayn/ suffix is thus not productive, as contrasted to the eastern /-ēn/, which may be attached to many types of nouns. Finally, whereas the pseudo-dual forms in other dialects may be paired with plural forms with which they closely correspond in usage (Blanc 1970:46), the Moroccan "pseudo-dual" /-īn/ is the only possible non-singular form for parts of the body.

Blanc uses these facts to support the distinction he makes between what he calls the "true" dual and the pseudo-dual. As Blanc notes, pseudo-dual constitutes a limited class shared by most, if not all, dialect regions (1970:43). But while the "true" dual in other dialects is a productive category, the only productive dual in Moroccan is the periphrastic construction /žūž d/ *two of* followed by a plural: /žūž d l-ktub/ *two books* (Harrell 1962:206; my informants give /ktūba/ for *books*).

Moroccan is the only dialect among the four whose only productive dual is periphrastic, but forms of periphrastic dual are found in all regions. The following section examines the forms and functions of these non-suffixed duals.

2.1.3 Periphrastic Duals

In addition to the Moroccan periphrastic dual /žūž d-/ *two of* with a following plural, two other dialects contain periphrastic dual constructions as well: Kuwaiti and a rural dialect in southern Syria. Holes notes that some Gulf speakers use a periphrastic dual form of the construction *plural noun + numeral two*, as in /kutub iṯnēn/ *two books*, which alternates with /kitābēn/ *two books* (1990:149). One example of this periphrastic dual occurs in my Kuwaiti data, from the oldest and least educated speaker:

K3 ريّال عندَه مرة حريم ثنتين، واحدة حلوة بس هو ما يحبها ، هاذيچ مو حلوة بس يحبها

rayyāl ʿinda mara ḥarīm t̲intēn, waḥda ḥilwa bass hu mā yḥibbha, had̲īč mū ḥilwa, bass yḥibbha
man at-him wife wives two, one pretty but he neg he-loves-her, that-one neg pretty but he-loves-her
A man is married, has two wives, one is pretty, but he doesn't love her, the other one isn't pretty, but he loves her

The fact that this example is used by an elderly uneducated speaker suggests that this periphrastic dual is not a recent development. The same form of periphrastic dual was used twice in conversation by an educated female speaker originally from Ḥūrān, a southern Syrian area whose dialect has a number of bedouin features (Cantineau 1946).

S	رجال اثنين	and	نسوان ثنتين
	rjāl it̲nēn		niswān t̲intēn
	men two (m)		women two (f)
	Two men		*Two women*

My Kuwaiti and rural Syrian examples of the periphrastic dual contain only human nouns.

It seems significant that Moroccan and Gulf dialects and a rural Syrian dialect all share the feature of periphrastic dual, since one would expect these regions to be more conservative linguistically than the central regions.[4]

Egyptian and Syrian speakers also make use of a periphrastic dual for certain classes of words. They have the option of using a periphrastic dual of the form *numeral two + plural noun* with human nouns. The following Egyptian example is also acceptable in Syrian:

E اتنين ضبّاط

itnēn ẓubbāṭ
two officers (Wise 1972:12)

[4]On the other hand, Ingham's description of Najdi syntax lists only a regular dual, and does not mention periphrastic dual forms. Ingham also notes feminine singular adjectival agreement with dual nouns (bētēnin zēnah/ *two good houses*, 1994:63), a construction rejected by informants from the four dialects areas examined here.

This periphrastic dual is obligatory in certain cases, as the dual suffix /-ēn/ cannot be affixed to certain classes of words.[5] Thus in Lebanon, one can only say *two Lebanese* using the periphrastic dual (below left), not the dual suffix (below right):

L	اتنين لبنانيّة	*لبنانيّين
	itnēn libnāniyye	* libnāniyyēn
	two Lebanese-p	* Lebanese-two

The dual of other word classes may be expressed with either the periphrastic dual or the dual suffix. Both of the following forms are acceptable:

L	اتنين اساتذة	استاذين
	itnēn ʾasātze	ʾistāzēn
	two teachers	*two teachers*

However, my Lebanese informant confirms that periphrastic /itnēn/ *two* does not modify inanimates, or even animals: the form /ḥmārēn/ means *two asses* of the animal kingdom, while /itnēn ḥamīr/ refers to the human variety.

Periphrastic dual constructions in which the numeral *two* either precedes or follows a human noun thus occur in all regions. This use of the numeral *two* parallels syntactically and functionally the use of the numeral /wāḥid/ *one* as a "new topic" marker (see 1.5). That is, like new topic article /wāḥid/ *one*, new topic *two* functions in part to indicate the relatively high individuation (animacy, specificity, and/or textual prominence) of the entities it introduces. Further evidence supporting this analysis follows.

2.1.4 Dual as New-Topic Marker

Blanc notes that the dual may be used to introduce two figures into a story, whereas mention of them after that is usually plural (1970:44, his sources: Spitta 1883, Blau 1960, and his own data). Cowell remarks that "[i]f the number happens to be two but is beside the point, or to be taken for granted, then the *plural* is used (1964:367, emphasis in original).

---

[5]Blanc remarks only that "[i]n all dialects, there are nouns that do not admit the dual at all" (1970:43). An inventory of morphological and lexical restrictions on the use of the dual suffix is a subject suitable for a morphological study.

The fact that dual marking often occurs on the first mention of nouns suggests its use is pragmatically marked, and not simply a case of free variation. Nouns marked with the dual suffix usually represent new topics; that is, they represent the first mention of textually prominent entities. Cowell notes that the dual is used in contrast to the singular, not the plural, and that expression of a quantity of two in definite possessed form uses the definite plural followed by the number *two* (1964:367):

S كتبي الاتنين
kətbi t-tnēn
books-my the-two
my two books

Further evidence that the dual ending represents a new-topic marker lies in speakers' avoidance of pronoun suffixes on dual nouns, with the exception of body parts. Holes points out that Gulf speakers refrain from using pronoun suffixes on dual nouns but not on human plural nouns ending in /-īn/ (1990:150), suggesting that the restriction on affixing pronoun suffixes to dual nouns has more to do with pragmatic factors than with rules of formal Arabic.[6] If the dual suffix reflects a kind of salience marking similar to the marking of new topics with the article /wāḥid/ *one*, then it is more likely to occur in the more individuating syntactic construction containing a genitive exponent than in construct genitives (see 2.4).

Moroccan speakers do not appear to make use of this kind of dual, and I have no evidence for its existence in Kuwait either. Both dialects use the periphrastic dual described in 2.1.3. The lack of this dual in the two peripheral, conservative dialects suggests that it has not always been a feature of spoken Arabic.

Language typology and the hierarchy of number marking posits that dual is marked relative to plural. As Croft notes: "Most commonly, the dual is marked with respect to distributional behavior. Frequently, dual forms are found only with personal and demonstrative pronouns"

---

[6]Rules for adding pronoun suffixes in formal Arabic dictate that the /n/ in both dual and sound masculine plural suffixes be dropped. In spoken Arabic, the /n/ may be retained, but the resulting construction is usually avoided.

(1990:100). Taken together with this general linguistic pattern, synchronic evidence from these dialects suggests that it is not so much a matter of spoken Arabic losing a productive dual with full agreement complement as of not having it in the first place. A future diachronic study of the dual in spoken Arabic might explore the possibility that the dual ending /-ēn/ as a new-topic salience marker represents a point of contact between formal and spoken Arabic, and a window on the role of pragmatics in the process of syntactic borrowing.

2.1.5 Pseudo-duals

As Blanc notes, pseudo-duals of parts of the body actually constitute a form of plural in Syrian and Egyptian. In fact, Cowell points out that a separate, "true" dual form also exists for such words in Syrian, formed by inserting a /-t-/ before the dual suffix /-ēn/. Cowell gives the following examples (1964:367):

S	اجرتينه	ايدتين	عينتين
	ʾəžərtēno	ʾittēn	ʿēntēn
	his two legs	*two hands*	*two eyes*

This "new dual" ending must have developed sometime after the original dual ending (Blanc's pseudo-dual) was reinterpreted as a plural. This development, the apparent result of speakers' "need" to express the quantity "exactly two" specifically for parts of the body, suggests that the historical development of the pseudo-dual has been divorced from that of the "true" dual. While Syrian /-t-/ distinguishes /ʾidēn/ *hands* from /ʾi(d)tēn/ *two hands*, it cannot be used to differentiate between /yōmēn/ *a couple of days* and /yomtēn/ *two days*. The fact that a particular dual ending exists for a specific semantic field does not necessarily mean that it extends to others, and any history of the dual in spoken Arabic must be category-specific, taking into account the fact that different kinds of dual exhibit different behavior. For example, Blanc points out that only pseudo-dual forms admit pronoun suffixes with the elision of the /n/ from /-ēn/ (as in formal Arabic), such as in Egyptian /riglayya/ *my legs* (1970:48). His "true" duals rarely admit such suffixes, except in formal registers of Arabic. This pattern suggests that the pseudo-dual may be older than the "true" dual in spoken Arabic.

Egyptian speakers have at their disposal plural forms that alternate with pseudo-dual forms, such as /ʿinēn in-nās/, pseudo-dual, and /ʿuyūn in-nās/, plural, both meaning *people's eyes.* It should not be assumed, as Blanc does, that at most "perhaps a shade of stylistic difference" (1970:46, n. 15) lies between them, because "stylistic difference" often points to an underlying pragmatic principle, perhaps a difference in degree of individuation. However, a larger corpus of contextualized examples needs to be examined before conclusions can be drawn.

2.1.6 Adverbial Dual

Another kind of dual, the adverbial, may not be dual in origin. A small, closed class of adverbial expressions found mostly in the Levant end in the suffix /-ēn/:

S	اهلين	صحّتين	مرحبتين	بعدين
	ʾahlēn	ṣaḥḥtēn	marḥəbtēn	baʿdēn
	welcome!	*bon appetit*	*welcome!*	*later*

Blanc claims that /ʾahlēn/ *welcome*, /ṣaḥḥtēn/ *bon appetit* and /marḥəbtēn/ *welcome* are duals; however, it seems more likely that the first two are actually cases of /ʾimāla/ *deflection*, or pronunciation of the vowel /a/ as a more fronted vowel, deflected towards /i/, known to occur in the Levant. At some later point /-en/ (or a stressed, lengthened /-ēn/) was then reanalyzed as a dual ending, and /marḥəbtēn/ was then formed by analogy. The vowel shift of /ʾimāla/ may also be responsible for the suffix /-ēn/ in /baʿdēn/ *after that*, the origin of which would in that case be /baʿd ʾan/ *after* (with following verb), found in Syria and Egypt.

2.2 Agreement Patterns of Plural Nouns

The Arabic plural has a number of subcategories.[7] Morphologically, Arabic distinguishes sound and broken plurals, and collective and distributive ones. Semantically, human nouns constitute a group distinct from inanimate ones. However, agreement patterns in spoken Arabic follow none of these delineations.

Agreement patterns of plural nouns in spoken Arabic seem at first to be fraught with difficulties; complicated sets of rules are found

[7]For an overview of plurals in educated spoken Arabic, see Sallam (1979).

in the grammars of several Arabic dialects. Holes notes for educated Gulf Arabic, which includes Kuwaiti, four "systems" of number/gender agreement, divided along gender and animacy lines (1990:155-7). Three of these 'systems' are found in Kuwait: (1) in the first, all plural nouns take masculine plural agreement; (2) the second system distinguishes between human and non-human, and all non-human nouns take feminine singular agreement; and (3) a third system combines rules from (1) and (2) and allows either masculine plural or feminine singular agreement with non-human nouns.[8] However, Holes admits that it is common for speakers to freely alternate between systems, a fact which would seem to preclude calling them systems.

Holes' analysis might stand as an example of interdialectic contact in the Gulf, except that dialects in other regions show similar overlapping agreement patterns. Adjectives and verbs modifying plural nouns alternate between feminine singular and plural marking.[9] Thus examples like the following occur in all dialect regions. In the first sentence, the plural subject /nās/ *people* takes deflected agreement (feminine singular) on the verb /bitfakkir/ *she thinks*, whereas the second sentence contains the same subject with a plural verb, /bisāfru/ *they travel*:

S3 بعرف ناس بيسافروا كل سنة
ba'rif nās bisāfru kill sine
I-know people indic-they-travel every year
I know people who go abroad every year

S2 فيه يعني ناس بتفكّر انّه شغلة عادي يعني
fī ya'ni nās bitfakkir ʾinnu šaġle ʿādi ya'ni
there-is that-is people indic-3fs-thinks comp-3ms thing (f) normal (m) that-is that-is
There are people who think that it is a normal thing, that is

[8]Holes (1990) does not include data on collective nouns, non-human animate nouns, or verbal agreement.

[9]The feminine singular agreement pattern, called deflected agreement, was regularized and codified in formal Arabic during its early history. However, the Quran and other early texts contain examples of both strict and deflected agreement (see Belnap 1991). It is reasonable to assume that these two types of agreement, deflected and plural, have coexisted for a long time.

Moreover, in the latter example, speaker S2 uses a masculine adjective, /ʿādi/ *normal*, to modify a feminine noun, /šaġle/ *thing*.

The agreement patterns in the examples cited above are difficult to explain in purely formal terms. Clearly, lexical items do not "control" agreement of nouns and adjectives; rather, the speaker determines the semantic or pragmatic content of the nouns themselves and chooses agreement patterns accordingly. Variation in agreement patterns appears to correlate with patterns of collective and individuated reference. In the case of feminine agreement cited above, /nās/ *people* is collective, referring to a group of people who all think alike. Individuation–or in this case, lack thereof–helps explain this pattern. Human nouns lower in individuation, not specified or modified, but rather viewed as being part of a collective whole, tend to take feminine singular agreement.

Several studies of agreement in spoken Arabic point to the role of individuation in determining verbal and adjectival agreement with plural nouns. Cowell notes that in Syrian, some plurals and collectives take feminine singular agreement "when collectivity or generality is emphasized rather than heterogeneity or particularity" (1964:423). This description suggests that the adjectival and verbal agreement of a plural noun depends on the degree to which the members of that plural set are individuated, and that agreement may be seen as a continuum ranging from collective to individuated.

Sallam shows that quantification affects agreement in the educated spoken Arabic of Egypt and the Levant (1979:37). He contrasts the unacceptability of a plural adjective with a collective plural noun in the first of the following minimal pair to the acceptability of the second, to which the quantifier /šwayyit/ *some, a few [pieces of]* is added (1979:37):

E *اشترينا ملابس كويّسين

* ištarēna malābis kwayyisīn

* bought-we clothes good-p

* *We bought nice (p) clothes*

E اشترينا شوية ملابس كويّسين

ištarēna šwayyit malābis kwayyisīn

bought-we some clothes nice-p

We bought some nice clothes

In the following two Moroccan passages (both taken from the same speaker and text), the same noun is given two different agreements, one feminine singular and one plural. In the first, the speaker treats the noun /n-nās/ *people* as an unspecified, unqualified, homogenous, generic group. The convergence of these features, all of them non-individuating, serves to push the noun to the non-individuated end of the individuation continuum. The low individuation of /n-nās/ *people* is manifested in the feminine singular form of the verb /mā katfəhəmš/ *they don't understand*, and the pronoun /ha/ on /baʿḍha/ *each other*. The second statement contains a different kind of reference to /n-nās/ *people*. In this case, a more specific group of people is named, and the noun is qualified by /wlād l-blād/ *sons of the town*. This higher degree of specificity is reflected in the plural agreement shown on the verb phrase /mā bqāwš kaymšīw/ *they no longer go*.

M10 الناس ما بقتش النوع د الاحترام ... الناس ما كتفهمش بعضها
n-nās mā bqatš n-nūʿ d l-əḥtirām ... n-nās mā katfəhəmš baʿḍha
the-people neg remained-3fs the-type gen the-respect ... the-people neg indic-3fs-understand each-other-f
People no longer [have] respect ... people don't understand each other

M10 كتشوف بزّاف د الناس ولاد البلاد ما بقاوش كيمشيوا البحر
katšūf bəzzāf d n-nās wlād l-blād mā bqāwš kaymšīw l-bḥar
indic-you-see a-lot gen the-people sons of-the-town neg remained-they indic-they-go the-sea
You see many people, town natives, no longer go to the beach

The feminine singular agreement on the reflexive pronoun /baʿḍha/ *each other* in the former sentence is worth noting, since reflexivity is one of the features Khan classifies as non-individuating (1984:470). However, not all reflexive nouns are entirely non-individuated, as the following Syrian example shows (Cowell 1964:425):

S هالألوان ما بيناسبوا بعضهن
ha l-ʾalwān mā bināsbu baʿḍon
[this the-colors neg indic-they-are-appropriate-for each-other]
These colors don't go together

Cowell argues that the reflexivity here adds to the individuation of these colors; however, the speaker's reference to certain specific colors suggests that individuation is a property of the colors themselves. Cowell himself observes that the same idea may be expressed by a feminine reflexive verb, /mā btətnāsab/ *they [3fs] don't match.*

The principle of individuation affects agreement patterns in the opposite manner as well, in that some morphologically "singular" nouns that refer to a collective group may take plural agreement. In the following two Syrian passages about premarital dating, the speaker comments that some people accept it and some do not. In both instances, she uses masculine nouns, /ʿālam/ (*people*, literally *world*) and /ši/ (literally, *thing*) with plural agreement. In each case, it is not the lexical item itself that determines the agreement, but its referent, a group of people:

S2 فيه عالم هيك وفيه عالم هيكي ، مشكّل يعني ، عالم بيقبلوا ...
fī ʿālam hēk wi fī ʿālam hēke, mšakkal yaʿni, ʿālam byiqbalu ..
there-is world like-that and there-is world like-that mixed-ms that-is world they-accept
There are people like this and people like that, it's mixed, that is, people who accept ...

S2 إلاّ يعني عالم اسوأ منها بكتير كتير يعني شي إلن ماضي كتير مشرشح منشان يقبلوا ياخدوا يعني هالبنت
ʾilla yaʿni ʿālam ʾaswaʾ min[h]a bi-ktīr ktīr yaʿni še ʾilon māḍi ktīr mšaršaḥ minšān yiqbalu yāxdu yaʿni ha l-binət
except that-is world worse than-her by-a-lot a-lot that-is thing to-them past very sordid in-order-to they-accept they-take that-is this the-girl
except for people who are much worse than her, that is, people who have a very sordid past, to accept to marry the girl

Yet another example from the same interview shows /əl-ʿālam/ *people* as subject of two feminine verbs, /taṭawwaret/ *developed* and /mā ʿādet/ *is no longer.* In this case, *people* is a collective whole, referring to people in general:

S2 لانه تطورت العالم ما عادت متل أول
la'innu tṭawwaret il-ʿālam, mā ʿādet mitil 'awwel
because-3ms developed-3fs the-world neg remained-3fs like first
Because people developed, they're no longer like they were before

Viewing the grammatical feature of plural agreement as a continuum allows a principled account of the variation that occurs, and reflects the speaker's control over this feature. At one end of the continuum lies collectivity, which corresponds to feminine singular agreement, and at the other, individuation, which corresponds to plural agreement. The choice of agreement depends on the features that influence individuation, especially specificity and agency. This continuum allows for the prediction that many plural nouns will not be limited to one agreement pattern: /nās/ *people* may be more or less individuated and thus may show either feminine singular or masculine plural agreement.

This view of number agreement also predicts that dual nouns take plural agreement rather than singular: by nature, a dual noun indicates some degree of individuation, and hence usually does not provide collective reference. Similarly, in the dialects that have an overlap of plural and pseudo-dual forms, the patterns of usage may be influenced by the degree of individuation of the noun phrase; in other words, the choice an Egyptian speaker makes between /ʿenēn in-nās/ *the eyes* (pseudo-dual) *of the people* and /ʿuyūn in-nās/ *the eyes* (plural) *of the people* may be based on the degree to which /in-nās/ *the people* is individuated.

In the most extensive study of agreement patterns in Arabic to date, Belnap investigates agreement patterns in Cairene Arabic, concluding that a number of factors combine to affect agreement, among them animacy (1991:61), salience (85), distance from the head noun to the modifier (85), and sentence typology (89). His study confirms that pragmatic ("functional and psychological") factors subsume formal and positional principles (99). Belnap also concludes that it is the speaker who really controls agreement patterns, not the head noun (143).

The following Egyptian example, from Belnap's data, provides another case in which the speaker controls agreement patterns, and suggests that individuation plays a central role in the selection of agreement. This speaker uses a feminine adjective, /ʿayyāna/ *sick*, and a plural verb, /biyiʾʿudu/ *they stay*, to modify the same noun within the same sentence (Belnap 1991:61):

E كل الناس عيّانة بالسكّر وبيقعدوا لوحدهم

kull in-nās ʿayyāna bi-s-sukkar wi-biyiʾʿudu li-waḥduhum
all the-people sick-f with-the-sugar and-they-sit by-themselves
All the people are sick with diabetes and live by themselves

Why does this speaker use a feminine adjective and a plural verb to describe the same group of people? In the first clause, people are viewed and treated as a homogenous group, whereas in the second, the adverbial phrase /li-waḥduhum/ *by themselves* adds individuation, since every single person lives alone. A similar example shows the agreement shifting from feminine singular /ha/ to plural /hum/ when the speaker moves from talking about /šiwayyit ḥagāt/ *some things* as a homogenous group to separating and ranking them (example from Belnap 1991:86; translation mine):

E شوية حاجات ... مش بترتيب اهمّيتها ... وبعدين نشوف اذا كنا نرتّبهم

šuwayyit ḥagāt ... miš bi-tartīb ahammiyyitha .. wi baʿdēn nišūf ʾiza kunna nirattibhum
some things ... neg by-rank importance-3fs ... and-then we-see if were-we we-order-them
... a few things ... not in order of their importance ... and then we'll see if we can order them

The 'distance from head noun' principle Belnap notes may be related to individuation. The more that is said about a noun, the more specified and textually prominent it becomes; therefore, if the "distance" between the noun and its modifier includes further mention or specification of that noun, its individuation will increase, and the probability of plural agreement will likewise increase. The following Syrian example echoes Belnap's Egyptian ones: while the first verb modifying /əl-ʾaṣdiqa/ *friends* is feminine, the rest of the sentence shows plural agreement (example from Grotzfeld 1965:97, translation mine):

S الاصدقا بتروح لعند بعضن وبيعايدوا على بعضن
əl-ʾaṣdiqa bətrūḥ la-ʿand baʿḍon w biʿāydu ʿala baʿḍon
[the-friends indic-3fs-goes to-at each-other and indic-they-wish-happy-holidays for each-other]
Friends go to each other's [houses] and wish each other happy holidays

Unfortunately, the Kuwaiti texts I collected have no examples that contrast deflected and plural agreement.

The speaker's perception of the individuation of a noun thus affects his or her choice of agreement. If a noun is highly individuated, animate, specific, textually prominent, or quantified, the speaker tends to choose plural agreement; conversely, if the noun is collective, non-specific, collective, and less prominent, the agreement will tend to be feminine singular. It makes sense to call these agreement patterns *individuated* and *collective*: individuated agreement referring to the use of plural verbs, adjectives, and pronouns, and collective agreement to feminine singular modification. These terms reflect the pragmatic choice made by the speaker in representing the nature of the entity she or he is describing.

One corollary of the theory that individuation underlies agreement patterns is that modified plurals will be more likely to take plural agreement than unmodified ones. An unmodified plural noun is less likely to be individuated, and thus more likely to be treated as a collective, taking a feminine singular verb or predicate, whereas adjectival modification automatically makes the noun more specified and thus more individuated. Examination of agreement data in the dialects yields several indications that agreement patterns of verb and subject differ from those of adjectives.

In Moroccan, Harrell notes that inanimate nouns only rarely, "in isolated idioms and stereotyped phrases," take feminine singular agreement (1962:158). My Moroccan corpus contains one instance in which a plural noun takes a feminine adjective, and here, the noun in question, /masāʾil/ *things*, belongs to the formal register of Arabic, which probably explains the feminine singular adjective /qbīḥa/ *ugly*:

M10 كيبقى يقول شي كلمة قبيحة، كيقول شي مسائل قبيحة
kaybqa yqūl ši kəlma qbīḥa, kayqūl ši masāʾil qbīḥa
indic-he-keeps indic-he-says some word ugly indic-he-says some things ugly
He keeps saying some nasty word, he says some nasty things

Caubet's Moroccan grammar includes a similar example, also somewhat formal in style (1993ii:274, translation mine):

M كاين أفلام هندية كيترجموها بالدارجة
kāyn ʾaflām hindiyya kaytəržmuha b-əd-dāriža
[there-is films Indian indic-they-translate-3fs in-the-colloquial]
There are Indian movies they translate into colloquial

The formal register of these examples notwithstanding, both contain indefinite, non-specific nouns low in individuation, which may also play a role in the use of collective agreement.

Sallam's study of agreement treats adjectival concord in educated spoken Arabic of Egypt and the Levant. He finds that non-Egyptians showed little acceptance of deflected adjectival agreement with human plurals (1979:42-9). The Egyptian pattern of collective (deflected) agreement with human groups is well-documented by Belnap (1991). However, my Syrian data and Cowell's grammar contain a number of examples in which human plural subjects collocate with a feminine singular verb. From my data:

S5 اغنى اغنياء أميركا عم تروح تسكن بهالمنطقة
ʾaġna ʾaġniyāʾ ʾamērka ʿam trūḥ tiskun bi-hā l-manṭʾa.
richest of-the-rich-p of-America prog 3fs-goes 3fs-lives in-this-the-region
The richest of the rich of America are going to live in this area

Cowell lists a number of examples containing subjects /nās/ *people*, /ʾahəl/ *people, folks*, and plurals ending in the feminine /e/ (a Syrian variant of /a/) such as /šaġġīle/ *workers*, and /ʾasātze/ *professors* (1964:424). All but one of Cowell's examples contain deflected verb-subject agreement, but not noun-adjective agreement. The exception contains two types of agreement with the noun, the plural pronoun /-hon/ *them* and the feminine adjective /kbīre/ *large* (1964:423):

S هالمغلفات هاللي جبتهن كبيرة
hal-ᵊmġallafāt halli žəbthon ᵊkbīre
[this-the-envelopes rel brought-you-3p big-f]
These envelopes [that] you brought are too large

This case of split agreement reflects a shift in the individuation of /mġallafāt/ *envelopes*: in the subject clause, the speaker identifies a specific, identifiable group of envelopes, while the predicate /kbīre/ *big* classifies them, in that they all belong to the class of envelopes that is too large.

In addition to adjectival modification, possession adds specificity as well. A contrasting pair of Egyptian sentences suggests that possessed nouns tend to take individuated rather than collective agreement. The first example contains the plural predicate /mitrabbiyīn/ *raised properly* modifying /ʿiyālu/ *his children*, while the second contains a collective verb /bitʿallaʾ/ *(3fs) hangs* modifying collective /il-ʿiyāl/ *children*:

E5 عياله مش متربّيّين
ʿiyālu miš mitrabbiyīn
children-his neg raised-properly-p
His children haven't been raised properly [aren't well behaved]

E4 في رمضان العيال بتعلّق فوانيس في الشارع
fi-ramaḍān l-ʿiyāl bitʿallaʾ fawanīs fi š-šāriʿ
in-Ramadan the-children indic-3fs-hangs lanterns in the-street
In Ramadan, children hang lanterns in the street

More evidence may be found in other varieties of Arabic. Rosenhouse notes a difference between verb-subject concord and noun-adjective concord in Palestinian bedouin dialects, such that the former tends to be feminine, the latter plural (1984a:116). And Belnap's study of agreement in Classical Arabic results in a much higher percentage of pronouns and verbs showing collective agreement than adjectives, reflecting the same patterns found in the dialects (1991:126). In general, then, collective (feminine singular) verb-subject agreement occurs more frequently than collective singular noun-adjective agreement, and this tendency is predicted by the higher degree of individuation associated with modified nouns.

Within this general pattern, individual dialects appear to show some degree of variation. Moroccan speakers appear to favor individuated (plural) agreement over collective (feminine) agreement, a tendency which parallels the Moroccan preference for a higher degree of individuation marking (see section 1.6). Cairene seems to fall at the other end of this spectrum: Belnap and Sallam both indicate that "Cairenes tend to use deflected [feminine] agreement more than speakers of other dialects" (Belnap 1991:64). This Cairene tendency to accord less syntactic attention to the individuation of nouns is mirrored as well in the absence in Egyptian of certain specifying articles and demonstrative forms found in other dialects (see Chapters 1 and 4).

2.3 Agreement Neutralization[10]

Agreement neutralization refers here to the absence of gender (feminine) or number (plural) grammatical agreement marking on verbs and adjectives whose subjects or head nouns are feminine or plural. Neutralization of adjectival agreement is prevalent in Egypt among certain classes of adjectives, and a few isolated cases may be found in the Levant and Kuwait. Neutralization of verb-subject agreement can occur in verb-initial sentences (VS typology), and represents a more general pattern found in most varieties of Arabic.

2.3.1 Neutralized Adjectival Agreement

Sallam's (1979) study of concord in the noun phrase examines data collected from a number of educated speakers from Egypt and the Levant, and notes a pattern of agreement loss or neutralization frequent among Egyptian speakers. Building on the research of Mitchell (1956, 1973), and Wise (1972), Sallam notes that certain adjectives, generally belonging to the morphological class of relational adjectives (Arabic /nisba/), especially those denoting place of origin or color, often show no gender or number agreement. His examples, most of them indefinite, include /ʾaṣīda ʿarabi/ *an Arabic poem*, and /rasma nglīzi/ *an English design* (1979:27). In both, the nouns are feminine and the adjectives neutralized (masculine).

---

[10]I have adapted the term *agreement neutralization* from Belnap 1991.

Sallam finds this phenomenon to be far less frequent in the Levant. Even so, evidence exists of agreement neutralization on certain relational adjectives when modifying nouns of low individuation. Sallam notes that most of his informants accept a masculine adjective in the phrase /līra libnāni/ *a Lebanese pound* (1979:41). And in the following Syrian proverb depicting a first-rate person or thing, the masculine classificatory adjective /ṣīni/ *china* modifies the feminine noun /zibdiyye/ *bowl* (example from Nelson et al. 1996:424). The low specificity of the noun phrase (any china bowl will do) may also help attract neutralized agreement.

S متل الزبدية الصيني منين ما رنّيتيها بترنّ
mitl iz-zibdiyye ṣ-ṣīni mnēn ma rannētīha bitrinn
like the-bowl the-china from-where nom rang-you-3fs indic-3fs-rings
Like a china bowl, wherever you tap it, it rings

The next two examples, from Syria and Kuwait, show the masculine adjective /ʿādi/ *normal* modifying feminine nouns of low individuation:

S2 بيكون عنده شغلة عادي
bikūn ʿandu šaġle ʿādi
indic-it-is at-him thing normal
It is for him a normal thing

K1 فظلّيت نص ساعة بعدين صارت السالفة عادي
fa-ḏ̣allēt nəṣṣ sāʿa baʿdēn ṣārət is-sālfa ʿādi
so-remained-I half hour then became-3fs the-talk (f) normal-ms
So I remained half an hour, then conversation became normal

Individuation thus seems to affect the neutralized agreement patterns of certain adjectives. Most of Sallam's examples consist of words for nationality, educational classes, such as class or course curriculum, and the like; in other words, they provide classificatory description (membership in a class) rather than the identification of a specific or particular item (1.2). Classificatory adjectives are more likely to show neutralized agreement. Sallam's data and Belnap's elicitation tasks both center on indefinite nouns, and thus do not provide adequate samplings covering the entire individuation continuum. Indirect evidence supporting this analysis lies in the parallel of neutralized agreement in Egyptian to the relative frequency of feminine singular agreement with plural nouns, as compared to other dialect regions (2.2). To really test this theory, however, a full range of both definite and indefinite data is needed.

Sallam's Egyptian data present a particular problem: while (a), (b), and (c) below are attested, his informants reject (d) as ungrammatical (1979:25-8; all these nouns are feminine, all the adjectives masculine):

(a) وردة بلدي
warda baladi
a home-grown rose

(b) قصيدة عربي
ʾaṣīda ʿarabi
an Arabic poem

(c) اللهجة المصري
il-lahga l-maṣri
the Egyptian dialect

(d) *وردة مصري
*warda maṣri
* *an Egyptian rose*

This pattern can be explained using the individuation hierarchies. The masculine adjective /maṣri/ *Egyptian* can modify the definite but abstract feminine noun /il-lahga/ *dialect*, but not the indefinite but otherwise individuated /warda/ *rose, flower*. The fact that /warda/ *one rose* can be modified by masculine /baladi/ *native, unsophisticated* is a function of the adjective /baladi/. Like other adjectives that tend to take neutralized agreement, viz., /tāni/ *other, another*, /ʿādi/ *usual, normal*, and /ktīr/ *many* (Belnap 1991:93), /baladi/ describes something completely unremarkable, and in that sense, unindividuated.[11]

An unexpected use of the infrequently used plural adjective /kutār/ *many*, usually neutralized as /ktīr/ (masculine singular form), not only supports this analysis, but also provides a sociolinguistic motivation for some of these agreement patterns. Belnap cites a rare instance of plural agreement /kutār/ *many* with both the plural /wuzara/ *ministers* and the (often) collective /nās/ *people* (1991:93):

---

[11]Sallam's observation that /baladi/ occurs in the feminine in the phrase /magālis baladiyya/ *local councils* (1979:27) is explained by the fact that /baladi/ in this latter case has a different meaning, referring to the local township (the phrase does **not** mean *native or unsophisticated councils*). I suspect that the adjective /maṣri/ *Egyptian* functions in a way opposite that of /baladi/, at least to some extent. For most Egyptian speakers, /maṣri/ carries a highly positive identity connotation, and in this sense should tend to show patterns of high individuation. A sociolinguistic investigation of this topic might produce interesting results.

E وزرا كتار كتار عملتلهم شغل ... اشتغلت مع ناس كتار في البلد
wuzara kutār kutār ʿamalt-ilhum šuġl ... ištaġalt maʿ nās kutār fi-l-balad
ministers many-p many-p did-I-for-them work ... worked-I with people many-p in-the-country
Many, many ministers, I did work for them ... I worked with many people in the country

The context of this example suggests a reason for the unusual plural form /kutār/ *many*. The speaker, a cabinetmaker, cites the many important people for whom he has worked. The plural agreement raises the individuation of /wuzara/ *ministers* and /nās/ *people*, heightening the speaker's portrayal of them as prominent and powerful individuals. In elevating their status, the speaker increases his own status by association, since they have sought him out. This use of agreement may reflect a kind of sociolinguistic posturing, a way for speakers to signal high individuation, and hence status, of themselves and others.

Sectarian identity in the Levant provides another possible example of the social use of agreement. In the following passage, a Syrian Christian attributes the rather strict mores of her society to the conservative Islamic country in which she lives. In modifying the feminine /baladna/ *our country*, the speaker uses feminine adjectives /mutaʿaṣṣibe/ *fanatic* and /muḥāfiḏa/ *conservative*, but uses the masculine form of /ʾislāmi/ *Islamic*:

S2 خاصة نحنا عندنا بلاد يعني بلدنا متعصبة بيقولوا عنها إسلامي ومحافظة
xāṣṣa niḥna ʿan[d]na bilād yaʿni baladna mutaʿaṣṣibe biqūlu ʿan[h]a ʾislāmi w muḥāfiḏa
especially we at-us country that-is country-our fanatical indic-3p-say about-3fs Islamic-m and conservative-f
Especially since we have a country -- our country is fanatical, so they say, Islamic and conservative

The context and seemingly deliberate use of a masculine *Islamic* followed directly by the feminine *conservative* suggest a kind of distancing posture assumed by the speaker.

Another text from northern Syria contains the noun /ʾislām/ *Islam* (rather than /muslimīn/ *Muslims*) to specify the sectarian identity of Muslims who moved into the (Christian) speaker's town of Sulaymaniyya (Behnstedt 1989:66, translation mine):

S ما كانت معمرة السليمانية، ما فيها خلق كتير. بعدين صارت
تتعمّر، صاروا العالم ينتقلوا وصارت هلّق هونيك يعني ناس،
صاروا اسلام.

mā kānet mʿammra s-sleymānīye, mā fīya xalʾ ᵊktīr. baʿdeyn ṣāret tətʿammar, ṣāru l-ʿālam yintəʾlu u ṣāret hallaʾ hawnīk yaʿni nās, ṣāru ʾislām.

neg was-3fs built-up-f Sulaymaniyya, neg in-3fs creation many. then became-3fs 3fs-get-built-up, became-3p the-world 3p-move and became-3fs now there that-is people, became-3p Islam

Sulaymaniyya was not built up, there weren't many people there (in it). Then it started getting built up, people started moving [there], and now, there, there [have] come to be, you know, people, they [have] come to be "Islam" [Muslims].

Does the use of /ʾislām/ *Islam* in this text also represent linguistic posturing? Lebanese informants confirm that the terms /ʾislām/ *Islam* and /masīḥiyye/ *Christian* or *Christianity* are often used by Lebanese of both religions to refer to the sectarian identity of groups of people (an informant insists that these terms do not refer to the religions themselves but rather to people). The use of the nominal form /ʾislām/ rather than the adjective, which would have to be the more individuating plural /muslimīn/ *Muslims*, may simply emphasize the collective identity rather than the individual.

As Belnap points out, the search for the purpose of agreement, syntactically redundant in many languages, has frustrated linguists for years (1991:25). What is the motivation for retaining a syntactic function that seems to carry little or no meaning of its own? Perhaps the reason lies partly in social meaning. Evidence from spoken Arabic suggests that agreement is a feature that allows speakers to claim for themselves or others a degree of social status or power, a kind of linguistic posturing.

Belnap notes among his informants a "general tendency of male speakers to favor deflected agreement more than female speakers," suggesting this finding as possible evidence of linguistic change in progress (1991:95). However, another plausible hypothesis is that social identity (in this case, gender) might affect agreement choice. In other words, adult male speakers, having a relatively high degree of status or agency vis-a-vis other social groups, tend to use non-individuating agreement patterns more than less privileged groups. If Belnap's results do reflect a general social trend, and if certain social groups use deflected agreement patterns to speak about others, the agreement might reflect or reinforce their own high status vis-a-vis the lower status of others.

2.3.2 Verb-Subject Number Agreement

Verb-initial sentences (V[erb] S[ubject] sentence typology) occur in all registers of Arabic. Formal Arabic has a rule that governs verb-subject neutralization in VS sentences: a verb that precedes its subject must show singular agreement. Gender agreement rules normally apply, except that a verb separated from its subject may show masculine singular agreement regardless of the number or gender of the subject. These patterns commonly occur in most dialects as well.

In VS sentences, then, verb-subject agreement may be neutralized in most (if not all) forms of Arabic. Cowell notes that this phenomenon most often occurs in Syrian when the subject is indefinite (1964:421-2). Belnap notes that this type of agreement pattern "sometimes occur[s]" in Egyptian; his example also contains an indefinite subject (1991:19):

E　مات منها اربع صبيان
māt-3ms minha ʾarbaʿ ṣubyān
died-he from-her four boys
Four boys of hers died

Normally, verbal idioms whose subjects express periods of time exhibit masculine singular agreement regardless of the subject's number and gender. In examples such as the following, the low individuation of the time period may affect the degree to which verb and subject agree:

En　بقالي ساعة مستنّيكي
baʾā-li sāʿa mistannīki
became-3ms-for-me hour (f) having-been-waiting-f-for-you
I have been waiting for you for an hour

S4 اسه ما صار لك جمعة، عشرة ايام ما صار لك

ʾissa mā ṣār lak jimʿa, ʿašr tiyyām mā ṣār-lak

yet neg became-3ms for-you week ten days neg became-3ms-for-you

You haven't even [been married] a week yet, not even ten days

Another example, from Behnstedt and Woidich's rural Egyptian Delta texts, introduces a stolen water buffalo. In the first sentence, indefinite feminine /gamūsa/ *(a) water buffalo* is preceded by a masculine singular verb, /insaraʾ/ *it was stolen,* while in the second, the now defined /ig-gamūsa/ *the water buffalo* is preceded by a feminine singular verb /insaraʾit/ *it was stolen* (Behnstedt and Woidich 1987:26, translation mine):

E في مرة من الأيام واحد عندنا، انسرق منه جاموسة من بيته. فلما انسرقت الجاموسة وخرجت ...

fi-marra min il-ʾayyām wāḥid ʿindine, insaraʾ minnu gamūsa min bētu. fa-lamma nsaraʾit ig-gamūsa wu xaragit ...

there-is once among the-days one-m at-us, was-stolen-3ms from-him water-buffalo from house-his. so-when was-stolen-3fs the-water-buffalo and got-away-3fs ...

There [was] one day a man among us who had a water buffalo stolen from his house. So when the water buffalo was stolen and got out ...

While verb-subject neutralization patterns in spoken Arabic often parallel formal Arabic rules, these formal rules themselves reflect the same pragmatic principles that other agreement patterns do. One pattern that emerges from the examples of verb-subject neutralization cited here is that the subject is often indefinite, non-specific, or non-human. In other words, these subjects are of low individuation. Another possible explanation for the agreement neutralization is that the indefinite subjects in some of these cases represent new topics; as such, they carry the pragmatic focus of the sentence. The verb, on the other hand, is thematic. Perhaps the neutralization of thematic sentence elements, such as sentence- or clause-initial verbs, lends greater prominence to the new topic.

Moroccan does not seem to show the same degree of agreement neutralization as do other dialects. Harrell and Caubet do not mention variation in verb-subject agreement in their grammars of Moroccan, and examples I found of verb-subject word order show plural agreement even with indefinite nouns, such as the following with plural /žāw/ *they came* preceding /drāri/ *kids* (Caubet 1993ii:273, translation mine):

M جاوا دراري يسوّلوا عليك
žāw drāri ysuwwlu ʿlīk
came-they kids they-ask about-you
[Some] kids came asking for you[12]

A Moroccan informant confirms this general pattern, and finds the singular verb /ža/ unacceptable here, but provides the following minimal pair contrasting a plural verb (right) with a neutralized verb (left):

M	مات لها اربعة د الولاد	ماتوا لها اربعة د الولاد
	māt-lha rəbʿa d l-wlād	mātu-lha rəbʿa d l-wlād
	died-3ms-of-hers 4 gen the-kids	died-p-of-hers 4 gen the-kids
	She had four kids die	*Four of her kids died*

The translations given for each sentence reflect my informant's explanation of the difference in terms of focus between them: in the example on the right, the focus is on the children who died, whereas the neutralized example on the left focuses on the woman herself. His intuition can be rephrased using the individuation hierarchy. In the example on the right, the children who died are more individuated, and hence plural agreement is used. By contrast, in the sentence on the left, the children have lower textual prominence, and hence less individuation, which helps to explain the neutralized agreement.

Moroccan speakers thus tend to favor plural agreement for both adjectives and verbs. If substantiated by further research, the lower frequency of collective and neutralized agreement variation I perceive in Moroccan would provide an interesting parallel to the Moroccan tendency to mark individuation, especially in human nouns (1.6).

---

[12]A Moroccan informant finds this example unusual, preferring /ši drāri/ *some kids* to the unmarked /drāri/ *kids* cited by Caubet. His intuition confirms the Moroccan tendency to favor marking individuation in human nouns noted in 1.6.

2.4 Genitive and Possessive Constructions

Spoken Arabic makes use of two constructions to express possessive and genitive relationships: the construct phrase (Arabic /iḍāfa/) that links two nouns together to specify a genitive or possessive relationship between them, and the so-called "analytic" genitive, which makes use of a genitive exponent to express that relationship. Harning's 1980 study of these two constructions includes all documented forms of spoken Arabic and is far more detailed and comprehensive than is possible here. Her use of the terms synthetic and analytic, respectively, to refer to them, and her characterization of the genitive exponent as a "dialectal innovation" (1980:10) reflect a widely shared view that spoken Arabic has long been in the process of shifting from a synthetic language to an analytic one whose syntactic relationships are expressed through strings of discrete morphemes.

Overlooked in this analysis is that Arabic has, throughout its documented history, had a number of alternative constructions to the iḍāfa. As Harning mentions, a number of "analytic" annexation particles are well-documented for Classical Arabic, most common of them /li-/ *for, belonging to* and /min/ *of*. The dialects also make use of these prepositions as genitive markers. Cowell includes among his examples two pairs of synonyms, on the left the construct phrase and on the right its near equivalent with an exponent (1964:460)

S	هالشقفة الارض	هالشقفة من الارض
	ha š-šaʾfet ᵊl-ʾarḍ	ha š-šaʾfe mn ᵊl-arḍ
	that piece of land	*that piece of land*
S	خارطة طرق	خارطة للطرق
	xārṭeṭ ṭəroʾ	xārṭa lə-ṭ-ṭəroʾ
	a road map	*a road map*

While it may be argued that the contexts of these preposition-exponents are limited in scope, the same holds true for the genitive exponents in most dialects (the main exception being urban Moroccan). Moreover, the construct phrase also has syntactic restrictions: its first term cannot be indefinite. In the following, the indefinite noun phrase /ʾarbaʿ ṣubyān/ *four boys* cannot take a possessive suffix, and /minha/ *of hers* indicates the possession (example from Belnap 1991:19):

E مات منها اربع صبيان
mãt minha ʾarbaʿ ṣubyān
died-he from-her four boys
Four boys of hers died

The use of /li-/ in formal Arabic is of particular comparative interest here. While it is grammatically possible to translate *The Yemeni Language Center* using a construct phrase, (a), the preferred rendering uses the preposition /li-/, (b):

	(a)	(b)
CA	مركز اللغات اليمني	المركز اليمني للّغات
	markaz al-luġāt al-yamanī	al-markaz al-yamanī li-l-luġāt
	center (of) the-languages the-Yemeni	the-center the-Yemeni for-languages

The preferred title, (b), places a contrastive focus on *Language* not conveyed by (a), and for this reason, presumably, is favored, since the title refers to the Yemeni *Language* Center, as opposed to the Yemeni *Cultural* Center, the Yemeni *Trade* Center, or any other center in Yemen. By contrast, (a) places a focus on *Yemeni*, and might refer to a *Yemeni* Language Center as opposed to an *Egyptian* or *Saudi* Language Center.

This function of /li-/ parallels one of the functions of the dialect exponents. Cowell provides examples from Syrian, including the following minimal pair, of which (a) is preferred over (b) (1964:460):

	(a)	(b)
S	الفرش الجديد تبع البيت	فرش البيت الجديد
	l-farš ᵊž-ždīd tabaʿ ᵊl-bēt	farš ᵊl-bēt ᵊž-ždīd
	the furniture the-new gen the-house	furniture of-the-house the-new
	the new furniture of the house	*the new furniture of the house*

I will show that constructions involving the exponents often convey specific pragmatic information that the construct phrase does not. The choice a speaker makes between the two constructions is governed by general principles shared to some extent by most dialect regions, even though the frequency of the exponents varies considerably.

Table 2-1 lists the most common genitive exponents in the four dialects:

Table 2-1: Genitive Exponents

Genitive Exponents			
	Masculine	Feminine	Plural
Moroccan	dyāl / d	---	---
Egyptian	bitāʿ	bitāʿit	bitūʿ
Syrian	tabaʿ	---	(tabaʿūl)
Kuwaiti	māl	(mālat)	(mālōt)

Gender and number agreement is obligatory only in Egypt. Syrian grammars give no feminine form corresponding to /tabaʿ/; Cowell gives two optional plural forms, /tabaʿāt/ and /tabaʿūl/ (1964:489). Kuwaiti masculine /māl/ often modifies feminine and plural nouns.

2.4.1 Harning's Study

Harning's (1980) comparative study of the construct and genitive exponents covers all documented Arabic-speaking regions, and explores the relative frequency of the genitive exponents and factors that motivate their use in Arabic dialects. Harning classifies the genitive exponents in six groups, mainly according to frequency, geography, and type of society (rural, bedouin, and urban), ranging from Group I, in which the exponents are limited to fixed expressions, to Group VI, in which the exponent is more productive than the construct (1980:158-60). She notes two "major dividing line(s)," one separating western North Africa from the rest of the region, and the other separating urban, rural, and bedouin societies (160-61).

The four dialects studied here represent three of Harning's six groups, ranging from the highest frequency count of Moroccan (Harning's Group VI) to the second lowest frequency of Kuwaiti and Syrian (Group II). In the middle range stands Egyptian (Group IV).

For the Persian Gulf dialects, Harning lists both /māl/ and /ḥagg/ as genitive exponents; according to my data, only the former fulfills that role in Kuwaiti. Johnstone (1967:90) confirms that Kuwaiti /ḥagg/

functions as an indirect object marker that may be used predicatively, and has the same meaning as /li-/ *to, for*. From my data:

K4 ذهب امها حگ نورا
dahab ummha ḥagg nūra
gold of-mother-her for Nura
Her mother's gold is for/belongs to Nura

The following typical examples show that /ḥagg/ usually (but not always) precedes nouns, whereas /l-/ normally occurs with pronoun objects:

K1 واگول حگ محمد صباح الخير
w agūl ḥagg mḥammad ṣabāḥ il-xēr
and I-say to Mohammed morning of-the-good
I say to Mohammed, 'Good morning'

K2 انا اگول لك
ʾāna agūl lak
I I-say to-you
I'll tell you

Harning observes that narratives tend to contain a higher percentage of exponents than dialogues, and proposes discourse motivation for the selection of that particular construction in certain narrative contexts (1980:36-38). However, not all narrative contexts are naturally conducive to the appearance of exponents. The absence of exponents from one of my Kuwaiti narrative texts is to be explained by its topic of arranging marriages, since genitive exponents tend not to be used to modify familial and marital relationships (for exceptions in Egyptian, see 2.4.5). Most of the examples of genitive exponents in my Kuwaiti data come from an interview with an elderly, illiterate woman, rather than the interviews with the younger, more educated speakers.

The aim of this brief overview of genitive constructions in the dialects is to investigate possible formal and pragmatic constraints or factors motivating the choice of construction. Harning's study makes several important observations about what she calls "stylistic" factors, which may be more precisely described as pragmatic and discourse functions. She notes, for example, that certain climactic passages in narratives tend to contain exponent phrases that give more weight to the passage, and that in parallel genitive constructions, the longer, weightier exponent phrases tend to occur at the end of the list, as a signal of closure (1980:37, 91, 143).

Rather than viewing the choice between the construct and the exponent phrase as a choice between "two parallel genitive systems" signalling "a dynamic process of language development" (Harning 1980:1), the exponent is better viewed as belonging to the same system as the construct, just as /li-/ and other prepositions have always provided alternatives to the construct in formal Arabic. The speaker chooses between a construct and an exponent on the basis of formal, semantic, and pragmatic considerations that will now be examined.

2.4.2 Formal Motivations for the Use of the Genitive Exponent

In a study of the genitive construction in North African dialects, Marçais (1977) points out that the morphological form and weight of the phrase play a role in the choice between the construct and an exponent. He attributes the use of the latter to a multi-term noun phrase, suffixed or otherwise modified nouns, or to a phrase in which direct annexation would "disfigure" the syllabic structure (1977:171). Harning lists similar motivations for the use of exponents in Kuwaiti (1980:35-6), Egyptian (90), and Syrian (52).

Borrowed words of foreign origin and words ending in a long vowel in general cannot take pronoun suffixes and do not readily fit into Arabic morphosyntactic patterns; therefore, they tend to occur with a possessive exponent rather than in a construct (see el-Tonsi 1982i:16). Duals (excluding the pseudo-dual parts of the body) also tend not to be used in construct phrases (Harning 1980:61; el-Tonsi 1982i:16; Marçais 1977:171), perhaps because of the morphological awkwardness of adding a suffix to the dual suffix /-ēn/. Pragmatics might play a role here as well, because the dual ending often indicates a degree of individuation, a factor that tends to favor the use of the genitive exponent.

The main formal motivations for the choice of the exponent include: multi-term annexation (three or more nouns), the presence of modifying adjectives, and parallel phrases with more than one head noun. Of the following Egyptian pair, el-Tonsi gives strong preference to (a) over (b) (1982i:19):

	(a)	(b)
E	ملعب التنس بتاع النادي	ملعب تنس النادي
	malʿab it-tinis bitāʿ in-nādi	malʿab tinis in-nādi
	court the-tennis gen the-club	court tennis the-club
	The tennis court of the club	*The tennis court of the club*

Cowell gives two possible Syrian variants for *my uncle's gasoline station*, both of which contain exponents (1964:461). The variant on the right carries an emphasis on *gasoline*, while the one on the left highlights *my uncle* as possessor. In each case, the exponent focuses attention on a particular piece of information:

S	محطة البنزين تبع عمّي	محطة عمي تبع البنزين
	mḥaṭṭeṭ ᵊl-banzīn tabaʿ ʿammi	mḥaṭṭet ʿammi tabaʿ ᵊl-banzīn
	[station the-gas gen uncle-my]	[station uncle-my gen the-gas]
	my uncle's gasoline station	*my uncle's* ***gasoline*** *station*

The following Kuwaiti sentence contains a complex phrase consisting of three nouns, one of which is a possessive pronoun: /rabʿ/ *friends*, /ha/ *her*, and /il-madrase/ *the school*. It is syntactically impossible to append a noun after a possessive pronoun, so this speaker has little choice but to use the exponent /māl/:

K3 ربعها مال المدرسة ييونها ويات امها وطردتهم
rabiʿha māl il-madrasa yiyūnha w yāt ʾummha w ṭradathum
friends-her gen the-school they-come-to-her and came-she mother-her and threw-out-them
Her friends from school would visit her and her mother came and threw them out

These structural factors parallel the pragmatics of information packaging. In the following section, I will show that the use of exponents allows a focus on the possessor not present in the construct phrase. Another possible motivation for avoiding multi-term constructs may lie in the ambiguity of the multiple relationships. In processing two possessive relationships at the same time, it may help the listener to know which one carries particular weight or focus. Hence, structural and pragmatic considerations seem to be at least partly related.

2.4.3 Pragmatic Functions

Harning notes for individual dialect areas "stylistic factors" that influence the choice of genitive construction, including the introduction of a new theme and contrast (1980:37-8, 63-4, 91-2). This observation may be more precisely phrased in pragmatic terms: the genitive exponents fulfill specific pragmatic functions that the construct phrase does not. First, the exponent places a focus on the *possessing* noun (in linear terms, the second noun) not conveyed by the construct phrase. In addition, the exponent lends a possessive phrase greater textual prominence, signalling a relatively high degree of individuation, contrastive focus, or the first mention of an entity in discourse. These features naturally overlap; thus it is not surprising to find more than one at work in many cases.

The exponent is likely to occur in genitive phrases that are specified or individuated. Cowell points out that Syrian /tabaʿ/ generally indicates identificatory annexion, and only rarely classificatory (1964:461). It is often used to express professional relationships, such as *his officer* in the following:[13]

S2 الضابط تبعه
iḍ-ḍābit tabaʿu
the-officer gen-his
his officer

In the following passage, the Egyptian speaker describes how an insect crawled into her ear. The insect is highly individuated, textually prominent and has the power to cause the speaker pain, all factors which help attract the use of the genitive exponent /bitāʿ/ in the phrase /l-mišwār bitaʿha/ *its journey*:

E2 هي دخلت، دخلت لحدّ عند الطبلة مش عارفة تعدّي فقاعدة تخبّط في طبلة ودني عشان تعدّي تكمّل بقى المشوار بتاعها
hiyya daxalit, daxalit li-ḥadd ʿand iṭ-ṭabla miš ʿarfa tʿaddi, fa-ʾaʿda tixabbaṭ fi ṭablit widni ʿašān tiʿaddi tikammil baʾa l-mišwār bitaʿha

---

[13]As Diem (1986) has shown, the concept of alienability helps explain why genitive exponents are not generally used to express relationships involving family and parts of the body, which are inalienable relationships.

it entered-3fs, entered-3fs to-extent at the-drum neg knowing it-pass so-sitting-f it-bang in drum of-ear-my in-order-to it-pass it-complete that-is the-journey gen-its
[The insect] entered, entered as far as the [ear]drum, not being able to pass, so it keeps on banging my eardrum in order to pass, to finish its journey

The exponent can also add contrastive focus to a genitive phrase, usually to the possessor. In this Moroccan example, the girl's possession of the room is singled out and contrasted in the absolute, *her very own room*:

M11 باها ملك سلطان، وناض دار لها البيت ديالها بوحدها
bb^{w}āha malik səlṭān w nāḍ dār-lha l-bīt dyālha b^{w}-uḥdha
father-her king sultan and got-up-he made-he for-her the-room gen-her by-self-her
Her father was a king, a sultan, and he up and made for her her very own room (suite)

The next passage contains both constructs and exponents, first the construct, /wəldha/ *her son*, then the exponent, /l-wəld dyālha/ *her son* (in boldface). After the first mention of the son, in construct, the narrator explicitly contrasts the identity of the man's two wives. The second mention of the son contains the exponent /dyālha/ *her [own]* in reference to the man's first wife, highlighting the focus on her identity as possessor, while simultaneously emphasizing the horror of her deed:

M11 گالت له آ الراجل، المرا كلات **ولدها** - هادي الضرّة - جوج د العيالات مجوّج الراجل المرا الاخرى گالت له المرا كلت **الولد ديالها**
gāt-lu ʾā r-rāžəl l-mra klāt **wəldha** - hādi ḍ-ḍərra - žūž d l-ʿyālāt[14] mžəwwəž r-rāžəl, l-mra l-x^{w}ra gā[l]t-lu l-mra klāt **l-wəld dyālha**
said-she to-him O the-husband, the-wife ate-she son-her--this the-second-wife--two gen the-women having married the-husband the-woman other said-she to-him the-woman ate-she the-son gen-hers

[14]The occurrence of /d/ in /žūž d l-ʿyālāt/ *two wives* is not a true possessive, but marks the specification of a quantity, in this case two. Moroccan /d/ fulfills this syntactic role for quantities between two and ten.

She said to him, 'Husband, the woman ate ***her son****–this is the second wife [talking]–two women the guy married, the other wife told him, the woman ate* ***her own son****.*

Kuwaiti /māl/ often occurs in phrases contrasting with other named or implied entities. In the first example, the speaker uses /māl/ to contrast the forgetfulness of old age with *that other kind*. In the second, she contrasts love in the old days with love in the post-oil era:

K3 لا — هاذا نسيان مال كبر، مو نسيان مال ذاك
lā -- hāḏa nisyān māl kubur, mū nisyān māl ḏāk
no--this forgetfulness gen old-age, neg forgetfulness gen that
No–this is forgetfulness of old age, not that other kind of forgetfulness

K3 حب أوّل .. مو مال الحين، الحين يحبّها ويروح، فلوس، وايد فلوس
ḥubb ʾawwal ... mū māl l-ḥīn, al-ḥīn yḥibbha w yrūḥ, flūs, wāyid flūs
love of-old-days ... neg gen now, now he-loves-her and he-goes, money, much money
Love in the old days ... not [like love] of today, these days he loves her and leaves [her], money, lots of money

Similarly, here one particular house of this member of the ruling family is contrasted to his other houses:

Kn بيت احمد الجابر مال الديرة
bēt aḥmad l-yābir māl id-dīra
house Ahmed al-Jabir gen-the-old-city
Ahmed Al-Jaber's house [the one] of the old city

Nouns that play a role as discourse topic, that is, figure importantly in a narrative, often attract special syntactic marking (1.5, 2.1). Genitive phrases with exponents often play a role as discourse topic. In the following, the *hair of a lion* will play a discourse role in the story, hence its first mention is marked with /māl/:

K3 روحي ييبي لي شعر مال سبع
rūḥi yībī-li šaʿar māl sibiʿ
go-f bring-f hair gen lion
Go bring me a hair of a lion

Another factor at work in this example is the identity of the possessor. Although the genitive phrase remains indefinite, the identity of the possessor is implicitly contrasted, since the woman is requested to get the hair of a lion, not the hair of any other animal.

Harning found Syrian to have one of the lowest frequencies of genitive exponents of any urban dialects (1980:158). One reason for this low frequency may be that Syrian speakers have at their disposal another construction that helps the speaker package (and helps the listener process) genitive information. This construction is the so-called "object marker" /la-/ (see further 10.3.5). The following example contains a complex possessive construction consisting of four terms, /sikirtēr(t)/ *secretary*, /mar(t)/ *wife*, /ra'īs/ *president*, and finally /əj-jāmʿa/ *the university*. The genitive is formed in a two-step process: first, the secretary's relationship to a female figure is established using a possessive pronoun, /sikirtērt[h]a/ *her secretary*, then the second figure is defined as /mart ra'īs əj-jāmʿa/ *the president of the university's wife*, using a three-term construct. The larger possessive consists of two parts, both genitive constructs, combined using the resumptive topic marker /la-/ (see further 10.3.5), which places a topical focus on the latter term.

S5 سكرتيرتها لمرة رئيس الجامعة دقّت تليفون

sikirtērt[h]a la-mart ra'īs ij-jāmʿa da''it talifōn

secretary-her obj-wife of-president of-the-university called-she telephone

The secretary of the president of the university's wife called

Although the primary function of /la-/ involves marking a resumptive topic, it often occurs in genitive constructions, where it fulfills a role similar to that of genitive /tabaʿ/ in that both particles allow the speaker to order and rank the relationships among multiple terms in a way that aids the listener to keep track of them. In Egyptian, the only acceptable way to express this idea would contain genitive /bitāʿ/ (or feminine /bitāʿit/):

E السكرتيرة بتاعة مراة رئيس الجامعة

is-sikritēra btāʿit mirāt raʿīs ig-gamʿa

the secretary gen wife of-president of-the-university

The secretary of the wife of the president of the university

Egyptian /bitāʿ/ shares with Syrian /tabaʿ/ syntactic restrictions and most semantic and pragmatic functions, the main exception being the greater Egyptian use of /bitāʿ/ in defining social relationships, as contrasted to Syrian /tabaʿ/ (see 2.4.5). From this perspective, the discrepancy Harning finds between the frequency of the exponents in these two urban areas is unexpected. However, the availability of /la-/ to Syrian speakers as an information packaging device helps to explain both the lower frequency of /tabaʿ/ and why Syrian speakers tend not to use it as often in describing social relationships.

2.4.4 Exponents and Individuation

The genitive exponents tend to reflect a high degree of specification or individuation as contrasted with the construct phrase. Syrian and Egyptian exponents seem to be limited to this pragmatic function for the most part. Moroccan and Kuwaiti, on the other hand, allow exponents to classify (rather than individuate) nouns. In syntactic terms, the exponents in Moroccan and Kuwaiti are more frequently used to modify indefinite nouns and/or nonspecific possessors than their Egyptian and Syrian counterparts.

Harning notes "qualification" as a common semantic characteristic of exponent phrases, but she does not make the distinction that Cowell does between classification and identification. Thus her examples of "qualification" include the use of exponents to individuate, such as Egyptian /il-kitāb bitāʿ is-siḥr/ *the book of magic*, which clearly refers to a specific book (87) and Moroccan /l-ma d[ə] l-bākor/ *le jus des figue-fleurs [sap of unripe figs]* (136), a classificatory identification.

It is important to make this distinction between classification (generic identity, low individuation) and identification (specific identity, high individuation), because it corresponds to a difference in the usage of the exponents in the dialects. Moroccan and Kuwaiti speakers use their exponents to classify and individuate, while Egyptian and Syrian speakers generally use the exponent to individuate but not to classify (except in certain idiomatic expressions noted below).

The following examples from Moroccan and Kuwaiti data show the exponents qualifying or classifying, but not individuating the nouns they modify. The nouns that constitute the first terms of these genitive phrases are all indefinite, and the possessors are generic rather than specific. The genitive phrase as a whole is thus low in individuation:

M6 شرا مگانة ديال الما
šra magāna dyāl l-ma
bought-he watch gen the-water
He bought a waterproof watch

M مشى جاب لي شي جلد د البگري
mšā žāb-li ši-žəld də-l-bəgri
[went-he brought-me some skin gen the-cow]
He went and bought me some old cowhide (Harrell 1962:183)

K3 أول ما ميش دخاترة، على زماننا، عيايز، اختراعات مال الحريم الكبار
ʾawwal mā mīš daxātra, ʿala zumānna, ʿayāyiz, xtarāʿāt māl əl-ḥarīm əl-kubār
first neg-there-is doctors on time-our, old-women, inventions gen the-women the -old
In the old days there [were] no doctors, in our time, [just] old women, the inventions of old women

In contrast to these Moroccan and Kuwaiti examples, in which the genitive exponent is used to classify rather than individuate, the following Egyptian example shows /bitāʿ/ in an individuating phrase. Although the first noun /ḥāga/ *thing* is indefinite and non-specific, the high individuation of /rabbina/ *God* allows the exponent /bitāʿit/, since *a thing of God's* is unique among all other things:

E10 زي ما قلت لحضرتك دا قسمة ونصيب وحاجة بتاعة ربنا
zayy ma ʾult li-ḥaḍritik da ʾisma wi naṣīb wi ḥāga bitāʿit rabbina
as nom said-I to-presence-your this fate and lot and thing gen Lord-our
Like I told you, Ma'am, this is fate, and something of God's

Syrian and Egyptian informants reject constructions with non-specific possessors as weak. Grammars of both dialects confirm: Cowell remarks that it is rare for Syrian /tabaʿ/ to annex an indefinite possessor (1964:489); for Egyptian, el-Tonsi specifies a limited set of idiomatic, predicated contexts in which /bitāʿ/ can annex an indefinite noun (1982i:20).

One of the few instances in which Egyptian and Syrian exponents /bitāʿ/ and /tabaʿ/ annexes an indefinite possessor is a shared idiomatic expression meaning *someone who likes* (a meaning I have not found for Moroccan /dyāl/ or Kuwaiti /māl/):

E	دا راجل بتاع نسوان	انا مش بتاع كلام
	da rāgil bitāʿ niswān	ana miš bitāʿ kalām
	that man gen women	I neg gen talk
	He likes women/is a ladies man	*I'm not all talk [and no action]*
L	هو تبع نسوان	انا ماني تبع حكي
	huwwe tabaʿ niswān	ana mānni tabaʿ ḥaki
	he gen women	I neg-I gen talk
	He likes women/is a ladies man	*I'm not all talk [and no action]*

This particular use of the exponent is not limited to urban dialects, however. Even conservative Najdi speakers make use of a parallel construction, /fēd/, which Ingham defines as (1994:182):[15]

> a possessive particle /fēd-ih/ *something belonging to him, concerned with him*, also used meaning *a sort of person fond of* ... as in /ana māni fēd hassuwālif/ *I am not the sort of person who likes this sort of thing.*

Exponents derived from nouns show varying degrees of grammatical agreement governed by the head noun. For Egyptian /bitāʿ/, agreement is obligatory according to most sources (Harning 1980:85, el-Tonsi 1982i:14). Kuwaiti and Syrian exponents, on the other hand, show agreement only occasionally. In the first example, plural /mālōt/ agrees with /l-ʾashum/ *stocks*, but in the second, masculine /māl/ modifies feminine /jāmʿa/ *university*. The first context is individuating, as particular stocks are indicated, whereas the second is merely descriptive, as the elderly, uneducated speaker does not know or remember the name of the university:

K4 حتى الاسهم مالوت الجمعية حوّلهم باسمه
ḥatta l-ʾashum mālōt əl-jamʿiyya ḥawwal-hum b-isma
even the-stocks gen the-association changed-he-them in-name-his

[15]Perhaps derived from /fī yad/ *in the hand of.*

Even the shares of the association he transferred them to his name

K3 خلّصوا الجامعة مال بغداد ، ياوا
xallaṣaw il-jāmʿa māl baġdād, yāw
finished-they the-university gen Baghdad, came-they
They finished [at] the University of Baghdad, they came back

Cowell's examples include plural forms /tabaʿāt/ and tabaʿūl/. In the following, the contrasting agreement on /tabaʿ/, first singular then plural, may reflect the relative importance of *the pictures* to each speaker. The first speaker lays no claim to them, and uses neutralized agreement; the second, on the other hand, owns the pictures, and in claiming possession, perhaps emphasizes their uniqueness or importance to him or her by using the plural /tabaʿūl/ (example from Cowell 1964:489):

S —— تبع مين هالصور ؟ —— تبعولي
-- tabaʿ mīn ha ṣ-ṣuwar? -- tabaʿūli
-- gen whom this the-pictures? -- gen-mine
-- *Whose pictures are these?* -- *Mine*

Moroccan /dyāl/, derived from a particle rather than a noun, does not show agreement in urban dialects.[16]

The partial agreement of certain exponents may find explanation in the individuation of the modified noun: the more individuated the genitive phrase, the greater the tendency for the exponent to agree in number and gender. Further evidence supporting this analysis is Harning's observation that agreement tends to be marked on /māl/ if the modifier is a personal pronoun suffix (1980:27), that is, in the framework used here, if the phrase as a whole is more individuated.

2.4.5 Sociolinguistic Motivations

Harning's study concludes by hypothesizing sociocultural reasons for the higher frequency and distribution of the analytic genitive in urban dialect groups. Harning notes that urban dialects tend to show a higher frequency of exponent phrases than rural or bedouin ones,

[16]Harning cites a claim by Lévi-Provençal that a certain rural dialect of Moroccan has feminine and plural forms of /dyāl/: /dyālt-/ and /dyāul/, but can find no attested occurrences (Harning 1980:132).

attributing this high frequency to the heterogeneity of urban society and the rapid social changes that can occur in such environments (1980:164-5). Evidence supporting this analysis includes the use of exponents to indicate certain kinds of extrafamilial social relationships.

Egyptian speakers appear to employ the most highly developed system of exponent use, reflecting a highly marked social order.[17] El-Tonsi provides a detailed explanation of the use of /bitāʿ/ to describe relationships between two human beings (adapted from 1982i:15):

> For human relationships the use of bitāʿ is limited to four circles:
> 1. Wife[18] (husband in rural dialects); euphemistic expressions for girlfriend and boyfriend.
> 2. Relationships with people lower in the social pyramid.
> 3. Relationships with people higher in job classification.
> 4. Service-based relationships with professionals.

In other words, Egyptian speakers usually use /bitāʿ/ to define relationships that are alienable, temporary, or contractual. Intuitively it seems possible that the physical distance caused by the exponent's separation of the two nouns might reflect relational distance as well. The use of the exponent in such cases may reinforce the social distance involved in these hierarchical and contractual relationships.

Professional relationships in other dialects appear to be expressed with an exponent optionally. In my Syrian data, a distancing authority is signalled with the exponent (see also Harning 1980:57):

S2 الضابط تبعن
id-ḍābiṭ tabaʿon
the officer gen-theirs
Their commanding officer

In the opposite direction socially, I have heard in Lebanon both /ṣānʿətna/ and /əṣ-ṣānʿa tāʿitna/ for *our maid* (Cowell confirms the use of both constructions in Syrian, 1964:460).

My Kuwaiti corpus contains one example of /māl/ modifying a human, the guard of the lion:

---

[17]For a sociolinguistic study of social hierarchy in Egypt, see Parkinson (1985).

[18]However, /is-sitt bitaʿti/ is necessitated by the use of /sitti/ to mean *my grandmother*.

K3 كل يوم تشتري فخوذ لحم وتروح تعطيها للحارس ماله
kil yōm tištiri fxūḏ laḥam w trūḥ ta‘ṭīha li-l-ḥāris māla
every day she-buys thighs meat and she-goes she-gives to-the-guard gen-3ms
Every day she would buy legs of meat and go give them to its (the lion's) guard

The same speaker uses a construct to express *her driver*:

K3 الحين العيوز دريولها واجف
al-ḥīn l-‘ayūz drēwilha wājif
we the-old-woman driver-her standing
Now, the old woman, her driver is standing by

However, the context here is that of a general statement, rather than a specific driver of a specific woman. The exponent tends to be used in cases which indicate a degree of specificity of either party, or both.

At the other end of the continuum, Moroccan speakers can use /dyāl/ to refer to any human relationship, even immediate family:

M الولد ديالها
l-wəld dyālha
the-son gen-hers
the son of hers, her son

2.4.6 Moroccan/ dyāl/

Of all the exponents in the four dialect regions, Moroccan /dyāl/ (variant /d/) shows the highest frequency.[19] Harning concludes that the exponent phrase is more productive than the construct, except in limited contexts of intimate relationships (1980:160; see Harrell 1962:194-201 for a list of "limited" contexts in which the construct is normally used). This high frequency is due at least in part to the wider range of syntactic roles that Moroccan /dyāl/ plays compared to its counterparts.

[19]Harning and Fischer and Jastrow, among others, claim that the particle /dyāl/ is "always" (Harning 1980:115) or "usually" (Fischer and Jastrow 1980:93) used with pronoun suffixes. Not only is that notion dismissed by several informants, but my data contain numerous counter-examples to such claims.

Moroccan /dyāl/ occurs in various semantic and syntactic contexts in which other exponents are rarely, if ever, used. One of these contexts is quantification with numbers from two to ten, which may not be expressed with the construct in other dialects.[20]

M9 خمسة د دراهم
xəmsa d drāhəm
five gen dirhams
five dirhams

Moroccan speakers also use /dyāl/ in expressions meaning *a lot of* and *how much of*:

M2 دوّزنا الايام بزّاف ديال الشقا
dəwwəzna l-iyyām, bəzzāf dyāl š-šqa
passed-we the-days, a lot gen the-toiling
We passed the days, [doing] a lot of hard work.

M2 ايوا، شحال ديال المسايل وشحال ديال هادا —
ʾīwa, šḥāl dyāl l-msāyl w šḥāl dyāl hāda --
yes how-much gen the-problems and how-much gen this --
So many problems and so much of this --

In most dialects, the genitive exponent may not modify an inalienable noun, but Moroccan /dyāl/ often does:

M1 الودنين ديالك
l-wədnīn dyālk
the-ears gen-yours
the ears of yours, your ears

M9 ما جات ف البال ديالي
mā žāt f l-bāl dyāli
neg came-3fs in the-mind gen-mine
It never entered my mind

These examples show that Moroccan /dyāl/ functions as a genitive case-marking particle that marks not only possession, but also

[20]Harning notes that a (century-old) text from the southwestern Moroccan dialect of Houwāra uses /ntāʿ/ as the normal genitive exponent (as does the entire region), but contains /d/ in the quantifying phrase /səbʿa d-l-ūlād/ *seven sons* (1980:131).

quantification, which the exponents of the other dialects may not do. The higher frequency of Moroccan /dyāl/ is thus partly explained by its greater functional capacity.

Chapter 1 demonstrated that animacy and specification seem to affect definite marking in Moroccan nominal phrases in such a way that Moroccan speakers tend to prefer definite marking on animate and specified nouns. It seems possible that the high frequency of /dyāl/ relative to exponents of other dialects may be partly related to the relatively wider use of the definite article in Moroccan speech, since /dyāl/ allows the definite article to be retained on one or both nouns in a genitive phrase.

2.5 Summary

This chapter has explored the influence of individuation on two types of noun modification, number agreement and possession. The discussion of number agreement included an exploration of the category of dual in spoken Arabic.

Examination of various phenomena of dual number and agreement led to several conclusions and a hypothesis concerning its historical development. Building on Blanc's distinction between dual and pseudo-dual (1970), I proposed further distinctions between productive and non-productive, and specific and non-specific duals. The category of dual consists of several different kinds of dual: frozen forms, most of which refer to body parts, a non-specific dual meaning *a couple of*, and a "new topic" dual that has specific pragmatic functions and is limited to individuated nouns. The productivity of the dual suffix /-ēn/ on nouns appears to be limited, either to certain classes of words in some cases, or to pragmatic functions in others. Periphrastic dual forms appear to be the norm in Morocco and Kuwait; and the dual suffix /-ayn/ is not a productive form in Morocco. This evidence led to a call for a reevaluation of the history of the dual in spoken Arabic, one that takes into account category-specific developments.

Number agreement patterns in the dialects were shown to be affected by the hierarchy of individuation. The agreement of adjectives, verbs and pronouns tends to be plural if the noun is highly individuated, i.e., is specific, definite, and/or high in textual or social prominence, an agreement pattern called here individuated plural agreement. By contrast, plural nouns that reflect collective, abstract, non-specific, and/or inanimate entities of low textual prominence tend to attract feminine singular or deflected verb and pronoun agreement (adjectival agreement less so, because adjectives tend to specify, giving the nouns they modify greater individuation). This latter agreement pattern is designated as collective plural agreement.

Similarly, the individuation of a possessive phrase, and particularly the possessor, influences the choice of genitive construction, such that the more individuated the phrase as a whole, or one of its members, the more likely the speaker to express that relationship using a genitive exponent. Formal and sociolinguistic motivating factors for the use of the exponent were also noted.

Within this general shared framework, slight variations occur. Moroccan speakers seem to have a greater tendency to use plural agreement patterns than speakers of other dialects. This tendency provides an interesting parallel to the high frequency of the genitive exponent /dyāl/ in Moroccan, and also the greater use of definite and specifying articles in Moroccan noted in Chapter 1.

A distinction is found between the two central dialects on the one hand and the two peripheral dialects on the other in the use of the genitive exponent (as opposed to the construct). Moroccan and Kuwaiti speakers can use genitive exponents to indicate classificatory as well as individuated identity, while Egyptians and Syrians tend to restrict the use of the exponents to individuated phrases. The fact that the Moroccan exponent /dyāl/ has a much higher frequency than Kuwaiti /māl/ is probably due in part to the Moroccan tendency to mark individuation in nouns and to its wider syntactic range (/dyāl/ also quantifies nouns between two and ten in number). Even so, this parallel between Moroccan and Kuwaiti in the use of genitive exponents bears watching for future developments.

3 Relative Clauses

3.0 Introduction

Ferguson (1959:630) includes the definite relative pronoun /illi/ as one of fifteen features common to most modern Arabic dialects.[1] Grammars of the dialects concur: Mitchell (1956:57) notes that the definite relative pronoun for Egyptian is /illi/; Cowell (1964:494) lists for Syrian /halli/ and /yalli/ as variants of /illi/;[2] Johnstone (1967) gives /illi/ for Kuwaiti; and Harrell (1962:164) notes /lli/ and /aš/ for Moroccan. These grammars specify that /illi/ only relativizes a definite head noun, and that no relative pronoun is used if the head noun is indefinite.

In his Moroccan grammar, Harrell claims that /lli/ in definite relative clauses "indicates specifically that the subordinate clause is a restrictive adjectival modifier" of the head noun (1962:164). This claim is not made for any other dialect, and it is refuted for Moroccan by this counter-example from my data in which /lli/ modifies the already restricted /l-wālida/, *[my] mother*:

M2 كانت خارجة الوالدة اللي جات عندي هي وعمّتي
kānt xārža l-wālida lli žāt ʿndi hiyya w ʿammti
was-she going-out the-mother rel came-she at-me she and aunt-my
My mother, who had come to my house, she and my aunt, was going out

This example shows that /illi/ can modify both restricted and non-restricted nouns in Moroccan, as it can in the other three dialect regions.

---

[1]Relativization in formal Arabic utilizes a set of definite relative pronouns inflected for gender and number (see Cantarino 1975iii:162), which contrast with the invariant pronoun /illi/ used in spoken Arabic.

[2]It is not clear whether /yalli/, /halli/ and /illi/ are free variations or reflect some nuance of meaning. Some of Cowell's examples suggest that /yalli/ tends to be restrictive, whereas /halli/ appears to be parallel to anaphoric demonstrative /ha/ in that the reference is to an established or otherwise identifiable referent, and is thus non-restrictive (Cowell 1964:495-8; see also 4.2). Cowell has few examples of /illi/, whereas my northern Syrian texts contain only /illi/; this discrepancy may reflect regional differences. Cowell prefers to call these particles attributives, since in his view they do not correspond to the English relative pronouns (1964:495).

Relativization in spoken Arabic thus seems at first glance to be almost uniform and highly analogous to the rules of literary Arabic in its distinction between definite and indefinite head nouns and clauses, the existence of a definite relative pronoun and the absence of an indefinite one, and the lack of distinction between restrictive and non-restrictive clauses. Formal Arabic and most of the dialects make use of what Keenan and Comrie (1977) call case-marking relativizing strategy; in Arabic relative clauses, a resumptive pronoun normally marks the syntactic position of the relativized noun.[3]

However, relativization in the four dialect regions turns out to be more complicated, and more interesting, than this simplified picture suggests. Relative clauses in spoken Arabic include a variety of structures. First, the pronoun /illi/ can relativize not only definite nouns, but also indefinite nouns, in all four dialect regions. Second, while /illi/ clauses normally leave a resumptive pronoun in the position of the relativized noun, the resumptive pronoun in the direct object position is optional in many varieties of Arabic.[4] Among the four regions examined here, Moroccan speakers in particular regularly omit the resumptive pronoun in direct object position, whereas Egyptian and Syrian speakers regularly reject its omission. My Aleppan data contain /illi/ clauses in which the head noun of the relative clause stands in construct (/iḍāfa/) with /illi/, rather than the more usual noun-modifier construction in which the head noun is marked definite. At the same time, the function of /illi/ extends beyond relative clauses. Several dialects use /illi/ as nominalizer and/or sentential complementizer in certain contexts that will be explored here.

Relativization with particles other than /illi/, while limited geographically, is of comparative interest. While non-attributive relative clauses headed by /illi/ are found in all areas, non-specific, non-attributive relative pronouns /ma/ and /mīn/ appear only in certain areas: /ma/

---

[3]Keenan and Comrie (1977) differentiate between word order relatives and case-marking relatives. The former is exemplified by English, in which the relativized position is moved to the head of the clause, while Arabic typifies the latter, leaving a resumptive pronoun as a "case-marker" of the relativized noun. In the case of relativized subjects, the pronoun is normally expressed as a verbal prefix, suffix, or circumfix, according to verb morphology.

[4]For Classical Arabic examples, see Wright (1898ii:320).

something, anything occurs only in my Moroccan data and /mīn/ *someone, anyone* only in Syrian.[5] The existence of non-specific relative pronouns provides an important parallel to the existence of an indefinite-specific article /ši/ in these two dialects (1.4). Moroccan speakers also have at their disposal an additional relativizing strategy in which oblique objects may be relativized with pronoun /fāš/ in a word-order type relative clause. The final section documents examples of a relative pronoun /d/ and variants in the speech of an elderly woman originally from rural northern Morocco.

How do speakers of these dialects manage this range of relative structures? A comparison of the contexts and types of nouns that appear in these various clauses reveals that the degree of individuation of the head noun affects the strategy used to relativize it. The more individuated the noun, the greater the tendency to use the standard /illi/ clause with resumptive pronoun. Temporal nouns, lower on the scale of individuation, have greater tendency to be relativized without resumptive pronouns. The use of /illi/ as nominalizer or sentential complementizer often occurs when a highly individuated noun appears anywhere in the preceding clause, suggesting that high individuation affects not only the noun phrase but also the sentence as a whole.[6]

This chapter will examine these relative structures and other clauses involving /illi/ in the four dialect areas.

3.1 Relativization of Indefinite-Specific Nouns with /illi/

The grammars of Cowell 1964 (Syrian), Harrell 1962 (Moroccan), Mitchell 1956 (Egyptian) and Holes 1990 (Gulf) all state that, in the construction of relative clauses, definite head nouns require the relative pronoun /illi/, whereas indefinite head nouns do not admit it. Examples of definite relative clauses from each dialect region:

---

[5]These two pronouns are reflexes of formal Arabic relatives /mā/ and /man/. Wright defines these relative pronouns as "either definite or indefinite" (1898ii:319), but a better description according to the analysis proposed here would be "partly specified."

[6]Cf. Hopper and Thompson's (1980) theory of transitivity, which argues for a symbiotic relationship among various sentence constituents such that features of "high transitivity," e.g., nominal salience, agency, perfective verbal aspect, tend to co-occur in highly transitive clauses.

M10 الحوت اللي ما كاينش عنده قيمة
l-ḥūt lli mā kāynš ʿəndu qīma
the-fish rel neg there-is at-it value
The fish that has no value

E3 الجيل اللي طالع الجديد
ig-gīl illi ṭāliᶜ ig-gidīd
the-generation rel coming-up the new
The new generation that's growing up

S5 الحياة الـ عشتها بأميركا حياة دالاس وداينستي
il-ḥayāt il ʿišt[h]a bi-ʾamērka ḥayāt dālās w dāynasti
the-life rel lived-I-it in-America life of-Dallas and Dynasty
The life I lived in America [was] the life of "Dallas" and "Dynasty"

K1 شلّتي مو هاذي اللي أبي أسافر ويّاها
šilliti mū hāḏi lli ʾabi ʾasāfir wiyyāha
group-my neg this rel I-want I-travel with-her
This is not my group [of friends] that I want to travel with

Examples of indefinite relative clauses include:

M10 عاود تاني كاين رزّة كيلبسها الراجل
ʿāwd tāni kāyn rəzza kaylbəsha r-rāžəl
then second there-is turban indic-he-wears-it the-man
Moreover, there is a turban that the man wears

E1 عايزة جهاز يتسجّل عليه حاجات
ᶜayza gihāz yitsaggil ʿalēh ḥagāt
wants-f machine be-recorded on-it things
She wants a machine that things can be recorded on

S2 فيه بنات بيقولوا ايه، متل بعضها
fī banāt biqūlu ʾēh, mitil baᶜḍ[h]a
there-is girls they-say yeah, like other-of-it
There are girls who say okay, that's alright

K2 اكو ناس يرضون، اكو ناس ما يرضون
ʾaku nās yirḍūn, ʾaku nās mā yirḍūn
there-are people they-agree there-are people neg they-agree
There are people who accept [this], there are people who do not accept

Based on this description and these examples, then, the use of the definite relative /illi/ appears to be controlled by the definiteness of the head noun of the clause. However, data from all dialects contain examples in which an indefinite head noun is relativized using the definite /illi/. Such data constitute clear violations of the "rules" for relative clause formation. While it might be argued that such sentences represent performance errors on the part of the speaker, the repeated occurrence of this structure should not be dismissed without further investigation. The traditional view that a head noun "controls" the syntax of a modifying clause cannot account for a range of naturally occurring data in which the structure of the modifying clause is at odds with the definiteness of the head noun. Rather, both the marking of the head noun and the marking of the relative clause are controlled by the speaker, who can combine definite and indefinite markings to indicate a range of specificity.

All four dialects allow indefinite head nouns to be relativized with the definite relative marker /illi/ (or Syrian variant /yalli/). A Moroccan informant supplied the following example (based on a sentence cited by Harrell 1962:165):

M3 بغيت طوموبيل اللي تمشي مزيان

bġīt ṭumubīl lli təmši məzyān

wanted-I car rel it-goes good

I want a car that will run good (elicited)

In the following Egyptian sentence, the indefinite noun /tamsiliyya/ *serial* is modified by a clause headed by the definite relative /(i)lli/:

E4 فيه تمثيليّة اللي كانوا بيجيبوها في التليفزيون اللي هي بتقول حبكت ياعمدة؟

fī tamsiliyya illi kānu biygibūha fi t-tilivizyōn illi hiyya bitʾūl ḥabakit ya ʿumda?

there-is serial rel were-they indic-they-bring-it in the-TV rel she she-says was-necessary-she O mayor?

There's a serial that they used to show on TV that says, Is it really necessary, Mayor?

To test for performance error, this sentence was repeated to two other Egyptian speakers, and both found it perfectly acceptable. Subsequent observation of Egyptian speakers has confirmed that similar examples occur with some regularity.

The individuation hierarchy provides a principled explanation for this syntactic behavior. In the example given above, the speaker appears to have in mind a specific serial program. He introduces this program using the indefinite form because he assumes that it is unfamiliar to or unidentifiable by his interlocutors, but at the same time, the use of /illi/ implies a particular, and presumably identifiable, serial. The noun in this case is thus not entirely indefinite, but rather falls in the indefinite-specific range. Lacking a syntactic indefinite-specific marker, however, the speaker utilizes a combination of indefinite and definite markings across the clause to represent the specific identity of the serial.

Cowell notes that "some [Syrian] speakers occasionally use /yalli/ to introduce clauses that are attributive to an indefinite term" (1964:499).[7] Cowell has no explanation for this infraction other than that "some speakers occasionally" do this (1964:499); to leave it at that would suggest that–as many native speakers of Arabic believe–colloquial has no rules. The answer here, as above, seems to lie in the indefinite-specific quality of the relativized nouns. Similar to the Egyptian example given above, the head noun in Cowell's data appears to fall in the indefinite-specific range; here, the speaker clearly has a specific entity in mind (1964:499):

S فيه واحدة يللي باتذكّرها فيها اسمها
fī wāḥde yalli bətzakkar[h]a fīha ʾəsm[h]a
[there-is one rel indic-I-remember-it in-it name-its]
There's one I remember that has her name in it

The inability of the definite/indefinite marking dichotomy to predict the occurrence/absence of the relative pronoun /illi/ shows that specificity is a feature that can extend beyond the noun to the noun phrase as a whole, affecting the interaction of nouns with modifiers. In the next example from Kuwait, the speaker uses the definite /illi/ to relativize the indefinite noun /bnayya/ *girl*. The speaker combines

---

[7]Similarly, Feghali's study of Lebanese syntax concludes that /elli/ can be used with indefinite as well as definite nouns and gives several examples resembling those cited here (1928:311).

these two markings, one indefinite and the other definite, to indicate the existence of some particular girl.

K2 ندوّر لَه بنية اللي تناسب لَه

əndawwir-la bnayya lli tnāsib-la

we-seek-for-him girl rel she-suits-him

We look for a girl for him that will suit him

This construction may be contrasted to the (normative) alternate, /bnayya tnāsib-la/, which would mean *a/any girl that would suit him*, the identity of such a girl being less specific.

In a number of examples of this type, the head noun is human, including /bnayya/ *girl* in the previous Kuwaiti example and /rayyāl/ *man* in the next:

K3 شوفي لو – كل ما يكون ريّال اللي يحب المرا شوفي بنتي ما يهمّه لا حچي هلَه ولا يهمّه حچي احد

šūfi lo -- kil ma yikūn rayyāl illi yḥibb il-mara šūfi binti mā yihimma lā ḥači hala wala yihimma ḥači ʾaḥad

see-f if -- every nom it-be man rel he-loves the-wife see-f daughter-my neg it-concerns-him talk of-family-his nor it-concerns-him talk of-anyone

Look, if -- whenever there is a man who loves [his] wife, see, my daughter, neither the words of his family nor anyone else's words concern him

Similarly, the following Syrian example contains the indefinite human noun /nās/ *people* relativized with /yalli/ (Cowell 1964:499):

S بهداك الوقت كان فيه كتير ناس يللي استغلّوا الموقف

b-hadāk əl-waʾət kān fī ktīr nās yəlli staġallu l-mawʾef

[in-that the-time was-it there-is many people rel exploited-they the-situation]

At that time there were a lot of people who took advantage of the situation

Since humanness is one of the most important features in the hierarchy of individuation, the tendency of this mixed marking to occur with human nouns lends further support to the theory that the individuation of a head noun can affect the syntax of relative clauses.

One might then ask why speakers only occasionally make use of this pattern, since indefinite nouns described by relative clauses by definition have a degree of specificity. In the following example, the speaker mentions an American friend who arrived recently, using an indefinite relative clause (Cowell 1964:497).

S فيه عندي صديق أميركاني اجا جديد ع البلاد
fī ʿandi ṣadīʾ ʾamerkāni ʾəža ždīd ʿal-ᵊblād
[there-is at-me friend American came-he new to-the-country]
I have an American friend who has just recently come to this country

The speaker obviously has a particular person in mind, and the combined features of specificity and animacy might be expected to "push" the speaker towards using /illi/ as an indication of the heightened specificity of the noun. However, native informants much prefer the indefinite clause to a definite clause introduced by /illi/. The following sentence was deemed unlikely to occur:

S * فيه عندي صديق أميركاني اللي اجا جديد ع البلاد
*fī ʿandi ṣadīʾ ʾamerkāni lli ʾəža ždīd ʿal-ᵊblād
*there-is at-me friend American rel came-he new to-the-country
**I have an American friend who has just recently come to this country*

The best explanation for these seemingly paradoxical data appears to lie in the pragmatic role of the noun itself. In this sentence, the noun /ṣadīʾ ʾamerkāni/ *an American friend* represents an entity being introduced for the first time. The speaker needs to establish both the new identity and the topical role of the person, and therefore must mark the noun as indefinite. Pragmatic and discourse roles thus also play a role in determining the use of definite and indefinite markings in relative clauses.

Relativization also provides further evidence that nouns marked with new-topic article /wāḥid/ (Moroccan /wāḥəd l-/; see 1.5) fall within the indefinite range of the definiteness continuum. In all dialects, nouns marked with this article are modified as indefinite nouns (Harrell specifies this rule for Moroccan, 1962:165). In the following, /wāḥəd ər-ržəl/ *one foot* heads an indefinite relative clause /fīh buzəllūm/ *it has arthritis*. Here, the absence of the definite /lli/ "balances" the specifying article /wāḥəd l/ so that the combination of syntactic markings does not overly "weight" the noun with definiteness.

M9 قال ليا آجي دلك له واحد الرجل حاشاك فيه بوزلّوم
qāl liyya ʾaži dlək-lu wāḥəd r-ržəl ḥāšāk fīh buzəllūm
said-he to-me come rub for-him one the-foot may-it-avoid-you in-it arthritis
He told me, come and massage for him a leg that had–may you be spared–arthritis

In contrast, Moroccan nouns with indefinite-specific article /ši/ are commonly relativized with /lli/ (Harrell 1962:165). Harrell cites an example containing /ši ṭumubīl/ *a car* (1962:165):

M بغيت شي طوموبيل اللي تمشي مزيان
bġīt ši ṭumubīl lli təmši məzyān
[wanted-I ši car rel it-goes good]
I want a car that will run good

More difficult to explain is the following Kuwaiti example, in which clearly non-specific /ay šay/ *anything* is modified using /illi/:

K2 اي شي عندچ مشكلة ام احمد احنا حاضرين. اي شي اللي تبين.
ay šay ʿindič muškila umm aḥmad iḥna ḥāḍrīn. ʾay šay illi tabīn
any thing at-you problem Umm Ahmed we present. any thing rel you-want
Any kind of problem you have, Umm Ahmed, we're here. Any thing that you want

The probable explanation for the use of definite /illi/ here is that the speaker wishes to give prominence to /ay šay/ *anything*, to stress that every single request will be granted.

Speakers from Egypt, Syria, and Kuwait thus make use of a combination of definite and indefinite markings to indicate a higher degree of specificity or individuation in head nouns of relative clauses. However, pragmatic and discourse factors seem to mitigate against the widespread use of this combination.

Classical Arabic grammars stipulate that relative clauses that modify a definite head noun must be headed by a definite relative particle, yet Wright cites the following Classical examples which violate this rule (1898ii:318):[8]

CA ما ينبغي للرجل يشبهك
mā yanbaġī li-r-rajuli yušbihuka
that which beseems the man who is like thee

كمثل الحمار يحمل أسفاراً
ka-maṯali l-ḥimāri yaḥmilu ʾasfāran
like the ass which carries books

كالجمر يوضع في الرماد
ka-l-jamrī yūḍaʿu fī r-ramādi
like the coal which is put among the ashes

The grammaticality of these sentences rests on an interpretation of each head noun as indicating "not a particular individual (animate or inanimate), but any individual bearing the name" (Wright 1898ii:318). Thus these definite nouns are somehow "less definite" than others, or more properly less individuated, and the syntax of the relative clause that modifies these nouns reflects that status.

The mirrored relationship between the dialect examples on one hand and Wright's Classical data on the other is worth noting: in the dialects, the noun is indefinite and the descriptive clause carries definite marking, whereas in Classical Arabic, the noun carries definite marking while the absence of the relative pronoun indicates the non-specific of the referent. Both varieties of Arabic use similar strategies in combining definite and indefinite markings to weight partly definite, partly specific nouns in relative clauses, except that Classical Arabic marks definite non-specific while the dialects, in general, mark indefinite-specific.[9]

In either case, the specificity of the head noun affects the syntax of the entire clause. The use of the definite relative pronoun /illi/ in relativizing an indefinite head noun cannot be predicted or explained

---

[8]Of the three examples Wright defines as relative clauses, native speakers of Arabic prefer to analyze the second and third as circumstantial clauses. However, the first example is difficult to dismiss.

[9]There appears to exist a certain parallel between Classical Arabic and Moroccan in that Moroccan speakers tend to use the definite article to mark non-specific nouns (see 1.6).

by purely formal rules, nor can it be judged grammatically "correct" or "incorrect;" rather, the combination of definite and indefinite marking represents a middle range of a continuum of specificity, and demonstrates one way in which speakers control the syntactic rules of the language to represent the world as they see it.

3.2 Non-attributive Relative Clauses

Two types of non-attributive relative clauses are found among the four dialects. The first type, which uses the relative pronoun /illi/ without a head noun or referent, is found across all four dialect regions.

M2 اللي يعاونك ما كاين واللي يحنّ فيك ما كاين
lli yʿāwnk mā kāyn w lli yḥənn fīk mā kāyn
rel he-help-you neg there-is and rel he-sympathize with-you neg there-is
There's nobody to help you, nobody to take pity on you

E1 اللي كنت باقيسه
illi kunt baʾīsu
rel was-I indic-I-try-on-it
The one I was trying on

S2 اللي ميّتة امّه يقدّم خطوة
illi mayyte ʾimmu yqaddim xaṭwe
rel having-died-f mother-his he-advance step
[Anyone] whose mother has died, [must] step forward

K2 اللي تگول مخلّص الثانوية واللي تگول مخلّص الجامعة ... illi tgūl mxəllaṣ it-tanawiyya, w illi tgūl mxəllaṣ il-jāmʿa ...
rel she-says having-finished the-high-school and rel she-says having-finished the-university ...
[There is someone] who says [my son] has finished high school and someone who says he has finished college ...

The second type of non-attributive relative clause employs non-attributive, non-specific relative pronouns /ma/ *what* or /mīn/ *who(m)*.[10]

[10]Some Moroccan speakers use /fāš/ as a non-attributive relative pronoun in indirect object position only (see 3.6).

Relative /ma/ commonly occurs in Moroccan speech:[11]

M1 ما كاين ما يتدار

mā kāyn ma yətdār

not there-is what he-be-done

There's nothing to do

M9 الله يعطيك حجّة ف قبر النبي ويعطيك ما تمنّيت عند الله

ḷḷāh yaʿṭīk ḥəžža f qəbr ən-nabi w yaʿṭīk ma tmənnīti ʿnd ḷḷāh

God he-give-you pilgrimage in grave of-the-prophet and he-give-you what wanted-you at God

God grant you a pilgrimage to the Prophet's grave and give you what you want from God

No examples of non-specific relative /ma/ occur in my Kuwaiti data, but Holes reports that /ma/ is used in this manner in educated Gulf Arabic, citing this example (1990:24):

G ما گال لك غلط

ma gāl lik ġalaṭ

[what told-he to-you wrong]

What he told you was wrong

Relative /ma/ does not appear to be a regular feature of Egyptian or Syrian speech, but Syrian speakers do make use of /mīn/ *anyone* as a non-specific, non-attributive relative pronoun. Cowell notes that this use of /mīn/ is limited to object position within the main sentence (1964:568); his example parallels the following one from my data:

S4 ما بدّن مين يخطب لن

mā biddon mīn yəxṭub-lon

neg want-they who they-arrange-marriage-for-them

They don't need anyone to arrange their marriage

It is worth noting that the usage of Moroccan /ma/ *what* and Syrian /mīn/ *who* as non-specific relatives parallel the existence in both

---

[11]While Egyptian, Syrian, and Kuwaiti speakers use /ma/ as a nominalizer, Moroccan speakers normally use /lli/ in this fashion:

M11 ...بحال اللي گلتي انت عاد مروّحها عروسة

... b-ḥāl lli gulti nti ʿād mrəwwəḥha ʿrūsa

.... like rel said-you you just having-taken-her bride

... *like you'd think he'd just taken her as a bride*

dialects of indefinite-specific article /ši/, suggesting that, in general, these two dialects incorporate into their syntax more structures that indicate a range of specificity or individuation in nouns than do Egyptian and Kuwaiti. While all four dialects employ various strategies to individuate or specify indefinite nouns, the number and kinds of strategies available differ. Moroccan in particular tends to mark partly definite, partly specific nouns with specifying or definite articles.

3.3 Aleppan Relative Pronoun /il/

In addition to /illi/, an abbreviated version, /il/, is found in the northern Syrian city of Aleppo. This /il/ might at first seem to be a variant of /illi/ (Ferguson 1959 implies so, and /al/ is attested as a variant of /allaḏi/ in Classical Arabic, Wright 1898i:269); however, the syntactic structure of the /il/ relative clause differs from that of /illi/: /il/ in fact nominalizes the relative clause so that the relative pronoun lies in construct with the head noun.

The following passage contains two examples of the /il/ construction, which together exhibit two syntactic features which distinguish the /il/ relative from the /illi/ construction: (a) the absence of the definite article on the head nouns, /manṭiʾt-/ *area* and /bēt/ *house*, and (b) the pronunciation of the feminine /t/ in /manṭiʾt-/.[12] These features clearly indicate that the head noun and the relative pronoun are in a genitive or construct state.

S5 أخدنا بيت كتير كويّس ، منطقة الـ أخدنا فيها كتير كويّسة وغنية كتير، وبيت الـ أخدناه كتير كويّس

ʾaxadna bēt ktīr kwayyis manṭiʾt il ʾaxadna fī[h]a ktīr kwayyse w ġaniyye ktīr w bēt il ʾaxadnā ktīr kwayyis

took-we house very nice area rel took-we in-it very nice and rich very and house rel took-we-it very nice

We took a very nice house, the area in which we lived was very nice and very rich and the house we took [was] very nice

Relative /il/ as nominalizer occurs in many other areas of the Levant as well, but in a more limited environment. Whereas Aleppan

[12]The feminine /t/ on nouns is only pronounced when the noun is in construct state with a following noun, pronoun, or nominal clause.

speaker S5 nominalizes a range of nouns in this way, examples from other parts of the Levant mainly contain temporal nouns /sāʿa/ *hour, time* or /waʾt/ *time*, as in the following example from a northern Syrian speaker:

S2 وقت الـ بيموت بيصير بيعملوه ملاك
waqt il bimūt biṣīr byəʿməlū malāk
time rel indic-he-dies indic-he-becomes indic-they-make-him angel
When he dies he becomes [such that] they make him out to be an angel

In his grammar of Lebanese, Feghali cites a number of similar examples of this construction with /sāʿt il-/ *the time that* (1928:308).

These constructions containing /sāʿt il-/ and /waʾt il-/ differ from those in the S5 passage cited above in one important respect: while the nouns /bēt/ *house* and /manṭiʾt-/ *area* in the S5 example are specific, the nouns /sāʿa/ *hour*, *time* and /waʾt/ *time* are non-specific. Evidence from all four dialects suggests that the relativization of non-specific temporal nouns constitutes a special case of relativization that is the topic of the following section.

3.4 Relativizing Non-specific Temporal Nouns

Data from the dialects show a range of constructions in which temporal nouns may be relativized. At one end of this range lie normative definite relative clauses containing /illi/ and resumptive pronouns, and at the other end are found nominalized clauses that resemble the construct-like clause headed by /il/. This latter use of /illi/ in temporal clauses does not follow normative relative patterns, in that /illi/ here functions as a nominalizer to adverbial phrases whose head noun refers to time, such as *day*, *hour*, and so forth. These clauses are not true relative clauses, since their head nouns are indefinite, and they function in the sentence as adverbial clauses. Pragmatically, these clauses often tend to be sentence-initial and thus thematic. In addition, the nouns used in this construction are low in specificity.

Moroccan, Syrian, and Kuwaiti speakers all use /illi/ in temporal clauses without resumptive pronouns. These Moroccan and Syrian sentences contain examples of temporal /illi/ with an indefinite head noun, the /illi/ clause being appended to it in construct state:

M11 نهار اللي كبرت گاللها آبنتي راني ما عنديش الولاد
nhār lli kəbrat gāl-lha ʾā bənti rāni mā ʿndīš l-wlād
day rel grew-up-she said-he-to-her O daughter-my see-me neg at-me the-children
When she grew up, he told her, My daughter, I do not have [other] children

S4 وقت اللي بيتجوّزوا بيقللك صار اختلافات معها
waʾt illi bitjawwazu biʾil-lak ṣār ixtilāfāt maʿha
time rel indic-they-marry indic-he-says-to-you became-it differences with-her
When they get married, he tells you, [there have] occurred disagreements with her

In the following Kuwaiti example, /illi/ modifies definite /ha s-sinīn/ *these years*, but no resumptive pronoun occurs within the relative clause:

K4 زين، يعني انت، هالسنين اللي مارست چذي، شفتي شنهو؟
zēn yaʿni inti ha s-sinīn illi mārasti čid̲i šifti šinnhu?
good that-is you this the-years rel practiced-you like-this saw-you what?
Okay, these years that you've practiced, what have you seen?

This temporal /illi/ syntactically parallels the Egyptian use of /ma/ as a temporal nominalizer, seen in the following:

E1 ولمّا منال شافته يوم ما جبته اتجنّنت
wi lamma manāl šafitu yōm ma gibtu, igganninit
and when Manal saw-she-it day that got-I-it, went-crazy-she
And when Manal saw it the day I got it she went crazy [over it]

This parallel suggests that /illi/, when in genitive construct with a following non-specific temporal noun such as /sāʿa/, acts as a nominalizer and not as a relative, which explains the absence of resumptive pronouns in these cases. Temporal nouns of low individuation seem to attract nominalization rather than relativization.

It is thus difficult to draw a well-defined boundary separating relative clauses from nominalized ones, at least in the case of temporal nouns. Rather, the modification of temporal nouns is probably best viewed as lying along a continuum of specificity. The lower the individuation of the noun, and the less salient the clause as a whole, the more likely it is to be nominalized and/or not contain a resumptive pronoun. Figure 2 diagrams the range of specificity of temporal nouns and the syntactic structures that relativize them.

Figure 2: Relativization of Temporal Nouns

Nonspecific:	Specific:
Nominalized with /illi/	Relativized with /illi/
or /ma/ in construct	and full resumption

Syntactically, there appears to be a gradual transition from relative clauses to nominalized clauses, particularly with non-specific temporal nouns in Moroccan and Syrian. Nouns with low specificity, especially those that appear in adverbial clauses, tend to take attributive clauses that are restrictive, so identified by the fact that they stand in construct with the following relative or nominalizing pronoun.

3.5 /illi/ as Complementizer

In addition to its use as a relative pronoun and a temporal nominalizer, /illi/ functions in certain contexts as a kind of conjunction or sentence complementizer. The limited yet strikingly parallel contexts in which /illi/ occurs in Morocco, Egypt, and Syria are worth noting.

Mitchell and El-Hassan note that /illi/ functions as complementizer for a "limited group of verbs (or verbal expressions)" in Levantine educated spoken Arabic (1994:113). Among their examples (114):

انبسطنا كتير اللي شفناك
nbasaṭna ktīr illi (or ʾinn iḥna) šufnāk
[were-happy-we very rel (or comp we) saw-we-you]
We were very happy that we saw you

عظيم اللي قدرت تخلّص بسرعة
ʿaẓīm illi (or ʾinnak) ʾdirt itxalliṣ b-surʿa
[great rel (or comp-you) were-able-you you-finish with-speed]
It is great that you were able to finish quickly

For Egyptian, Badawi and Hinds give one of the meanings of /illi/ as *seeing that, since* and note that it has functions as a conjunction in this sense (1986:33; see also Woidich 1980a). They cite the following examples (33):

E انا أُشكَر اللي قدّمتك له
ʾana ʾuškar illi ʾaddimt-ak lu
[I I-be-thanked rel introduced-I-you to-him]
I should be thanked, since [that] I introduced you to him

E الحقّ عليّ اللي طاوعتك
il-ḥaʾʾ ʿalayya ʾilli ṭawiʿtak
[the-right on-me rel obeyed-I-you]
it's my fault for obeying [that I obeyed] you

I elicited a number of similar examples from a Moroccan informant native of Meknas, including:

M3 فرحنا اللي شفناك
frəḥna lli šəfnāk
became-happy-we rel saw-we-you
We were happy that we saw you or *We're happy to see you*

M3 طار لي اللي ما جيتيش
ṭār-li lli mā žītīš
flew-it to-me neg came-you
I was upset [I lost it] that you didn't come

While Badawi and Hinds define this /illi/ as *seeing that, since,*it may not be freely used in any context with this meaning. Native informants reject sentences like:

M * ما قدرناش نجيوا اللي جاونا ضياف
* mā qdərnāš nžīw lli žāwna ḍyāf
* neg were-able-we we-come rel came-he-to-us guests
* *We weren't able to come seeing that we had guests*

E * نمت كويس اللي اتحسّن الجوّ
* nimt kwayyis illi itḥassan ig-gaww
* slept-I good rel improved-it the-weather
* *I slept well seeing that the weather has improved*

S * تعبت اللي اشتغلت كتير اليوم
* tiʿibt illi štaġalt ktīr il-yōm
* got-tired-I rel worked-I much today
* *I got tired since I worked a lot today*

What the previously cited examples all have in common–and what is missing from the ungrammatical examples–is not syntactic but semantic: an emotional reaction, such as happiness, anger, relief, or resentment. The "relativized" /illi/ clause is linked to that emotional state in that it contains the underlying reason or cause of that state. The /illi/ clause thus becomes a relative clause modifying an underlying or understood *reason* or *cause* for the emotional state.

Speakers from all dialect areas report common usage of the construction /il-ḥamdu li-l-lāh illi/ *Thank God that*, as in the Egyptian expression:

E الحمد لله اللي جت على قدّ كدا
il-ḥamdu li-l-lāh illi gat ʿala ʾadd kida
the-praise to-God rel came-it on extent of-that
Thank God it wasn't worse

In this case, it may be the highly individuated status of the noun *God* that attracts the relative pronoun /illi/.

3.6 Moroccan Word-Order Relatives: /fāš/ and Interrogatives

The relative clauses examined so far have all used a case-coding relativization strategy in which the syntactic role of the relativized noun is marked by a position-marking resumptive pronoun in the relative clause (Keenan and Comrie 1977). However, Moroccan Arabic has a second kind of relative clause which operates with a word-order relativization strategy, using a different relative pronoun, /fāš/, and having no resumptive pronoun within the body of the clause.[13] This kind of clause relativizes oblique objects of low individuation whose sentential role is generally locative or temporal. Harrell notes the

[13]It was noted previously that Moroccan relative clauses with /lli/ also do not normally code the direct object position with resumptive pronouns. Whether this point of similarity between the two constructions bears theoretical implications is left to future research.

relative /-āš/, used in combination with prepositions /f/ and (less commonly) /b/ "in those cases where a human being is not referred to" (1962:164; /bāš/ does not occur in my data).[14] In the following three examples, /faš/ relativizes the nouns /wəqt/ *time*, /līla/ *night*, and /magānāt/ *watches*. In the first, /l-wəqt/ *the time* is clearly not highly specified or textually prominent. In the second, /l-līla/ *the night* refers to a particular night, but the exact identity of that night seems less important here than what happened at the time. In the third, /l-magānāt/ *the watches* are generic rather than specific.

M11 الوقت فاش دارت معايا بغيت نولد ...
l-wəqt fāš dārət m^{c}āya bġīt nūləd
the-time rel did-it with-me wanted-I I-give-birth
When [labor] started with me [and] I was about to give birth ...

M7 عقلتي الليلة فاش كنا عند السي الجيلالي؟
^{c}qalti l-līla fāš kunna ^{c}nd s-si ž-žīlāli?
remembered-you the-night rel were-we at Mr. Jilali?
Do you remember the night when we were at Mr. Jilali's?

M6 شرا مگانة ديال الما، عرفتي دوك المگانات فاش تيهبطوا – سميته
šra magāna dyāl l-mā, ^{c}rafti dūk l-magānāt fāš tayhabṭu -- smiyytu
bought-he watch gen the-water found-out-you those the-watches rel indic-they-go-down -- name-its
He bought a water-proof watch, you know, those watches with which they go down [in] -- what's its name

These examples suggest that relativization with /fāš/ tends to modify nouns low in specification or individuation.

In the following, /fāš/ stands as a non-specific, in this case non-attributive relative pronoun:

M11 ما صابت مسكينة لا ما تاكل لا فاش تگمّط داك الولد
mā ṣābət məskīna lā ma tākul lā fāš tgəmməṭ dāk l-wəld
neg found-she poor neg what she-eat neg rel she-wrap that the-boy
She found, poor thing, neither a thing to eat nor a thing in which to wrap the boy

---

[14]Marçais cites a construction combining the two pronouns that my Moroccan informants found strange: /əl-^{c}ām əlli fāš mšīt/ *"l'année oú je suis parti"* [lit., *the year that in which I left*] (1977:205).

Northern Moroccan speakers I interviewed did not use this relative pronoun, but the data I collected contains several examples of a similar construction using the interrogative particle /fīn/ *where*:

M10 كيجي واحد خور عاود تاني سكران ويجي ويتكب له على البلاصة فين گالس هو والمرا دياله وولاده

kayži wāḥəd xūr ʿāwd tāni səkrān w yži w yətkəbb-lu ʿla l-blāṣa fīn gāls hūwa w l-mra dyālu w wlādu

indic-he-comes one other then again drunk and he-come and he-throw-up on the-place where sitting he and the-wife of-his and children-his

Then again another one comes along drunk and comes and throws up on the place where he's sitting, he and his wife and children

The same construction also occurs in the speech of a woman from the Middle Atlas region:

M11 احنا غادي نمشيوا البلاد اللي ما تعرفيهاش، غادي تتبعي غير ديك الرماد والنخالة حتّى لديك البلاصة فين غادي نحطوا

ḥna ġādi nəmšīw l-blād lli mā təʿrfīhāš, ġādi ttəbʿi ġī[r] dīk ər-rmād w n-nəxx^{w}āla ḥtta l-dīk l-blāṣa fīn ġādi nḥəṭṭu

we will we-go the-place rel neg you-know-it fut you-follow only that the-ashes and the-chaff until to-that the-place where will we-alight

We are going to the place you don't know, you will follow just these ashes and chaff until that place where we will alight

There appears to be some overlap in function between /lli/ as a nominalizer for non-specific temporal nouns and /faš/ as a relativizing particle for non-specific nouns or nouns of low individuation. As with temporal relative/nominalizer /lli/, relative clauses with /fāš/ and /fīn/ contain no resumptive pronouns. This overlap may reflect regional variation, or perhaps constitutes evidence of a shifting paradigm in which different relativization strategies stand in competition.

Relativization with /fāš/ parallels relativization with /lli/ in Moroccan in a lower degree of resumptive marking as compared to relative clauses in other dialects. Resumptive pronouns in Moroccan /lli/ clauses are only required when the relativized noun is a genitive or the object of a preposition, and the occurrence of a resumptive pronoun in direct object position in Moroccan is unusual (Harrell 1962:164). However, the immediately preceding example contains a resumptive pronoun in direct object position: /l-blād lli mā taʿrfīhāš/ *the place you don't know [it].* The following is more typical; here /l-basṭiyyāt/ *the pills* is relativized from direct object position with no resumptive pronoun in the relative clause itself:

M9 آ سيدي احمد ديك البسطيات اللي عطيتيني ديك النهار!
'ā sīdi ḥmǝd dīk l-basṭiyyāt lli ʿṭitīni dīk n-nhār!
O Mr. Ahmed those the-pills rel you-gave-me that the-day!
Mr. Ahmed, those pills that you gave me the other day!

A Moroccan informant I questioned about this variation in the occurrence of the resumptive pronoun in direct object position offered the observation that resumptive pronouns tend to be used in negative constructions, such as /l-blād lli mā taʿrfīhāš/ *the place you don't know [it].* The use of the resumptive pronoun in such cases may lend a kind of emphatic or categorical negation to the clause by specifying the negated object: *the place you don't know at all.*

3.7 Moroccan Relative Pronoun /d/

A relative particle unrelated to the /illi/ pronouns exists in the mountains of northern Morocco, among speakers known as /žbāla/ *mountain Arabs.*[15] The following examples are all taken from an interview with one speaker, an elderly, uneducated woman:

M9 يصلّي واحد الفقيه دنّه يعرف شنّو كاين
yṣalli wāḥǝd l-fqīh dǝnnu yǝʿraf šǝnnu kāyn
he-pray one the-learned rel he-knows what there-is
A religious scholar who knows what's up [was] praying

M9 بنادم اللي مزيان، كله تقول مزيان وبنادم دنّه قبيح ...
bnādǝm lli mzyān, kulla tqūl mzyān w bnādǝm dǝnnu qbīḥ ...
person rel good, always you-say good and person rel-he bad ...
The one who is good, always you say [he's] good, and the one who is bad ...

---

[15]See also Fischer and Jastrow (1980:258), who note variants of this pronoun /iddi/, /dī/, and /d/ among the /žbāla/.

M9 قال له آوليدي انتينا احسن من هادم د حجّوا
qāl-lu ʾā wlīdi ntīna ḥsən mən hādəm d ḥəžžu
said-he-to-him O son-my you better than those rel they-made-pilgrimage
He told him, Son, you are better than those that made the pilgrimage

In the first and second examples, the particle /dənnu/ modifies singular, highly individuated nouns, while in the third, /d/ modifies a less specified plural. In the second sentence, /dənnu/ in the second clause mirrors /lli/ in the first, which also regularly occurs in this woman's speech, and which is used by the community in which she has lived for years. The third example contains the basic relative particle is /d/, which is for most Moroccan speakers a variant of the genitive /dyāl/. This speaker uses /dyāl/ overwhelmingly, if not exclusively, in genitive constructions. She also uses in the following sentence the interrogative particle /š/ as a non-attributive relative pronoun:

M9 شرا لها، آ الحبيب، ش كيخصّها
šrā-lha, ʾā l-ḥbīb, š kayxəṣṣha
bought-he-for-her the-dear what indic-it-is-necessary-for-her
He bought for her, my dear, what she needed

These data indicate that this dialect also shows a range of relative constructions parallel to the urban dialects. However, the speaker I recorded has lived for a long time in the town of Larache, and her speech is mixed. Relativization strategies in this dialect area warrant further investigation.

3.8 Summary

While definite relative pronoun /illi/ is found in all dialect regions, several alternative constructions coexist with it in certain areas. Moreover, the use of /illi/ itself does not quite follow the rules given for it in the dialect grammars.

Relative clauses whose head nouns are morphologically indefinite reflect a semantic continuum that ranges from indefinite, non-specific to indefinite-specific. An indefinite, non-specific head noun is followed by an indefinite relative clause. An indefinite but specific noun, on the other hand, may be joined to its attributive clause by the (otherwise definite) particle /illi/. The use of definite relative /illi/ to partly define or specify indefinite nouns is a regular, if not common, feature of spoken Arabic. While the dialects normally follow formal varieties of Arabic in distinguishing between definite and indefinite head nouns, the definite pronoun /illi/ can mark a relative clause describing an indefinite-specific head noun.

Data from spoken Arabic point to links between relativization and other syntactic constructions. Northern Syrian speakers can relativize using /il/ in a clause in which the head noun stands in construct with the following clause, and the mountain Arabs of northern Morocco use variants of /d/ in both relatives and genitives. Relativization also overlaps with nominalization in temporal clauses, as speakers from Morocco, Syria, and Kuwait sometimes use /illi/ to "relativize" temporal nouns in constructions where the head noun is marked indefinite, but is modified by an /illi/ clauses that stands in construct with it. /illi/ in these clauses parallels the Egyptian nominalizer /ma/.

Moroccan dialects show additional relativization strategies not found elsewhere in my data pool. The relative pronoun /fāš/ may be used to relativize non-human nouns that appear to be of low specification and less individuation. At the same time, Moroccan speakers normally do not use resumptive pronouns to mark relativized direct objects, except in negated clauses.

In addition to clarifying aspects of the usage of indefinite articles, patterns of number agreement, and genitive exponents (Chapters 1 and 2), the continuum of individuation also helps explain certain patterns of relativization in the dialects. A relatively high degree of individuation of an indefinite noun, or low individuation of a definite one, may be reflected in a mix of definite and indefinite syntactic markers, or the use of nominalized as opposed to relativized temporal nouns. Moroccan and Syrian speakers both use non-attributive, non-specific relative pronouns, Morrocan /ma/ for inanimates and Syrians /mīn/ for humans. strategies that parallel their use of indefinite-specific articles to indicate a middle range on the individuation continuum. Relativization thus provides further evidence that, to varying extents, speakers of all dialects use of a range of strategies to represent the continuum of individuation and specification that exists in the natural world.

4 Demonstrative Articles and Pronouns

4.0 Introduction

This chapter will explore the main syntactic and discourse functions of demonstrative articles and pronouns in the four dialects. The primary aim will be to look for pragmatic patterns of demonstrative syntax across dialects–not an easy task, given the number of forms and their distribution, some marked for gender, some not, some pre-nominal, some post-nominal. Nonetheless, evidence suggests that most of these dialects share demonstrative patterns and functions.[1]

Moroccan, Syrian, and Kuwaiti dialects are characterized by considerable flexibility and variety of demonstrative forms and syntax, especially in comparison to Egyptian.[2] In the former group, demonstratives may precede or follow the noun, whereas in Egyptian, the syntax of demonstrative-noun phrases is fixed and homogenous: demonstratives must follow the nouns they modify. The range of demonstrative patterns in Moroccan, Syrian, and Kuwaiti parallels a range of pragmatic functions as well, and these functions will be explored in this chapter.

In Arabic, nominal, pronominal, and adjectival forms normally show gender distinction, so it may be surprising to find a lack of gender distinction in some of the forms examined here.[3] Three of the four dialect areas (the exception being Egyptian) have genderless unstressed demonstratives. The syntactic and pragmatic functions of these pronouns will be explored here.

---

[1]This discussion is limited to the most commonly occurring demonstratives. For an exhaustive catalogue of demonstrative forms in spoken Arabic, see Fischer (1959). The analysis here relies chiefly on my own data because context has been crucial in trying to determine discourse functions of the various demonstrative pronouns.

[2]Demonstratives in spoken Arabic show greater syntactic flexibility than do demonstratives in formal Arabic, which precede the noun except in genitive constructions.

[3]Rosenhouse attempts to explain away Fischer's citation of ungendered demonstrative forms in the Ṣanʿāʾ (Yemen) dialect (Rosenhouse 1984b:254, citing Fischer 1959:71).

The basic function of demonstratives is to manage discourse topics.[4] Demonstratives identify, recall, highlight, and contrast entities that play important roles in discourse. In spoken Arabic, demonstratives perform these functions with anaphoric, deictic, topic recall, specification, and contrastive reference. All non-deictic demonstratives are anaphoric, but a distinction must be made between those pronouns that are only anaphoric, and not contrastive, and those that involve at least some degree of contrast.

It is important to distinguish between unstressed and stressed demonstrative forms (except in Egyptian, which apparently lacks an unstressed form). The unstressed forms serve only to signal anaphoric reference, either to an entity that has already been mentioned, or to an entity that the speaker presumes is shared with or identifiable by the interlocutor, or physically present. The "stressed" forms and functions of demonstratives likewise show similar patterns across dialects. It is well-known that the proximal and distal forms of demonstratives function deictically to refer to near and far objects in both time and space; in addition, these two sets of forms can indicate "discourse distance:" that is, when used to recall a topic previously mentioned in the discourse, the form of the demonstrative helps to signal the degree of proximity in a figurative sense, that is, the degree of "retrievability" of the topic.[5] Finally, it is primarily the distal forms that are used to signal contrastive reference, perhaps because through distancing two entities from each other, their separate identities are more clearly highlighted.

4.1 Proximal and Distal Demonstrative Forms

Grammars of the dialects subdivide demonstrative pronouns into two sets, proximal and distal, referring either to temporal or locative distance. With the exception of Egyptian, the forms of these pronouns are relatively homogenous. Common forms of the proximal set are summarized in Table 4-1, and the distal set in Table 4-2.

[4]"Discourse topic" is used here in a non-technical sense, to refer to any entity that plays an important role in the discourse.

[5]Lord and Dahlgren's (1997) study of anaphora in newspaper articles was helpful in formulating this analysis.

Table 4-1: Proximal Demonstrative Pronouns

Proximal Demonstrative Pronouns			
	masculine	feminine	plural
Moroccan	hāda	hādi	hādu
Egyptian	da	di	dōl
Syrian	hād(a)	hāy(ye)	hadōl(e)
Kuwaiti	hāḏa	hāḏi	(ha)ḏēla

Parentheses indicate an optional segment of the pronoun. More complete lists of demonstrative forms may be found in Fischer (1959), Harrell (1962), Cowell (1964), Fischer and Jastrow (1980), and Holes (1990). Egyptian in particular has a large number of alternative forms to the ones given here (see Badawi and Hinds 1986:273).

Table 4-2: Distal Demonstrative Pronouns

Distal Demonstrative Pronouns			
	masculine	feminine	plural
Moroccan	(hā)dāk	(hā)dīk	(hā)dūk
Egyptian	dāk, dukha	dīk, dikha	dukhum
Syrian	hadāk	hadīk	hadolīk
Kuwaiti	(ha)ḏāk	(ha)ḏīč	(ha)ḏēla

A cursory glance at Tables 4-1 and 4-2 reveals similar proximal and distal forms in all dialects except Egyptian, in which the absence of the morpheme /ha/ from all demonstrative forms is immediately apparent.

4.2 Unstressed Anaphoric Demonstrative Articles /ha/ and /hād/

In addition to the forms given in Tables 4-1 and 4-2, Moroccan, Syrian, and Kuwaiti Arabic share a kind of short, ungendered, pre-nominal, unstressed demonstrative that can only occur prefixed to a following noun. I will call these forms demonstrative articles, adapting the term from Harrell (1962:147) with a modified definition. Harrell uses the term for all forms that are used with the definite article and precede the noun they modify, gendered and ungendered, short and long forms (1962:147-48, 190). It is necessary to maintain a distinction between forms that only occur prefixed to a following noun, and those that can occur independently, a distinction that happens to parallel the absence or presence of gender marking as well. Table 4-3 lists the forms of the demonstrative article.

Table 4-3: Unstressed Demonstrative Articles

The Demonstrative Article	
Moroccan	hād
Egyptian	--
Syrian	ha
Kuwaiti	ha

Harrell describes the function of Moroccan /hād/ as having "generalized demonstrative meaning" with "none of the implications of **distinguishing** between near and far as do the English demonstratives *this* and *that*" (1962:147, emphasis mine). The lack of ability of /hād/ to distinguish between objects suggests that its function is anaphoric. Similarly, Cowell, analyzing examples of Syrian /ha/ from his corpus, concludes that /ha/ may be used in either an anaphoric or a "deictic" sense[6] (1964:556). By the latter he means present in the immediate

[6]Cowell uses deictic as "presentational," referring to an entity in the immediate speech context, and calls /ha/ a "demonstrative prefix" (1964:556).

environment, as is clear from the example he gives, in which /ha l-bināye l-ḥamra/ *that red building* stands clearly in view of the interlocutors (1964:556):

S وين فيه مطعم منيح هون؟ --- شايف هالبناية الحمرا؟ وراها
wēn fī maṭʿam ᵊmnīḥ hōn? --- šāyef ha l-bināye l-ḥamra? warāha
[where there-is restaurant good here? having-seen this the-building the-red? ... behind-it]
Where is there a good restaurant around here? --- Do you see that red building? Behind it.

Cowell's analysis can be simplified by noting that this particular kind of deictic function falls within discourse anaphora, for entities within the physical view of the speakers belong to the current discourse registry because they are known and therefore retrievable.

Both /ha/ and /hād/ share certain grammatical characteristics and pragmatic functions. They are numberless and genderless, and do not show agreement with the noun they modify. They are sometimes called 'unstressed' demonstratives, reflecting the fact that they are never used to specify or contrast.[7] Rather, they are only used to mention entities whose unique identity is already known to both speaker and listener. They belong to a class of demonstratives Croft (1990) calls the "anaphoric demonstrative."

Croft defines the difference between anaphoric demonstratives, deictic demonstratives, and definite articles (1990:219):[8]

> [A]naphoric demonstratives differ from "true" (deictic) demonstratives in that they may refer to an object previously mentioned in the discourse, but they differ from "true" definite articles in that they are not used to refer to uniquely identifiable objects not previously referred to (as in *I found a jar and unscrewed **the** lid*).

This general definition of anaphoric demonstratives helps us to identify the function of /ha/ and /hād/ by contrasting their function to that of the

---

[7]Compare to Wald's discussion of "unstressed that" in English, where "that" marks the first mention of an entity that is presumed to be shared knowledge. Wald's example: "My sister works in--you know that deer?" (1983:113).

[8]The unstressed demonstrative pronoun /ha/ has been noted by Rosenhouse, who claims it is used "more or less as a definite article"–an inexact description (1984:251).

proximal and distal forms (which also have anaphoric functions, as I will show), but it needs to be slightly modified to fit Arabic.

As Croft notes, in languages that have both anaphoric demonstratives and definite articles, the former "competes with" the latter (1990:219). However, unlike English *that*, and like the Arabic definite article, Arabic /ha/ and /hād/ may refer to uniquely identifiable objects not directly referred to in the discourse, but which exist in the permanent registry,[9] or can be implied or "retrieved" from the context or the registry of topics already established in the current discourse. These anaphoric demonstratives serve to "retrieve" or recall the noun from that permanent registry. Another distinction between the definite article and the anaphoric demonstratives lies in the specificity of the modified noun. The definite article in Arabic can modify generic and abstract nouns, whereas the anaphoric demonstratives always refer to specific entities, which also have a degree of textual prominence.

Like definite marking and number agreement, the use of the anaphoric demonstrative is subject to a degree of speaker control. The choice between the anaphoric demonstrative and the definite article depends on the speaker's choice of representation of the textual prominence of the noun. Nouns modified by the anaphoric demonstrative are more individuated, and play a more important role in the discourse, than nouns modified only by the definite article.

4.2.1 Syntactic Functions of Demonstrative Articles

Of all demonstrative forms, only the anaphoric demonstrative article has syntactic license to modify any definite noun regardless of number, gender, or genitive status.

The following two Moroccan sentences pair /hād/ with a masculine singular, /l-insān/*person*, and a human plural, /n-nās/ *people*:

M9 الدار د هاد الانسان اللي الجار ديالك
d-dār d hād l-ʾinsān lli ž-žār dyālk
the-house gen this he-person rel the neighbor gen-yours
the house of that person who is your neighbor

[9]The "permanent registry" refers to unique objects known to everyone, such as *the sun* (see Chafe 1976).

M2 هاد الناس د الزمان
hād n-nās d zmān
this the-people gen old
those people of long ago

Next follow analogous examples from Syrian and Kuwaiti, in which /ha/ modifies masculine, feminine, and plural nouns:

S2 بيروحوا بهالعتمة وبهالليل
birūḥu b-ha l-ʿatme w b-ha l-lēl
indic-they-go in this the-darkness (f) and in-that-the-night (m)
They go in that darkness and that night ...

K4 هالسنين اللي مارست
ha s-snīn illi mārasti
this the-years which practiced-you
in all these years you've practiced ...

Harrell and Cowell note that the demonstrative article can precede genitive constructions (not permitted in formal Arabic). The following Moroccan examples contain /hād/ modifying possessed nouns:

M هاد صاحبي
hād ṣāḥbi
[this friend-my]
this friend of mine (Harrell 1962:191)

M9 فين هاد داري؟
fīn hād dāri?
where this house-my?
Where is this house of mine?

Likewise, in Syrian and Kuwaiti, /ha/ may precede genitive constructions. In this construction, /ha/ assimilates the definite article /l-/ into a combined article that modifies the entire construct, not just the first noun (Cowell 1964:459):

S هالفنجان القهوة
ha l-fənžān ᵊl-ʾahwe
[this the-cup of-the-coffee]
this cup of coffee

My Kuwaiti data contains a parallel example:

K3 تشتري كل يوم هالفخوذ اللحم
tištri kil yōm ha l-fxūḏ il-laḥam
she-buys every day this the-legs-of-meat
She buys every day these legs of meat

The demonstrative article is thus syntactically distinguished from the deictic stressed demonstrative pronouns by virtue of the former's ability to modify masculine and feminine, singular and plural nouns, as well as genitive and possessive constructions. These unique syntactic features parallel specific pragmatic roles this article plays in discourse.

4.2.2 Discourse Functions of the Demonstrative Article

The anaphoric demonstrative article in Syrian, Kuwaiti, and Moroccan modifies a unique referent that is already established in the conversational registry in one of the following ways: (a) it has been previously mentioned in the discourse, directly or indirectly; (b) it is in the permanent registry; or (c) it is present in the immediate environment. The anaphoric demonstrative normally occurs with the first or second mention of a noun. Unlike the definite article, the anaphoric demonstrative only modifies individuated, textually prominent nouns. Unlike the deictic demonstrative, the article may not be used in contrastive reference; that is, it can be used to establish coreference just when there is only one possible referent. By highlighting the anaphoric nature of the reference, /ha/ and /hād/ add cohesion to the discourse in several ways. Examples from Moroccan, Syrian, and Kuwaiti demonstrate the discourse roles these demonstrative articles play.

In the following Kuwaiti passage, /fxuḏ il-laḥam/ *legs of meat* is repeated, the second time with the anaphoric demonstrative, reiterating the specific identity of the meat and its importance to the story:

K3 كل يوم تشتري فخوذ لحم وتروح تعطيها للحارس مالَه. تشتري كل يوم هالفخوذ اللحم
kil yōm tištiri fxūḏ laḥam wi trūḥ taʿṭīha li-l-ḥāris māla. tištiri kil yōm ha l-fxūḏ il-laḥam
every day she-buys legs of-meat and she-goes she-gives-them to-the-guard gen-it. she-buys every day this the-legs of-the meat

Every day she buys legs of meat and goes and gives them to the guard of [the lion]. She buys every day these legs of meat

The interview from which the following question is taken centers around the experience of a Kuwaiti professional matchmaker. After a discussion of the matchmaker's years of experience, the interviewer frames the following question with /ha s-sinīn/ *these years*, referring to and summarizing this experience:

K4 انت هالسنين اللي مارست چذي شفتي شنهو، يميلون حگ اي نوعية من البنات؟

ʾinti ha s-sinīn illi mārasti čiḏi šifti šinhu, ymīlūn ḥagg ay nawʿiyya mn əl-banāt?

you this the-years which practiced-you like-this saw-you what they-incline to which type of the-girls

In all these years you've practiced like this, you have noticed what? They are inclined toward which kind of girls?

The previous example contrasts with the following, in which the elderly Kuwaiti speaker tells her life story, including all of the places she has lived. Among them she mentions *this house*, using /hāḏa l-bēt/, because it is only one among a set of possible referents:

K3 من نزلنا الحين هاذا البيت تدرون چم؟ خمسة وعشرين سنة

min nizalna l-ḥīn hāḏa l-bēt tadrūn čam? xamsa w ʿišrīn sina

from moved-in-we now this the-house you-know how-many? five and twenty year

Do you know how long now since we moved into this house? 25 years

Similarly, in the next passage, the function of the deictic demonstrative /hāḏi/ *this* in /hāḏi l-mara/ *this woman* contrasts with that of the anaphoric /ha/ in /ha š-šay/ *this thing*. The fact that /l-mara/ is further modified with a relative clause tells us that she is not uniquely identifiable, whereas /ha š-šay/ has only one referent, and it is the discourse topic here: the protocol of matchmaking.

K2 انا ، يعني ، من مارست ويّا هاذي المرا اللي تخطب يعني، وانا على هالشي، على المكشوف

K2 ʾāna yaʿni min mārast wiyya hādi l-mara illi tixaṭib yaʿni w ana ʿala ha š-šay ʿala l-makšūf
I that-is from practiced-I with this the-woman who she-arranges-marriages that-is and I on this the-thing on the-exposed
I, since I began practicing with this woman who arranges marriages, I've been [doing it] this way, out in the open.

In the lion-taming Kuwaiti parable from which the next example is taken, anaphoric /ha/ modifies the one and only lion, /ha s-sibiʿ/ *that lion*. Moreover, the syntactic position of *that lion* indicates that it functions as the topic of the sentence, which in turn reflects its importance to the narrative:

K3 يعني ها سبع، شلون گدرتي تاخذين منَّه شلون؟
yaʿni ha sibiʿ šlōn gədartey tāxdīn minna šlōn?
that-is this the-lion how were-able-you you-take from-it how?
That lion, how did you take [a hair] from it, how?

The next speaker is a Moroccan woman recalling the harsh treatment she received at the hands of her mother-in-law. In mid-sentence, she extends her complaint to the entire older generation, already identified and known by extension from the mother-in-law, with /hād n-nās/ *those people*:

M2 ها عگوزتي تنوّت، گالت دابا وهادي شوف اش عطات لامها ولاّ اش
مخّرت ولا اش دارت ولاّ — هاد الناس د زمان كانوا صعوبة بزّاف
ha ʿgūzti tnuwwat gālt dāba w hādi šūf aš ʿṭāt l-^{u}mmha wlla š maxxrat wlla aš dārt wlla - hād n-nās d zmān kānu ṣuʿūba bəzzāf
here mother-in-law-my caught-on-she said-she now and this-one look what gave-she to-mother-her or what stole-she or what did-she or -- this the-people gen the-time were-they difficulty
Here my mother-in-law has caught on. She said, Now look what this one has given to her mother or what she has stolen or what she has done or -- Those people of those days, they were a great difficulty

In the following two passages, elderly Moroccan and Syrian speakers compare the past and the present. When these speakers shift the topic to the present generation, they introduce the latter with the anaphoric articles /hād/ and /ha/, respectively, which serve here to indicate both temporal "presence" of *this generation* and its role as a new topic of conversation.

M2 حنايا كنّا تنخافوا من خيالنا. هاد الجيل آ سيدي اللي طالع ما خايف ما - ما والو

ḥnāya kunna tanxāfu mən xyālna. hād ž-žīl ʾā sīdi lli ṭālʿ mā xāyif mā -- mā wālu

we were-we indic-we-fear from shadow-our. this the-generation O sir which coming-up neg fearing neg -- neg nothing

We used to be afraid of our shadow. This generation, sir, that is emerging, is not afraid or anything

S4 عادات الاوّلية - ابهاتنا وجدودنا - كانوا ما يشوفوا العروس لليلة العرس. هلّق هالجيل هالموجود بيخطبوا بعضن هنّن

ʿādāt il-awwaliyye, abbahātna w ždūdna, kānu mā yšūfu l-ʿarūs la-lēlt l-ʿərs. hallaʾ ha j-jīl ha l-mawjūd buxṭbu baʿḍon hinnin

customs of-the-first-ones, fathers-our and grandfathers-our, were-they neg they-see the-bride until-the-night of-the-wedding. now this the-generation this the-present indic-they-arrange-marriage each-other they

The customs of the old [generations], our fathers and grandfathers, they used to not see the bride until the wedding night. Now, this generation, they arrange their own marriages themselves

In the following Syrian passage, /ha ṭ-ṭalʿa/ *this going out* and /ha l-fawte/ *this going in* are both anaphoric references to the movements implied by the verbs /birūḥu/ *they go* and /bīžu/ *they come*.

S2 ما بيروحوا ما بيجوا يعني اكتر اوقاتن بالبيت وما فيه، ما فيه لا هالطلعة ولا هالفوتة

mā birūḥu mā bižu yaʿni ʾaktar ʾawqāton bi-l-bēt w mā fī, mā fī lā ha ṭ-ṭalʿa wala ha l-fawte

neg indic-they-go neg indic-they-come that-is most times-their in-the-house and neg there-is neg there-is neg this the-going-out nor this the-entering

They don't go out or in, that is, most of their time is at home, and there isn't -- there is neither this going out nor that going in

Another Syrian passage from the same text contains two anaphorically modified nouns whose previous mention is indirect. From the phrase /min iṣ-ṣəbəḥ/ *from the early morning*, the listener can infer the state of darkness and night mentioned directly afterwards. In this case, the use of /ha/ to modify /l-ʿatme/ *the darkness* and /l-lēl/ *the night* heightens the semantic impact of these nouns by bringing them into the immediate environment: because /ha/ carries the implication of physical presence, the speaker can use it to summon physical sensations associated with the nouns.

S2 كانوا كل سبت لمدّة سنة يروحوا يشعّلوا بخّور من الصبح، بيروحوا بهالعتمة وبهالليل يروحوا يشعّلوا بخّور وشمع ويبكوا وكذا ع الميت

kānu kill sabət li-middit sine yirūḥu yšaʿʿlu baxxūr mn əṣ-ṣəbəḥ, birūḥu b-ha l-ʿatme w b-ha l-lēl yrūḥu yšaʿʿlu baxxūr w šamʿ w yibku w kaza ʿa l-mayyit

were-they every Saturday for-period of-year they-go they-light incense from the-morning, indic-they-go in this the-darkness and in-this the-night they-go they-light incense and candles and they-cry and so-forth over the-deceased

They would go every Saturday for a whole year to light incense in the early morning, they go in that darkness and in that night, they would go and light incense and candles and cry and so forth over the deceased

In the next Moroccan example, the identity of the house is not in question, since the character has only one house. Rather, the meaning of the anaphoric article here is subverted and sarcastic: the boy has taken the sheep to the wrong house, and the man who sent him uses /hād/ to let him know that he has confused its unique identity with that of another house:

M9 قال له فاين الحولي؟ قال له ادّيته لدارك. قال له فاين هاد داري؟!

qāl-lu fāyn l-ḥawli? qal-lu ddītu l-dārk. qāl-lu fāyn hād dāri?!

said-he-to-him where the-sheep? said-he-to-him took-I-it to-house-your. said-he-to-him where this house-my?!

He said to him, Where is the sheep? He said, I took it to your house. He said, Where is this house of mine?!

Objects in the physical vicinity of the speaker are normally identified with the anaphoric demonstrative. The next speaker was pointing to a cemetery within sight of the house in which the audience was sitting while recounting this passage:

M11 بقات غادية ياللاه ياللاه .. حتى قرّبت حداهم، تابعة غير ديك الطريق، التعليمة ديال الطريق، وصلت بحال وصلت لهاد القبور

bqāt ġādya, yāḷḷāh yāḷḷāh ... ḥtta qarrbat ḥdāhum, tābʿa ġī[r] dīk ṭ-ṭrīq, t-taʿlīma dyāl ṭ-ṭrīq. wəṣlat bḥāl wəṣlat l-hād-l-qbūr

kept-she going-f come-on come-on ... until neared-she next-to-them following-f only that [the-road] the-marking gen the-road, arrived-she as-if arrived-she to-that-the-graves

She kept on going and going ... until she got close to where they were, following just the marking on the road, [until] she arrived, as if she had come up to where those graves are

Also within the realm of the immediate physical environment is the current time frame, regardless of whether the speaker specifies it as hour, day, week, month, or year. The demonstrative article is normally used in such cases, indicating the immediate temporal environment that is the only possible referent:

M10 انا العام الاخر مشيت شي خمسة وهاد العام مشيت شي تمانية

ʾāna l-ʿām l-āxur mšīt ši xəmsa w hād l-ʿām mšīt ši tmanya

I the-year the-other went-I some 5 and this the-year went-I some 8

Last year I went about 5 [times] and this year I went about 8

In all of its functions, then, the demonstrative article serves to indicate the established identity of a noun, its presence in or importance to the speech context itself, whether physical, temporal, or topical.

One final observation may be made concerning unstressed /ha/. This pronoun also occurs in Moroccan and Kuwaiti speech as an adverbial demonstrative, as these two examples show:

M9 خلّى الدار دياله ها فاين وعطاه لواحد الجارة ها فاين

xəlla d-dār dyālu ha fāyn w ʿṭāh l-wāḥd ž-žāra ha fāyn

left-he the-house of-his this where and gave-he-it to-one the-neighbor this where

He passed his house here and gave it to a neighbor here

K4 رحت عند الگلاّف سوّالي كرسي ها طوله
rəḥt ʿind l-gaḷḷāf sawwā-li kərsi ha ṭūlah
went-I to the-shipbuilder made-he-me chair this height-its
I went to the shipbuilder and he made me a chair this high

4.3 Unstressed Distal Demonstratives

The unstressed anaphoric demonstrative articles are by virtue of their form and function proximal forms. However, one particular distal demonstrative pronoun, Moroccan /dīk/, functions as an unstressed form in certain environments. In Moroccan, /dīk/ functions as the short form of the feminine distal demonstrative, corresponding to masculine /dāk/ and feminine /dūk/. The following sections propose a distinction between distal, gendered /dīk/ and unstressed, ungendered /dīk/.

4.3.1 Ungendered Moroccan /dīk/ and /dāk/

Moroccan speakers from the area surrounding Tangiers use the distal form /dīk/ in ways analogous to the (proximal) anaphoric /hād/. That is, when it functions as an anaphoric demonstrative, /dīk/ is numberless and genderless. The following sentences, taken from recorded interviews in the coastal town of Larache, contain nominal phrases in which /dīk/ modifies masculine nouns. In all of these contexts, /dīk/ functions anaphorically, modifying a previously mentioned or known entity (analogous to unstressed English *that*). It should also be noted that the referent nouns in these contexts are of low individuation, such as /ši/ *thing*, and /ḥawli/ *sheep*:

M10 كيشريوا ديك الشي كامل
kayšrīw dīk š-ši kāməl
indic-they-buy that the-stuff all
They buy all this stuff

M9 الله ديك الشي اللي عطاه
ḷḷāh dīk š-ši lli ʿṭāh
God that the-thing which gave-he-him
That's what God gave him

M9 مول ديك الحولي دابا اللي شرى
mūl dīk l-ḥawli dāba lli šra
owner of-that the-sheep now which bought-he
The owner of that sheep that he bought, now

M10 ديك [الحوت] اللي كيكون فيه الشراوط ما كانش كيعطيه قيمة
dīk [l-ḥūt] lli kaykūn fīh š-šrāwəṭ mā kānš kayəʿṭīh qīma
that [fish] which in-it-m rag-things neg was indic-he-gives-it value
That [fish] that has rag-like[fins], [no one] valued it

Moroccan speakers commonly use /dīk/ as an unstressed demonstrative. In the following sentence, the use of /fin/ to relativize /dīk l-blāṣa/ shows that the demonstrative phrase is non-specific:

M11 غادي تتبعي غير ديك الرماد والنخالة حتى لديك البلاصة فين غادي نحطّوا
ġādi ttəbʿi ġī[r] dīk ər-rmād w n-n^{u}xx^{w}āla ḥtta l-dīk l-blāṣa fīn ġādi nḥəṭṭu
fut you-follow only that the-ashes and the-chaff until to-that the-place where fut we-alight
You will just follow those ashes and chaff until [you get to] the place where we will alight

The absence of examples in which /dīk/ modifies masculine human nouns supports the interpretation of its function as modifying nouns of low individuation.

Caubet's data from Fez and the surrounding region contain several examples in which masculine /dāk/ modifies feminine and plural nouns. In the following sentence, /dāk/ modifies feminine /əl-ləhža/ *the dialect* (Caubet 1993ii:6):

M ... الفرنساويين، هادا ... كيهدروا داك اللهجة ...
əl-fransāwiyyīn, hāda ... kayhədru dāk əl-ləhža ...
the-French-p, this.. indic-they-speak that the-dialect
The French, that [is] .. they speak that dialect ...

In the next example, masculine /dāk/ modifies plural /l-iyyām/ *the days* (Caubet 1983:309, translation mine):

M داك الايام اللي فاتوا، كنت مريضة
dāk əl-iyyām lli fātu, kunt mrīḍa
that-m the-days rel passed-they, was-I ill
Those past days, I was ill

Both masculine /dāk/ and feminine /dīk/ are thus attested as non-gendered forms, perhaps regional variants of non-stressed, non-specifying demonstrative forms.

4.3.2 Non-specific Temporal Demonstrative /dīk/

Moroccan /dīk/ commonly occurs with non-specific temporal nouns, such as /sāʿa/ *time* and /nhār/ *day*.[10] These two Moroccan passages both contain /dīk/ modifying a temporal noun, the first masculine, /nhār/ *day*, and the second feminine, /sāʿa/ *hour*.

M9 آسيدي احمد ديك البسطيات اللي عطيتيني ديك النهار!
ʾā sīdi ḥmad, dīk l-basṭiyyāt lli ʿṭitīni dīk n-nhār!
O Mr. Ahmed those the-pills which you-gave-me that the-day!
Mr. Ahmed, those pills that you gave me the other day!

M11 ديك الساعة اللي زادت
dīk s-sāʿa lli zādət
that the-hour which was-born-she
That time that she was born

The fact that these nouns lack specific reference suggests that /dīk/ is non-specifying. Rather, /dīk/ here indicates temporal distance. Moreover, this non-gendered use of /dīk/ is not limited to Moroccan, but is also attested in rural Egyptian, Syrian, and Kuwaiti speech. Badawi and Hinds report /dīk in-nahār/ *the other day* from rural Egypt (1986:274):

E كنت عنده ديك النهار
kunt ʿandu dīk in-nahār
[was-I at-him that the-day]
I was at his place just the other day

[10]Caubet also gives several examples, including /dīk əl-ʿām/ [*the other year*] (1993ii:317).

In Kuwaiti, the regular feminine distal form, /d̠īč/, ends in /č/,[11] but in these two expressions, an otherwise unattested /d̠īk/ is used:

K3 الفلوس ذيك الساعة ما ميش
il-flūs d̠īk is-sāʿa mā mīš
the-money that the-hour neg-there-is
At that time there was no money

K4 ذيك اليوم گلت حگ احمد ...
dīk il-yōm gilt ḥagg ʾahmad
that the-day said-I to Ahmad ...
The other day I told Ahmad ...

My Syrian data yields only /hadāk/, a long form marked for gender:

S2 هداك اليوم
hadāk il-yōm
the other day

However, Cowell reports that the feminine /hadīk/ is commonly used with masculine /yōm/ *day* (Cowell 1964:557):

S هديك اليوم
hadīk əl-yōm
That day

In all attested cases, the use of /dīk/ as an ungendered form is limited to non-specific temporal expressions *day* and *time* (/yōm/, /nhār/, /sāʿa/). While these are clearly idiomatic expressions, the degree of similarity from Morocco to Kuwait is striking. Data cited in Chapter 3 shows that non-specific temporal nouns across dialects may be relativized in a kind of genitive relative clause not used with other nouns; here is a second instance in which the non-specific nature of temporal nouns appears to affect their syntactic behavior.

4.4 Demonstrative Pronouns in Post-Nominal Position

While demonstratives obligatorily occur in post-nominal position in Egyptian, the other dialects exhibit both pre- and post-nominal demonstrative constructions. Post-nominal placement of full

---

[11]For the shift of /k/ to /č/ in Gulf dialects, see Holes (1991).

demonstrative forms in Moroccan, Syrian, and Kuwaiti is obligatory when the modified noun occurs in genitive constructions. This discussion is concerned only with situations in which the post-nominal placement is optional.

Harrell (1962) does not mention post-nominal demonstrative constructions in his Moroccan grammar, but several examples occur in my data. For Syrian, Ambros remarks that demonstratives "may be placed before or after the head noun" (1977:73). Holes notes that demonstratives in Gulf Arabic may follow the noun phrase (1990:62). In this section, I will examine possible pragmatic motivation for placement of the demonstrative pronoun after the noun.

Post-nominal demonstratives occur in two types of constructions, which appear to have distinguishable pragmatic functions. In the first type, the noun is followed by a demonstrative pronoun, proximal or distal. In the second, the noun is preceded by the anaphoric demonstrative article (/hād/ or /ha/) and followed by a proximal demonstrative, resulting in a "double-demonstrative" construction. The nature of the reference in both of these constructions appears to be highly individuated, but not contrastive, suggesting that the degree of individuation plays a role in the choice of word order in demonstrative phrases.

4.4.1 Post-Nominal Demonstratives

Both proximal and distal demonstrative forms occur post-nominally in all dialects. Obligatory and unmarked in Egyptian, this construction seems to represent marked usage in Moroccan and Syrian, judging by the lower frequency of its occurrence in those dialects. For Syrian, Cowell notes that "[l]ess commonly, the demonstrative follows a single noun" (1964:558). The examples he gives are without context, and I have not yet found examples in my data pool. On the other hand, I have found a relatively high frequency of this construction in Kuwaiti data, where it may be less marked than in Moroccan and Syrian.[12]

The post-nominal position does not seem to be deictic, nor does it manage discourse topics, that is, contrast or distinguish among a

[12]For Najdi Arabic, Ingham lists both pre- and post-nominal constructions as equally possible (1994:55-56).

number of possible referents. Since post-nominal position is normally adjectival, its meaning might be expected to be descriptive rather than identificatory. In general, examples I have found in Moroccan and Kuwaiti data share two characteristics: the references are clearly anaphoric, to previously mentioned nouns, and the discourse contexts in which they occur contain no other topics which might compete for attention. The post-nominal demonstrative does not seem to contrast the modified noun with another possible referent, but rather to reinvoke a previous discourse topic, uniquely identifiable but not current or physically present. Its function thus differs slightly from that of the demonstrative article /ha(d)/, which establishes coreference with a current discourse topic or an entity in the immediate environment.

The Moroccan speaker of the following statement has been talking about her special healing powers. After mentioning a particular man whose arthritis she healed, she reinvokes the topic of her healing gifts with the reference /š-ši hāda/ *that thing*:

M9 وشحال د الحباب يعرفوني على الشي هادا
w šḥāl d l-ḥbāb yʿarfūni ʿla š-ši hāda
and how-many gen the-friends they-know-me for the-thing this
And so many friends know me for this thing

This post-nominal demonstrative construction occurs regularly in Kuwaiti speech. In the first passage below, the matchmaker specifies the people she takes with her to meet a prospective bride: her partner and her customer. The man she mentions, /š-šaxṣ hāḏa/ *that person*, has already been mentioned, and moreover he is the only plausible referent in this case. She uses /hāḏa/ to refer back to the previous mention of the man and recall him into the present context.

K2 اودّيها. اودّي منهي؟ اودّي المرا الچبيرة واودّي الشخص هاذا معي
awaddīha, awaddi mənhi? awaddi l-mara l-čibīra w awaddi š-šaxṣ hāḏa maʿi
I-take-her, I-take who-she? I-take the-woman the-old and I-take the-person this with-me
I take her. I take who? I take the old woman and I take that person with me

The *sheikhs* and *the girl* in the next two examples are not to be contrasted with other sheikhs and girls, but rather represent resumed topics:

K3 تشاركين الشيوخ هذيلا؟
tšārkīn iš-šyūx hadēla?
share-you the-sheikhs those?
You would share [the wealth of] those sheikhs?!

K4 زين امّ احمد يعني شلون تگدرين مثلاً تشرحين للولد؟ هل توصفين لَه البنت او تگولين لَه والله البنت هاذي حلوة وزينة وچذي
zēn umm aḥmad yaʿni šlōn tigədrīn maṯalan tišraḥīn l-il-walad? hal tōṣafīn-lah l-bint aw tigūlīn-la waḷḷa l-bint hāḏi ḥilwa w zēna w čiḏi
okay Umm Ahmed that-is how you-can for-example you-explain to-the-boy? ques you-describe-to-him the-girl or you-say-to-him by-God the-girl this pretty and good and thus
OK, Umm Ahmed, how can you, let's say, explain to the boy? Do you describe the girl to him or do you say to him, Really, this girl is pretty and good and so forth

The post-nominal demonstrative thus functions to alert the listener to recall a previously mentioned topic.

4.4.2 "Double" Demonstrative Constructions

The second type of post-nominal construction combines the pre-nominal anaphoric demonstrative article with a post-nominal proximal demonstrative pronoun, resulting in a "double" demonstrative. The combination of /ha/ or /hād/ and the proximal demonstrative gives this construction both anaphoric reference and heightened specificity or immediacy, similar in force to the English adjective *particular*. It seems to have an effect somewhat like a "zoom-in" camera shot in the way it focuses attention on the noun it modifies. This construction also appears to add cohesion to the discourse, signalling either the closure of a particular topic, or a heightened focus on the topic at hand. Cowell, analyzing his Syrian data, gives the basic meaning of this construction as contrastive, but the examples cited here will show that specificity is a more exact description, since any contrast with another possible referent is indirect at best. Cowell too notes the cohesive role played by this construction in one of his examples (1964:558).

The first example is taken from a narrative about the invasion of the Moroccan resort town of Larache by rude tourists. After discussing the problem at some length, the speaker summarizes his analysis with the phrase /hād l-qaḍiyya hādi/ *this particular problem*:

M10 احنا متلاً، عزري ماشي بحال مجوّج... العائلة، اللي كيقول الإنسان، ما بقاوش كيهوّدوا عائلات، العزري، حتى العزارى ديال ولاد البلاد ما بقاوش كيهوّدوا، قلال. ها انت كتلاحض **هاد القضية هادي**، كتشوف هاد الناس بزّاف

ḥna matalan, ʿazrī māšī b-ḥāl mžəwwəž ... l-ʿāʾila, lli kayqūl l-ʾinsān, mā bqāwš kayhawwdu ʿāʾilāt, l-ʿazrī, ḥtta l-ʿazāra dyāl wlād l-blād mā bqāwš kayhawwdu, qlāl, ha nta katlāḥəḍ **hād l-qaḍiyya hādi**, katšūf hād n-nās bəzzāf

We, too, for example, the bachelor is not like the married man ... the family, what one calls [the family], families no longer go [to the beach], the bachelor, even bachelors native to the town no longer go, very few. You yourself notice ***this particular problem****, you see those people a lot*

In the following two Syrian examples, /ha l-māšṭa hāy/ *this dressing-woman* and /ha ṣ-ṣabi hāda/ *this boy* signal anaphoric reference to the immediate topic. Neither reference is contrastive, rather, the use of this construction adds cohesion to the narratives by signalling the immediacy of the current discourse topic.

S1 فيه واحد عطاه استاذه ورقة، قال له ما بتفتحها لحتّى تيجي لتموت. هالصبي هادا ضلّ مشغول هيكي ...

fī waḥed ʿaṭā istāzu waraʾa, ʾal-lu mā btiftaḥha la-ḥatta tiži la-tmūt. ha ṣ-ṣabi hāda ḍall mašġūl hēki ...

there-is one gave-he-him paper, said-he-to-him neg fut-you-open-it until you-come to-you-die. this the-boy this remained-he preoccupied thus

There was a [boy], his teacher gave him a piece of paper. He said to him, You will not open it until you are about to die. This boy remained preoccupied like that ...

S4 يجيبوا لها الماشطة ... هالماشطة هاي مرا كانت تشتغل بالحمّام
yžību-l[h]a l-māšṭa ... ha l-māšṭa hayy mara kānit tištiġil bi-l-ḥammām
they-bring to-her the-dressing-woman ... this the-dressing-woman this woman was-she she-work in-the-bath
They would bring her the dressing woman ... this dressing woman is a woman who used to work in the bath

This construction is often used to modify temporal expressions of present time, not to contrast the present with another time, but to heighten the immediacy of the present. In the next set of examples, the double demonstrative phrases highlight the specificity and immediacy of *this year*, *this moment*, and *these days*:

M10 اش ع نقول لك عاود تاني، هاد العام هادا تمانية وتمانين بصراحة تمانية وتمانين جا مفلّس
ʾaš ʿa nqūl-lək ʿāwd tāni hād l-ʿām hāda tmanya w tmānīn b-ṣarāḥa tmanya w tmānīn ža mfəlləs
what fut I-tell-you again again, this the-year this eighty and eight in-honesty eighty and eight came-it bankrupt
What am I going to tell you, again, this particular year, '88, honestly, '88 has been bankrupt

S لاح شوفه بهالإيّام هاي
laḥa-šūfo b-ha l-ʾiyyām hayy
[fut-I-see-him in-this the-days this]
I'll see him any day now [these very days] (Cowell 1964:558)

K2 ما نگدر نردّ عليچ بها الدگيگة هاذي
mā nigdar nrədd ʿalēč bi-ha d-dgīga hāḏi
negwe-can we-answer for-you at-this the-minute this
We can't answer you this very minute

K2 يبون البيضا هالايام هاذي كلّه يبون البيظ
yabūn əl-bēḏa ha l-iyyām hāḏi killa yabūn əl-bīḏ
they-want the-white-f this the-days these all-it they-want the white-p
They want the fair-skinned [girl], these days, they always want fair-skinned [girls]

This double-demonstrative construction focuses attention on a discourse topic to heighten its immediacy, or to add cohesion to the discourse by further highlighting the relevance of the noun to its context.

4.5 Discourse Functions of Distal Demonstratives

The choice between the proximal and distal forms of the demonstrative pronoun in any given context is a relative one involving the speaker's perception of distance. Moreover, this distance may be physical, temporal, or what will be called here "discourse distance:" that is, the relative accessibility of the topic in question within the context of the discourse itself. The choice between proximal and distal forms often reflects the speaker's judgement about the relative presence or distance of the noun in question in the mind of the audience, and the relative ease or difficulty of recalling or retrieving it.

Speakers tend to use proximal demonstrative forms to indicate topics close at hand. In the following Kuwaiti passage, the speaker uses /hāḏa/ twice, in each case to refer to the immediately preceding referent because it represents the closer and more easily retrieved topic:

K2 ساعات يردّون عليّ يعني في نفس الكلام، يگول والله ام احمد،
عجبتني البنية وشوفي ردّ البنية بعد شنو، وساعات والله يگول
انشالله يصير خير. **هاذا** اللي يگول لچ يصير خير اعرف ان هو
ما يبي البنية واللي يگوللچ والله سئلي البنية شوفي ايش گالت
عني ش رايها فيني **هاذا** اعرف ان هو يعني لَه خاطر بالبنية

sāʿāt yrəddūn ʿalayy yaʿni fi nafs il-kalām, ygūl waḷḷa umm aḥmad, ʿəjibatni lə-bnayya w šūfi radd lə-bnayya baʿd šənu, w sāʿāt lā waḷḷa, ygūl inšaḷḷa yṣīr xēr. **hāḏa** lli ygul-lič yṣīr xēr, aʿrəf inna mā yabi l-bnayya, ʾeh, w illi ygul-lič waḷḷa siʾli l-bnayya šūfi eš gālit ʿanni š rāyha fīni, **hāḏa** aʿrəf inna hu yaʿni la xāṭir b-l-bnayya

Sometimes they answer me in the same words, [one] says, well, Umm Ahmad, I liked the girl, see what the response of the girl is, then, and sometimes he says, hopefully things will work out for the best. ***That one*** *who says may things work out for the best, I know that he doesn't want the girl, and* ***the one*** *who tells you, Well, ask the girl, see what she said about me, what her opinion of me is, this one, I know he is interested in the girl.*

Distal demonstrative forms, by contrast, refer to relatively difficult to retrieve topics, distant in time, space, or discourse. They often mark topic switches in discourse. Distal demonstratives also serve to contrast possible referents, by putting distance between them. When contrasting between two possible referents, most speakers choose the distal form to refer to both. Examples from Moroccan, Syrian, and Kuwaiti provide representative contexts in which distal demonstratives fulfill these functions.

In the first Moroccan example, the stressed distal pronoun /hādīk/ signals both that /š-šfra/ *the knife* is not physically present, and that it is, in contrast to all other possible knives, the specific one the speaker wants:

M9 قالت له آ سيدي، عندي غير الشفرة د العيد، مانحبّش نعطيها قال لها
هاديك بغيت انا، آراها باش ندبح
qalt-lu ʾā sīdi, ʿndi ġī[r] š-šfra d l-ʿīd, mā nḥəbbš naʿṭīha. qāl-lha **hādīk** bġīt ana, ʾārāha bāš nədbaḥ
said-she to-him O sir at-me only the-knife gen the-feast neg I-like I-give-it. said-he-to-her **that** wanted-I I, give-here-it so-that I-slaughter
She said, O sir, I have only the knife of the feast, I wouldn't like to give it [to you]. He said, ***that one*** *I want, give it here so I can slaughter*

The following excerpt from a joke represents an instance in which /hādīk/ is used to signal to the listener within the joke itself to retrieve the topic, /d-dār/ *the house* from a distance. The house has been a previous topic of conversation but is not immediately under discussion; it is retrievable but relatively distant.

M6 گال ليه كي جاتك **هاديك** الدار؟ گال ليه الله يعمّرها دار زعما
gāl-līh, kī žātk **hādīk** d-dār? gāl-līh aḷḷāh yʿammərha dār zaʿma
said-he to-him how came-it-to-you **that** the-house? said-he to-him God he-make-it-flourish house that-is
He said, How do you like ***that*** *house? He said, It's a great house*

In the next example, /hādīk/ is used three times, each time to contrast and put "distance" between the two wives:

M11 **هاديك** عندها سبعة د الولاد **هاديك** ادّاها عاد باش تولد ...
ناضت **هاديك** مولاة سبعة كانت حاملة غادي تولد

hādīk ʿandha səbʿa d l-wlād **hādīk** əddāha ʿād bāš təwləd ... nāḍt **hādīk** mūlat səbʿa kānt ḥāmla ġādi təwləd

that at-her seven gen the-children **that** took-he-her then so-as-to she-give-birth ... got-up-she **that the-woman** owner-of seven was-she pregnant will she-give-birth even she

That one *had seven children,* ***the other one*** *he married too to bear [him] children ...* ***That woman****, the one who had seven [children], was pregnant and was about to give birth*

The next Moroccan passage contains a number of distal demonstratives, and illustrates how the speaker manipulates these forms on several different levels. Of particular note here is the shift among stressed and unstressed distal forms: the stressed forms recall discourse topics to the center of attention, helping to anchor them in the narrative, while the unstressed forms are used once the topic has been sufficiently established and anchored, usually by the second or third mention of the topic.

M5 واحد النهار كانت عندنا الاستادة ديال اللغة الفرنسية - ماشي
مغربية، استادة يهودية هي، يهودية وتعرفي مشكل قضية العرب
مع اليهود ... ايوا **هاديك الاستادة** - المهم، ف الدورة الاولى كنّا
تنقراوا - كنت ممتازة، تناخد النقاط الاوّلين، دايماً تتعطيني النقطة
الاولى، الدورة الاولى كنت الاولى، ف الدورة التانية، وقع مشكل
مع **ديك الاستادة** . **هاداك المشكل** هو انني اوّل مرة تنشري جلاّبة
- تعقلي اَ اختي - **ديك الجلاّبة** اللي كنت شريتي لي؟

wāḥd ən-nhār kānt ʿəndna l-ʾustāda dyāl l-luġa l-faransiyya -- māši maġribiyya, ʾustāda yəhūdiyya hiyya, yəhūdiyya, w tʿarfi muškil qaḍiyyt l-ʿrab mʿa l-yhūd ... ʾiwa, **hādīk lʾustāda** -- l-muhimm, f d-dawra l-ʾūla kunna tanqrāw -- kunt mumtāza, tanāxud n-nuqāṭ l-ʾuwwlīn, dāyman tatəʿṭīni n-nuqṭa l-l-uwla, d-dawra l-ʾūla kunt l-ʾūla, f d-dawra t-tānya wqaʿ muškil mʿa **dīk l-ʾustāda. hādāk l-muškil huwwa** ʾənnani ʾuwwəl mərra tanšri žəllāba -- tʿaqli ʾā uxti--**dīk ž-žəllāba** lli kunti šrītī-li?

One day we had [a] French teacher, she wasn't Moroccan, she was a Jewish teacher, she was Jewish, and you know the problem of the Arab-Israeli cause. Anyway, ***that teacher*** *-- the point is, in the first term we were studying, I was excellent, I always got the highest marks, she always gave me the highest mark, the first term I was the first. In the second term I had a problem with* ***that teacher.*** ***That problem*** *was that for the first time I bought a jellaba--remember, sister,* ***that jellaba*** *that you had bought me?*

The next speaker, from Syria, uses /hadīk/ to signal the temporal distance of /marra/ *time*, and the necessity for the speaker to retrieve it from that (relatively) long ago time:

S2 لازم نعمل له شي مقدّمة لحتى ما ينصدم متل هاديك المرّة

lāzim niʿmil-lu ši muqaddime la-ḥatta mā yinṣədim mitil hadīk il-marra

must we-make for-him some introduction for-so-that neg he-gets-shocked like that the-time

We must give him some sort of preparation so that he won't go into shock like that last time

A female speaker from Aleppo uses both proximal and distal demonstrative forms in the following passage, proximal /hadōl(e)/, and distal /hadōlīk/. The patterned distribution of these two forms reveals that the proximal form is non-contrastive and refers to the immediate topic at hand, while the distal form marks contrastive reference:

S5 دولة تانية أكيد الشرق عن الغرب. **هادوليك**، الغرب باظنّ أغنى ...

واكتر السكّان فيها من الدول السكاندناڤيّة ... **هادولي**، فينلاندا،

النورويج، **هادول** ارقى دول العالم

dawle tānye ʾakīd iš-sarʾ ʿan il-ġarb. **hadōlīk**, il-ġarb, baẓənn ʾaġna ... w aktar əs-səkkān fīha mn id-duwal əs-skandināviyye ... **hadōle,** finlanda, in-norwēž, **hadōl** ʾarqa duwal il-ʿālam.

country second sure the-east from the-west. **those**, the-west, indic-I-think richer ... and most of-the-residents in-it from the-countries the-Scandinavian ... **those**, Finland, Norway, **those** most-advanced of-countries of-the-world

[It's] another country, certainly, the east [of the US] from the west. ***Those*** *[people], the west, I think, are richer ... Most of the residents there are from the Scandinavian countries ...* ***Those*** *[countries], Finland, Norway,* ***those*** *are the most advanced countries in the world*

The final Kuwaiti example shows stressed distal /hadīč/ indicating both contrast and distance. The story revolves around two characters; proximal /hādi/ indicates the central character, the jealous first wife, while the distal form refers to the mentally "farther" or lesser topic of the second wife. The post-nominal position of /hādi/ indicates that, despite the presence of two women, the central character is clear in the mind of the speaker, and she expects it to be clear to the listener as well. The main character then later uses /hadīč/ to refer to her co-wife in a distancing and disparaging gesture:

K3 ريّال عندَه مرا، حريم ثنتين واحدة حلوة بس هو ما يحبّها **هاذيچ** مو حلوة بس يحبّها. نزين. گامت **المرا هاذي** ، چان تگول أنا ليش حلوة أنا، ما يحبّني وهاي الكريهة يحبّها؟ أنا اروح حگ المطوّع اسوّي لَه شي علشان يحبّني. راحت حگ واحد مطوّع يعني گالت لَه رايلي عندَه مرا وانا ما يحبّني و**هاذيچ** كريهة ويحبّها

rayyāl ʿinda mara ḥarīm ṯintēn waḥda ḥilwa bass hu mā yḥibbha, **haḏīč** mū ḥilwa, bass yḥibbha. nzēn. gāmat **il-mara hāḏi** čan tgūl ʾāna lēš ḥilwa ʾāna, mā yḥibbni w hāy l-karīha yḥibbha? ʾāna arūḥ ḥagg lə-mṭawwaʿ ʾasawwi-la šay ʿalašān yḥibbni. rāḥat ḥagg wāḥid mṭawwaʿ yaʿni gālit-la rāyli ʿinda mara w āna mā yḥibbni w **haḏič** karīha w yḥibbha

A man is married, has two wives, one is pretty but he doesn't love her, ***the other one*** *is not pretty but he loves her. OK.* ***This woman,*** *she would say, Why, I am pretty, doesn't he love me whereas this ugly one, he loves? I am going to the sheikh to get a spell put on him so he will love me. She went to one sheikh and told him, My husband has a (second) wife, he doesn't love me and* ***that one*** *is ugly but he loves her.*

My Egyptian data contain no distal pronouns, but Badawi and Hinds give the following example, which shows clearly the contrastive function of the distal forms (1986:274):

E الفستان دا احلى من دكها

il-fustān da ʾaḥla min dukha

the-dress this prettier than that

This dress is prettier than that other one

Badawi and Hinds cite a number of variant demonstrative forms in Egyptian, and Belnap notes that sociolinguistic interviews he conducted in Cairo showed "considerable social evaluation of the distant deixis demonstratives" (1991:155). These forms, and their discourse functions, deserve an in-depth study in their own right.

4.6 Summary

Moroccan, Syrian, and Kuwaiti dialects distinguish between unstressed, anaphoric demonstratives and deictic demonstratives. These dialects share an unstressed anaphoric demonstrative article (Syrian and Kuwaiti /ha/, Moroccan /hād/), a genderless, numberless demonstrative whose function is to modify a textually prominent, highly individuated noun. Deictic demonstratives consist of proximal and distal forms, and Moroccan speakers have both stressed and unstressed distal forms at their disposal. While proximal forms tend to be used to establish the coreference of entities in discourse, distal forms are more likely to have contrastive reference.

Unstressed demonstratives that modify non-specified temporal nouns do not always agree in gender with the noun they modify. A feminine form, /dīk/, occurs in rural speech across dialects in certain fixed expressions involving temporal nouns of low specificity. This non-specific feminine marking may be parallel to the feminine singular agreement used with collective plurals, both representing a kind of neuter gender.

Proximal and distal demonstrative forms, too, have discourse functions in addition to their deictic meaning. The former tend to modify discourse topics close at hand, while the latter indicate the relative "mental" distance of a topic and signal the need for the listener to retrieve it from (relatively) far away.

Speakers from all four regions employ demonstrative constructions in which the demonstrative pronoun follows the noun (this position is obligatory in Egyptian). Post-nominal demonstratives in the other dialects are not contrastive, but rather add physical or temporal immediacy to the noun or cohesion to the discourse.

The absence of an anaphoric demonstrative article in Egyptian seems to parallel the absence of an indefinite-specific article (1.4), and perhaps also the higher frequency of neutralized adjectival agreement in this dialect (2.3). Perhaps additional synchronic and diachronic research will reveal whether or not this pattern has resulted from syntactic levelling involving several different types of nominal marking.

5 Categorizing Verbs

5.0 Introduction

This chapter provides a brief overview of the category "verb" in spoken Arabic. The boundaries that separate linguistic categories are not absolute, and for some lexical items, membership in one category does not preclude membership in another as well. The category of verb itself overlaps with pseudo-verbal elements that may indicate verbal meanings without containing all the normal morphological traits of verbs, such as voice, subject marking, and tense forms.

Descriptions of the dialects often cite certain verbs that perform auxiliary functions or show modified syntactic behavior, such as a partial loss of agreement. As Eisele (1992) shows, while a fixed category of auxiliary verbs in English can be defined in terms of syntactic behavior patterns,[1] no such syntactic tests exist for "auxiliary" in Egyptian Arabic. Eisele thus finds no *syntactic* justification for the category of auxiliary in Egyptian Arabic, although he proposes a lexical subclass of auxiliaries based on patterns of sentence complementizers, embedding, and subject coreference (1992:160ff.). Eisele's analysis will be modified here, with particular attention to different types of embedding that occur in compound verb phrases.

The chapter begins with a brief overview of verbs in spoken Arabic. It will then propose three categories of verbs that can be shown to exhibit special patterns of syntactic behavior and/or function: verbs of motion (also called translocative verbs), temporal verbs, and pseudo-verbs. Following Eisele, "category" is understood here to be "fuzzy," that is, consisting of core and peripheral members, with the core members providing the basis for the syntactic and functional definition of the category (1992:160).

---

[1]Eisele cites a number of syntactic characteristics that have been shown to define English auxiliaries, among them subject-auxiliary inversion in yes-no questions (*Have you seen?*), negative contraction (*wouldn't*), and "do-support" (*do* cannot negate auxiliaries) (1992:148).

5.1 Overview of Verb Forms

The two basic morphological stems of spoken Arabic are called here the *perfective* (/faʿal/, also called suffix-stem and perfect tense) and the *imperfective* (/yifʿal/, also called prefix-stem and imperfect tense). The more commonly used terms for these two forms are 'perfect' and 'imperfect,' respectively; however, the term 'perfect' is used here and in general to designate a specific formal aspect, to which the Arabic /al-māḍī/ does not correspond. The terms perfective and imperfective more clearly describe the aspectual nature of the Arabic morphological stems, and the use of these terms in Slavic for a similar aspectual distinction makes them preferable to any other. Following Eisele (1988), the term *tense* is defined here to refer only to a morphological verb stem; calling the two morphological verb forms "tenses" does not imply that their basic meaning is one of time reference.

For Moroccan, Egyptian, and Syrian dialects, a further distinction must be made between marked and unmarked forms of the imperfective. This distinction is largely modal, rather than aspectual: one of the primary functions of the unmarked imperfective is to indicate subjunctive mood, while marked forms of the imperfective represent indicative, future, and, in the eastern dialects, progressive and/or intentive moods. Kuwaiti, on the other hand, makes no morphosyntactic distinction between subjunctive and indicative, and this lack of distinction has implications for the modal system of this dialect. These topics will be explored in Chapter 8.

The active (and to a slightly lesser extent, passive) participle presents an interesting nexus linking verb and non-verb. Participles in spoken Arabic have nominal, adjectival, and verbal meanings and functions. When used verbally, participles are tenseless (see Chapter 7) , but carry aspect (discussed in Chapter 6), and show certain syntactic behavior patterns of verbs, such as negation (Chapter 9).

The perfective stem of the Arabic verb describes a completed event, and relative past time reference. Its aspectual meaning has been described as "realized" (Mitchell and El-Hassan 1994) and "complete" (Eisele 1990a). The perfective also functions as the prescribed norm in formal Arabic for expressing the protasis in most conditional sentences;

however, most forms of spoken Arabic allow both the perfective and the imperfective stems in conditional sentences. This perceived move away from the perfective as the conditional mood has led some to speculate that modern spoken Arabic is moving away from an aspectual distinction towards a tense-based one (e.g., Holes 1995:177). Chapter 8 will argue that the variation of tense forms used in conditional sentences reflects not temporal location but rather a combination of aspectual and modal distinctions.

The verb system of spoken Arabic also includes lexical items that are capable of carrying verbal meaning and sharing some of the syntactic functions of verbs. These latter are called here pseudo-verbs, after Qafisheh (1975); their main syntactic characteristics are outlined in this chapter.

Finally, the imperative stem of the verb does not differ significantly from one variety of Arabic to another, except in its phonological realizations. Prohibitives in all four dialects are formed using the unmarked imperfective with negating particles /mā/ or /lā/. The imperative and prohibitive are not of syntactic contrastive interest and thus will not be treated in this study.

5.2 Auxiliaries and Other Categories

The problem with defining auxiliary verbs across languages lies partly in the fact that auxiliary is by nature a category that arises out of diachronic developments in a particular language's verbal system (Givón 1979a:221-2). "Auxiliary" in English includes both temporal and modal verbs, and their Arabic lexical counterparts have been described as auxiliary as well. Thus Harrell calls a number of different Moroccan verbs and particles auxiliaries: /bġa/ *to want*, /kān/ *to be*, /xəṣṣ/ *must*, future marker /ġādi/, and others (1962:178-85). Mitchell and El-Hassan join Harrell in naming these kinds of verbs auxiliaries, classifying them as auxiliaries of aspect (according to their definition of aspect, 1994:36). However, taken together, the members of these "auxiliary" categories have little in common in either syntactic behavior or function. Harrell's grouping appears to consist of lexical items that are derived from verbs but lack a full conjugation. Any cross-dialect analysis of verbal syntax must begin with a description of the syntactic functions of different types of verbs before any kind of classification can be made.

The task of describing the verbal syntax of spoken Arabic may be streamlined by distinguishing among several types of verbs and verb-related particles. A number of verbs having to do with the temporal location and/or contour of events, such as onset, cessation, and continuation, share certain characteristics of behavior, including frequent use in compound verb phrases (phrases consisting of two or more verbs that belong to the same clause).[2] These kinds of verbs may be grouped into two "fuzzy" categories: one consisting mostly of translocatives, or verbs of motion, whose core members perform special functions in narrative contexts, and one consisting of verbs whose primary function is to establish time reference, which I will call temporal verbs. In addition to their special narrative functions, the syntactic behavior of temporal verbs and verbs of motion in compound verb phrases sets them apart from other verbs.

Eisele tests for a lexical class of auxiliary, including /kān/ *to be* and "aspectualizers" (some of which are designated here as temporal verbs), using four subcategorizing and selectional features. He identifies four characteristics shared by the core members of his auxiliary class: (1) they may not take a sentence complementizer (/inn-/ *that*); (2) they exhibit obligatory subject coreferentiality among members of the verb phrase; (3) they admit both modal and non-modal embedding (i.e., unmarked and marked imperfectives); and (4) they do not allow embedded verbs to carry deictic time reference (1992:160-1). This discussion will focus on the nature of verbal embedding, thus excluding by definition verbs that take sentential complements. Of interest here, then, are claims (2), (3), and (4).

---

[2]As Eisele (1992) points out, asyndetic coordination is a regular feature of spoken Arabic clauses and sentences, because complementizers can often be omitted (unlike formal Arabic, in which a subordinate relationship is normally signalled by the use of complementizers). However, the relationship of sentential complements (clauses that complement verbs such as *to think*, *to understand*, *to say*, and so forth) to main verbs does not concern us here, because the sentential complement constitutes a separate, finite clause that can be distinguished semantically and that has no syntactic restrictions on the type of verb that may occur in it. (The temporal relationship between main clauses and sentence complements is treated in 7.1)

Eisele cites obligatory subject coreferentiality for /kān/ *to be* and other "aspectualizers" and modal verbs in Egyptian. However, while it is normal for /kān/ to exhibit coreferentiality with subordinated verbs, this feature is not obligatory, as the following example shows. In this sentence, the feminine gender of the masculine /kān/ *was-3ms* is not coreferent with either the feminine subject /sakta ʾalbiyya/ *heart attack* or the feminine verb /ḥatgī-li/ *fut-3fs-come to me*:

E3 كان حتجي لي سكتة قلبية
kān ḥatgī-li sakta ʾalbiyya!
was-3ms fut-3fs-come-to-me stroke (f) heart
I was going to have a heart attack!

Non-coreferentiality with /kān/ and /ṣār/ *to become* occurs regularly in Syrian Arabic. In the following Syrian sentence, the plural verb /ṣāru/ *they started* does not share the singular subject of /yiʿzim/ *he invites*:[3]

S5 وصاروا يعني كلّ واحد يعزمنا
w ṣārū yaʿni kill wāḥid yiʿzimna
and became-they that-is every one he-invite-us
They started, every person would invite us

Subject coreferentiality, then, cannot be used as a definitive criterion for membership in a cross-dialectal auxiliary class.

As Eisele's analysis suggests, verbs in spoken Arabic can be embedded in two ways: modally and temporally. Modal embedding consists of the obligatory use of a subjunctive verb form (in Moroccan, Egyptian, and Syrian; Kuwaiti has no distinct form), and is mandatory with deontic modals (such as *to want*, *to be necessary*, *to be able*) and "causatives" such as *to make, to encourage*, and *to advise* (Eisele 1992:164). Examples of modal embedding from Moroccan, Egyptian, and Syrian include:

M7 ش بغيتي ندير لك؟
š bġīti ndīr lək?
what wanted-you I-do for-you ?
What do you want me to do for you?

---

[3]This problem is investigated in 10.2.2, where an analysis is offered that /kān/ and /ṣār/ in such cases are topicalized.

E2 ما قدرتش اخلّص المشاوير
mā ʾidirtiš axaḷḷaṣ il-mašawīr
neg was-able-I I-finish the-errands
I wasn't able to finish the errands

S2 ما لازم نخبّره فجأة
mā lāzim nxabbru faž'atan
neg must we-inform-him suddenly
We mustn't tell him suddenly

Temporal embedding, on the other hand, is a regular feature of time reference in Arabic. This point will be argued in more detail in Chapter 7, but briefly, time reference in a main clause, or the head verb of a main clause, is normally relative to the moment of speech, and the time reference of any subordinate verb or clause is relative to that of the main clause, where perfective signals relative past and imperfective, relative non-past (see 7.1 for discussion and examples).

Modal and non-modal embedding may be contrasted in the following Egyptian minimal pair cited by Eisele (1992:153). Both verbs /rāh/ *he went* and /yirūḥ/ *he go* are temporally embedded by the pseudo-verb /lāzim/ *it is necessary*: the imperfective /yirūḥ/ *he go* signals concurrence with /lāzim/, while the perfective /rāḥ/ signals relative past, *he must have gone*, the act of *going* having taken place prior to the time indicated by /lāzim/. However, only the verb /yirūḥ/ *he go* on the right is modally embedded, signalling deontic modality. On the left, /rāḥ/ *he went* is not modally embedded, being a finite form with epistemic, not deontic meaning. (The clausal boundary may be reconstructed semantically: *it must be [the case] that he went*).

E,S	لازم راح	لازم يروح
	lāzim rāḥ	lāzim yirūḥ
	it-is-necessary went-he	it-is-necessary he-go
	he must have gone	*he must go*

The relationship between two or more verbs in any given sentence is thus indicated in part by the type of embedding involved: given a compound verb phrase, the second may be modally and temporally embedded by the first, or temporally embedded, or, in one exceptional case, not embedded at all. Of the two fuzzy categories examined here, temporal verbs embed other verbs temporally but not modally, while certain verbs of motion, such as /rāḥ/ (Moroccan /mša/) *to go*, and /ʾām/ (Moroccan /nāḍ/, Kuwaiti /gām/) *to get up, begin*, do not embed following verbs either modally or temporally, as the following section will show.

5.2.1 Verbs of Motion

Certain core members of the category verbs of motion (also called translocative verbs) exhibit special syntactic characteristics. Some grammars call these verbs auxiliaries, referring perhaps to the absence of temporal embedding exhibited by some of these verbs in narrative contexts. Harrell lists /mša/ *to go* and /ža/ *to come* as the most common "auxiliary verbs of motion" in Moroccan (1962:182). Mitchell and El-Hassan specify /ʾām/, *to get up* /rāḥ/ *to go*, /iža/ *to come*, and /rižiʿ/ *to return* as punctual auxiliaries common in Egypt and the Levant (1994:76-7).

Across the four dialect regions, the most commonly occurring verbs of motion in narratives are verbs meaning *to go*, *to come*, *to get up*, and *to sit*. The actions of *getting up* and *sitting* are usually meant figuratively, not literally, referring to the onset or finality of an action. The following examples represent typical usages of these verbs, highly parallel across dialects:

M9 مشى شرى لها المسكين العطور
mša šrā-lha l-mskīn l-ʿṭūr
went-he bought-he for-her the-dear the-incense
He went and bought her, the dear soul, the incense

M11 ناض گال لها انا خصّني الولد
nāḍ gāl-līha ʾāna xəṣṣni l-wəld
arose-he said-he to-her I necessary-for-me the-son
He up and said to her I need [a] son

E1 راحت جابت الموف
rāḥit gābit il-mōv
went-she got-she the-mauve
She went and got the mauve [outfit]

S4 امّه مصرية، وقامت راحت خطبت له بنت اخوها
ʾəmmu məṣriyye, w ʾāmit rāḥit xaṭbit-lu bint ʾaxū[h]a
mother-his Egyptian, and got-up-she went-she arranged-engagement-she for-him daughter of-her-brother
His mother is Egyptian, and she (up and) went and got him engaged to her niece

K3 راحوا چذّبوها
rāḥaw čaḏḏabūha
went-they made-a-liar-they-her
They (went and) made her out to be a liar

K1 گعدت شربت
gaʿadt šribt
sat-down-I drank-I
I (sat down and) drank

These verbs, M /nāḍ/ *to get up*, and /mša/ *to go*, E /rāḥ/ *to go*; S /ʾām/ *to get up* and /rāḥ/ *to go*; and K /rāḥ/ *to go* and /gaʿad/ *to sit*, all occur in compound verb phrases without embedding the following verb either temporally or modally. In each case, the two verbs are not sequential but simultaneous: that is, the people whose actions are described above did not first *get up* or *sit* and then perform the other actions. It may be argued that the two verbs in these cases actually constitute two separate main clauses, and that the conjunction *and* is merely omitted. However, native speakers I consulted find the addition of /wa/ *and* to these sentences to be either questionable, unacceptable, or different in meaning.

Another reason for viewing verbs of motion as a distinct group is that their participles give a progressive aspectual meaning not associated with other participles (see further 6.4). The special functions involving the sequencing and aspectual contouring of events in narrative contexts are examined in more detail in section 6.5.

5.2.2 Temporal Verbs

Temporal verbs include the copula /kān/ *to be*, verbs meaning *to become, to begin*, signalling entry into a state or onset of habitual action, verbs meaning *to continue*, indicating continuation of a habit or state, and the verbal expression *to no longer [do]*, signalling loss of state or cessation of habitual activity. Several dialect grammars designate some of these verbs as either "auxiliary verbs" or "aspectualizers" (Harrell 1962:179-185; al-Najjar 1984; Mitchell and El-Hassan 1994:36). Badawi and Hinds call some of the Egyptian variants "preverbs" (see e.g. 1986:59,91). None of these terms elucidates the function of these verbs, which is not to lend a formal aspectual character to the verb phrase, but rather to set the time frame for other actions and states. Temporal verbs differ from other verbs in that they embed other verbs temporally but not modally.

As the archetypal temporal verb, /kān/ differs from all other verbs in spoken Arabic as the only verb that can embed all three verb forms, perfective, imperfective, and participle,[4] in compound verb phrases. The meanings and functions of the verb /kān/ are almost identical across dialects, and it has unique semantic and syntactic status as a verb that marks only the time frame of an action relative to the moment of speaking, not aspect.[5] The formation of various tenses with /kān/ embedding perfectives, imperfectives, and participles is detailed in Table 5-1.

Temporal verbs embed other verbs temporally but not modally. Unlike other verbs, temporal verbs can embed participles (a non-finite verb form). Examples from Moroccan, Egyptian, and Levantine:

M11 بقت غادية
bqat ġādya
remained-she going-f
She kept going

E فضل قاعد
fiḍil ʾāʿid
remained-he sitting
He kept sitting

L ضلّينا واقفين ساعة
ḍallēna wāʾfīn sāʿa
remained-we standing-p hour
We remained standing there for an hour

---

[4]The acceptability and meaning of participles in temporal phrases is affected by the aspectual nature of the verb from which the participle is derived (see 6.4).

[5]In addition, /kān/ functions in conditional clauses as a marker of conditional mood (8.7).

Table 5-1: Time Reference with /kān/

Time Reference with /kān/				
	Moroccan	Egyptian	Syrian	Kuwaiti
past state *was doing*	kān gāləs *he was sitting*	kān ʾāʿid *he was sitting*	kān ʾāʿid *he was sitting*	kān gāʿid *he was sitting*
pluperfect *had done*	kān ža *he had come*	kān ga *he had come*	kān ʾiža *he had come*	čān ya *he had come*
past progressive *was/ used to be*	kān kayqra *he was/ used to be studying*	kān biyidris *he was/ used to be studying*	kān yədrus *he used to study* kān ʿam yidrus *he was studying*	kān yadris *he was/ used to be studying*
future in relation to past *was going to*	kān ġādi yəlʿab *he was going to play*	kān ḥa-yilʿab *he was going to play*	kān raḥ yilʿab *he was going to play*	kān raḥ yilʿab *he was going to play*
future progressive *will be doing*	ġādi ykūn kayqra *he will be studying*	ḥaykūn biyidris *he will be studying*	bikūn/raḥ ykūn ʿam yədrus *he will be studying*	biykūn gāʿid yadris *he will be studying*
future perfect *will have done*	ġādi ykūn wṣəl *he will have arrived*	ḥaykūn wiṣil *he will have arrived*	bikūn/raḥ ykūn wəṣil *he will have arrived*	biykūn wuṣal *he will have arrived*

Forms given here are adapted from a number of sources: my data, Harrell (1962:179-80), Cowell (1964:340-2), Johnstone (1967:143), Qafisheh (1975:224ff), el-Tonsi (1982), Al-Najjar (1984:212-3), and Eisele (1988, 1990b). Al-Najjar restricts the use of the future progressive to sentences with no overt subject (1984:130-1); he gives only participle forms for the future perfect. My Kuwaiti corpus contains few examples of compound tenses.

Moroccan speakers normally use marked imperfective with all temporal verbs (presumably the reason Harrell designates them as auxiliaries, 1962:179ff). In this example, /tayxəmməm/ *he thinks* represents an indicative mood:

M6 بقى تيخمّم مع راسه
bqa tayxəmməm mʿa rāsu
remained-he indic-he-thinks with self-his
He thought to himself for awhile

In Syrian, temporal verbs embed either a marked or an unmarked imperfective. In the first of the following two examples, the verb embedded by /ṣār/ *to become* is unmarked, while in the second the embedded verb is marked with the progressive particle /mma/ (a variant of /ʿam/):

S5 كلّن صاروا يدقّوا تليفونات يسلّموا علينا
killon ṣāru ydiʾʾu talifōnāt ysallmu ʿalēna
all-them began-they they-call telephones they-greet on-us
All of them started to call us up and welcome us

S2 صارت هالعادة مّا تتبطّل
ṣāret ha l-ʿāde mma titbaṭṭal
became-it this the-custom prog it-stops-itself
This custom has begun to die out

As a rule, the use of the /b/ indicative marker in Syrian and Egyptian is more restricted in temporal clauses than the Moroccan indicative /ka/ (variant /ta/). Egyptian speakers normally use indicative /b/ only with /kān/:

E8 كان بيغزّي بلاد افريقيا كلّه من اللحوم دي
kān biyġazzi bilād ʾafriqya kullu min il-luḥūm di
was-he indic-he-feeds countries of-Africa all-of-it from the-meats this
He used to feed the whole of the African countries from that meat

Temporal verbs are described in more detail in 7.2.

5.3 Pseudo-Verbs

A number of expressions belonging to the verb phrase but are not fully verbal themselves have been labelled auxiliary verbs, modals, preverbal elements (Eisele 1988, Ingham 1994), and pseudo-verbs (Qafisheh 1975). I adopt here the term pseudo-verb, since it best describes the partially verbal syntactic nature of these expressions.

Pseudo-verbs function as main verbs in a sentence: they are negated as verbs, and many can modally embed other verbs. Predictably, the membership of many lexical items in the pseudo-verbs class is not stable, for several reasons. Some lexical items have both verbal and non-verbal meanings. In addition, some verbs and verb-like elements are undergoing processes of evolution by which they are gaining or losing verbal characteristics. These changes are neither unidirectional nor recent; nor are they limited to urban, high-contact areas.

Most if not all varieties of spoken Arabic contain lexical items that do not belong to the morphological category of verb but do occupy a slot within the verb phrase and often share certain features of verbal syntax. In the following sentences, prepositions are used to establish existence or possession. The prepositions /fī/ *there is* and /ʿand/ (/ʿind/) *at* take the sentence-initial verb position, and are negated with standard verbal negation, in Egyptian /mā - š/, Syrian and Kuwaiti /mā/. [6]

E ماфيش مشكلة
mā fīš muškila
neg there-is problem
There's no problem

S2 لا أبوي ما له علاقة
lā ʾabuyi mā lu ʿalāqa
no father-my neg-to-him relationship
No, my father has nothing to do with it

K2 ما عندَه شهادة
mā ʿinda šahāda
neg at-him degree
He does not have a degree

K4 انا بعد ما لي حظّ
ʾāna baʿd mā-li ḥaḏḏ
I then neg-to-me luck
I, now, I have no luck

---

[6]Word order typology is discussed in Chapter 10, where it is contended that VSO is a normal sentence typology for spoken Arabic. Chapter 9 describes the system of negation in spoken Arabic and the distinction between verbal and predicated negation forms.

Membership in the pseudo-verb category is not lexically but semantically determined, and lexical items whose semantic domains incorporate a range of verbal and non-verbal meaning do not always function as pseudo-verbs. For example, the Syrian preposition /ʾil-/ *to have* or *belong(ing) to* may be verbal or locative. Both of the following sentences contain /ʾilak/ *belonging to you*, but the underlying structures of the sentences differ. The first example shows a more verbal structure and meaning, marked by word order and the verbal negative particle /mā/, while in the second /ʾilak/ is clearly predicated, and negated with the predicating negative particle /mū/.

S1 ما إلك شغل عندي
mā ʾilak šəġəl ʿandi
neg to-you business at-me
You do not have a job with me

S3 الكاس مو إلك
il-kās mū ʾilak
the-glass neg to-you
The glass is not yours

The "fuzzy category" of pseudo-verbs is useful in describing the syntactic behavior of certain lexical items in certain semantic and syntactic contexts. The constellation of features shared by pseudo-verbs include verbal negation, the ability to subordinate, semantically and (in most cases) syntactically, and the ability to take pronoun subjects and logical objects. A number of lexical items can be seen to behave sometimes, but not always, as pseudo-verbs.

5.3.1 Characteristics of Pseudo-Verbs

In general, most pseudo-verbs consist of either prepositions that give locative or possessive meaning, or of nominally derived forms that give modal meaning (particularly obligatory mood). Pseudo-verbs are characterized by one or more semantic or syntactic features. A pseudo-verb can be a nominal or prepositional phrase that is used semantically to convey a verbal meaning, often but not necessarily possessive or existential in nature. This type of pseudo-verb may take its logical subject in the form of a pronoun object. Modal pseudo-verbs that take a verbal complement normally subordinate the verb syntactically, requiring the verb to be subjunctive. Pseudo-verbs are usually negated with verbal negation (see 9.3). Finally, a few pseudo-verbs appear to have developed in an opposite direction: rather than arising out of non-verbal elements that took on verbal function and (subsequently) verbal structure, these pseudo-verbs appear to be the result of partial loss of verbal status.

The semantic feature is an essential part of the definition, because, as seen above, many lexical items that often function as pseudo-verbs have other, non-verbal roles as well. On the other hand, the expression of logical subject as object is not limited to pseudo-verbs, since some verbs, such as /ʿažab/ *to please*, have the same construction.

The best syntactic test for determining whether a particular word may belong to this category is negation: many lexical items that function as pseudo-verbs are negated in the same way as verbs. In the following examples from Morocco and Egypt, possessive pseudo-verbs /ʿ[a]nd/ and /li/ take the verbal negation pattern of /mā - š/:

M6 اللي عنده الوراق واللي ماعندوش
lli ʿndu l-wrāq w lli mā ʿndūš
which at-him the-papers and which neg at-him
[He] who has [his] papers and he who doesn't have [them]

E ما ليش نفس
mā līš nifs
neg at-me appetite
I don't feel like it

The main exception to this rule of thumb is found in Cairo,[7] where pseudo-verbs derived from participles are normally negated with the predicate negating particle /miš/ rather than the verbal negative particle /mā - š/ (negating particles are discussed in Chapter 9):

E2 مش عايزة تطلع تاني
miš ʿayza ṭiṭlaʿ tāni
neg wanting-f she-goes-out second
It doesn't want to come out again

---

[7]Behnstedt and Woidich find negation with /mā - š/ to be common in many parts of Egypt (1985).

The characteristics that make up the loose category of pseudo-verbs are thus better envisioned as syntactic norms rather than hard and fast rules, since particular lexical items may be "more" or "less" pseudo-verbal in nature. In Syrian Arabic, /baʿd/ *yet* functions as a pseudo-verb meaning *to still [be]*:[8]

S3 بعدني بالبيت
baʿdni b-əl-bēt
still-me in-the-house
I'm still at home

The verbal nature of this expression appears in the use of the direct object pronoun /ni/ *me* as an object of /baʿd/. However, /baʿd/ may be "less verbal" than many other pseudo-verbs in that it cannot be negated; Syrian speakers reject sentences such as */mā baʿdni bi-l-bēt/ *I am not still at home.*

A number of pseudo-verbs expressing necessity or obligation (E, S, K /lāzim/, M /xəṣṣ/ *must*), ability (E, S /fī/ *able*), desire (S /bidd/, K /wudd/, E /ʿāyiz/ *want*, E /nifs/ *appetite*), and so forth, behave syntactically like main verbs in that they subordinate their verbal complement. This subordination can be demonstrated in Moroccan, Egyptian, and Syrian, because subordinate verbs in these cases must be unmarked imperfective. (Kuwaiti, on the other hand, does not morphosyntactically mark subordination.) The following contain subordinating pseudo-verbs:

M3 خصنا نطيّبوا العشا
xəṣṣna nṭəyybu l-ʿša
necessary-for-us we-cook the-dinner
We must cook dinner

E2 دخلت لحدّ عند الطبلة مش عارفة تعدّي
daxalit li-ḥadd ʿand iṭ-ṭabla miš ʿarfa tʿaddi
entered-it to-until at the-drum neg knowing-[how] it-cross
[The insect] went in as far as the eardrum, not being able to cross

---

[8]The pseudo-verb /baʿd/ *[to be] still [doing]* is also common in the Najd (Ingham 1994:107-8), but does not occur in my Kuwaiti data. This meaning is verbal in most varieties of Arabic (compare to formal Arabic /mā zāla/ *to remain, to not cease*).

S2 قال انه ما لازم نخبّره فجأة
qāl ʾinnu mā lāzim nxabbru fažʾatan
said-he that-it neg must we-inform-him suddenly
He said, We mustn't inform him too suddenly

Some Syrian prepositional pseudo-verbs, such as /ʿand/ *at* (possession) and /fī-/ *can, be able*, have adopted accusative marking for their objects (which represent in some cases the logical subject). In the following, /fī-/ takes the accusative first-person singular pronoun obejct /ni/ (first-person singular is the only pronoun whose accusative form, /ni/, differs from its genitive, /i/). :

Sn ما فيني اروح معك
mā fīni rūḥ maʿik
neg in-me I-go with-you
I'm not able to go with you

Second, certain Syrian pseudo-verbs can take grammatically marked direct objects, because pronoun direct objects are clearly indicated by the accusative marker / yā-/:

Sn عندي ياهن
ʿandi yāhon
at-me object-them
I have them

In addition to the more common pseudo-verbs cited above, these four dialects appear to share a pseudo-verb /ʿumr-/ (Moroccan /ʿam(m)ər-/) meaning *never*. The following constructions demonstrate the optional use of this particle as a pseudo-verb (it may also be used adverbially):

M ما عمّرني كنخدم
mā ʿamməmi kanəxdəm
neg life-me indic-I-work
I never work (Harrell 1962:153)

E5 ما عمريش عملت كدا
mā ʿumrīš ʿamalt kida
neg life-mine did-I like-that
I never did that (elicited)

Sn كنت صغير ما عمري اتنعشر سنة
kint ṣġīr mā ʿumri itnaʿašar sine
was-I young neg age-my twelve year
I was young, my age wasn't even twelve

K1 گلت لَه أو كي ... ما عمري سوّاها ويّاي
gilt-la ʾō kē ... mā ʿumri sawwāha wiyyāy
said-I-to-him o.k. neg life-my he-did-it with-me
I told him, O.K. ... never in my life did he do this to me

Most interesting about this pseudo-verb in particular is its semantic resemblance to temporal verbs, which delineate the time frame of an action. *To never [do]* bears semantic affinity with *to no longer [do]*, and this affinity may have helped to attract verbal syntactic behavior to the noun /ʿumr/.

5.3.2 Pronouns as Copulas

Subject pronouns that "separate" subjects and predicates in copulative sentences optionally occur in all dialects. Khan explains the tendency for this kind of topic-comment construction to occur in certain environments in Semitic by noting that these pronouns, which he calls agreement pronouns, appear in equational sentences whose predicate is highly individuated (1988:50). Cowell identifies this structure as marked, calling it "extraposition;" among the examples he cites is the following, containing subject pronoun /hiyye/ *it* as copula (1964:434):

S اهم شي بكلّ دكتوراه هي الاطروحة
ahamm šī bi-kəll doktōrā hiyye l-ʾəṭrūḥa
[most-important thing in-each doctorate it the-dissertation]
The most important thing in every doctorate is the dissertation

Of interest here is that this "agreement pronoun" has become in some dialects a full-fledged, pseudo-verb copula.[9] This kind of copula development is noted as a regular cross-linguistic phenomenon by Li and Thompson (1977).

Moroccan speakers can use masculine and feminine third person pronouns in equational sentences whose subject is first person. This

---

[9]See also Eid (1991, 1992) on agreement patterns in Egyptian copulas.

copula shows gender agreement only, either masculine /huwwa/ or feminine /hiyya/, and appears only with highly individuated predicates.

M6 انا هو هادوك الناس؟
ʾāna huwwa hādūk n-nās?
I he those the-people?
Am I those people?

M11 تتگول له انا هي امّك
tatgūl-lu ʾāna hiyya mm^{w}ək
indic-she-says-to-him I she mother-your
She tells him, I am your mother

Eid cites similar Egyptian examples that show third person masculine pronoun /huwwa/ as a non-gendered copula (1992:122):

E	انا هو انا	انت هو انت	انا هو المدير
	ana huwwa inta	inti huwwa inti	ana huwwa il-mudīr
	I am you (m)	*You (f) are you (f)*	*I am the director (m)*

I have not found examples of this construction in Kuwaiti, and attempts to elicit sentences similar to the examples above from Lebanese and Syrian speakers have proven unsuccessful. Evidence suggests, then, that the pronoun has developed into a copula only in the western dialect regions. However, all four dialects make use of a negative copula, consisting of a verbally negated pronoun; this copula will be surveyed in section 9.3.5.

5.3.3 Pseudo-Verbs in Rural Northwestern Syria

It was noted above that pseudo-verbs normally subordinate a verbal complement so that the subordinate verb must be non-finite. However, evidence from a female ʿAlawite speaker from a northwestern village near Lattakia shows the use of certain pseudo-verbs meaning *be able to* and *have* with finite verbal complements, including perfective verbs. The following two examples show pseudo-verbs /fī/ *be possible for* and /ʾil-/ *belonging to* playing an ambiguous role in the grammar of the verb phrase. In the first, /fī-/ *be possible for* is negated as a verb with /mā/, but followed by the perfective /rəḥət/ *I went*, rather than the expected subjunctive /rūḥ/ *I go*. Similarly, in the second example, /ʾili/

I had occupies a verbal position following /mā ʿād/ *no longer* (lit., *it did not come back*, yet the semantically subordinate verb /rəḥət/ *I went* is also perfective. In the third sentence, /fī-/ carries the future particle /raḥ/ normally restricted to verbs:

S1 ما فيني رحت
mā fīni rəḥət
neg possible for-me went-I
I wasn't able to go

S1 صار «ريمي»، ما عاد إلي قلب رحت
ṣār rīmi, mā ʿād ʾili ʾalb rəḥət
became-it "Rimi," no longer to-me heart went-I
[The program] "Rimi" came on, I no longer had the heart to go

S1 ما رح فيني
mā raḥ fīni
neg fut possible for-me
I won't be able to

These constructions do not occur in the other varieties of spoken Arabic examined here. On the one hand, /fī-/ *able* is more verbal than its counterpart in other dialects, taking verbal future marking, and on the other hand, it is less verbal, in that it does not subordinate a verbal complement. Does this ambiguity mean that /fī/ in this dialect is less developed, or developing in a different fashion, than it is in urban dialects of the region? Or do these examples result from dialect-switching, since the speaker in question is also a student at the University of Damascus, and her speech shows adaptation to the norms of this prestige dialect in a number of ways (for example, she normally changes her native /q/ for the more prestigious urban /ʾ/)? More research into these kinds of construction is needed.

5.3.4 Loss of Verbal Status

The process by which certain non-verbal lexical items acquire features of verbal behavior is mirrored by a process of verbs losing verbal characteristics. This process is evident in the dialects as well.

Of the impersonal Moroccan verb /xəṣṣ/ *it is necessary*, Harrell remarks that the marked imperfective /kayxəṣṣ/ is "sometimes" used, but that “[t]his distinction is not made absolutely consistently by all speakers” (1962:185). In my data, /kayxəṣṣ/ occurs only in the north:

M10 كيخصه تكون البلايا دياله كلّها
kayxəṣṣu tkūn l-plāya dyālu kullha
indic-it-is-necessary-for-him it-be the-beach gen-his all-of-it
He wants the beach to be all his

Some verbs have undergone partial agreement loss in another way: certain functions of the verb lose markings. This phenomenon is evident in Kuwaiti /čān/, derived from /kān/ *to be*. The latter retains full conjugation as a verb, but appears in the frozen form /čān/ without subject marking when it marks mood (see Chapter 8).

K3 انا لو اعرف اكتب واگرا چان يصير مسلسل ماميش مثلَه
ʾāna lo ʾaʿarf ʾaktib w agra čān yṣīr musalsil māmīš mitla
I if I-know I-write and I-read would he-become serial not-there-is like-it
I, if I knew how to write and read, there would be a serial like no other

Other verbs that have lost or are in the process of losing verbal features include Moroccan /ʿād/ *then, again* and Syrian /mā ʿād/ *no longer*. The particle /ʿād/, originally a verb, *to return*, has become in many areas a frozen particle whose discourse function lies in signaling a subsequent event in a logical chronology. Examples include:

M11 ما بغاش يسمّيها تا كبرت وعاد سمّت راسها
mā bġāš ysəmmīha ta kəbrat w ʿād səmmat rāsha
neg wanted-he he-name-her until grew-up-she and again named-she self-her
He didn't want to name her until she grew up, then she named herself

M11 هاديك عندها سبعة د الولاد وهاديك ادّاها عاد باش تولد الولد
hādīk ʿəndha səbʿa d-l-wlād w hādīk əddāha ʿād bāš təwləd l-wəld
that-one at-her seven gen the-children and that-one took-he-her again in-order she-bear the-son
That one had seven children [girls] and the other one he married then to bear [him a] son

Nor is this process limited to the urban dialects: the Gulf and Najdi dialects show traces of this process too. The presence of such particles in Najdi indicates that this kind of development is neither new nor tied to the spread of Arabic outside the Peninsula. In Najdi, the frozen particle /ʿād/ means *still, anymore*, the antonym of /mā ʿād/ *no longer, no more*, as Ingham's examples show (1994:107-8):

N عادك بدوي
ʿād-ik bduwi
You are still a bedouin

N اخيراً صرت ما عاد الگاه ع التليفون
axīran ṣirt mā ʿād algāh ʿa t-tilifōn
Finally I became unable to get him on the telephone

This process is more or less complete in some cases: what presumably began as time frame and narrative contour verbs, Moroccan /ʿād/ *then, again*, Egyptian /tann/ *kept on, then*, and Kuwaiti /čān/ *would* are now frozen particles (see 6.5.2, 8.5).

In other cases, this process seems still to be underway. Syrian /mā ʿād/ *no longer* shows subject agreement much of the time, especially with first and second person subjects, but is beginning to lose agreement in some cases, especially with third-person subjects. In the following, /mā ʿād/ lacks number agreement with the plural subject *they* that is marked on the subordinated verbs /yismaʿu/ *they listen to* and /yəšʿalu/ *they turn on*:

S2 ما عاد يسمعوا موسيقى، ما عاد يشعلوا التليفزيون
mā ʿād yismaʿu musīqa, mā ʿād yəšaʿʿlu t-tilvizyōn
no longer-ms they-listen music, no longer-ms they-turn-on the-television
They no longer listen to music, they no longer turn on the television

Clearly, processes of grammaticization, Bybee, Perkins, and Pagliuca's (1994) designation for the diachronic development of grammatical morphemes, show a number of parallels across dialect regions. A comparative study of the evolution of verbal morphemes across all dialect regions, especially in light of grammaticization theory, would make an important contribution to the field.

5.4 The Participle

The Arabic participle presents several problems to the would-be analyst.[10] The classification and description of the active and passive participles in formal Arabic describe a form more nominal than verbal, reflecting the more common nominal and adjectival usages of the participle in formal Arabic. In spoken Arabic, however, the participle maintains a primarily verbal function (see further 6.4 and 7.3). Participles can be used to refer to actions and events that have taken place, are taking place, or will take place in the future. At times the participle seems to describe a completed event, at others a state, and at other times a continuous activity. The reason for this ambiguity lies in part in the attempt to include time reference in the definition of the participle, and in part in the conflation of formal aspect with lexical aspect, problems to which I will return in Chapters 6 and 7. The participle is included in this survey of categories that are verbal in nature, without being full-fledged verbs.

The verbal features of the participle have been well documented by Mitchell (1952), Harrell (1962), Cowell (1964), Wild (1964), and Eisele (1988). The most obvious characteristic that participles share with verbs is that active participles can take both direct and indirect objects, as the following examples show:

M11 ديك اللي مربياه
dīk lli mrəbbyāh
this which having-raised-him
The one who had raised him

E1 لسّه جايباه النهاردا
lissa gaybā n-naharda
just having-brought-f-it today
I('ve) just got(ten) it today

---

[10]Participle here refers to the active and passive forms /ism fāʿil/ and /ism mafʿūl/ and their derived forms. I will avoid here the question of the relationship of the /faʿlān/ form to /fāʿil/ and its derivations. It appears that /faʿlān/ is most productive in Syrian (see Grotzfeld 1965:30); my data contain very few examples of it, and these are purely stative, e.g. /kānt nafsīytha taʿbāna/ *her emotional state was tired* (Kuwaiti). This form is of limited productivity in the western dialects, and does not occur at all in my Moroccan data.

S5 اللي باعتُّن للجيران
illi bāʿitton li-j-jīrān
which having-sent-fs to-the-neighbors
The ones she had sent to the neighbors

K2 الأم داگّة لي تليفون
il-ʾumm dāggat-li tilifōn
the-mother having-called-me telephone
The mother has called me

The examples cited above raise a point of comparative interest involving the morphosyntactic behavior of feminine participles. Within the four dialect groups treated here, an east-west isogloss exists for the pronunciation of the feminine suffix /-a[t]/ when direct and indirect pronoun objects are suffixed to it (as in S5 and K2 above). In the western dialects, the /-t/ is not pronounced, and the /-a/ is lengthened, whereas in Syrian and Kuwaiti the /-t/ is pronounced, as if the participle were a noun in construct. It is not an absolute east-west isogloss, since Mitchell's (1952) description of Libyan shows the /-t/ pronounced as in the eastern dialects. The pronunciation of /-t/ may be historically related to the /tanwīn/ suffix /-in/ on participles in Peninsular bedouin dialects (see Ingham 1994: 49); in any case, it deserves further study.

Participles carry gender inflection for subject, but not person.. An exception to this rule is found in the Syrian area, where active participles whose subject is second-person feminine have developed an ending that looks very much like a perfective verbal suffix. The following example shows a feminine singular participle, /šayfa/ *having seen*, with the genitive pronunciation /-t/, and the addition of the feminine second-person verbal suffix /-i/:

Sn شايفتيه لأحمد؟
šāyəftī la-ʾaḥmad?
having-seen-you-f-him obj-Ahmed?
Have you (f) seen Ahmed?

The motivation for this development seems to lie in the quasi-verbal nature of the participle, and in particular an aspectual association between it and the perfective, an association discussed further in Chapter 6.

Variations in the negation patterns of participles show that the participle sometimes functions as a verb, and at other times takes its syntactic position within the predicate (see Chapter 9). Chapter 7 will show that the participle may be used in past, present, and future time frames, a fact which prevents its formal association with any particular tense or time reference.

5.5 Summary

The category of verbs in spoken Arabic contains both core and peripheral members. The latter group includes members called here pseudo-verbs, defined not lexically but syntactically, as non-verbal expressions that show certain aspects of verbal behavior, such as negation patterns and syntactic objects, which often represent logical subjects. Two other subcategories of verbs were also proposed: verbs of motion and temporal verbs. Verbs of motion exhibit unique syntactic behavior in their occurrence in non-embedding compound verb phrases. While other types of verbs embed temporally and modally, the core group of motion verbs do neither, and some verbs of motion have special narrative functions (see Chapter 7). Temporal verbs, which function to delineate the time frame of an event, also consist of core and peripheral members. Temporal verbs embed other verbs temporally but not modally. The quintessential temporal verb, /kān/ *to be*, embeds a full range of perfective, imperfective, and participle forms, something no other Arabic verb can do. Other members of this class may embed participles; the extent to which they embed indicative imperfectives varies from dialect to dialect, being most common in Morocco and least common in Egypt. (Kuwaiti has no distinct indicative forms.) Chapter 7 contains further discussion on the syntactic behavior of temporal verbs.

6 Aspect

6.0 Introduction

Comrie defines aspect as consisting of "different ways of viewing the internal temporal constituency of a situation" (1976:3). For example, events and actions may be represented as punctual, i.e., having no internal dimension, or as durative, i.e., action-as-process.[1] Comrie's (1976) discussion includes three main cross-linguistic aspectual distinctions: perfective, imperfective, and perfect. I will argue here that these three cross-linguistic categories are realized in Arabic as the morphological forms of the verb, perfective, imperfective and participle.[2] The primary aim of this chapter is to provide a basic description of the aspectual meanings of these Arabic forms with particular attention to narrative contexts.

An important step in describing the nature of verbal aspect in Arabic has been Eisele's recognition of the distinction between two different types of aspect, 'formal' and 'lexical' (1990a:190; cf. Comrie 1976:6, n. 4). Formal aspect refers to the way in which the action in question is represented: as a complete, punctual event, as a duration or process, or as a resultant state. Lexical aspect (also called aktionsart, *type of action*), on the other hand, refers to a semantic feature inherent

---

[1]Mitchell and El-Hassan define aspect as "first and foremost a matter of duration, of progress from one location in time or space to another" (1994:74). Their study of aspect in the educated spoken Arabic of Egypt and the Levant concerns itself with interrelationships among aspect, tense, and modality, and explores a number of fine distinctions in meaning. This discussion treats these three verbal categories as distinct from one another.

[2]Arabic has both active and passive participle forms (/ism fāʿil/ and /ism mafʿūl/), and both forms can give verbal, nominal, and adjectival meanings. The term participle as used throughout this chapter refers to participles with verbal meaning. Active participles occur more commonly than passive ones, and most of the examples in this chapter happen to be active, but passive participles can also carry perfect aspect, as the passive participle /maḥṭūṭ/ *having been put* demonstrates here:

L ليش الصحن مش محطوط بالبرّاد؟
lēš əṣ-ṣaḥən miš maḥṭūṭ bə-l-barrād?
why the-dish neg having-been-put in-the-refrigerator?
Why hasn't the dish been put in the refrigerator?

in an individual verb, such as punctuality or duration, telic or atelic meaning, or stative or dynamic (Comrie 1976). Lexical aspect is not itself a syntactic category, but it does have implications for syntax in that interpretations of contextualized meanings of the imperfective and the participle depend in part on the lexical nature of the verb.

6.1 Lexical Aspect

A number of studies have investigated lexical aspect in various registers of Arabic, and examined the ways in which different interpretations of surface meaning are explained or predicted by the semantic nature of the individual verb. McCarus (1976, Syrian), el-Tonsi (1982, Egyptian), Eisele (1990b, Egyptian), Ingham (1994, Najdi) and al-Najjar (1984, Kuwaiti) have proposed classifications of verbs according to their lexical aspect. These classifications range in complexity from Ingham's bifurcation of aktionsart into state/motion and action (1994:89-90), to McCarus' rather elaborate system based on analyses of aspect in English.

Harrell classifies Moroccan verbs in four categories: durative, punctual, state/motion, and a fourth unnamed category whose description matches that of inceptive verbs (1962:176-177). These verbs refer

> either to an immediate activity or a necessary resultant of that activity, e.g. *rkeb* 'to mount' or 'to ride' (mounting being a necessary prerequisite to riding), *lbes* 'to put on' (clothing) or 'to wear' (putting something on being a necessary prerequisite to wearing it (1962:177).

McCarus (1976) compares lexical aspect in formal Arabic, Syrian, and English, and proposes a semantic categorization of lexical aspect based on the meanings of the participle and the imperfective. He distinguishes among a number of aktionsart categories, including state, movement, accomplishment, achievement, developmental, and inceptive.

Eisele (1990b) demonstrates the ways in which lexical aspect interacts with formal aspect in Cairene Arabic, affecting the semantic interpretation of a given verb in its active participle and marked imperfective forms.

Al-Najjar's study of aspect in Kuwaiti conflates lexical and formal aspect. His primary aim is to describe the roles and meanings of certain verbs he calls "aspectual markers" (1984:11). Ingham's approach to aspect in Najdi more closely conforms to the goal here, which is a simplified description of verbal behavior. Ingham describes Najdi as "exhibit[ing] an Aktionsart category dividing verbs into two classes (1) Action and (2) State/Motion verbs" (1994:87). He recognizes that verbs of all types can have multiple interpretations, telic and atelic, inceptive and non-inceptive, and that this multivalence of verbs makes their categorization problematic (1994:91).[3]

Most of these studies classify the possible lexical aspect or aktionsart readings given by the various verb stems. Depending on whether the verb is stative, motion, inceptive, or act, the marked imperfective allows habitual, progressive, and/or gnomic meanings, and the participle allows perfect, "present state" (called here resultant state), present progressive, or simple future interpretations. A comparative analysis of Egyptian and Syrian studies, combined with extrapolations from Moroccan and Kuwaiti data, reveals similar patterns of lexical aspect form and meaning throughout all four dialect regions. Table 6-1 summarizes the results of this analysis in chart form.[4]

Even in the brief summary presented in Table 6-1, the semantic classification of verbs looks rather complex, and there remains a good deal of overlap among the various categories The main shortcoming of this kind of approach lies in the attempt to classify verbs lexically in these categories. Many Arabic verbs contain within their semantic fields more than one lexical aspect, and may thus belong to more than one semantic category.

Ingham's distinction between telic and atelic verbs–or, more precisely, verb meanings–proves central to understanding verbal semantics. Ingham defines telic verbs as verbs whose action "leads up to a definite conclusion, as in *to build a house* or *to write a letter*"

---

[3]Ingham's discussion of aspect in Najdi, and his insights on the telic/atelic distinction were crucial in the formulation of the analysis presented here (see also Comrie 1976:44-48).

[4]Sample verbs are given in English due to the practical difficulty of including transcriptions from four different dialects.

(1994:89). Atelic verbs, by contrast, describe an action with no definite conclusion, such as *to work* or *to read.* A telic/atelic classification of verb meanings simplifies the classification of lexical aspect, particularly of the participle.

Table 6-1: Classification of Lexical Aspect

Lexical Aspect in the Dialects			
Verb Type	Perfective	Imperfective (Indicative)	Participle
stative, sensory, psychological *to understand*	entry into a state *understood, came to understand*	habitual or gnomic (general statement) *understands*	progressive or resultant state *has understood, understands*
motion *to leave*	completion *left*	habitual *leaves*	progressive or resultant state *is leaving, has left*
durative (no change or event) *to wait for*	completion *waited*	habitual *waits*	progressive *waiting*
inceptive: durative or punctual *to wear, put on (clothes)*	onset of action *wore (once), put on*	habitual or progressive *wears, is putting on*	resultant state *wearing, having put on*
act *to read*	completion *read*	habitual or progressive *reads, is reading*	resultant state *having read*

Eisele reports two different aspectual readings for the participle /mʾaggara/ *having rented* in the following sentence (1990b:210):

E هدى لسه مأجّرة شقة في درب الاحمر
huda lissa m'aggara ša''a fi darb il-'aḥmar
[Huda just/still having-rented apartment in Darb al-Ahmar]
Huda has just rented an apartment in Darb al-Ahmar or
Huda is still renting an apartment in Darb al-Ahmar

The two readings of this sentence reflect two different lexical aspects of the verb /'aggar/ *to rent*: telic *to make a rental agreement*, and atelic *to be or begin renting (a place)*. The combination of telic with the action nature of the verb results in a perfect reading of the participle in the former, and the atelic, stative character of the verb in the second gives a progressive reading. Mitchell gives a similar example containing the participle /mʿaddi/ *having crossed, crossing* (1978:249):

E شفته معدّي الشارع
šuftu miʿaddi iš-šāriʿ
[saw-I-him having-crossed the-street]
I saw him crossing the street or *I saw he had crossed the street*

The motion verb /ʿadda/ *to cross* may be atelic, signalling the entry into the state of motion but not its completion, or it may signify the act of *crossing the street* in its entirety, a telic act. These multiple readings suggest that it may not be desirable–or possible–to assign a given lexical item to just one aktionsart class.

The semantic analysis of verbs can be simplified by allowing verbs membership in more than one category, depending on context. Many verbs in Arabic have both telic and atelic meanings that are realized by both form and context, such that /nām/ can mean either *to fall asleep* or *to sleep*, /qaʿad/ *to sit down* or *to be sitting*, /daras/ *to study* or *to study something*, /ʿirif/ *to know* or *to find out*, depending on the context and the morphological form used. The verb /ḏākar/ *to study, review [a lesson]* can be either telic or atelic, and hence punctual or durative, in some dialects. Ingham admits only an atelic meaning for Najdi, and thus cannot give a reading for the active participle (1994:91). In Egyptian, however, telic use of this verb is common, and gives rise to a perfect interpretation of the participle: /'ana mizākir id-dars/ *I have studied the lesson*.

A general reluctance to designate a reading of resultant state for verbs of motion seems to be based mainly on the usage of the verb /rāḥ/ *to go*, which cannot give a resultant meaning in some dialects. However, other verbs of motion commonly give resultant state meanings, among them /ža/ *to come, arrive* and /miši/ *to leave*:

S	بعدني جايي	E	هو لسّه ماشي
	baʿdni jāye		huwwa lissa māši
	just-me having-arrived		he just having-gone
	I have just arrived		*He has just left*

The verb /ḥabb/ has both a stative, atelic meaning, *to love*, and an inceptive, telic meaning, *to fall in love with*. The speaker's choice to use the participle /ḥābbe/ *having fallen in love with* rather than the imperfective /bitḥibb/ *she loves* in the following sentence stresses the telic meaning, that she has fallen in love or had a love affair. The telic meaning emphasizes the completion of the act, and implies that the girl in question has stepped over the line of acceptable social behavior:

S2 هاي كانت حابّة فلان هاي كانت تطلع معه هاي كانت تتمشّى معه
hayy kānit ḥābbe flān hayy kānit tiṭlaʿ maʿu hayy kānit titmašša maʿu
this was-she having-fallen-in-love-with so-and-so this was-she she-go-out with-him this was-she she-go-walking with-him
This [girl] was in love with so-and so, she would go out with him, she would go out walking with him

These semantic categories, then, can best be viewed as categories of verb *meanings*, and not categories of verbs. The complexities of lexical aspect analysis can be reduced by classifying meanings rather than verbs. Since verbs can have both telic and atelic, or inceptive and non-inceptive meanings, depending on context and lexical item; these features provide the key to a simplified classification. The analysis proposed here will focus on the participle because it represents the most problematic of all verb stems.

Both the completion of an action and entry into a state share telic meaning, and both are commonly expressed with the perfective and the participle. Using Ingham's bifurcation of verbs into action and state/motion categories, two patterns emerge. (1) Participles of action verbs can only give perfect meaning when they are telic. (In fact, participles of atelic action verbs are rarely, if ever, used in spoken Arabic.) In the following sentence, /ʾāri/ gives a telic meaning, *to read [and finish reading] something*; it cannot give the reading *I am still reading this book.*

E لسّه قاري الكتاب دا
lissa ʾāri k-kitāb da
just having-read the-book that
I've just read this book

(2) Participles of stative and motion verbs are used both in telic and atelic meanings. An atelic lexical aspect gives rise to interpretations of stative or progressive aktionsart, such as /ʾaʿda/ *sitting* in the following Egyptian sentence (el-Tonsi 1982:41):

E انت قاعدة هنا نصّ ساعة؟
inti ʾaʿda hina nuṣṣ-ə sāʿa?
you sitting here half hour
Will you be sitting here for (another) half an hour?

Telic lexical aspect, on the other hand, gives rise to a perfect or resultant state reading:

L بعدني قاعد! ليش بدّك ياني اقوم؟
baʿdni ʾāʿid! lēš beddik yāni ʾūm?
just-me having-sat! why want-you me I-get-up?
I've just sat down! Why do you want me to get up? (elicited)

Table 6-2: Lexical Aspect and the Participle

Lexical Aspect and the Participle		
	Telic	Atelic
State/Motion	resultant state	progressive
Action	resultant state	---

The aspectual reading of the participle can thus be linked directly to the context-specific meaning of its verb. If the meaning is telic, the participle will give a resultant state (perfect aspect) reading. If the meaning is atelic, the participle may be used only to express a progressive reading for states and verbs of motion. These findings, summarized in Table 6-2, have obvious implications for the aspectual nature of the participle, which will be explored in section 6.4.

6.2 Formal Aspect

Formal aspect refers to the way in which a verbal form describes the contour of a particular action as an event, process, or state. As such, formal aspect cannot always be judged according to grammatical correctness; rather, the speaker chooses to describe an action as, for example, a process that extends over time, as a completed event viewed in its entirety, or as a resultant state. The remainder of this chapter will be concerned with the roles that formal aspect plays in the verbal system of spoken Arabic, with particular attention to narrative contexts.

The three main categories of aspect discussed by Comrie (1976) are perfective, imperfective, and perfect.[5] These three categories map onto the Arabic system quite neatly, finding expression in the imperfective, perfective and participle, respectively. Though these three Arabic verb stems may not correspond exactly with perfective and imperfective aspects in other languages, they do conform closely to the defining characteristics of these aspects as listed by Comrie (1976:18-21, 24-26). The perfective aspect presents the action as a completed, indivisible whole, and contrasts to the imperfective, which describes the action internally, as a non-complete process, which may be iterative, habitual, or progressive. The perfect describes an action as a state that bears relevance to the moment of speaking.

Several dialect grammars have approximated this analysis without committing to this terminology and framework. For Moroccan, Harrell describes perfective and perfect without using the terms, and he calls the imperfective "durative" (1962:173). For Egyptian, Eisele prefers not to equate Arabic tense forms with Slavic aspect, but sees an aspectual

---

[5]See also Li, Thompson, and Thompson (1982:19) and references therein.

correspondence between the English 'event' or simple tense forms (e.g., *go, went*) and the Arabic perfective on one hand, and between the English 'process' or compound forms (e.g., *was going, am going*) and the Arabic imperfective (1990a:191). Al-Najjar (1984:6) uses the terms perfective, imperfective, and perfect as I do here, although his study of aspect in Kuwaiti focuses on lexical aspect. Ingham also uses the terms perfective and imperfective (1994:87), and describes the participle as a perfect in the cases noted above (1994:89).

It is important to distinguish clearly between the perfect and perfective aspects. The overlap in terminology is unfortunate, but commonly occurs, and is unavoidable at present, since it would be even more confusing to invent new terms for old concepts (see further Comrie 1976:12 and Lyons 1977:714-15). Comrie uses the term perfect to designate "a past situation which has present relevance;" the perfective, on the other hand, "denotes a situation viewed in its entirety, without regard to internal temporal constituency" (1976:12).

These aspects are familiar from other languages. Slavic in particular grammaticalizes perfective and imperfective aspect in a more elaborate system than Arabic, and English has a perfect which is similar to the Arabic. However, these three aspects are not necessarily grammaticalized in exactly the same way in all languages. It need not be claimed that Arabic perfective and imperfective are equivalent to Slavic, nor that the Arabic perfect matches the English perfect, for these terms to be used. It must only be shown that the meanings of these Arabic forms conform to general linguistic definitions of these aspects.

Slavic languages have a highly developed aspectual system, with separate verb stems for the perfective in various tenses, so that a future event can be described as perfective, as a complete, punctual event. Arabic does not have separate tenses, and so the expression of a present or future event as perfective, as a punctual whole, is much less common than the expression of a past event as such (although punctuality may be implied by the participle, see 6.4). Arabic may have a less elaborate aspectual system than Slavic, but this does not mean that Arabic verbs are less aspectual. While the meaning of the Slavic perfective is highly *punctual*, that of the Arabic perfective appears to be more focused on the *completed* nature of the event. Mitchell and El-Hassan seem to concur: "The difference between that which has been realized (fulfilled, accomplished, brought about) and that which has not is at the root of Arabic distinctions of tense and mood" (1994:8). Cross-linguistically, perfective aspect consists of a constellation of features, and its realization in a given language may favor one particular feature over others. In Arabic, the "completed" feature of the perfective plays a primary role.

In addition, the 'perfectiveness' of the perfective may vary somewhat among different varieties of spoken Arabic. Mitchell contrasts the following two Jordanian examples, the first judged by his informants to be ungrammatical and the second acceptable (1978:237):

J قرأت الكتاب عدة ساعات
* qara't il-kitāb ʿiddit sāʿāt
* [read-past-I the-book several hours]
* [*I read the book for several hours*]

J قرأت في الكتاب عدة ساعات
qara't fi il-kitāb ʿiddit sāʿāt
[read-past-I in the-book several hours]
I read (in) the book for several hours

In the second example, the aspectual nature of the perfective /qara't/ *I read* is altered by the preposition /fi/, which permits an atelic interpretation of the action that correlates with the adverb /ʿiddit sāʿāt/ *(for) several hours.* This use of /fi/ as an aspectual "durative" particle is common in Morocco, Egypt, and the Levant. However, a sentence based on Mitchell's Jordanian example and translated into Moroccan was rejected by Moroccan informants, who corrected the sentence to:

M1 تلاتة د سوايع وانا كنقرا ف واحد الكتاب
tlāta d swāyəʿ w āna kanqra f wāḥəd l-ktāb
three gen hours and I indic-read-I in one the-book
I've (I had) been reading a book for three hours (elicited)

This judgement suggests that some educated Moroccan speakers, in contrast to educated Jordanian speakers, have difficulty associating the perfective with a duration of time. The educated register of Mitchell's Jordanian speaker, indicated by the glottal stop in /qara't/ *I read* (which in a less formal register would be /ʾarēt/) may also play a role in usage here. In any case, a blanket statement on the use of the perfective in spoken Arabic is not yet warranted, and more research is needed both into regional and social variation.[6]

At the other end of the dialect spectrum lie the following examples, taken from an interview with an elderly Kuwaiti woman. In this passage, she reports a conversation with a male relative, speaking in his voice. Noteworthy here is the use of perfectives /rəḥt/ *I went* and /ṭagget/ *she called* juxtaposed with imperfectives /arūḥ/ *I go* and /mā aʿyi/ *I am not aware* in the same narrative context, even though both verbs clearly refer to the same temporal frame. These perfectives indicate recurring events, but describe the events as punctual ones fitting within a larger series of events.

K3 عاداتها ماهي زينة. انا اروح الشغل. [ا]لا رحت الشغل، طگّت امها
عليها تليفون وما اعي إلاّ وين رايحين، المعرض، ويوم رايحين ما
ادري وين يگولون ولا تحچّيت، هدّت امّها لسانها عليك

ʿādātha māhi zēna. ʾāna arūḥ iš-šuġəl. la rəḥt iš-šuġəl, ṭagget ummha ʿalēha talifōn w mā aʿi ʾilla wēn rāyḥīn, il-maʿraḍ, w yōm rāyḥīn mā adri wēn yigūlūn w la tḥaččēt, haddat ʾummha lisānha ʿalēk

habits-her neg good. I I-go the-job. when went-I the-job, called-she mother-her at-her telephone and neg I-aware except where going-p, the-exhibition, and day going-p neg I-know where they-say and if spoke-you, loosed-she mother-her on-you

Her habits are not good. I go to work. When I go to work, her mother calls her–on the phone–and before I am aware of it where are they off to–to the exhibition, and another day I don't know where they say they're going, and if you say anything, her mother lets her tongue loose on you.

Similarly, the following passage about how Kuwaiti society used to deal with infertility "in the old days" contains perfectives /yāt/ *she came* and /tzawwəjaw/ *they got married*, contrasting with imperfective /yanṭurūn/ *they wait*:

---

[6]See also Mitchell and El-Hassan (1994) for a detailed comparison of aspectual usages in the educated spoken Arabic of the Levant.

K3 شوفي يعني حين اوّل لا يات المرا لا تزوّجوا، عگب الزواج ينطرون عليها شهر، شهرين

šūfi ya‘ni ḥīn ʾawwal la yāt il-mara la tzawwəjaw, ‘ugub iz-zawāj yanṭurūn ‘alēha šahər, šahrēn

you-see that-is when old-days if came-she the-woman when they got married, after the-marriage they-wait for-her month month-2

You see, in the old days, when the woman came when they got married, they would wait a month or two

The perfective moves the narrative forward, and serves to foreground the events it represents, in contrast to the use of the imperfective to provide background descriptions. Foregrounding and backgrounding will be explored further in section 6.5.1.

6.3 Translation and Speaker Point of View

Anderson's study of aspect as a cross-linguistic category rests on the premise that "[a] grammatical category, such as the '[p]erfect,' will not have exactly the same range of uses in one language as it does in another" (1982:227).[7] In trying to determine the aspectual meanings of verb forms, it is important to allow for two kinds of variables: problems that arise in translating across languages, and the degree of control maintained by speakers in representing actions and events. For the first, if a certain aspectual distinction is made by one language but not another, translations that maintain the original distinction may be difficult to find. In the case of speaker control, two speakers may report the same event or elicit the same information using different aspectual forms, depending on the way she or he chooses to represent that event or question. The following, while not the only means of asking, represent common variants for *Do you remember?* in each dialect:

M1 عقلتي؟	E5 فاكر؟	S3 بتتذكّر؟	K1 تذكرين؟
‘qəlti?	fākir?	btətzakkar?	tiḏkərīn?
remembered-you	having-remembered	indic-you-remember	you-f-recall

[7]Anderson proposes a schema for the mapping of uses of the perfect in a variety of languages; unfortunately, his discussion of (formal) Arabic focuses on what is called here the perfective, not the participle.

Do these different verb stems mean that the aspectual systems of the dialects differ? Not necessarily. Lexical aspect, formal aspect, and speaker attitude all affect the formation of these questions. As the Moroccan version suggests, the perfective in Moroccan sometimes has a performative function, at least in certain common expressions, such as the generalized use of the perfective /bġīt/ *I want* and /xəṣṣ/ *must, it is necessary*. By contrast, in using the imperfective, the Syrian and Kuwait questions stress the act of remembering as a process. The Egyptian participle contains an implied perfective event as well, but adds to it a relevant resultant state. Moreover, the use of the participle in this case goes beyond a request for information to a social interaction: by phrasing the request in terms of a resultant, relevant state, the speaker adds connotations of shared experience, relevant to the present moment, and hence a reinforcing of social or emotional ties. The use of different verb stems in these questions may tell us as much about speaker attitudes as about the nature of verbal aspect in these dialects.

Lexically stative verbs, such as *to know*, interact with aspect in a way that defies translation. The context of the following Kuwaiti example clarifies the reason for the speaker's choice of the participle /ʿārif/ *having learned*. An interviewer has asked the speaker about her opinion of marriage at a young age. In her reply, the speaker stresses that a man should have already come to understand the responsibilities of marriage. The use of the participle /ʿārif/ *having learned* adds this dimension of completed comprehension, while the imperfective would stress comprehension as an ongoing process.

K2 يعني ودّچ الواحد الولد يتزوّج عمرَه خمسة وعشرين، ستة وعشرين،
عارف الحياة، عارف مسؤوليات الزوجة

ya‘ni wuddič il-wāḥid il-walad yitzawwaj ‘umra xamsa w ‘išrīn, sitta w ‘išrīn, ‘ārif il-ḥayāt, ‘ārif mas’ūliyyət iz-zōja

that-is desire-your the-one the-boy he-marries age-his five and twenty six and twenty, having-learned the-life, having-learned the-responsibilities of-the-wife

You would like the boy to marry at the age of 25 or26, having [already] learned [about] life, having learned the responsibilities of [having a] wife

Adjectives, participles, and verbs can all be stative. In addition, the lexical aspect of a number of verbs is "stative." Thus Mitchell and El-Hassan (1994:86-87) claim "synonymy" between /ʾana ʿārif tārīx al-ʿarab/ *I know Arab history* and /ʾana baʿrif tārīx al-ʿarab/, *I know Arab history*, not only because of the "stative" nature of the act of knowing in both cases, but also because English has only one form to express states of knowing. By way of investigating Mitchell and El-Hassan's claim, I elicited from a linguistically trained Lebanese speaker a number of sentences containing the participle /ʿārif/ *knowing, having found out* and the imperfective /baʿrif/ *I know*, from which the following four have been chosen as representative:

a بعرف كيف كلّ واحد بيفكّر
baʿrif kīf kill wāḥid bifakkir
indic-I-know how each one indic-he-thinks
I know how each one thinks

b بعرف اسامي كلّ التلاميذ
baʿrif ʾasāmi kill it-tlāmīz
indic-I-know names of-all of-the-students
I know the names of all the students

c مانّي عارف الله وين حاططني
mānni ʿārif ʾaḷḷah wēn ḥāṭiṭni
neg-I having learned God where having-put-me
I don't know where God has put me [what's going on with me]

d انا عارف شو عم بحكي
ʾana ʿārif šu ʿam biḥki
I having-learned what prog indic-I-say
I know what I'm saying

Is it possible to determine the motivation behind the choice of verb forms in these contexts? Eisele (1990a:204) claims that, in certain contexts, the perfective and the perfect can "imply" events and states not primarily grammaticalized by the verb form; if this is so, then the imperfective should have similar capability. A possible motivation for the use of the imperfective in examples (a) and (b) is to imply the underlying *process* of learning a certain body of knowledge, here the way certain people think and the names of the students. Examples (c) and (d), on the other hand, contain no body of knowledge to be learned through a process. Rather, the participle indicates a completed knowing, or not knowing, as a resultant state that has special relevance to the speech act (see 6.4).

The use of the participle in these and other contexts conforms to Li, Thompson, and Thompson's (1982) pragmatics of perfect aspect in Chinese. I will cite their findings here not to propose that the Arabic perfect is equivalent to the Chinese, but to offer a cross-linguistic perspective on the functions of perfect aspect.

6.4 Perfect Aspect

Li, Thompson, and Thompson (1982) examine the discourse properties of the Mandarin Chinese perfect. They see the same two essential, defining properties of the perfect in Chinese that the Arabic participle has: stativity, and relevance to reference time. The pragmatic functions of the perfect in Chinese include (adapted from 1982:28-37):

1. to indicate change of state, or change of perception on the part of the speaker;
2. to correct a wrong assumption;
3. to report progress so far, update, relevance;
4. to signal what happens next, in a narrative sequence;
5. to close a statement, marking 'speaker contribution.'

Of special interest here are functions (1) and (2), because they explain the use of the participle in examples (c) and (d) above.[8] Example (c) represents a loss of perception on the part of the speaker, which falls under the rubric of a change in perception. From the point of view of the speaker, example (d) corrects the erroneous assumption on the part of the interlocutor that the speaker does not know what he is talking about. The use of the participle in these particular contexts thus seems to follow certain aspectual principles.

The lack of an equivalent distinction in English between participle /ʾana ʿārif/ *I know* and imperfective /baʿrif/ *I know* does not preclude a difference in perspective expressed in the Arabic. Just as speakers

[8]Other functions also prove relevant to the Arabic perfect, in particular (4) "what happens next," which will be discussed further in section 6.5.3.

control the degree to which they specify or individuate nouns (see 1.3), they also retain a degree of control in choosing the aspectual representation of an event.

Eisele 1990a and Mitchell and El-Hassan 1994 are reluctant to assign a direct relationship between perfect aspect and the participle in part because the English perfect is often used to translate the Arabic perfective. However, the use of one form to translate another form from another language does not necessarily establish a grammatical equivalence between the two forms. In a number of European languages, the semantic field of the perfect has been gradually expanding at the expense of the simple past (Comrie 1976:11). Conversely, the English perfect has syntactic restrictions that the Arabic perfect does not. As Comrie notes, in English, the specific time reference of the prior event may not be expressed. "[O]ne cannot say *I have got up at five o'clock this morning*" (Comrie 1976:54). In several dialects of spoken Arabic, on the other hand, such a sentence is perfectly acceptable, as these elicited sentences show:

M اليوم راني فايق من الستة
l-yūm rāni fāyq mən s-sətta
today here-I-am having-woken-up from the-six
Look here, today I (have) got(ten) up at six (elicited)

E النهاردا صاحي الساعة ستة
in-naharda ṣāḥi s-sāʿa sitta
today having-awaken the-hour six
Today I got up (have) got(ten) up at six o'clock (elicited)

L اليوم فايق الساعة ستة
il-yōm fāyiʾ is-sāʿa sitte
today having awaken the hour six
Today I (have) got(ten) up at six o'clock (elicited)

Arabic allows temporal conflation of the prior event and the resultant state in a way English does not. In these examples, *six o'clock* represents both the time of the prior event and the onset of the relevant state. In contrast, the English perfect precludes overt reference to the exact time of the previous event itself, but almost requires overt expression of the non-specific time frame of the resultant state. Hence one can say in English *I have just gotten up*, but not *I have gotten up five minutes ago.*

In the following excerpt, a Kuwaiti matchmaker describes the first steps in arranging a marriage. The problem here is the translation of the participle /dāggat-li/ *having called me*. An idiomatic English translation would favor the use of the English past tense rather than the present perfect: *the mother called* sounds more natural in this context than *the mother has called.*

K2 امّ البنية ترجع تگول لي يا امّ احمد انت تعرفينَه؟ اگول لها والله
انا ما اعرفَه الامّ داگّة لي تليفون تگول ابيچ تخطبي حگّ ولدي

ʾumm lə-bnayya tirjaʿ tgul-li ya umm aḥmad, anti taʿrfīna? ʾagul-lha lā waḷḷa, ʾāna mā aʿrfa, il-umm dāggat-li telifōn tgūl ʾabīč txaṭbi ḥagg wildi

mother of-the-girl she-returns she-says to-me O Umm Ahmad you you-know-him? I-say to-her by-God I neg I-know-him, the-mother having-called-me telephone she-says I-want-you you-arrange-marriage for son-my

The girl's mother comes back to me saying, Umm Ahmad, do you know him? I tell her, I don't know him, the mother has called me saying, I want you to arrange a marriage for my son

On the other hand, as Eisele notes, the Arabic perfective may often be rendered more idiomatically into English using the English present perfect, especially in the case of inchoative verbs (1990a:202):

E خلاص، زهقت

xalāṣ, zihiʾt

finished, I-became-bored

Enough already, I've become annoyed (I'm annoyed)

Here again, the difference lies in idiomatic expression. English does not generally accord grammatical attention to the punctual entry into a state, especially if that state is still on-going and relevant. Arabic speakers, on the other hand, can choose to represent either the entry into the state as a punctual event, or the state resulting from that event. Eisele notes that the Arabic perfective "asserts" the event and "implies" the resulting state (1990a:204); this implication is not grammatical but contextual and translational.

6.4.1 Perfect Aspect and the Participle

The meaning and function of the active participle in spoken Arabic has been under investigation for some time. Johnstone (1967:142) notes of Eastern Arabian dialects that "the syntax of these dialects does not differ greatly from that of literary Arabic ... except in the extended use of the active participle." Johnstone undoubtedly refers to the widespread use in spoken Arabic of participles with verbal force, as opposed to participial forms serving as adjectives, impersonal predicates or frozen forms (such as /lāzim/ *must, it is necessary*), a distinction maintained here as well.

But if it is correct to assign perfect aspect to the participle, as is claimed here, then its near absence from written genres with a verbal meaning does not result from difference in syntax between written and spoken Arabic so much as in differences in discourse type and context. Written language is often distanced from the force of relevance to the speech act. It may be precisely the relevance aspect of the participle that precludes its extensive use in most written contexts, especially expository writing. The perfect aspect would therefore be a feature of language more naturally associated with spoken, not written, language.[9]

The aspectual nature of the participle in a number of dialects has been analyzed by Wild (1964), Woidich (1975), Mitchell (1978), el-Tonsi (1982), Al-Najjar (1984), Eisele (1988, 1990a), and Ingham (1994). Some of these analyses have attempted to codify the use of the active participle with various time references; all have investigated the nuances of its aspectual meanings.

Terms like 'resultative' and 'stative' are often used to describe the participle. Mitchell (1978:230), Al-Najjar (1984), and Holes (1990) hint at a relationship between perfect aspect and the active participle, but stop short of associating the two. Ingham recognizes the perfect

---

[9]Li, Thompson and Thompson's research on Chinese supports this theory: they find that the Chinese perfect is "very rare in expository and scientific writing and practically non-existent in news-reporting, speeches, lectures ... [and descriptive writing]" (1982:26). Only in narratives is the Chinese perfect likely to occur. In Classical Arabic, then, one would expect to find participles with perfect aspect in literary anecdotes and narratives. It is my impression that this is precisely the context in which this use of the participle most frequently occurs; however, this speculation awaits further research.

nature of participles in Najdi Arabic: "it [is] possible to interpret the [a]ctive participle as meaning *having begun to* ... or *having performed the initial action which results in the state of* ..." (1994:91). However, he too is reluctant to assign perfect aspect to the participle because of the progressive reading of participles of certain state and motion verbs.

Eisele (1990a) labels the participle as "stative." While the participle clearly represents a state, stativity is not in and of itself the defining characteristic of the participle. First, as noted above, the term 'stative' is also used to denote one type of lexical aspect. Verbs of epistemic knowledge in most languages are stative: *to know*, *to perceive*, and *to believe* all refer to states of knowledge rather than acts. Thus 'stativity' is not limited to the participle, but is also a lexical quality inherent in certain types of verbs. Secondly, copulative sentences, including those containing a null-copula, may also be said to represent a state, whether permanent or not. Finally, it is not the stative quality of participles alone that lends them their aspectual nature. Rather, it is the resultative and relevance features that allow participles to be associated with the perfect aspect. Stativity is therefore a necessary but not sufficient quality of the perfect aspect.

The following examples demonstrate the importance of the resultative (relevance to speech act) character of the participle. In each case, the participle denotes a state resulting from a prior act and concurrent and relevant to the speech context. (The question of time reference will be taken up in Chapter 7.)

The female character in this story is able to recognize her son years later because the angels *had marked him* when he was born with certain birthmarks, and the resultant state is crucial to her recognition:

M11 ياقوتة بين عينيه وياجورة بين سنّيه معلّمينه الملايكات منين زاد

yāqūta bīn ʿinīh w yāžūra bīn sənnīh mʿallmīnu l-malāykāt mnīn zād

sapphire between eyes-his and brick between teeth-his having-marked-him the-angels when was-born-he

A sapphire[-shaped mole] between his eyes and a brick [-shaped gap] between his teeth, the angels having marked him when he was born

In the story from which the next sentence is taken, the man has lost a valuable sheep that *had been bought* for a large sum of money:

M9 مشى الراجل حمق، ايوه الحولي مشري بألف والزيادة
mša r-rāžl ḥmaq, ʾīwa l-ḥawli məšri b ʾalf w z-zyāda
went-he the-man went-mad-he, well, the-sheep having-been-bought with thousand and more
The man went crazy–the sheep had been bought for upwards of a thousand

Recording a list of chores with her friend, the scribe notes that she *has already written* this one, correcting her friend's assumption that this chore is not yet on the list:

E1 --- ولازم تصلّحي الفرامل --- انا كاتبة دي
--- wi lāzim tiṣallaḥi l-farāmil --- ʾana katba di
--- and must you-repair the-brakes --- I having-written this
--- *And you have to fix the brakes.* --- *I've written that down.*

The next speaker has just been asked if she has a prospective husband in mind. Her reply stresses that, as far as she knows now, her decision has been made:

S2 حالياً مختارته
ḥāliyyan muxtārtu
currently having-chosen-him
As of now, I've chosen him

This Kuwaiti woman proudly describes putting the finishing touches on her new chalet using perfective verbs. Her friend then asks if the electricity has been connected yet, so that it is ready to be inhabited:

K4 --- سوّيت له القنافات، خلّصتهم --- الكهربا واصلة؟
--- sawwēt-le l-qənāfāt, xaḷḷaṣthum --- il-kahraba wāṣla?
--- made-I-for-it the-sofas, finished-I-them --- the-electricity having-reached?
— I got the sofas for it, I finished them. --- Has electricity arrived?

These participles all fit the definition of perfect aspect: the resultant state of a prior action that has special relevance to the speech act.

6.4.2 Participles of Motion

The biggest problem presented by the participle as a grammatical form is that a small category dominated by participles of motion[10] seem to behave in an altogether different manner than the participles cited above. Rather than indicating the resultant state of a prior act, these particular motion participles often indicate a progressive act. Hence E,S /māši/ can mean both *going* and *having left*, and E, S, K /nāzil/ either *going down/out* or *having gone.* The participle /wāṣil/, on the other hand, can only mean *having arrived* in all four dialects.

In Egyptian, /rāyiḥ/ means only *going*, not *having gone.* Kuwaiti speakers, however, use this participle in both meanings. In the following passage, the speaker recounts his last birthday party, listing the preparations undertaken by his friends. Past time reference is established by contextual framing. The participle of motion /rayḥīn/ *having gone* is clearly parallel in aspect to /msawwīn/ *having made*, /šarīn/ *having bought*, and /yāybīn/ *having brought.*

K1 فيوم عيد ميلادنا، مسوّين لنا حفلة، عيد ميلادنا انا ويّاه، بيننا وبينَه اسبوع رايحين شارين كيكة ويايبين المشروب

fa yōm ʿīd milādna msawwīn-lina ḥafla, ʿīd milādna ʾāna wiyyā benna w bēna isbūʿ, rāyḥīn šārīn kēka w yāybīn l-mašrūb

so day feast birth-our having-made-p for-us party, anniversary-our I with-him between-us and between-him week having-gone-p having-bought-p cake and having-brought-p the-drink

So the day of our birthday they had arranged for us a party, our birthday, mine and his, between [me] and him is a week, they had gone and bought us a cake and brought the drinks

Al-Najjar notes, but does not explain, the use of /rāyiḥ/ going and other participles of motion with both progressive and perfect meanings (1984:145).

The existence of what appear to be two contradictory usages of the same form has motivated various analyses of the participle along

[10]Mitchell and El-Hassan (1994) point out that *translocation* is a more appropriate term for this category of verbs, since it is verbs expressing movement from one location to another that exhibit this behavior. I will use *motion* in the sense of *translocation*.

semantic lines, as seen in section 6.1. Eisele's solution to this problem is to call the perfect usage "non-characteristic" with respect to aspect (1990a:204). An alternate explanation is offered here, one that views this as an historical problem, resulting in the development of a secondary, stative meaning.

As any dictionary of Arabic shows, many Arabic verbs have a range of meanings both telic and atelic. The problem of the motion class participles is resolved by viewing the range of telic and atelic meanings inherent in each verb. The verb /miši/ can mean, in different contexts, *to walk, to go*, and *to set out to go somewhere, leave.* If /miši/ is understood to mean to *set out to go* rather than the process of *going*, the semantic extension of /māši/ from perfect *having set out* to progressive *in a state of going* is not problematic, but well within the normal parameter of perfect meaning. Verbs meaning *to go* can carry both telic (*to go somewhere*) and atelic (*to set out*) meanings; it is the atelic meaning of these verbs that gives rise to the interpretation of the participle as motion in progress.

The overwhelming preponderance of evidence from a number of dialects thus confirms that the basic aspectual nature of the participle is perfect. The question of time reference, however, is a different one entirely, and will be examined in Chapter 7.

6.5 Aspect in Narrative Contexts

This overview of aspect in spoken Arabic will conclude with a brief look at aspect in narratives across dialects. Narratives provide a range of meanings of forms and structures. While ostensibly about another time and place, narratives are often present in a way that emphasizes the relevance to the moment of speaking: to be as close as possible to the audience, the narrative context is brought into the here and now. Narrative uses of verb forms are strikingly similar across dialects, and reflect the centrality of aspect to the verbal system of Arabic.

The use of the so-called "historical present," the progressive present that relates past events, is a well-known cross-linguistic phenomenon also common in Arabic. The following Kuwaiti narrative shifts abruptly from perfective to imperfective at a moment of tension, when the narrator discovers that his friend is no longer speaking to him. Perfective verbs /ga'adt/ *I got up*, and /ṭala' rāḥ/ *he left [and] went*, move the plot forward, while the imperfective forms, /'agūl/ *I say*, and /mā yḥāčīni/ *he doesn't speak to me*, as a kind of historical present, heighten the immediacy of these actions:

K1 ثاني يوم گعدت الصبح واگول حگ م. صباح الخير، ما يحاچيني، طلع راح الدوام

ṯāni yōm ga'adt əṣ-ṣəbḥ w-agūl ḥagg M ṣabāḥ il-xēr, mā yiḥāčīni, ṭala' rāḥ id-dawām

second day got-up-I the morning and I-say to M. morning the-good neg he-speaks-to-me left-he want-he the-work

The next day I got up in the morning and I say good morning to M. and he doesn't talk to me! He left and went to work.

However, the historical present does not by itself explain non-past usage of imperfective forms in spoken Arabic. The historical present in English often consists of event forms, like a recent television commercial for a kind of toothpaste, in which the speaker relates a past event using present forms: *My dad picks me up at the airport, and right there on the highway he starts examining my teeth!* As Eisele notes, the English event form is parallel to the Arabic perfective (1990a), so the use of present tense event forms in English narratives cannot be equated with the use of the imperfective in Arabic which, while conveying the narrative immediacy of a relative non-past occurrence, describes the event in a different fashion. Another unexplained feature of Arabic narratives is that many of them combine perfective and imperfective forms, both describing past events. Clearly, aspect is involved in the choice of forms in narrative. The next four sections describe different strategies Arabic speakers use in narration.

6.5.1 Foregrounding and Backgrounding

Hopper has identified what he calls "a universal of narrative discourse," a phenomenon he calls foregrounding and backgrounding (1979:213). These terms refer to the "parts of the narrative which relate events belonging to the skeletal structure of the discourse," and the "supportive material which does not itself narrate the main events" (1979:213). This discourse universal is realized with different strategies across languages, but a number of core syntactic and semantic phenomena can be identified, including aspect. Several languages studied by Hopper use "event" forms to move the narrative along, and "process" forms to describe the internal content of supporting or descriptive material. Arabic follows this pattern as well: the perfective and the imperfective verb stems are used to narrate and describe, respectively. The perfective relates the event or action as a completed whole, while the imperfective provides a picture of event as process, and opens it up for internal viewing.[11]

A typical narrative, the following text contains both perfective and imperfective forms. The choice between them is motivated by status of the events themselves within the narrative: the former represent actions that move the plot forward, the latter descriptive or scene-setting material. Background is given using imperfective forms /tʾul-lu/ *she says to him* and /tšūf/ *she looks*, in both cases preceded by the participle of motion /gayya/ *coming*. The plot of the narrative moves forward through the perfective verb forms, /ʾal-laha/ *he told her*, /miši/, *he left*, and /laʾit/ *she found.*

E6 هي جايّة تقول له على الله تكون القهوة عجبتك. قال لها كويسة، بعد ما مشي جايّة تشوف في الفنجان لقت القهوة زيّ ما هي.

hiyya gayya tʾul-lu ʿal-aḷḷa tkūn il-ʾahwa ʿagabit-ak ʾal-laha kwayyisa. baʿd ma miši gayya tšuf fi l-fingān laʾit il-ʾahwa zayy ma hiyya

she coming she-say-to-him upon-God it-be the-coffee pleased-it-you. said-he-to-her good. after left-he coming she-look in the-cup found-she the-coffee like it

She comes and tells him, I hope [to God] you liked the coffee. He told her, [it was] good. After he left, she's coming to look at the coffee cup, she found the coffee as it [was before].

---

[11]Hopper's analysis suggests that he would see the historical development of the Arabic perfective and imperfective as, in part, a natural consequence of this discourse universal. Arabic features such as word order and the suffixed and prefixed forms of the verb stems seem to fit his framework.

The next passage, from Morocco, shows similar use of the verb forms. The only event that belongs to the plot here is the king's setting up a private room for his only daughter, /dār-lha/ *he made for her.* The background description of the room itself is carried out using imperfective verb forms, /mā txrəžš/, *she doesn't go out*, /mā tdxəlš/, *she doesn't come in*, /makatnūḍš/ *she doesn't get up*.

M11 بّاها ملك سلطان وناض دار لها البيت ديالها بوحدها بالخدّامة، ما تخرجش ما تدخلش. ما كتنوضش من الدار، گاع ما كتخرج برّا.

bb^wāha malik səlṭān w nāḍ dār-lha l-bīt dyālha b^w-uḥdha b-l-xəddāma, mā txrəžš mā tdxəlš. mā katnuḍš mən d-dār, gaʿ mā katxrəž bərra

father-her king sultan and got-up-he made-he-for-her the-room gen-hers by-self-her with-the-servants, neg she-go-out neg she-go-in. neg indic-she-gets-up from the-house, at-all neg she-go-out outside

Her father [was] a king, and he up and made her her own room all by herself, with servants, she wouldn't go out or in. She doesn't leave the house, doesn't go out at all.

This next excerpt shows more of the story's plot, and most of the verbs are perfective. The imperfective verb, /tatbāt/ *she spends the night* stands out as a description tangential to the main plot events:

M11 فين هي مسكينة ملّي مشاوا عليها بالطريق وتتبات برّا ما نعستش نعست ملّي دخلت الدار نعست.

fīn hiyya məskīna məlli mšāw ʿlīha bə-ṭ-ṭrīq w tatbāt bərra mā naʿsatš, naʿsat məlli dəxlat d-dār naʿsat

where she poor when left-they on-her in-the-road and indic-she-spends-the-night outside neg slept-she slept-she when entered-she the-house slept-she

Where is she, poor thing? When they left her on the road, and she was spending the night outside, she didn't sleep. She went to sleep when she entered the house, she went to sleep.

The choice of verb form in narrative, then, has at least as much to do with aspect as with tense or time reference. The descriptive, scene-setting events and states reported with the imperfective in these passages are not unimportant to the narrative, just to the forward motion of its basic plot. Indeed, the background descriptions are what make the narrative vivid; without them, there would be a plot but no story.

Alternating between perfective and imperfective forms can have other uses as well. In the following text, a Kuwaiti match-maker describes her work. She has been relating the process of taking a man to see a prospective bride. She uses the perfective aspect to summarize the events she narrated in the previous section, presenting these events as points along a time line, seen externally. Returning to the imperfective opens up the internal description of an action, permitting the speaker to describe events as processes, rather than as one-time events.

K2 تسألَه، گعدنا وسألها وسألتَه، سلام، مع السلامة، طلعنا، طلعنا، أنا طبعاً أنا اسأل الولد بالسيّارة، اگول لَه هه، ش عجبتك البنية وليدي ولاّ ما عجبتك؟

tisʾəḷa, gaʿədna, w saʾalha w saʾəlta, salām, maʿ s-salāma, ṭalaʿna, ṭalaʿna. ʾāna ṭabʿan ʾāna ʾasʾal il-walad bi-s-sayyāra, ʾagūl la ha, š ʿəjibtak lə-bnayya wlīdi wəlla mā ʿəjibtak?

she-asks-him, sat-we, and asked-he-her and asked-she-him, bye, good-bye, left-we left-we I of-course I I-ask the-boy in-the-car, I-say-to-him, hm, ques pleased-she-you little-son-my or neg pleased-she-you?

She asks him, we sat, and he asked her and she asked him, good-bye, good-bye we went out, we went out, I of course I ask the boy in the car, I say to him, Well, did you like the girl my son or did you not like the girl?

The following Egyptian narrative contains a background description involving three verbs: /biyiʾfiz/ *he jumps*, /nisi/ *he forgot* and /yiliff/ *he would run around*, all in parallel syntactic construction, and all taking place in immediate succession, and yet they alternate between perfective and imperfective. Particularly surprising is the use of the perfective /nisi/ *he forgot* in between two imperfective verbs. This may be a consequence of the interaction of formal and lexical aspect, in that the imperfective /byinsa/ *he forgets* can only give a habitual reading, whereas the context clearly calls for what Eisele (1990b) calls an "event form." Here, the perfective /nisi/ *he forgot* must be used to give the force of an event, emphasizing the momentary lapse of consciousness.

E9 فلقيت لك أخويا احمد دا أوّل الأهلي ما حطّ جون بيقفز في السقف
ونسي نفسه ويلفّ في الصالة
fa-la'ēt lak axūya 'aḥmad da 'awwal il-'ahli ma ḥaṭṭ gōn biyi'fiz fi s-sa'f w nisi nafsu w yiliff fi ṣ-ṣāla
so-found-I for-you brother-my Ahmad that soon the-Ahli as put-he goal indic-he-jumps in the-roof and forgot-he himself and he-run in the-parlor
Then I found my brother Ahmad, as soon as the Ahli scored a goal, jumps to the ceiling and forgot himself and [goes] running around the room

The next passage contains a Syrian's description of a year of living in the United States. The events all took place in the past, yet they are described here using imperfective forms, because they are viewed and presented by the speaker as habitual or recurring actions. Conversely, the use of the perfective here, as for example /kānu ʿam bimaššu klābon/ *they were walking their dogs*, would indicate that the action occurred only once, for /ʿam/ cannot mark habitual action. Context dictates a past-time reference for these events, because the speaker was no longer residing in the U.S. at the time of the interview, and so these events could not have been occurring in a (then-)present time frame.

S5 عم بقِللك هولي يكونوا عم بيمشّوا كلابن، يكونوا عم بيتمشّوا
بالشارع، يدقّوا الباب عليّ ويقولوا لي عندك مانع نشرب قهوة؟
ʿam ba'il-lik, hōle ykūnu ʿam bimaššu klābon, ykūnu ʿam bitmaššu bi-š-šāriʿ, yidi''u l-bāb ʿaleyy w y'ūlū-li ʿandik māniʿ nišrab 'ahwe?
prog indic-I-say-to-you those they-be prog indic-they-walk dogs-their, they-be prog indic-they-walk in-the-street they-knock the-door at-me
I'm telling you, they would be walking their dogs, they would be strolling in the street, they'd knock at my door and say to me, Do you have any objection to us having a cup of coffee?

However, foregrounding and backgrounding do not explain all of the verb form usages in narrative texts. Two other patterns of usage may be detected in spoken Arabic narratives. One is the use of certain verbs, mainly verbs of motion, to give narrative texts aspectual contour, and the other involves the use of imperfective and participle forms in special constructions to highlight sudden events. Both of these constructions contour the sequencing of events, indicating a sudden or important event. The use of the participle in these contexts bears striking parallel to Li, Thompson and Thompson's function of the perfect in Chinese to signal the next event in a narrative (see 6.4).

6.5.2 Aspect and Narrative Contour

Discourse foregrounding and backgrounding help explain the choice of aspectual forms in narrative. In addition, a group of verbs consisting of certain verbs of motion seem to play a role in highlighting narrative events. Al-Najjar 1984 examines some of these verbs at length in his study of aspect in Kuwaiti. He calls these verbs "aspectual," and so they are, but theirs is lexical aspect. Since they seem as a group to mark the twists and turns of narrative events, I will tentatively call their function "narrative contour." Some of these verbs seem to allow verb phrases to combine two lexical aspects, punctual and stative/progressive, for certain narrative purposes.

Speakers use this tool in two ways. Some of these verbs control the narrative "dimension" of actions, to add some highlight to a backgrounded action or event, or to add a stative or progressive dimension to a foregrounded event. Another function is to give contour to the narrative as a whole, by drawing the attention of the listener to the next in a series of foregrounded events.[12] The most commonly occurring "contouring" verbs in my data are listed in Table 6-3. This partial listing should suffice to give a general idea of this proposed group, which contains striking semantic parallels across dialects. Even where individual lexical items differ, their semantic fields correspond (e.g., *to get up,* Moroccan /nāḍ/ and Egyptian and Syrian /ʾām/).

Syntactically, these verbs exhibit unique behavior in that they may be followed by non-embedded (modally or temporally) verbs in

---

[12]Palva (1991) and Caubet (1995) have studied uses of the verb /ža/ *to come* in Jordanian and Moroccan dialect narratives respectively, analyzing the narrative functions of this particular verb.

asyndetic construction. Mitchell and El-Hassan dismiss this feature as simple coordination (1994:113); while this may be true, the fact remains that no other verbs may be coordinated asyndetically in this manner.

Table 6-3: Narrative Contour Verbs

Narrative Contour Verbs				
	Moroccan	Egyptian	Syrian	Kuwaiti
go: next action	mša	rāḥ	rāḥ	rāḥ
come: next action	ža	ga	ʾiža	ya
get up: new or sudden action	nāḍ	ʾām	ʾām	gām
sit down, continue: action verbs	bqa	ʾaʿad	ʾaʿad	gaʿad
complete: state/ motion verbs	təmm	tann	tamm	tamm
return: resume previous action	ʿāwəd	rigiʿ	rižiʿ ʿād	rijaʿ

Verbs meaning *to go* combine the idea of physical motion, the act of going somewhere, with the end result, expressed by the following (often) perfective verb. The asyndetic coordination in this case allows the different lexical aspects to color or contour each other so that the motion and the end result are conveyed together as a whole, seen from both perspectives at once.

M6 غادي نمشي نجيب غير الگارّو ونجي
ġādi nəmši nžīb ġīr l-garru w nži
fut I-go I-bring only the-cigarettes and I-come
I'm just going to go and get cigarettes and come back

M9 مشى شرى لها مسكين العطور
mša šrā-lha mskīn l-ʿṭūr
went-he bought-he-for-her dear the-incense
He went and bought her, the dear, incense

E1 راحت جابت الموف
rāḥit gābit il-mōv
went-she got-she the-mauve
She went and got the mauve

K3 راحوا چذّبوها
rāḥaw čaḏḏabūha
went-they made-a-liar-they-her
They went and made her out to be a liar

The verb *to come* is used similarly in the dialects, and differs from *to go* in physical or psychological perspective, depending on where the speaker locates himself or herself with respect to the actions involved.

Subsequent actions in narrative, and particularly sudden or surprising ones, are often introduced by verbs whose lexical meaning is *to get up, stand up*: Moroccan /nāḍ/, Egyptian and Syrian /ʾām/, and Kuwaiti /gām/, as these examples show:[13]

M11 واحد الراجل عنده المرا تتولد غير البنات، ما عندهاش الولد. ناض
گال ليها أنا خصني الولد. ناض تجوّج مرا خرى
wāḥəd r-rāžl ʿndu l-mra tatəwləd ġi[r] l-bnāt, mā ʿndhāš l-wəld. nāḍ gāl-līha ʾāna xəṣṣni l-wəld. nāḍ tžəwwəž mra x^wra
one the-man at-him the-wife indic-she-bears only the-girls neg at-her the-son. got-up-he said-he-to-her I necessary-for-me the-son. got-up-he married-he wife another

---

[13]This narrative use of /gām/ in Kuwaiti differs slightly from another use of this verb as a temporal verb, discussed in Chapter 7. In the latter, /gām/ indicates the onset of an action or a change of state, and is followed by an imperfective. In narrative usage, /gām/ signals subsequent action and may be followed by a perfective verb, or a participle in some dialects.

[There was] a man who had a wife who bore only daughters, she had no son. He told her, I need [a] son. He up and married another woman.

S4 امّه مصرية، وقامت راحت خطبت له بنت اخوها
ʾəmmu məṣriyye, w ʾāmit rāḥit xaṭbit-lu bint axū[h]a
mother-his Egyptian, and got-up-she went-she arranged-marriage-she-for-him daughter of-her-brother
His mother is Egyptian, and she up (and) went (and) got him engaged to her niece

K3 گامت سعاد گالت اعطيچ المية واربعين
gāmat suʿād gālat aʿaṭīč lə-mya w arbaʿīn
got-up-she Suʿād said-she I-give-you the-hundred and forty
Suʿād up and said, I'll give you the hundred and forty

These verbs also function as verbs of beginning (see further7.2).

Verbs meaning *to sit down* combine with following imperfectives (of action verbs only, not stative or motion verbs) to lend continuous or progressive aktionsart to an action. In Kuwaiti, the participle of this verb functions as a progressive marker for imperfective verbs (8.3.3).

The verb /tamm/ *to complete* occurs in all dialect regions. Harrell notes that /tamm/ (originally, *to complete*) in Moroccan is used with participles of motion (1962:184).[14] If his definition is expanded to include stative participles, it can apply to Egyptian and Syrian as well. Harrell does not give a meaning for /tamm/, noting that it adds "tense" to the following participle. His description can be refined: as a narrative contour verb, /tamm/ allows the combination of completed or punctual aspect and the continuous aktionsart of the following participle to give both a sense of the duration of a state or translocation and its completion up to a certain (often implied) point in time, as these examples show:

M7 تمّيت جاي
təmmīt žāy
continued-I coming-ms
I continued walking (coming)

---

[14]Harrell's counterexample of /tamm/ followed by a perfective is arguably a misinterpretation: reading /tamm mhuwwed/ for Harrell's /tamm huwwed/ *he went down* (1962:184), all attested examples contain participles.

E5 تمّيت رايح
tammēt rāyiḥ
remained-I going-ms
I kept going

S1 صار ريمي، ما عادإلي قلب رحت، ما عم بمشي، من يومها تمّيت قاعدة
ṣār rīmi, mā ʿād ʾili ʾalb riḥət – mā ʿam bimši – min yōm[h]a tammēt ʾāʿde
became-it Rimi, neg remained-it to-me heart went-I – neg prog-I-walk – from day-it continued-I sitting
"Rimi" came on, I no longer had the heart to go–I'm not walking–from that day, I've remained sitting

The Egyptian pseudo-verb /tann/ probably derives from this verb. Badawi and Hinds note that /tann/ signals "the continuousness or habitualness of an action or state" or "the immediate succession of one action or state to another" (1986:139), and give its truncated conjugation forms which show a partial loss of subject agreement and acquisition of the logical subject as an object. Their examples include the following pair, both of which show the combination of continuousness with the perfectivity of completion. Here, the implied end or completion points are not temoral but physical: the interior of a structure and the arrival at the company, respectively.

E تنّي داخل
tann-i dāxil
further and further in I went

E شافوا الجرنال وتنّهم طايرين ع الشركة
šāfu g-gurnāl wi tann-u-hum ṭayrīn ʿa š-širka
they saw the newspaper and rushed straight off to the company

Kuwaiti /tamm/ seems to focus on the second meaning that Badawi and Hinds give for /tann/, the immediate succession of events (a function that all narrative contour verbs share, but in different senses). In my Kuwaiti data, /tamm/ occurs only in the speech of one elderly woman, who uses it with a following perfective, as if to signal a logically subsequent event, or movement forward chronologically and logically. In the first example, the speaker has been describing a series of meetings with an acquaintance of hers. After he got married:

K3 تمّيت غطّيت سنة بعد ، إلاّ ملاگيني : هه شلونچ ام محمد
tammēt ġaṭṭēt sina baʿd, ʾilla mlāgīni: hah, šlōnič umm mḥammad
remained-I covered-I year then suddenly meeting-me hey, how-you Umm Mḥammad?
I passed another year, there he is meeting me, [saying] Hey, how are you Umm Muhammad?

In the next passage, part of a Kuwaiti "Romeo and Juliette" story, the parents have prevented the girl and her beloved from marrying. The next event is:

K3 البنت تحبّه، تمّت طاحت مريضة
əl-bint tḥibba, tammat ṭāḥat marīḏ̣a
the-girl she-loves-him, completed-she fell-she sick
The girl is in love with him, she fell sick

Verbs meaning *to return, resume* signal either a narrative return to or the resumption of a previously mentioned action, with the effect of bringing a section of narrative "full circle." The first example shows the use of Moroccan /ʿāwed/ *to return* to indicate the close of a circular series of events (example from Harrell 1962:184-5):

M فوقما كيجي للسوق كيجي يسلّم علي ويمشي يتقضّى حاجة ويعاود يجي يشوفني
fūq-əmma kayži lə-s-sūq, kayži ysəlləm ʿlīya w ymši itqəḍḍa ḥāža wə ʿāwəd yži yšūfni
when indic-he-comes to-the-market, indic-he-comes he-greet on-me and he-go he-shop thing and return-he he-come he-see-me
Every time he comes to the market, he comes to greet me and [then] goes shopping and [then] comes to see me again

The following Syrian passage demonstrates the use of /ʿād/ *to return* to mark a return to a previous action. Here the speaker describes a rather involved process of renting a house in the United States, a process that includes her landlady acquiring the approval of the neighbors. The use of /ʿādit/ *she went back* followed by perfective /ʾajjaritna/ *she rented to us* returns the narrative explanation to the point of origin and closes the narrative circle, signalling the end of this part of the narrative.

S5 أجّرتنا البيت لأنّ عن طريق عميد كلية العمارة أجرتنا اياه. ومن بعد ما بعتت رسالة لكل الجيران عم تشرح لن مين نحن واشّو وضعنا اشّو شغل جوزي واشّو نحن بالواحد ... يعني كاتبة الن تفاصيل عنّا طويلة عريضة لأنَ تركت النا رسالة بالبيت منشان نقرا اللي باعتّن للجيران. بقى من وقت الـ وصلنا – مو باعتة للجيران هالرسالة؟– ووافقوا انّه تأجّرنا البيت، **عادت أجّرتنا** البيت.

ʾajjaritna l-bēt laʾinnə ʿan ṭarīʾ ʿamīd killiyit il-ʿamāra ʾajjaritna yyā. w mən baʿd ma baʿatit risāle la-kill ij-jīrān ʿam tišraḥ-lon mīnon niḥna w ʾeššu waḍəʿna ʾeššu šuġl jōzi w ʾeššu niḥna bi-l-wāḥid ... yaʿni kātibt-əlon tafāṣīl ʿanna ṭawīle ʿarīḍa laʾinni tarkit-əlna risāle bi-l-bēt mišān niʾra lli bāʿitton li-j-jīrān. baʾa min waʾt il wṣəlna, -- mū bāʿte li-j-jīrān ha r-risāle? -- w wāfaʾu innu tʾajjirna l-bēt, **ʿādit ajjaritna** l-bēt

She rented us the house (because) through the Dean of the School of Architecture she rented it to us. After she sent a letter to all the neighbors explaining to them who we were and what our situation was and what my husband's job was and what we were, each and every one ... She had written to them in great detail, because she left us a letter in the house so that we could read what she sent to the neighbors. So as soon as we arrived–hadn't she sent that letter to the neighbors?–and they approved her renting us the house, she ***[went back and] rented*** *us the house.*

The next passage shows Syrian /biržaʿu/ (lit., *they return*) used in the same way. Here, the family of a young person who gets married without their blessing will eventually go back and make up.

S2 بدّن يزعلوا فترة، اذا زعلوا بدّن يرضوا غصباً عنّن لأنّ بنتن أو ابنن ما فيّن يتخلّوا عنّن يعني. ايه. بيرجعوا بيتراضوا متل ما كانوا

biddon yizʿalu fatra, ʾiza ziʿlu biddon yirḍu ġaṣban ʿannon laʾann binton ʾaw ibnon mā fī[h]on yitxallu ʿannon yaʿni. ʾēh. biržaʿu byitrāḍu mitil ma kānu

want-they they-get-angry period, if got-angry-they want-they they-acquiesce in-spite of-them because daughter-their or son-their neg able-they they-abandon them that-is. yeah. indic-they-return indic-they-reconcile-with-each-other like were-they

They will get angry for a while, if they get angry they will acquiesce in spite of themselves because [it's] their daughter or son, and they can't abandon them. They go back and all make up with each other just like they were before.

The striking parallels in meanings and functions of these verbs across dialects suggest that verbal narrative devices in spoken Arabic warrant further comparative attention.

6.5.3 *Suddenly, all of a sudden* with Participle

Most of these dialects (I lack evidence for Moroccan) make use of participles in narrative in similar ways, preceded by a verb of motion and indicating a next event. This usage of the perfect aspect coincides with the description of one the functions of the Chinese perfect by Li, Thompson, and Thompson: to signal "what happens next, this has just happened/is about to happen" (1982:36). This function explains the use of the aspectual nature of the participle to highlight sudden or important plot events.

Egyptian favors the verbs /rāḥ/ *to go* and /ʾām/ *to get up* with the participle. In this passage, from a film plot narrative, the villain /ʾām ḥāṭiṭ/ *up and put* his briefcase, an act intended to confuse the heroine:

E6 تاني يوم جه الصبح، ما كانتش هي في المكتب. قام حاطط لها شنطة
tāni yōm geh ṣ-ṣubḥ, mā kanitš hiyya fi-l-maktab. ʾām ḥāṭiṭ laha šanṭa
second day came-he the-morning neg was-she she in the-office. got-up-he having put for-her briefcase
The next day he came in the morning, she wasn't in the office. He (up and) put a briefcase for her [to find]

The next passage shows the function of /rāḥ/ with a following participle to indicate subsequent action. When the captain of the ship tells the mate to *stop* /waʾʾaf/ the ship, the narrator says, /ruḥna muwạʾʾafīn/ *[and so] we went and stopped* (Behnstedt 1980:42, translation mine):

E قال: وقّف الفلوكة! رحنا موقفين
ʾāl: waʾʾaf il-filūka! ruḥna muwaʾʾafīn
said-he: stop the-boat! went-we having-stopped-p
He said, Stop the boat! So we went and stopped

Several examples of /yi'ūm/ with participle occur in my Syrian data, among them:

S1 حمل حاله وراح. ومن ورشة لورشة، وكل ما شاف صاحب المحلّ الورقة يقوم كاعره

ḥamal ḥālu w rāḥ. w min warše la-warše, w kill ma šāf ṣāḥib il-maḥall il-wara'a y'ūm kā'ru

carried-he self-his and went-he. and from shop to-shop, and all that saw-he owner of-the-store the-paper he-get-up having-thrown-out-him

He picked himself up and left. And from shop to shop [he went], every time the store owner saw the paper he would up and throw him out

Kuwaiti narratives often contain /illa/ or/willa/ *suddenly* followed by a participle:

K3 تمّيت غطّيت سنة بعد إلاّ ملاگيني، هه، شلونچ؟

tammēt ġaṭṭēt sina ba'd 'illa mlāgīni, hah šlōnic?

continued-I covered-I year after suddenly having-met-me well how-you?

I then passed a year after that, suddenly he is meeting me:hey, how are you?

K1 وقت المغرب ولاّ انا مستاء

waqt əl-maġərb willa 'āna mistā'

time of-the-sunset suddenly I angry

When it got to be evening, now I'm angry

6.5.4 *Suddenly* with the Imperfective

Finally, the two peripheral dialects use the imperfective in ways that do not seem to be paralleled in the central dialects. Harrell identifies a Moroccan construction he calls a circumstantial clause (/ḥāl/) as a commonly used narrative technique. Structurally, this construction does resemble the circumstantial clause, in that it consists of /w/ followed by a pronoun and an unmarked imperfective; however, the meaning of this construction differs, as it does not denote an event simultaneous to a main verb, but rather a sequential action. Harrell notes that this construction "carries the implication of *thereupon* or *forthwith, suddenly*" (1962:175). The following passage contains an example, /w huwwa yəržaʿ/ *suddenly he returns*:

M6 دازت واحد السيمانا گلس فيها وهو يرجع
dāzt wāḥəd s-simāna gləs fīha w-huwwa yəržaʿ
passed-it one the-week sat-he in-it and-he he-return
A week passed during which he stayed, and suddenly he returns

This unusual use of the imperfective may function as a kind of historical present.

Similarly, in Kuwaiti narratives, the modal /čān/ *had, would* precedes an imperfective to indicate a foregrounded action, sometimes sudden. This device occurs frequently in the narratives of a young male speaker:

K1 يوم كامل وانا على حرگة اعصابي ، وقت المغرب والا انا مستاء .
مرّة واحدة چان يدگّ علَي راشد
yōm kāmil w āna ʿala ḥirgət aʿṣābi, waqt əl-maġərb willa ʾāna mistāʾ. marra wāḥda čān ydəgg ʿalay rāšid
day whole and I on burning of-nerves-my, time of-the-sunset then I angry. time one čān he-rings on-me Rashid
My nerves were on edge [the] entire day. When it got to be evening, now I'm angry. All at once Rashid called/calls me

In other cases, this use of /čān/ with an imperfective looks very much like a kind of historical present, and it will be revisited in that context in section 7.1.

6.6 Summary

This discussion of aspect in spoken Arabic has distinguished between lexical aspect, which refers to semantic features inherent to the meaning(s) of a particular verb, and formal aspect, which is viewed here as being grammaticalized in Arabic in the morphological forms perfective, imperfective, and participle.

Previous studies of lexical aspect have classified verbs in a number of categories according to the meanings of the morphological forms, resulting in a complex representation of the interaction of formal and lexical aspectual meaning. The aspectual meanings of the participle present a special problem in Arabic, since some participles carry perfect aspect (a relevant, resultant state) while others give a stative or progressive aktionsart, resembling an imperfective aspect. This problem is solved by distinguishing between telic and atelic lexical meanings, resulting in a simplified prediction of participial meaning. Telic verbs have perfect aspect, and atelic verbs of motion and stative verbs give rise to progressive interpretation. Atelic action verbs cannot be used in participial form.

Formal aspect, following Comrie (1976) and others, is defined as a way of describing the internal constituency of an action or event. The three verb stems, perfective, imperfective, and participle, correspond to the three major cross-linguistic types of formal aspect in language: perfective, imperfective, and perfect. The usage of the participle across dialect regions corresponds closely to descriptions of perfect aspect in other languages, among them Chinese. Functions of the perfect in both Arabic and Chinese include indicating a change of perception, correcting a wrong assumption, and signalling sudden or important events in a narrative (Li, Thompson, and Thompson 1982).

I have argued here for the primacy of aspect to the verbal system of spoken Arabic, especially in the choice of verb forms in narrative contexts. As a means of representation, aspect is controlled by the speaker, who chooses aspectual representation according to his or her perspective of an action or event. In narrative contexts, Arabic speakers consistently choose aspectual representation over external (deictic) temporal representation.

A certain core group of verbs of motion, parallel across dialects, plays important roles in narrative texts, signalling subsequent or immediately successive action, the ordering of events, the beginning and final actions in a logical series, and the combination of lexical aspects in a single action. Speakers of all dialect regions employ narrative contour verbs in strikingly similar fashion to give aspectual depth to narratives.

These conclusions are not meant to deny a role for time reference in the verb system of spoken Arabic, the topic of the next chapter.

7 Tense and Time Reference

7.0 Introduction

After years of debate over the temporal or aspectual nature of Arabic verbs, the trend in most recent studies has been to view the verbal system of spoken Arabic as combining aspect and time reference (Eisele 1988, Ingham 1994). Chapter 6 presented evidence supporting the centrality of aspect to the verbal system of spoken Arabic . If the morphological forms of the verb are aspectual and temporal, as has been argued, what role does time reference play? This chapter will examine mechanisms through which time reference is established in the four dialects.

Following Eisele, a distinction will be made here between the terms tense and time reference (1988:49). Tense refers to morphological verb forms, and time reference to the role of these forms (and other sentence elements) in establishing the location in time of actions, events and states with respect to the reference time. In other words, the Arabic perfective and imperfective represent morphological categories that interact with other grammatical features to produce time reference. Time reference is understood in this study to be a feature of the sentence as a whole, and even beyond the bounds of the sentence, of the discourse unit.[1] Time reference may be determined by a number of different sentential and contextual means, including verbs, clausal structure, discourse context, and, in some dialects, certain non-deictic adverbs.

Most previous studies of Arabic verbal systems have aimed to establish the basic or context-independent meaning of verb forms, as opposed to context-specific meaning. Full investigation has yet to be made of the use and meaning of verbs in narrative and conversational contexts. The goal here is to describe naturally occurring speech patterns, with particular attention to narrative contexts.

Eisele's study of tense, aspect and time reference in Cairene Arabic (1988, 1990a) represents the first serious attempt to define the

[1] The term 'discourse unit' has yet to be defined in terms of length or composition, but it has been shown to exist by studies of definiteness and referentiality (see e.g. Wald 1983, Khan 1988).

relationship between tense and aspect in spoken Egyptian Arabic. His analysis of the context-independent meaning of the verb forms in Egyptian Arabic forms concludes that tense forms in Cairene Arabic have "two primary meanings ... time reference and aspect" (1990a:190). Eisele characterizes the verbal system of Cairene as a past/non-past dichotomy of the morphological tenses, a framework taken as the point of departure here. However, this chapter will expand his context-independent framework to include context-dependent tense as well.

It is maintained here that Comrie's (1976:80) assessment of Classical Arabic, that the perfective and imperfective represent relative past and relative non-past respectively, holds true for the dialects as well. Two mechanisms can shift relative time reference from the moment of speaking to another point, past or future: embedding, which shifts the reference point to the main clause, and tense neutralization, a discourse mechanism. These two mechanisms allow aspect to play a greater role than time reference in the choice of verb form in many contexts. In addition, a special class of verbs called here temporal verbs has as its primary function the establishment of time reference. Finally, it will be argued that some of the confusion over the interpretation of the meaning of the participle arises from the attempt to associate time reference with it. As Holes notes, the participle is a tenseless form that does not signal any particular time reference (1990:189).

7.1 Relative Time Reference in Arabic

The Arabic tense system is inherently tied to context. Cowell (1964:340) and Mitchell and El-Hassan (1994:65) define main clause time reference as being relative to the moment of speaking. In fact, it can be argued that this "default" reference of the moment of speech is grammaticalized in Arabic, because time reference is not marked in copulative *to be* (also called equational) sentences unless it is past or future. In the following sentences, the absence of a tensed form indicates that the time reference is understood to be the moment of speech.

M6 هادي نكتة عليه هو
hādi nukta ʿlīh huwwa
this joke about-him he
This is a joke about him

E1 لا مش قديم لإن الموديل بتاعه حلو قوي
la' miš 'adīm li'inn il-mōdēl bitā'u ḥilw 'awi
no neg old because the-style of-it pretty very
No it [the dress] is not old because its style is very pretty

S2 حياتن غير شي
ḥayāton ġēr ši
life-their another thing
Their life is something else!

K4 اسم الله عليكم — انتو زينين وهي زينة
'ism aḷḷa 'alēkum -- 'intu zēnīn w hiya zēna
name-of-God upon-you -- you good and she good
God protect you--you are good and she is good

The perfective and imperfective also locate an action relative to the moment of speech, as past and non-past, respectively. However, this point of reference may be overridden or shifted by grammatical processes or discourse contexts. These processes and contexts are the subject of the following sections.

7.1.1 Adverbs and Relative Time Reference

In the eastern dialects, the temporal reference point may be shifted from the moment of speech to a past or future point by means of adverbs. Evidence from Kuwaiti in particular indicates that non-deictic adverbs can collocate with imperfective verb forms to establish past time reference. In the first example, the adverb /'awwal/ *in the old days* shifts the reference point of the verb /'axāf/ *I [was] afraid.*

K2 گال لي روحي، اهو صرّح لي يعني، أوّل اخاف انّ اروح وايي
gal-li rūḥi, 'uhuwa ṣarraḥ-li ya'ni, 'awwal 'axāf inn 'arūḥ w 'ayi
said-he-to-me go-f he permitted-he-me that-is first I-am-afraid comp I-go and I-come
He told me, Go, he gave me permission, that is. Before, I [used to be] afraid to come and go

Both grammars of Gulf Arabic agree on this point, and give supporting examples. Johnstone notes that "the imperfect[ive] indicates an incomplete act in the present or future, less frequently an incomplete event in the past" (1967:143). His example:

K يروحون الكويت
yrūḥūn il-kwēt
[they-go the-Kuwait]
They used to go, would go to Kuwait

Holes is even more explicit (1990:26-7):

> It is frequently the case, in certain types of discourse, that an adverbial clause of time is used to set a 'past' time frame for the main clause ... In such cases, the main clause verbs do not need to be marked for past time.

Holes identifies this mechanism as narrative-specific; however, the narrative context may be quite limited in scope, since time reference is easily "retrieved" by native speakers from a number of dialects. Egyptian and Syrian speakers easily accept a past time reference for sentences like the immediately preceding Kuwaiti one. A Syrian informant judged the following elicited sentence acceptable:

S3 ايام زمان الناس بتزور بعضها
ʾayyām zamān in-nās bitzūr baʿḍ[h]a
days of-(old)-time the-people indic-she-visit each-other
In the old days, people [would] visit each other

Mitchell and El-Hassan cite an example from Jordan containing imperfectives /byšraḥ/ *he explains* and /byaʿṭi/ *he gives* referring to past events (1994:66).

J تصوّر ... إنّه المدرّس بيشرح الدرس امبارح وبيعطي امتحان في غيابي
taṣawwar ... ʾinnu(h) il-mudarris byšraḥ id-dars imbāriḥ ʾuw byaʿṭi ṭ-ṭullāb imtiḥān fi ġyābi
[imagine ... comp the-teacher indic-he-explains the-lesson yesterday and indic-he-gives the-students exam in absence-my]
Imagine ... that the teacher explained the lesson yesterday and gave the students an exam in my absence

Moroccan informants, by contrast, categorically reject sentences like:

M *ف القديم عباد الله ناشطين، كيمشيوا ...
* f-l-qdīm ʿbād ḷḷāh nāšṭīn, kaymšīw..
* in-the-old servants of-God active, indic-they-go ...
* *In the old days, people [are] active, they go ...*

However, my Moroccan corpus includes a number of examples of imperfective verbs referring to past events, including imperfective /tatəbqa/ *she remains* in the following, taken from a passage in which the speaker recalls problems with her mother-in-law as a young bride:

M2 ايوا وتتبقى تتخاصم وتتبقى تت —

ʾīwa w tatəbqa tatxāṣm w tatəbqa tat --

well indic-she-remains indic-she-quarrels and indic-she-remains indic-she --

She [would] keep quarrelling, and she [would] keep -- [pause]

The larger context of this utterance marks its past context, and hence interpretation. A possible conclusion would be that Moroccan speakers cannot retrieve past narrative reference as easily as speakers of other dialects. Time reference in discourse will be discussed in 7.1.3; for now, I will note in passing that the two dialects whose aspectual system is arguably the most "conservative," or closest to classical Arabic usage, appear to differ in their acceptance of adverbially marked relative time reference. Moroccan speakers seem to have the most difficulty accepting past readings of imperfective, while Kuwaiti speakers more easily retrieve past time reference for imperfective verbs. This unexpected contrast suggests that aspect and time reference do not necessarily relate reciprocally; that is, a loss or shift in one category does not have automatic implications for the other.

7.1.2 Relative Time Reference in Complement Clauses

While time reference in the main clause is relative to the moment of speaking, time reference in complemental clauses is relative to that of the main clause (cf. Cowell 1964:340). This tense shift represents a syntactic means of transferring the reference point from the moment of utterance to another point in time.[2] The imperfective in this case indicates concurrence with the main verb, while the perfective signals past relative to the main clause, or a pluperfect.

[2]Comrie's (1985) investigation of tense and time reference as a cross-linguistic syntactic category makes a parallel distinction between what he calls "absolute" and "relative" tense. Relative tense has to do with subordinate tense relations, or other means of establishing time reference such as adverbs (1985:63).

Sentential complements show relative tense to the main clause. The following pairs contrast relative past and relative concurrent or future reference (examples elicited):

E,S	قال انه مشغول ʾāl innu mašġūl said-he comp busy *He said that he was busy*	قال انه كان مشغول ʾāl innu kān mašġūl said-he comp was-he busy *He said that he had been busy*
E,L	افتكرته حيروح iftakartu ḥayrūḥ thought-I-him going I *thought he was going to go*	افتكرته راح iftakartu rāḥ thought-I-him went-he *I thought he had gone*
M	عرفت باللي مشى بحاله ʿrəft b-əlli mša b-ḥālu found-out-I comp went-he with-himself *I found out that he had left*	عرفت باللي غادي يمشي بحاله ʿrəft b-əlli ġādi yəmši b-ḥālu found-out-I comp fut-he-leave with-himself *I found out that he was going to leave*

Relative clauses also show relative tense. The first example, from Morocco, shows a relative clause containing a perfective, /žāt/ *she had come*, signalling a pluperfect time reference with respect to the main clause verb phrase, /kānt xārža/ *she was going out*:

M2 كانت خارجة الوالدة اللي جات عندي
kānt xārža l-wālida lli žāt l-ʿndi
was-she going-out the-mother rel came-she at-me
My mother, who had come to my house, was going out

The Egyptian speaker here uses a perfective /ištarētī/ *you bought* in a relative clause that is subordinate to the main verb, /raggaʿti/ *you returned*:

E1 رجّعت الفستان اللي اشتريتيه من سان ميشيل؟
raggaʿti l-fustān illi štarētī min sān mīšēl?
returned-you the-dress which bought-you-it from St. Michel?
Did you take back the dress you had bought from St. Michel?

The next example shows the participle, /bāʿitton/ *she having sent them*, in a relative clause giving a past perfect reading, even though the participle has no time reference of its own (see further 7.3):

S5 كاتبةلن تفاصيل عنا طويلة عريضة لأن تركت لنا رسالة بالبيت مشان نقرا اللي باعتّن للجيران

kātibt-əlon tafāṣīl ʿanna ṭawīle ʿarīḍa laʾinn tarkit-əlna risāle bi-l-bēt mišān niʾra lli bāʿitton li-j-jīrān

having-written-she to-them details about-us long wide because left-she for-us letter in-the-house in-order we-read rel she-having-sent-them to-the-neighbors

She had written to them extensive details about us, [we knew] because she left a letter in the house [we rented from her] so that we could read [the letters] she had sent to the neighbors

In the following Kuwaiti example, the time reference of imperfective /ʾabi/ *I want[ed]* is concurrent with the main verb /gəṭṭni/ *he dropped me off*:

K3 گطني المكان اللي ابي

gaṭṭni il-mekān illi ʾabi

dropped-he-me the-place rel I-want

He dropped me off at the place I wanted

Equational sentences that are subordinate to a main clause are understood to be concurrent with the time frame of that main clause. Circumstantial clauses (Arabic /ḥāl/), which describe the state or circumstance of a sentence agent or topic, are by definition concurrent with the main clause they help modify. Typical examples of circumstantial clauses, marked and subordinated by /w(i)/ *and, when*, include:

E6 وهمّ ماشيين، نسي شنطته معاها

wə humma mašyīn, nisi šanṭitu maʿāha

and they leaving-mp, forgot-he bag-his with-her

When they were leaving, he forgot his briefcase at her place

K2 ثلاثة سنين وانا اركض مع هالمرا بدون شي يعني

t̲alāt̲a snīn w āna arkaḍ maʿ ha l-mara bidūn šay yaʿni

three years and I I-run with this the-woman without thing that-is

Three years I have been running around with this woman without compensation

Other subordinate clauses, too, contain imperfective verbs whose time reference is present relative to the main clause. The following Syrian example shows an adverbial clause with imperfective /iḥki/ *I talk* referring to a past recurring event:

S5 تعلّمت اللغة من جيرانا، قدّ ما احكي معهن واضطرّ احكي معهن تعلّمت منن اللغة

t‘allamt il-luġa min jīrānna, ʾadd mā aḥkī ma‘on w aḍṭarr aḥkī ma‘on t‘allamt minnon il-luġa

learned-I the-language from neighbors-our, amount that I-talk with-them and I-be-forced I-talk with-them learned-I from-them the-language

I learned the language from our neighbors, so much I talked with them and was forced to talk with them I learned the language from them

7.1.3 Discourse Shift of Time Reference: Tense Neutralization

It was noted in 7.1.1 that Holes correlates the syntactic shift of time reference associated with non-deictic adverbs with narrative contexts. Even a sentence-length narrative frame suffices to allow shifts in time reference. Moreover, narrative contexts allow relative past time reference even without adverbs. Comrie calls this process tense neutralization (1985:103-104). Tense neutralization, which occurs in narrative sequencing, provides for one verb to establish a past time reference for subsequent non-past verbs, when the discourse proceeds as an uninterrupted sequence (similar to English speakers' use of the 'historical present'). This discourse mechanism for shifting time reference depends in part on the assumption of a "natural" interpretation of events as being sequential and chronological, and allows aspect to play a primary role in the choice of verb form.

The following examples show that time reference may be established outside the sentence, either by other sentences which are marked for past time, or by the context of the discourse itself. In the following Moroccan passage, the speaker establishes the time frame initially, with the perfective verb /dəwwəzna/ *we passed*, and once having done so, does not need to repeat the past time reference; the remainder of the clauses contain imperfectives or the zero-copula:

M2 دوّزنا الايّام بزّاف ديال الشقا والوليدات ف ضهرنا تنشقاوا بيهم واللي يعاونك ما كاين واللي يحنّ فيك ما كاين واللي -- كلها مشغول وكلها مشطون وانتيا تَتـ -- سمُه -- والضيفان والشقا، الطحين تنغربلوه

dəwwəzna l-iyyām, bəzzāf dyāl š-šqa w l-wlīdāt f ḍharna tanšqāw bihum w lli yʿāwnk ma kāyn w lli yḥənn fīk ma kāyn w lli -- kullha mašġūl w kullha məšṭūn w ntiyya tat -- smu w ḍ-ḍīfān w š-šqa, ṭ-ṭḥīn tanġarblūh

passed-we the-days, much gen the-work and the-kids on back-our indic-we-work with-them and rel he-help-you neg there-is and rel sympathize with-you neg there-is and rel -- all-f busy and all-f preoccupied and you indic - name-its and the-guests and the-work, the-flour we-sift-it

We spent the days, a lot of work with the kids on our backs, we work with them [there], and to help you there's no-one, there's no-one to sympathize and -- everyone's busy, everyone's preoccupied, and you do -- what's it called, and the guests and the work, the flour we sift

The next passage contains a number of imperfective verbs referring to past events, time reference being established by /kān/ *he/it used to*:

E8 وقت الملك فيصل كان ممنوع الدبح برّا المجزر – وتدبحي مش حتاخدي – المجزر يدبح لك، حتاخدي تاخدي. الضحية اللي بتسيبيها سيبيها في المجزر. كان بيغزّي بلاد افريقيا كلّه من اللحوم دي، وبتتنضّف وبتتّلّج

waʾt il-malik fēṣal kān mamnūʿ id-dabḥ barra l-magzar -- wi tidbaḥi miš ḥa-taxdi -- il-magzar yidbaḥ-lik, ḥa-taxdi taxdi. iḍ-ḍaḥiyya lli bitsibīha sibīha fi-l-magzar. kān biyġazzi bilād ʾafriqya kullu min il-luḥūm di, wi btitnaḍḍaf wi btittallig

time of-the-king Faisal was-it forbidden the-slaughtering outside the-slaughterhouse -- and you-slaughter neg fut-you-take -- the-slaughterhouse it-slaughter-for-you, fut-you-take, you-take. the-sacrifice rel indic-you-leave-it leave-f-it in-the-slaughterhouse. was-he indic-he-feeds countries of-Africa all-it from the-meats these, and indic-they-are-cleaned and indic-they-are-frozen

The days of King Faisal it was forbidden to slaughter outside the slaughterhouse--if you slaughter you wouldn't take--the slaughterhouse would slaughter for you, [what] you want to take, take. The sacrifice that you [want to] leave, leave in the slaughterhouse. He used to feed the whole of the African countries from that meat, it would be cleaned and frozen

Finally, a Syrian speaker talks about a period of time she spent in the United States. She establishes past time reference with /inbasaṭət/ *I enjoyed myself*, then describes her activities using the imperfective:

S5 المعشر اللي عاشرته كله من هالمستوى، كتير كويس كتير انبسطت
... كلهن يعزموني نروح شوپنغ وقت اللي يعزموني نروح شوپنغ،
ايشو نقضّي النهار من الصبح للمسا، كتير مننبسط

l-maʿšar illi ʿāšartu killu min ha l-mustawa, ktīr kwayyis, ktīr ənbasaṭət ... killon yiʿzmūni nrūḥ šopping. waʾt illi yiʿzmūni nrūḥ šopping, eššu nʾaḍḍi n-nhār min iṣ-ṣubuḥ la-l-masa, ktīr mnənbəsiṭ

the-group rel lived-among-it all-of-it from this the-level, very good very enjoyed-self-I ... all-them they-invite-me we-go shopping time rel they-invite-me we-go shopping, what we-spend the-day from the-morning until-the-evening very enjoyed-self-I

The group of people I lived among was all of this level--very good, I enjoyed myself a lot ... All of them would invite me to go shopping. When they'd invite me to go shopping we'd spend the whole day from morning until evening, we'd have a great time.

In the final example, from Kuwait, the adverb /ʾawwal/ *in the old days* establishes past time reference:

K3 لا أول ماميش دخاترة، على زماننا، عيايز، اختراعات مال الحريم الكبار

lā, ʾawwal mamīš daxātra ʿala zumānna, ʿayāyiz, xtarāʿāt māl il-ḥarīm il-kubār

no first neg-there-is doctors on time-our, old-women, inventions gen the-women the -old

No, in the old days there [were] no doctors, in our time, [just] old women, the inventions of old women

7.1.4 Kuwaiti /čān/: Historical Present?

The Kuwaiti particle /čān/ (a frozen reflex of the verb /kān/ *to be*) shares with other Peninsular dialects a modal conditional meaning, *would* (see 8.5). In addition, it appears to function in narrative contexts to give a non-present or non-indicative meaning to certain imperfective verbs, especially /yigūl/ *to say*. The following passages contain /čān/ (marked in bold) prefixing an imperfective verb:

K1 مرّة واحدة **چان** يدگّ علَي
marra waḥda **čān** yidigg ʿalay
time one **čān** he-rings on-me
Suddenly he called/calls me

K3 رايحين هناك، عگب ما رحنا **چان** اگول حگّ نورا هه نورا، ما تيوّزين ندى؟
rayḥīn hnāk, ʿugub mā ruḥna **čān** agūl ḥagg Nūra hah Nura, mā tyawwizīn Nada?
going-pl there, after nom went-we, **čān** I-say to Nura, hey, Nura, neg you-marry-off Nada?
*We're going there, after we went, **I say** to Nura, Hey, Nura, aren't you going to marry off Nada?*

K3 تمّيت غطّيت سنة بعد إلاّ ملاگيني، هه شلونچ ام محمد شلونچ شلون بنيّتچ. **چان** يگول طلگتها. ليش؟ گال عندي بعد ولد
tammēt ġaṭṭēt sina baʿd ʾilla mlāgīni, hah šlōnič imm Mḥammad šlōnič šlōn bnayytič. **čān** yigūl ṭallagtha. lēš? gāl ʿindi baʿd walad
finished-I covered-I year after suddenly having-met-me, hey how-you Umm Mḥammad how-you how-girl-your. **čān** he-say divorced-I-her. Why? said-he at-me yet child
I passed a year after that then suddenly he meets me, [saying] 'Hey Umm Muhammad how are you? How's your daughter?' He says, 'I divorced [my wife].' 'Why?' He said, 'And I even have a child by her.'

K3 ريّال عنده مرا حريم ثنتين، واحدة حلوة بس هو ما يحبها، هاذيچ مو حلوة بس يحبها. نزين. گامت المرا هاذي **چان** تگول انا ليش حلوة انا، ما يحبني وهاي الكريهة يحبها

K3 rayyāl ʿinda mara ḥarīm ṯintēn waḥda ḥilwa bass hu mā yḥibbha hāḏīč mū ḥilwa, bass yḥibbha. nzēn. gāmat il-mara hāḏi **čan** tgūl ʾāna lēš ḥilwa ʾāna, mā yḥibbni w hāy l-karīha yḥibbha
man at-him woman women two, one-f pretty-f but he neg he-loves-her, that-f neg pretty-f but he-loves-her. good. got-up-she the-woman this **čān** she-say I why pretty-f I, neg he-loves-me and this the-ugly-f he-loves-her
A man is married, has two wives, one is pretty but he doesn't love her, the other one isn't pretty but he loves her. This woman up and **says** *I, why, I'm pretty, he doesn't love me and that ugly one he loves her?*

Functioning like the colloquial American English expression *I go*, this /čān/ often precedes the verb /gāl/ *to say*, ostensibly to alert the listener to ensuing direct speech central to the narrative. Unlike the conditional use of /čān/ (see 8.7), the mood here is not counterfactual but factual. Clauses introduced with /čān/ seem to play a key role in Kuwaiti narratives, much like clauses using the historical present in English. If indeed these uses of /čān/ indicate the development of a narrative historical present marker, it represents a unique development among these dialects, and bears watching for future developments.

7.2 Temporal Verbs

Chapter 5 proposed a category of temporal verbs, motivated by their semantic function, to mark onset, duration, cessation, or continuity of an action or state, and their behavior as temporal but not modal embedders. Table 7-1 includes a list of common temporal verbs.

Some of the verbs included in this group, such as /nāḍ/ and /gām/ *to get up, begin*, and /ʾaʿad, gaʾad/ *to sit, continue*, also function as narrative contour verbs, verbs that combine time reference with lexical and formal aspect to give an internal contour to narrative actions or events (6.5.2). Temporal verbs combine time reference and lexical aspect, and the two groups show a degree of overlap. However, temporal verbs are not limited to narrative contexts. And while translocative verbs occur asyndetically conjoined to following verbs or participles in narrative contexts without subordinating them, temporal verbs as a group show more complex relationships to the verbs whose time frame they provide. I will examine here certain syntactic characteristics particular to temporal verbs, with the caveat that some of these characteristics pertain only to core members of this set.

Table 7-1: Temporal Verbs

Temporal Verbs				
	start, enter into (state or habit)	begin (action verbs)	no longer	continue, keep doing
Moroccan	ržaʿ wəlla	nāḍ bda	ma bqāš	bqa
Egyptian	baʾa	baʾa ibtada	ma baʾāš	fiḍil ʾaʿad
Syrian	ṣār	ṣār (ballaš)	ma ʿād ma baʾa	ḍall
Kuwaiti	gām (ṣār)	gām bida	ma ʿād	gaʿad

Kuwaiti /ṣār/ occurs in my data with non-verbal predicates only, such as /ṣār-li mašākil/ *I've started to have problems.*

7.2.1 Temporal Verbs in Compound Verb Phrases

Chapter 5 argued that temporal verbs constitute a unique class of verbs because they embed other verbs temporally but not modally. Here the dialects will be compared according to the syntactic restrictions on embedding by temporal verbs in Moroccan, Egyptian, and Syrian (Kuwaiti does not mark syntactic embedding).

Moroccan speakers allow a following indicative with all temporal verbs. Harrell's examples include (1962:181-2):

M بدا كيعوم
bda kayʿūm
[began-he indic-he-swims]
he began/has begun to swim

بقت كتعاينهم
bqat ka-tʿāyenhom
[kept-she indic-she-awaits-them]
she kept waiting for them

Other examples from my data pool:

M10 كيبقى يقول شي كلمة قبيحة
kaybqa yqūl ši kəlma qbīḥa
indic-he-keeps indic-he-says some word ugly
He keeps saying some nasty word

M2 كنت تنخاف منها بزّاف
kunt tanxāf mənha bəzzāf
was-I indic-I-am-afraid from-her a-lot
I was very afraid of her

Syrian speakers have two marked imperfectives at their disposal: an indicative with /b/ and a progressive with /ʿam/ (regional variant /mma/). The latter is commonly used with temporal verbs, as the following examples with /kān/ *to be* and /mā ʿād/ *no longer* show:

S5 هولي يكونوا عم بيمشّوا كلابن يكونوا عم بيتمشّوا بالشارع ...
hōle ykūnu ʿam bimaššu klābon, ykūnu ʿam bitmaššu bi-š-šāriʿ ...
those they-be prog indic-they-walk dogs-their they-be prog indic-they-walk in-the-street ...
They'd be walking their dogs, they'd be walking in the street ...

S2 هلّق صايرين البنات مّا يطنّشوا ما عاد مّا يهمّن
hallaʾ ṣāyrīn l-banāt mma yṭannšu, mā ʿād mma yhimmon
now having-become-p the-girls prog they-ignore no-longer prog it-interests-them
Now, girls have started to ignore [society], they no longer care

However, the unmarked imperfective more commonly marks a past habitual action embedded by /kān/. Cowell (1964:336) and Mitchell and El-Hassan (1994:98) note that the b-imperfective following /kān/ is generally reserved for use in conditional environments (see also 8.4). The following example shows /kān/ with an unmarked imperfective signalling past habitual action:

S2 بالاوّل كانوا يشوفوا اتنين ماشيين مع بعضن يا لطيف جريمة
bi-l-awwal kānu yšūfu tnēn māšyīn maʿ baʿḍon ya laṭīf žarīme
at-the-first were-they they-see two walking with each-other-them O Merciful crime
At first they would see a couple walking together, my God, what a crime

Egyptian shows more restricted use of marked imperfective forms in temporal compound phrases than do Moroccan and Syrian. Cairene speakers allow indicative forms only with /kān/:

E3 كان بيغزّي بلاد افريقيا كلّه من اللحوم دي
kān biyġazzi bilād ʾafriqya kullu min il-luḥūm di
was-he indic-he-feeds countries of-Africa all-it from the-meats this
He used to feed the whole of the African countries from that meat

Other temporal verbs normally embed unmarked imperfectives or, in the case of stative verbs, participles:

En ما بقيتش اعزف عود
ma baʿitš ʾaʿzif ʿūd
no longer-I I-play oud
I no longer play the oud (lute)

En حتفضلي قاعدة هنا لغاية امتى؟
ḥatifḍali ʾaʿda hina li-ġāyit ʾimta?
fut-you-remain-f sitting-f here until when?
How long are you going to remain sitting here?

7.2.2 Topicalization of Temporal Verbs[3]

In some sentences containing /kān/ *to be*, the syntactic position of this verb is difficult to determine. In these cases, /kān/ seems to occupy a syntactic sentence position only tenuously related to the remainder of the main clause.

At times, the subject agreement of /kān/ differs from that of the temporally embedded verb in any obvious way. In the following, the syntactic subject of /kānit/ *she was* refers back to the topic of the previous sentence, the /māšṭa/ *woman who dresses brides for weddings*,

[3]"Topic" as a sentence category is treated at length in Chapter 10.

and is co-referential with the direct object /yāha/ *her*, not the subject of the verb /yijību/ *they bring*.

S4 هالماشـطة هاي مـرا كانت تشـتـغل بالحمـام ... كانت اول يجيبوا لها ياها تحنّي لها اجريها

ha l-māšṭa hāy mara kānit tištiġil bi-l-ḥammām ... kānit ʾawwal yjību-l[h]a yāha tḥannī-l[h]a ijrē[h]a

that-the-dressing-woman this woman was-she she-work in-the-bathhouse ... was-she first they-bring for-her her she-puts-henna-for-her legs-her

This "dressing woman" [was] a woman who used to work in the bathhouse. In the old days they used to bring her to her [the bride] to henna her legs for her

In order to make syntactic sense of this sentence, it is necessary to posit a sentence category that /kān/ can occupy. This position cannot be called auxiliary, because of the discrepancy between the subjects of /kān/ and the subjects of the main verbs in the example cited above. The syntactic role of /kān/ in such sentences may be better analyzed as thematic or topical. The facts that support this analysis include: (a) in these sentences, /kān/ always occupies sentence-initial position, and (b) the subject pronoun of /kān/ in such cases is not coreferent with the main-clause subject. All four dialects all exhibit this use of /kān/.

In this Kuwaiti sentence, the relationship of /kān/ to the rest of the sentence is difficult to explain structurally, since /kān ʾāna/ *it was I* is ungrammatical. Here, /kān ʾawwal/ *it was in the old days* sets the temporal frame for the rest of the passage:

K3 كان أول هني انا اللي اطبخ أنا اللي اربّي العيال وانا اللي اسوّي كل شي

kān ʾawwal hni ʾāna lli ʾaṭbax ʾāna lli ʾarabbi l-ʿyāl w āna lli ʾasawwi kil šay

was-it first here I which I-cook I which I-raise the-kids and I which I-do every thing

It was in the old days here I who cooked, I who raised the kids and I who did everything

While it could be argued that the entire sentence is the syntactic subject of /kān/, this analysis does not satisfactorily explain other examples.

The subject of /kān/ *it was* in the next sentence is not coreferent with either the subject of /ḥatgī-li/ *going to come to me*, or any other sentence constituent. Here /kān/ can only be understood as establishing past time reference outside the clausal boundaries of the rest of the sentence.

E3 كان حتجي لي سكتة قلبية
kān ḥatgī-li sakta ʾalbiyya!
was-3ms fut-3fs-come-to-me stopping heart!
I was going to have a heart attack!

The next Syrian sentence shows similar structure. In Arabic syntax, the main negating particles normally precede the initial verb, but in this sentence, /kān/ *it was* precedes the negative /mā/:

S4 كان ما فيه تفكير متل هلّق
kān mā fī tafkīr mitil hallaʾ
was-it neg there-is thinking like now
There wasn't [the same] thinking as nowadays

This sentence does not represent an isolated instance of such a construction, for Woidich lists similar Egyptian examples (1968:41). Often /kān/ will frame an embedded negative verb phrase to give a habitual reading, which may be related to the topical position of /kān/.

In the following passage, the second occurrence of /kān/ *it was* does not agree with the embedded verb /kaysəyybūh/ *they throw it out.* The most likely referent is the discourse topic, /l-ḥut/ *the fish.*[4]

M10 اللي كيكون فيه الشراوط ما كانش كيعطيه قيمة كان غير كيسيّبوه
lli kaykūn fih š-šrāwaṭ mā kānš kayaʿṭīh qīma kān ġī[r] kaysəyybūh
which indic-it-is in-it rag-like [fins] neg was it-neg indic-he-gives-it value was-3ms only indic-they-leave-it
The [fish] that has rag-like fins, [no one] valued it, they just threw it out

Syrian /ṣār/ can also be topicalized. In the following passage, the subject of /ṣār/ is unclear, but it would be difficult to assign that role to /il-ʿālam/ because the following verb, /itʿawwdu/, shows that

[4]Another problematic use of /kān/ in this sentence is that the singular subject of /ma kanš kayaʿṭih/ *he didn't use to give it* has no clear referent, unless an elided *one* is postulated.

/il-ʿālam/ is plural in this context. Moreover, the perfective verb /itʿawwdu/ *they became accustomed to* cannot belong to the same clause as /ṣār/, which does not embed a perfective verb:

S2 صار شويّ العالم اتعوّدوا انّه يشوفوا اتنين ماشيين مع بعضن
ṣār šwayy il-ʿālam itʿawwdu ʾinnu yšūfu itnēn māšyīn maʿ baʿḍon
became-it a-little the-world got-accustomed-they that they-see two walking-p with each-other
People have gotten a bit used to seeing two people going together

Similarly, in the following, /ṣār/ has no subject, since the main verb /mma yitqaddmu/ *they are progressing* shows a plural subject:

S2 هلّق يعني صار شويّة شويّة مّا يتقدّموا
hallaʾ yaʿni ṣār šwayye šwayye mma yitqaddmu
now that-is became-it little little prog they-progress
Now it started slowly they are progressing

It is difficult to translate the next two examples in a way that reflects their structure. The verb /ṣār/ *to become* occurs three times, and in no case does it agree with the syntactic subject of its sentence. Rather, all three verbs agree syntactically with their topics: in the first sentence, /ṣārit/ refers to a hypothetical girl while /ṣār/ has no clear syntactic referent; in the second example, /biṣīr/ *he becomes* refers to the hypothetical deceased:

S2 هلّق وقت بتكون متعلّمة وكذا وصارت عندها منتوج وبتطلع بتشتغل صار يعني بتلاقي غير مجال انّه تلاقي شريك حياتها المناسب الكويّس
hallaʾ waqt bitkūn mitʿallme w kaza w ṣārit ʿand[h]a mantūž w btiṭlaʿ btištiġil ṣār yaʿni bitlāqi ġēr mažāl innu tlāqī šarīk ḥayāt[h]a il-munāsib il-kwayyis
now time indic-she-is educated-f and so-forth and became-she at-her been-produced and indic-she-goes-out indic-she-works became-it that-is indic-she-finds other area that-it she-find partner of-life-her the-appropriate the-good
Now, when she is educated and so forth and she has come to be productive and she goes out and works, she has come to find other area[s] in which to find her life partner

S2 وقت الـ بيموت، بيصير بيعملوه ملاك
waqt il bimūt, biṣīr byəʿməlū malāk
time rel indic-he-dies, indic-he-becomes indic-they-make-him angel
When he dies, (he becomes) they make him out to be an angel

Kuwaiti /gām/ *to begin*, a semantic equivalent to Syrian /ṣār/, can be topicalized as well. In most Arabic dialects (as in formal Arabic), questions are formed by fronting the interrogative particle. Thus in the following, interrogative /š/ *what* precedes the verb /tsawwi/ *she does.* However, the sentence-initial /gāmat/ *she began* falls outside these normal syntactic parameters, preceding the interrogative:

K3 گامت ش تسوّي، كل يوم تشتري فخوذ لحم
gāmat š tsawwi, kil yōm tištiri fxūḏ laḥam
began-she what she-does, every day she-buys legs of-meat
She began to do what? every day she [would] buy legs of meat

Numerous cases exist in which /kān/, Syrian /ṣār/, and Kuwaiti /gām/ exhibit an unusual relationship to the sentence they modify. It will be argued in Chapter 10 that the sentence position these verbs occupy may be defined as a topic position. Other temporal verbs, meaning *to start/begin* and *to cease/no longer [do]* show interesting cross-dialectal parallels, as the next sections demonstrate.

7.2.3 *To start, begin*: Stative and Non-stative

Most dialects have two sets of verbs that indicate the onset or inception of a state or action with a following imperfective, one group whose literal meaning is *to become*, and another whose meaning is *to begin.* The former set tends to place semantic focus on the change of state or habit, including motion, while the latter signals the onset of an activity. The following pairs demonstrate the use of these verbs.

The first Moroccan example shows /ržaʿ/ *to become* with a verb of motion, emphasizing the state of rushing about, while the second contains /nāḍ/ *to begin*, indicating what the woman started doing next:

M2 ورجعت تتسبق
w rəžʿat tatsbəq
and became-she indic-she-rushes
She started rushing about

M11 ناضت تتسرح ديك المرا

nāḍət tatsraḥ dīk l-mra

got-up-she she-shepherds that woman

That woman began to shepherd [animals]

Examples contrasting Egyptian /baʾa/ *to become* and /ibtada/ *to begin* include the following. In the first, /baʾēt/ *I became* signals entry into a state of confinement, while in the second, /ibtadat/ *it began* indicates the onset of melting (Badawi and Hinds 1986:91, 59):

E بعد الجواز بقيت امنعها من الخروج

baʿd ig-gawāz baʾēt ʾamnaʿ-ha min il-xurūg

[after the-marriage became-I I-forbid-her from the-going-out]

After we got married I did not allow her to go out

E الشمس ابتدت تسيّح الاسفلت

ʾiš-šams ibtadit tisayyaḥ il-ʾasfalt

[the-sun began-it it-melt the-asphalt]

The sun began to melt the asphalt

The Syrian ice-cream joke (cited in full in 1.5) contains both /ṣār/ *to become* and /ballaš/ *to begin.* The former emphasizes a change of expected state, namely, the unexpectedness of eating ice cream with bread, while the latter notes the ensuing action of the waiter:

S2 جاب له صحن بوظة صار ياكله بالخبز. بلّش الگارسون يتضحّك عليه

žāb-lu ṣaḥn būẓa ṣār yāklu bi-l-xubəz. ballaš ig-garsōn yitḍaḥḥak ʿalē

brought-he to-him plate of-ice-cream started-he he-eat-it with-the-bread. began-he the-waiter he-laugh at-him

[The waiter] brought him a plate of ice cream, he started eating it with bread. The waiter began to laugh at him

My Kuwaiti corpus includes only /gām/ *to get up, begin* for both changes of state and the onset of activity (but see Al-Najjar for composed sentences containing /bida/ *to begin*, 1984:30-32). From my data:

K3 لكن أنا دشّني شوية الخراف. گمت انسى

lākin ʾāna daššni šwayya lə-xrāf. gimt ansa

but I entered-it-me a-bit the-senility. began-I I-forget

But senility has set in me a bit. I have started to forget

K2 بس الوقت الحالي هذا الحين گاموا يقررون اهم
bass il-waqt il-ḥāli hāḏa al-ḥīn gāmu yqarrirūn ʾuhuma
but the-time the-present this now got-up-they they-decide they
But at this present time, now, they started deciding themselves

7.2.4 *No longer*: /ma bqaš/, /ma baʾā(š)/, /ma ʿād/

Two verbs designate cessation of a previous progressive or habitual action: /mā bqāš/ and /mā baʾāš/ in Morocco and Egypt (with /mā baʾa/ occurring also in Aleppo and Beirut), and /mā ʿād/ in Syria and Kuwait.

M10 ما بقاوش كيمشيوا
mā bqāwš kaymšīw
neg remained-they-neg indic-they-go
They no longer go

S2 ما عاد عندن شغلة غير خلص، مات
mā ʿād ʿandon šaġle ġēr xalaṣ māt
neg remained at-them occupation except finish died-he
They no longer have any concern save "that's it, he's dead"

The following Moroccan conversation shows perfective /mā bqīnāš/ *we no longer remained* used in a description of habitual annual events. The use of the perfective rather than the imperfective may be due to the focus on the cessation of the habit.

M1,9 —— وف رمضان كيف كتديري معاه؟ —— ف رمضان آوليدي ما بقيناش فيه .. سبحان الله العظيم نقيلوا صايمين وحتى المغرب ونشربوا هاديك الزلافة د الحريرة
--- w f ramḍān kīf katdīri mʿāh? --- f ramḍān ʾā wlīdī mā bqīnāš fīh ... subḥān ḷḷāh l-ʿaḍīm nqāylu ṣāymīn w ḥtta l-maġrəb w nšərbu hadīk z-zlāfa d l-ḥrīra
--- and in Ramadan how indic-you-do with-it? --- in Ramadan O son-my neg remained-we in-it .. praise of-God the-great we-spend-afternoon fasting and til the sunset and we-drink that the-bowl gen the-Harira
--- And in Ramadan what do you do about it [your tobacco habit]? --- In Ramadan, my son, we no longer do it ... Praise God Almighty, we spend the afternoon fasting until sunset, and we drink that bowl of Harira soup

More importantly, the eastern dialects in particular show that /mā ʿād/ is losing its status as independent verb, perhaps on its way to becoming a frozen particle. In third-person contexts, /mā ʿād/ no longer shows agreement with plural subjects, as may be seen in the following, in which /mā ʿād/ is dependent on /yišaʿʿlu/ *they turn on* for subject agreement.

S2 مثلا عنّا وقت مثلا بيموت واحد أهله ما عاد يحضروا افراح ما عاد يشعّلوا التليفزيون ما عاد يسمعوا موسيقى ما عاد يطلعوا مشاوير

masalan ʿanna waqt masalan bimūt wāḥid ʾahlu mā ʿād yiḥḍaru afrāḥ mā ʿād yšaʿʿlu t-tilvizyōn mā ʿād yismaʿu musīqa mā ʿād yiṭlaʿu mšāwīr

for-example at-us time for-example indic-he-dies one family-his neg remained they-attend weddings neg remained they-turn-on the-television neg remained they-hear music neg remained they-go-out outings

For example, in our [village], when someone dies, his family no longer attends weddings, no longer turns on the television, no longer listens to music, no longer goes out [recreationally]

The loss of agreement however is (at this synchronic juncture) partial. A Beiruti informant claims that first and second person subjects require subject agreement, and even in the third person, /mā ʿād/ retains full agreement with its subject if it does not temporally embed another verb, as in the following:

S2 فيه يعني ناس بتفكّر انّه شغلة عادي يعني طبعاً لأنّه تطوّرت العالم ما عادت متل أوّل

fī yaʿni nās bitfakkir ʾinnu šaġle ʿādi yaʿni ṭabʿan laʾannu ttạwwaret il-ʿālam mā ʿādet mitil ʾawwal

there-is that-is people indic-3fs-thinks that-it thing usual that-is of-course because-it developed-3fs the world neg remained-3fs like first

There are people who think that it's a normal thing, of course, because people have changed, they're no longer like before

My Aleppan data show /mā baʿa/ in place of /mā ʿād/. However, unlike the western usage, in which /mā baʾa/ is fully conjugated, Aleppan (and Beiruti) /mā baʿa/ usually occurs as a fixed form that does not show subject agreement (similar to its Damascene counterpart /mā ʿād/). In the following example, /mā baʾa/ does not agree in gender with the following feminine verb /btifriʾ/ *it makes a difference*:

S5 ما بقى بتفرق معي يعني انّي آخد مثلاً كورس تاني
mā baʾa btifriʾ maʿi yaʿni inni ʾāxud kamān masalan kūrs tāni
neg remained-3ms 3fs-differentiates with-me that-is comp-I I-take course for-example another
It no longer made a difference for me to take another course

7.3 The Participle and Time Reference

Analyses of the role of the active participle in the verbal system of spoken Arabic have been troubled by meanings that appear at first to be contradictory: the participle is used in sentences that have past, present, present perfect and future time reference. Harrell says of the active participle in Moroccan that it "functions as a verb in the sense that it takes objects and *indicates various degrees of time* and manner of verbal action" (1962:173, emphasis mine).

In all four dialects investigated here, the active participle is commonly used in past, present and future time contexts. As Eisele notes for Egyptian, logical analysis of the time reference of the participle shows that the participle has no time reference, and that the time reference is supplied by the context, as is the case with non-present uses of the imperfective verb (1990a:206). The time reference of the resultant state expressed by the participle may be indicated in several ways.

The fact that the participle itself has no time reference of its own is demonstrated by the fact that adverbs of all different time frames correlate with it. Eisele has determined that the collocation of various time adverbials with the participle in Cairene Arabic may be explained by the association of the adverbials with the underlying (perfective) event implied by the participle (1990a:204-6). The same analysis applies to the other dialects as well, for all of them allow reference to be made to the implied event underlying the participle. In the following sentences, adverbs /šḥāl hādi/ *for a long time*, /imbāriḥ/ *yesterday*, and /min zamān/ *for a long time* all correlate with the perfective events assumed and subsumed by the participles:

M1 هما واخدينها شحال هادي
huma wāxdīnha šḥāl hādi
they having-taken-mp-it how-long this
They've had it for long time

E2 لسّه شايفاه امبارح
lissa šayfā imbāriḥ
just having-seen-f-him yesterday
I've just seen him yesterday

K4 — سعاد شلونها؟ — بالمستشفى
— ش فيها بعد؟ — وي! منيّمينها من زمان
--- suʿād šlōnha? --- b-il-mustašfa
--- š fīha baʿd? --- wī! mnayymīnha min zamān
--- Suʿād how-she? --- in-the-hospital
--- what in-her then? --- well! having-put-in-bed-her from (long)-time
--- *How is Suad?* --- *In the hospital.*
--- *What's wrong with her then?* --- *Oh! They've had her in bed for a long time*

Moreover, when the resultative state of the participle is not relevant to the moment of speech, past time reference must be specified by /kān/, as these examples show:

M2 كانت خارجة الوالدة اللي جات عندي
M2 kānt xārja l-wālida lli žāt ʿndi
was-she leaving-fs the-mother who came-she at-me
My mother, who had come to visit me, was leaving

E3 واللهِ ما كنت متصوّرة دي
waḷḷāhi mā kunt mitṣawwara di
by-God neg was-I having-imagined-f this
By God, I had never imagined this

In contexts whose past time reference has been established, the participle can even express pluperfect time reference. The immediately preceding Egyptian example is translated *had never imagined* (rather than *didn't imagine*) according to its context, the narration of a past event. My corpus contains many examples of pluperfect time reference:

M11 دخل لعند ديك امّه اللي مربياه
dxal l-ʿənd dīk mm^{w}u lli mrəbbyāh
entered-he into that mother-his who having-raised-f-him
He went into her house, the mother who had raised him

Sn اخدتها امبارح —. صار لي جمعة شايفها
ʾaxadt[h]a mbāriḥ -- ṣār-li žimʿa šāyif[h]a
took-I-it yesterday -- became-it to-me week having-seen-it
I took it yesterday -- I had seen it a week ago

K3 انا ظلموني ... كلّه ببيت امّي ، شارية بيت م.، شاريتَه امّي
ʾāna ḏ̣lamūni ... killa b-bēt ummi, šārya bēt M, šārīta ʾummi
I wronged-they-me all-of-it in-house-of-mother-my having-bought-f house of-M., having-bought-f-it mother-my
They wronged me. All of it was at my mother's house. (She) had bought the house of M., my mother had bought it

The problem of future time reference may be solved in the same way, if, instead of restricting the 'present relevance' of the perfect to a 'past event,' the perfect is defined as having *present relevance to an event* past or future. Since the participle itself carries no specific time reference, the event implied by the participle may be either past or future, correlating respectively with past or future adverbs and other time referents. In the following examples, the adverbs /bukra/ and /ġədda/ *tomorrow* refer to the future time of the perfective event of setting off or leaving, and obviously not to the duration of the trip.

E5 همّ ماشيين بكرة
humma mašyīn bukra
they having-left tomorrow
They're leaving tomorrow

M1 غدّا انا مسافر
ġədda ʾāna msāfər
tomorrow I travelling
Tomorrow, I'm leaving

Both of these examples may also be translated as ... *will have left*. In all dialects, certain participles of motion commonly refer to future actions such as *leaving*, *coming*, and *going*.

The use of non-motion participles to refer to the future appears to be limited to contexts of swearing an oath, and in particular negative oaths, as the following examples suggest. These participial oaths emphasize that the event to which they refer will not take place under any circumstance, strongly negating any possible resultant state from such an occurrence. It is in part the speech act itself, the act of swearing, that gives rise to the future interpretation of these sentences.[5]

M1 ما واكلش!
mā wāklš
not having-eaten-ms
I am not eating! or I will not eat!

M7 وحتّى انا من هاد الكوتشي ما نازلش!
w ḥtta ana mən hād l-kūtši mā nāzilš!
and-even I from this the-carriage not going-down!
I too am not getting/will not get out of this carriage!

E5 والله مانا واكل!
waḷḷāhi māna wākil!
by-God not-I having eaten
By God, I will not eat!

L والله مانّي طابخة لك شي اليوم
waḷḷa manni ṭābxit-lak ši l-yōm
by-God neg-I having-cooked-for-you thing the-day
By God, I'm not cooking you anything today! (elicited)

K3 چان تگوللي انا بطگچ ؟! ماني طاگتچ بس چذي جدّام عمچ
čan tgul-li ʾāna baṭəggič? mānī ṭāggitič bass čiḏi jiddām ʿammič
would she-say-to-me I fut-I-beat-you? not-I having-beaten-f-you just like-that in-front-of uncle-your
She told me, will I beat you? I won't beat you, just in front of your uncle

The next Kuwaiti example confirms that participles of motion can be used in oaths as well:

[5]This function of the participle in spoken Arabic parallels the use of the perfective in Classical Arabic to deny the occurrence of an event in the future (see Wright 1898ii:2).

K4 شارين شاليه ... ان شا الله تييوننا ... ما حد داخلَه گبلكم

šārīn šālē... nšāḷḷa tyūnna ..mā-ḥad dāxla gabilkum

having-bought-mp chalet ... God-willing you-come-us .. not-one having-entered-ms-it before-you

We've bought a chalet ... hope you'll come visit us ... no one [will] enter it before you

The participle thus constitutes an aspectual verb form that represents a resultant state of a perfective action or event. As Eisele (1990a) suggests, the implied event can be a past or a future one, and thus the resultant state can refer to past, present, or future time relative to the moment of speaking. This time reference, however, is established through the use of adverbs or contextual meaning.

7.4 Summary

While Chapter 6 described the aspectual content of the Arabic morphological verb forms, the perfective, the imperfective, and the participle (perfect), this chapter has explored their role in establishing time reference. Comrie's (1976) assessment of Classical Arabic verb forms as representing relative past and relative non-past applies equally to the verb system of spoken Arabic. The relative nature of time reference in Arabic manifests itself in a number of ways.

Time reference in Arabic is inherently relative to the moment of utterance, so much so that "present tense" requires no verb form at all. Verbless copulative ("equational") sentences rely on the moment of speech to temporally frame their propositions.

However, while the most basic reference point for time reference is the moment of speech, that point may be fairly easily shifted by means of temporal sentence elements, such as adverbs, or by the larger discourse context. Two mechanisms play a role in shifting relative time reference from the moment of speaking to another point, past or future: syntactic embedding, which shifts the temporal reference point to the main clause, and tense neutralization, a discourse mechanism by which a single past time reference may set the narrative frame for an entire passage. These two mechanisms allow aspect to play a greater role than time reference in the choice of verb form in many contexts.

A special class of verbs called here temporal verbs maintain as their primary function the establishment of time reference, especially of non-punctual events and states. These verbs embed other verbs temporally, but not modally (see also 5.2.2). Temporal verbs exhibit striking parallels across all four dialect regions. Finally, the participle itself carries no tense or time reference; rather, its time reference is established through relative tense, speech contexts (especially swearing oaths), adverbs, and temporal verbs.

8 Mood

8.0 Introduction

Palmer defines modality as "the grammaticalization of speakers' (subjective) attitudes and opinions" (1986:16), in other words, the speaker's characterization of the event as possible, desirable, necessary, and so forth.[1] However, while modality refers to a feature often marked on the verb, it "does not relate semantically to the verb alone or primarily, but to the whole sentence" (Palmer 1986:2). In Arabic, as in other languages, mood can be expressed through a number of different means, lexical, morphological, and syntactic. Mitchell and El-Hassan (1994) note a number of sentence elements other than the verb that affect the interpretation of modality in educated spoken Arabic. They provide an extensive study of mood in the educated spoken Arabic of Egypt and the Levant, in which they explore the full range of means through which modality is expressed. What follows here falls far short of such an enterprise; I aim to compare the basic grammatical functions of the imperfective with its various markers across dialect regions. Excluded from this discussion are lexical mood markers such as /lāzim/ *must*, /yimkin/ *may*, and so on, which Mitchell and El-Hassan examine at length. These lexical items contribute to the mood of a sentence by indicating the specific attitude of the speaker, that is, whether he or she presents the event as possible, desirable, necessary, and so forth. What is of concern here is the modal contribution of the morphological form of the verb itself, to the extent that it can be disengaged from lexical mood markers and other sentence elements.

[1]Mood in formal Arabic consists of three forms of the imperfective, called indicative, subjunctive, and jussive. In general, the unmarked imperfective in spoken Arabic combines the functions of the Classical subjunctive and jussive forms (Mitchell and El-Hassan use the term jussive for the unmarked imperfective in their study of mood in educated spoken Arabic, 1994:12-13). Cowell calls the subjunctive and jussive of Classical Arabic "not full-fledged grammatical categories, but only automatic syntactic alternates" (1964:343). That is, in formal Arabic, the choice of mood is often determined by one of several negative, conditional, or nominalizing particles, and not by speaker attitude. Hence, the analysis presented here is an attempt to classify moods of spoken Arabic without reference to formal Arabic.

The number and type of moods that are expressed morphologically (marked on the verb itself) vary from dialect to dialect in the four areas under study here. The imperative has its own morphological inflectional stem, consistent in all dialects. Moroccan, Egyptian, and Syrian all distinguish between the indicative mood, which represents an *actual* event, and the subjunctive, which indicates a *potential* event. Kuwaiti makes no such grammatical distinction, although it does have a particle /čān/ that can indicate non-actuality when used with the imperfective (see 8.5). Table 8-1 summarizes these and other moods, using terminology adapted from Palmer (1986) and Mitchell and El-Hassan (1994).

Table 8-1: Moods in the Dialects

Moods in the Dialects			
Mood	Meaning	Grammatical Marking	Dialects
Indicative	actuality duration	marked imperfective	M, E, S
Subjunctive	possibility desirability	unmarked imperfective	M, E, S
Intentive	intention/will	marked imperfective	S, K
Future	futurity	marked imperfective	M, E, S, K
Imperative	command	imperative stem	M, E, S, K
Conditional, Hypothetical	hypotheticality/ counterfactual	/kān/ or perfective	M, E, S, K
Commissive	oath	perfective, perfect (negated)	M, E, S, K

Also included here is a brief discussion of the marked forms of the imperfective that indicate future time reference. Grammarians of Levantine Arabic in particular decline to classify these markers as future because of the tense implications of that term (see Cowell 1964:322; Mitchell and El-Hassan 1994:13). But according to Lyons, "[f]uturity is never a purely temporal concept" (1977:677), and Bybee, Perkins, and Pagliuca note that, cross-linguistically, "future is less a temporal category and more a category resembling agent-oriented and epistemic modality, with important temporal implications" (1994:280). Palmer cites a number of languages in which the future has a modal sense, and modals are used to indicate future events (1986:217-8).[2] I will thus use the term *future* to refer to a grammatical mood rather than a morphological tense, since Arabic marks the future in the same way it marks other moods.

Mitchell and El-Hassan classify the mood of the perfective as indicative (1994:14), and its unmarked usage is so, but the perfective also has a non-indicative marked use in oaths (in modal terms, *commissives*, Palmer 1986:115) and conditionals, which will be examined in the final sections of this chapter.

8.1 Marked and Unmarked Imperfectives

Moroccan, Egyptian, and Syrian speakers distinguish between marked and unmarked imperfective forms (Table 8-2 lists the main imperfective markers found in the four dialect areas). Marked forms of the imperfective represent indicative and future moods. The morphologically unmarked form of the imperfective serves as a subjunctive mood, with non-indicative, potential, hortative, or optative meaning, and also functions as a subordinate, non-finite verb. In addition, the subjunctive in Moroccan and Egyptian can express polite questions, possibility, and desirability, similar to English modals *would, should, could,* and *might*. The marked imperfective, or indicative, contrasts with the unmarked imperfective, or subjunctive, in both syntactic distribution and modal function.

Syntactically, the unmarked imperfective functions as a non-finite verb in subordinate clauses in all three dialects; the marked imperfective may not assume this function. The following pairs of Moroccan and Egyptian examples contrast grammatical sentences with embedded

---

[2]One such future modal is the imperfective inflection of the energetic mood of Classical Arabic, which generally refers to future actions (Wright 1898ii:24).

unmarked imperfectives on the left and ungrammatical sentences with embedded marked imperfectives on the right (examples elicited):

M1	بغيت نعيّط لفاروق	*بغيت كنعيّط ...
	bġīt nʿayyaṭ l-fārūq	* bġīt ka-nʿayyaṭ ...
	wanted-I I-call to-Faruq	* wanted-I indic-I-call ...
	I wanted to call Faruq	* *I wanted I call ...*
E2	ما قدرتش اخلّص المشاوير	* ما قدرتش باخلّص ...
	ma ʾidirtiš axallaṣ il-mašawīr	* ma ʾidirtiš baxallaṣ ...
	neg was-able-I I-finish the-errands	* neg was-able-I indic-I-finish
	I wasn't able to finish the errands	* *I wasn't able I finish ...*

Table 8-2: Imperfective Markers

Imperfective Markers				
Dialect	Future	Intentional	Indicative	Subjunctive
M	māš(i) ġa(di)	-	ka- ta-	-
E	ḥa-	-	bi- (ʿammāl)	-
S	raḥ	b-	b- (ʿam)	-
K	bi- raḥ	bi-	(gāʿid)	(čān)

The two Moroccan forms reflect northern and southern usage respectively. Indicative forms in parentheses represent progressive markers; Kuwaiti /gāʿid/ (masculine) has feminine and plural forms /gāʿda/ and gāʿdīn/ (see 8.3.2). Kuwaiti /čān/ carries special modal meaning (see 8.5). Other local variants of these particles exist alongside the forms given here. Moroccan data containing future particle /ʿa-/ in place of /māš/ was recorded in the town of Larache along the Atlantic coast, and future /ʿa/ is also found in rural Egypt (Behnstedt and Woidich 1985ii:224). Behnstedt and Woidich note indicative /ʿa/, /ʿam/ and variants in some rural Egyptian areas (1985ii:221). Many Syrian speakers add /b-/ to progressive prefix /ʿam/, resulting in /ʿam b-/. Variant /mma/ for /ʿam/ occurs in some of my northern Syrian data.

In the following Syrian passage, the unmarked imperfectives /niṭlaʿ/ *we go out*, /nishar/ *we stay up at night*, /nfūt/ *we go*, in /nidrus/ *we study*, /nitmašša/ *we go walking*, and /nrūḥ/ *we go* are all subordinate to /bḥibb/ *I like*. Marked imperfectives (*/bniṭlaʿ/ *we go out*, */bnishar/ *we stay up*, and so on) would be ungrammatical this context.

S2 بحبّ مثلاً نحنا مجموعة نطلع نسهر نفوت وندرس مثلاً سوا ونتمشّى سوا ونروح ع المعهد سوا

bḥibb masalan niḥna mažmūʿa niṭlaʿ nishar nfūt w nidrus masalan sawa w nitmašša sawa w nrūḥ ʿa l-maʿhad sawa

indic-I-like for-example we group we-go-out we-stay-up we-enter and we-study for-example together and we-walk together and we-go to the-institute together

I'd like, for instance, for us as a group to go out at night, come back and study together, go for walks together, go to school together

The modal distinction grammaticalized by the marked/indicative and unmarked/subjunctive forms of the imperfective aspect corresponds to the distinction between *actual* and *potential*. Mitchell and El-Hassan note that "the subjunctive indicates unrealized verbal action" (1994:29). I prefer the term *potentiality*: the subjunctive represents a potential event without reference–or speaker commitment–to actualization. The following minimal pairs demonstrate the actual and potential modal distinction as grammaticalized by unmarked and marked forms of the imperfective in Egyptian. Column (a) contains unmarked imperfectives, column (b) marked counterparts:

	(a)	(b)
E	تشربي شاي؟	بتشربي شاي؟
	tišrabi šāy?	bitišrabi šāy?
	you-drink-f tea	indic-you-drink-f tea
	Would you like to drink some tea?	*Do you drink tea?*
E	لازم تطبخ	لازم بتطبخ
	lāzim tuṭbux	lāzim bituṭbux
	must she-cook	must indic-she cooks
	She has to cook	*She must be cooking*

Each of the dialects marks the imperfective with different modal prefixes, and it is here that these dialects show the greatest individuality. However, differences in the prefixes themselves do not always parallel differences in usage. Egyptian and Moroccan dialects share the same basic system of marked and unmarked imperfectives, even though the prefixes they use derive from different lexical sources. And Egyptian and Syrian share the indicative marker /b(i)-/, but while a number of its functions overlap, others differ. Syrian stands out among these three dialects in having the most complex system of imperfective markers.

The discussion will begin with a comparison of the unmarked imperfective in Moroccan, Egyptian, and Syrian dialects, followed by a comparison of the marked forms, with special attention to Syrian /b-/.

8.2 Unmarked Imperfective: Subjunctive

In addition to its grammatical role as a non-finite, embedded verb form, the subjunctive may express hortative and optative moods, or it may function as a kind of potential deontic mood,[3] that is, it suggests the possibility, necessity, or desirability[4] of performing an action. In Moroccan and Egyptian, the subjunctive plays a number of roles as a main clause verb, appearing in main clauses expressing event-as-potentiality, and reflecting a non-assertive stance on the part of the speaker. It often expresses a degree of politeness in social interaction. Contrast the subjunctive in the Moroccan and Egyptian version with the indicative in the Syrian version of *Would you [like to] drink some tea?*:

M	تشربي اتاي؟	E	تشربي شاي؟	S	بتشربي شاي؟
	tšərbi ʾātāy?		tišrabi šāy?		btišrəbi šāy?
	you-drink tea		you-drink tea		**b**-you-drink tea

Mitchell and El-Hassan point out that Egyptians, in contrast to Levantine speakers, typically omit /bi-/ from the imperfective of certain verbs of knowing, remembering, liking, and other "mental" verbs

[3]*Deontic* is used here, following Palmer (1986:96), to refer to moods involving human will, such as obligation, permission, and necessity.

[4]Mitchell and El-Hassan propose the term *desiderative* for these exhortatory meanings (1994:29), but *desiderative* is used by other linguists to mean an unrealizable wish: *would that ...* (Palmer 1986:10).

(1994:22-3). Presumably, the polite speaker does not want to commit too much to the truth of opinions or presume to know the mind of another person. In the following, the absence of /bi-/ may reflect the speaker's doubt that her listener knows her:

E6 قالت له، انت حضرتك تعرفني؟
ʾalit-lu, ʾinta ḥaḍritak tiʿrafni?
said-she-to-him, you sir you-know-me?
She said to him, you, sir, Do you know me?

Syrian speakers, in contrast, tend to use /b-/ imperfectives with verbs of thinking and knowing (example from Cowell 1964:483; see also Mitchell and El-Hassan 1994:23):

S بتعرف لي شي بنت بتقعد صانعة؟
btaʿrif-li ši bint btiʾʿod ṣānʿa ?
[indic-you-know-for-me some girl indic-she-sits maid]
Do you know any girl who would work as a maid?

Moroccan patterns appear to follow Egyptian ones. Here a speaker uses the subjunctive /taʿqəli/ *you remember*:

M5 اوّل مرّة تنشري جلابة — تعقلي اختي، ديك الجلابة اللي شريتي لي
ʾuwwəl mərra tanšri žllāba -- taʿqəli ʾuxti, dīk əž-žllāba lli šrītī-li
first time indic-I-buy dress--you-remember sister-my, that the-dress rel bought-you for-us
[It was] the first time I bought a jellaba [type of dress]–remember, sister, that jellaba you bought me?

Mitchell and El-Hassan claim that subjunctive "refers to a formal *subjoining* of sentence elements" (1994:13), and this appears to be true in general for some of the Levantine dialects. According to Mitchell and El-Hassan as well as Beiruti informants, Levantine speakers use the indicative marker /b-/ in polite requests, for possibility, or a deontic modal meaning *might*, *could*, *would* (1994:20ff).[5] Cowell, on the other

[5]Mitchell and El-Hassan note the following exception in their data from Lebanon (1994:32):

L كمّل حديثي أو بكتفي اني سمعت صوتك؟
kammil ḥadīsi ʾaw biktifi ʾinni smiʿət ṣōtik?
[I-finish speech-my or fut-I-be-satisfied comp-I heard-I voice-your?]
Shall I finish what I have to say or shall I be satisfied with having heard your voice?

hand, grants a wider range of meaning to the Syrian subjunctive, admitting to it suggestivity (1964:344):

S اعمل قهوة، ولاّ شاي؟
ʾaʿmel ʾahwe, wəlla šāy?
[I-make coffee, or tea?]
Shall I make coffee, or tea?

This use of the unmarked imperfective is rejected by my Beiruti informants, who insist on the /b-/ imperfective here. The conflicting data and judgements of various Syro-Levantine grammars and speakers remain unsolvable at this juncture, and suggest dialect variation and possibly syntactic change in progress. The wider modal range of Syrian /b-/ as compared to Egyptian /bi-/ invites further analysis; this topic will be revisited in 8.4.

In all three dialects, the definiteness or individuation of a verb's subject or topic may affect its modal marking. Cowell observes that the subjunctive often appears in clauses modifying an indefinite head noun (1964:356; cf. Mitchell and El-Hassan 1994:42). In such cases, the non-specific reference of the indefinite noun may "attract" the subjunctive as an expression of lack of speaker commitment to an actual event or state of affairs. In the following, the Syrian speaker mentions /bint/ *a girl* who /mā tkūn/ *might not be* (subjunctive) a virgin, a *potential* rather than an *actual* case:

S2 مستحيل هوني عندنا واحد يقبل انّه ياخد بنت ما تكون عزراء
mustaḥīl hōni ʿan[d]na wāḥid yiqbal ʾinnu yāxud binət mā tkūn ʿazrāʾ
impossible here at-us one he-accept that-he he-take girl neg she-be virgin
It's impossible here for anyone to agree to marry a girl who isn't/might not be a virgin

Moroccan data also suggest a tendency for unindividuated nouns to occur with subjunctive verbs. One of Harrell's Moroccan texts contains two examples parallel in structure, but containing different moods. In the first, a negated subjunctive /mā tʿažbək-ši/ *you might not like* modifies a partly specified /ši ḥāža/ *something*. In the second, indicative /katʿarfu/ *you know* modifies /ši ḥadd/ *someone*, an indefinite-specific human, which is of higher individuation than /ši ḥāža/, and hence may attract the indicative marking on the verb (1962:224; translations mine):

M غادي تشوفي شي حاجة اللي ما تعجبكشي
ġādi tšūfi ši ḥāža lli ma tʿažbek-ši
[fut you-see some thing rel neg it-please-you]
You will see something that you might not like

M اعرف بان مات شي حد كتعرفه وغادي يجيك خباره
ʿrəf bin māt ši ḥadd katʿarfu w ġādi yžīk xbāru
[know comp died-he some one indic-you-know-him and-fut it-come-to-you news-his]
Know that someone you know died and you will get news of this

Another factor may also affect the speaker's choice of verb mood here: the negated verb in the first example, /ma tʿažbek-ši/ *you might not like.* Since a negated verb does not represent an expected action, there is little need for speaker commitment to the actuality of the event. In fact, the use of indicative forms in negative clauses should reflect a strong speaker commitment to the *non-actuality* of the event or state.

Section 6.5 has shown that speakers of all four dialects often choose the imperfective to represent non-punctual past events in narrative. While this usage of the imperfective usually entails indicative forms, the subjunctive is occasionally used. In describing habitual events, speakers may use the unmarked imperfective to give a non-indicative reading. In the next example, an elderly Moroccan speaker addicted to sniffing tobacco uses unmarked imperfective forms /nəbqa/ *I remain*, /nṣīb/ *I find*, /nḥibb/ *I want*, and /nqūl/ *I say*, to describe events that occur repeatedly, whenever she tries to give up the habit:

M9 لصقت لصقة واحدة، آه شحال انا نبقى يومين وتلت ايام مللي نصيب الدنيا تدور بيّ ونحب نلقي الفتنة في الدار نقول لابني ارجع ارجع نفّح
laṣqat laṣqa wāḥda ʾāh šḥāl ana nəbqa yumayn w tlət iyyām məlli nṣīb d-dənya tdūr biyya w nḥibb nlqi l-fətna f d-dār nqūl l-ibni ržəʿ ržəʿ nəffəḥ
stuck-it sticking one, oh how-much I I-remain two-days and three days when I-find the-world it-spin with-me and I-want I-stir-up the-trouble in the-house I-say to-son-my go-back go-back sniff

[The tobacco habit] has stuck, stuck completely. How often I [might] stay [without it] two, three days, when I]'ll] find the world spinning and go looking for trouble at home, I['ll] tell my son, go back [to sniffing], go back, sniff.

In the next Syrian passage, an Aleppan speaker describes her experience with her American neighbors while living in the U.S. for a year. Here, the unmarked imperfectives /ykūnu/ *they would be*, /ydiʾʾu/ *they would knock*, and /yʾūlū-li/ *they say to me* give modal, past habitual readings:

S5 عم بقِللك هولي يكونوا عم بيمشّوا كلابن، يكونوا عم بيتمشّوا بالشارع، يدقّوا الباب عليّ ويقولوا لي عندك مانع نشرب قهوة؟

ʿam baʾil-lik, hōle ykūnu ʿam bimaššu klābon, ykūnu ʿam bitmaššu bi-š-šāriʿ, ydiʾʾu l-bāb ʿaleyy w yʾūlū-li ʿandik māniʿ nišrab ʾahwe?
prog indic-I-say-to-you, those they-be prog indic-they walk dogs-their, they-be prog they-go-walking in-the-street, they-knock the-door on-me they-say-to-me at-you objection we-drink coffee?
I'm telling you, they would be walking their dogs, they would be strolling in the street, they'd knock on my door and say to me, Do you mind if we have some coffee?

One usage of the unmarked imperfective seems to be distinctively Moroccan. Harrell observes that Moroccan speakers use the unmarked imperfective as an immediate future, as well as a future in the apodosis of conditional clauses (1962:173-5). His observation is born out in the following excerpt from a Moroccan folktale, in which the highlighted unmarked imperfective /ndīrha/ *I do it* clearly refers to a future action:

M11 هاديك سهيهة البهيهة اللي دارتها بالرجال قبل لا يديروها بها. هاي هاي هاي والله تا نديرها بها انا، **نديرها** بها انا!

hādīk shīha l-bhīha lli dārətha bə-r-ržāl qbəl la ydīrūha bīha. hāy hāy hāy waḷḷāh ta ndīrha biha ʾāna, **ndīrha** biha ʾāna!
that Shiha Bhiha rel did-she-it to-the-men before nom they-do-it to-her. ho ho ho by-God until I-do-it to-her I **I-do-it** to-her I!
That is Shiha Bhiha who does it to men before they can do it to her. Ho ho ho, [just wait] 'til I do it to her, ***I [will] do it*** *to her!*

Here, as well as in some of Harrell's examples, there seems to be more intentional commitment to acts expressed with an unmarked imperfective.

Perhaps the omission of an indicative or future marker represents a deontic expression of speaker intention, as contrasted to an epistemic expression of the speaker's commitment to the actuality of the event.

8.3 Marked Forms of the Imperfective

This section will briefly treat the moods of the various marked imperfectives. The main focus here will be on Syrian, since it has the most complex system of imperfective marking, with particular attention paid to the functions of Syrian verbal prefix /b-/. Kuwaiti, on the other hand, will receive less attention, because its modal system does not make extensive use of verbal prefixes.

8.3.1 Future and Intentive Moods

Table 8-2 (section 8.1) reveals a partial overlap across adjacent dialect areas in the case of particles /b(i)-/ and /raḥ/. Syrian and Kuwaiti share the particle /b(i)-/ as an intentive future, while Egyptian, Syrian, and urban Kuwaiti share the particle /raḥ/ (Egyptian /ḥa-/). The existence in Syrian and Kuwaiti of two future particles, /b-/ and /raḥ/, necessitates a distinction between future and intentive moods. The western dialects, on the other hand, have only one future marker each, with regional variants.

The most common future particle in Moroccan is /ġā(di)/, my data include regional variants /ʿa-/ and /māš/ in the area surrounding Tangiers and Tetouan.

M10 ش ع نقول لك، البلايا مزيانة وعيّانة
š ʿa-nqūl-lk, l-plāya mzyāna w ʿəyyāna
what fut I-say to-you, the-beach good and bad
What shall I tell you, the beach is good and bad

M1 بحقّ ماش نجيش دابا
b-ḥaqq māš nžīš dāba
but neg fut I-come now
But I'm not coming now

M11 غادي نمدّ لك رجلي من الشرجم
ġādi nmədd-lək rəžli mn š-šəržəm
fut I-stretch to-you leg-my from the-window
I will put out my leg from the window for you

In Egypt, most speakers use the particle /ḥa-/ (less frequently /ha-/) to signify future reference:

E1 حاخلّي منال تجيبه لمّا تيجي
ḥa-xalli manāl tigību lamma tīgi
fut-I-make Manal she-bring-it when she-come
I'll have Manal get it when she comes

The derivations of these future particles help shed light on their modal meanings. While Moroccan and Egyptian future particles derive from lexical variants of the verb *to go*, the Kuwaiti future marker /b-/ has its origin in the imperfective stem /(y)abi/ *(he) wants*, as the use of the full form shows (see also Al-Najjar 1984:87-90):

K3 يبي يطگّني
yabi yṭəggni
he-wants he-beats-me
He [was] about to beat me

Kuwaiti /b-/ appears to indicate both future time reference and intentionality (Al-Najjar calls it "volition," 1984:119), at least in the speech of an older Kuwaiti woman. In the first of the next pair, both taken from an interview with an elderly woman, /biydišš/ *he will enter* must signal future time reference, since one cannot exercise control over one's age. In contrast, /biytaṭallagūn/ *they want to get divorced* in the second clearly indicates the intention of the participants to get divorced:

K3 بيدشّ العشرين
biydišš il-ʿišrīn
will-enter-he the-twentieth
He's going to be twenty

K3 راحَوا المحكمة بيتطلّگون
rāḥaw l-maḥkama biytaṭallagūn
went-they the-court will-they-get-divorced
They went to the court wanting to get divorced

A young Kuwaiti male, on the other hand, uses both /b-/ and /raḥ/, the former in contexts reflecting a degree of personal will or intention, and the second as a future marker: In the first of the two examples taken from his narrative about a trip to Morocco, the speaker uses /b-/ to indicate the intention of his friends for the group to go to Egypt:

K1 وعدوني انّا بنروح مصر
wa'adūni inna bi-nrūḥ maṣər
promised-they-me comp-we b-we-go Egypt
They promised me that we will go to Egypt

When the promise falls through, they encourage him to go visit Morocco, and the future particle /raḥ/ marks what will happen if he does:

K1 روح المغرب، تجربة رح تكون، لو الشخص اللي ويّاك مو زين، لو ما تعرفَه عدل، رح تعرفَه بالسفر
rūḥ il-maġrib, tajriba raḥ tkūn, lo iš-šaxṣ illi wayyāk mū zēn, lo mā ta'arfa 'idil raḥ ta'arfa bi-s-safar
go Morocco, experience fut it-be, if the-person with-you neg good, if neg you-know-him well, fut you-know-him in-the-traveling
Go to Morocco, it will be an experience, if the person you're with isn't good, if you don't know him well, you will get to know him in traveling

The intentive nature of Kuwaiti /b-/ is not limited to human will. In the following, the subject of /bitṣīr/ *will happen* is /maṣāyib/ *catastrophes*, as if problems will single out the speaker:

K1 هاذي اول مصيبة، عيل بتصير لي مصايب بالمغرب!
hāḏi 'awwal muṣība 'ayal bitṣīr-li maṣāyib bi-l-maġrib
this first catastrophe then b-3fs-happen-to-me catastrophes in Morocco
This is the first catastrophe, then [more] catastrophes will happen to me in Morocco!

Syrian speakers also have at their disposal the same two functionally distinct particles that refer to future events, /b-/ and /raḥ/. Cowell names /raḥ/ a "particle of anticipation," and classifies the future meaning of /b-/, which he describes as either "annunciatory" or "dispositional," as a subcategory of the indicative (1964:322-27). Mitchell and El-Hassan subsume under "nonpast tense" both the "intentive" mood marked by /ḥa/ and the "indicative" marked by /b-/ (1994:14), and note that, "[i]n the Levant especially, b-nonpast is often of straightforward future reference" (1994:13). Both of these studies thus include the future meaning of /b-/ as a subclass of the indicative mood. I will argue that a distinction should be maintained between the two meanings, and suggest separate origins for intentive /b-/ and indicative /b-/ in 8.4.

Both /b-/ and /raḥ/ indicate future actions and events in Syrian, but each one has a distinct modal implication. The following four examples all occur in the Syrian play *Wādī al-Misk*:

S6 شو رح تسمي المولود؟
šu raḥ tsammi l-mawlūd?
what fut you-name the-newborn
What are you going to name the baby?

S6 امتى رح تزيد لنا المعاش؟
ʾimta raḥ tzīd lna l-maʿāš?
when fut you-increase-for-us the-salary
When are you going to increase our salary?

S6 بلا ما تضيّعي وقتك هاتي بحطّ لك اياه بطريقي
bala ma tḍayyʿi waʾtik, hāti, b-ḥəṭṭ-lik yā b-ṭarīʾi
without that you-waste-f time-your, give, will-I-put-for-you obj-it on-way-my
Don't waste your time, I'll drop it off for you on my way

S6 ها المرة ان شا الله ما بنسى
ha l-marra nšaḷḷa mā binsa
this the-time God-willing neg will-I-forget
This time, hopefully, I won't forget

Two significant differences in context emerge between the first two sentences, which contain /raḥ/, and the latter two, with /b-/. First, /raḥ/ is used with questions that specifically ask about future events: naming a child and seeking a pay raise, while /b-/ appears in statements about intended actions on the part of the speaker. (The fact that the /b-/ future often occurs on first-person verbs lends further support to the intentive reading of this particle.) Second, the first two examples with /raḥ/ consist of questions seeking information. In the judgement of a

Lebanese informant, /b-/ cannot be used to seek factual information, such as *what* or *where*, about a future event; he rejects the following as ungrammatical:

L * شو بتجيب معك؟
* šu bitžīb maʿak?
* what int-you-bring with-you
* *What will you bring with you?*

However, /b-/ may be used in informational questions if the question focuses on the addressee's intention:

L امتى بتزيد لنا المعاش؟
imta bətzīd lna l-maʿāš?
when int-you-increase for-us the-salary
When do you plan to raise our salary? (elicited)

The Levantine modal use of /b-/ in polite questions–a usage not shared by Egyptian speakers–further supports its interpretation as an intentive particle expressing will:

L بتشرب شاي؟
btišrab šāy?
int-you-drink tea?
Would you like to drink some tea? (elicited)

Another special use of Syrian /b-/ combines it with a negative particle to express a commissive mood, a commitment on the part of the speaker that an event will not, or must not happen. In this case /b-/ gives a future modal meaning to the verb. The following two passages, taken from the same text, show modal future uses of /b-/ in /mā btiftaḥha/ *you must not open it* and /mā biṣīr/, which commonly carries the meaning *it must not be, [one] must not ...*

S1 والله يا ماما عطاني استاذي ورقة وقال لي ما بتفتحها لحتّى تموت
wal̤l̤a ya māma ʿaṭāni ʾistāzi waraʾa w ʾāl-li mā btiftaḥ[h]a la-ḥatta tmūt
By-God O mother gave-he teacher-my paper and-said-he-to-me neg **b**-you-open-it to-until you-die
Well, Mama, my teacher gave me a piece of paper and told me, You must not open it until you die

S1 يا بابا عطاني الاستاذ ورقة وقال لي ما بيصير تشوفها
ya bāba ʿaṭāni il-ʾistāz waraʾa w ʾāl-li mā biṣīr tšūf[h]a
said-he-to-him O Papa gave-he-me the-teacher paper and said-he-to-me neg b-it-happen you-see-it
Papa, the teacher gave me a piece of paper and told me it must not happen that I see it (I must not see it)

This and other meanings of Syrian /b-/ will be discussed further in 8.4.

8.3.2 Indicative Mood

The indicative mood represents action as realized process, depending on the lexical aspect of the verb, habitual, progressive, or stative. Table 8-3 lists the indicative prefixes in the dialects.

Table 8-3: Indicative Markers

Indicative Markers		
Dialect	Progressive	Durative
M	--	ka- / ta-
E	(ʿammāl)	bi-
S	ʿam	b-
K	gāʿid (gāʿda, gāʿdīn)	--

Moroccan /ka-/ and /ta-/, Egyptian /bi-/, and Syrian /b-/ (disregarding its intentive meaning) all share the meaning of action-as-state-of being, or a combined habitual/stative aktionsart.[6] Harrell calls Moroccan /ka/ the *durative*, a term that neatly combines the habitual and the stative meanings, leaving the interpretation of specific examples to the lexical aspect of the verb and other sentential and discourse factors (section 6.1 shows that stative and progressive readings depend

[6]Comrie defines habituality to include non-iterative acts, such as *used to believe* (1976:27, but see Mitchell and El-Hassan for arguments against this analysis, 1994:100-1).

in large part on the lexical aspect of the verb). Examples from my Moroccan and Egyptian data include:

M11 ما تتخرجش من الدار
mā tatxrəž[š] mn d-dār
neg indic-she-leaves from the-house
She doesn't go out of the house

E1 أصل عمّ احمد بيضرب عود
ʾaṣl ʿamm aḥmad byiḍrab ʿūd
since uncle Ahmed indic-he-plays lute
You see, Uncle Ahmad plays the lute

The western dialects, Moroccan and Egyptian, do not grammatically distnguish between indicative and progressive moods, using their indicative markers for both. Syrian and Kuwaiti, on the other hand, mark progressivity with other particles.

The progressive prefix in urban Syria is /ʿam/, followed by the imperfective with or without the /b-/ prefix:

S5 عم بقللك !
ʿam ba'il-lik!
prog indic-I-say to-you!
I'm telling you!

Some northern Syrian speakers use /mma/ as a variant of /ʿam/ (presumably reflexes of /ʿammāl/, intact in Egyptian as an intensifier):

S2 هلق صايرين البنات مّا يطنّشوا، ما عاد مّا يهمّن
hallaʾ ṣāyrīn il-banāt mma yṭannšu, mā ʿād mma yhimmon
now having-become-p the-girls prog they-ignore, neg remained-it prog it-concerns-them
Nowadays girls have come to ignore [social pressure], it no longer matters to them

Egyptian speakers have at their disposal an intensifying progressive /ʿammāl/ (Badawi and Hinds 1986:602):

E عمّال ياكل
E ʿammāl yākul
continuous he-eat
He keeps on eating

Kuwaiti speakers, who have no indicative marker, use /gāʿid/ (f /gāʿda/, p /gāʿdīn/) to mark the progressive. From my Kuwaiti data:

K1 رفيجي اللي يمبي گاعد يشرب ويسكي
rifīji lli yam[b]i gāʿid yišrab wiski
friend-my rel beside-me prog he-drinks whiskey
My friend who is next to me is drinking whiskey

Al-Najjar's examples show subject agreement in all cases, among them the feminine /gāʿda/ here (1984:212):

K مريم گاعدة تفرش بيتها هالايام
maryam gāʿda tafriš beytha ha l-ayyām
Maryam prog-f she-furnishes house-her this the-days
Maryam is furnishing her house these days

Syrian and Kuwaiti thus grammaticalize the progressive, while Moroccan and Egyptian do not.

8.4 The Multiple Meanings of Syrian /b-/

Syrian /b-/ presents a puzzle. Although lexically identical to the Egyptian /bi-/, its syntactic range is broader than its Egyptian counterpart. Syrian /b-/ occurs in a number of contexts with different meanings, summarized in Table 8-4. Most of these functions have already been discussed in 8.3, except for the use of /b-/ as a modal future.

Unlike indicative prefixes Egyptian /bi-/ and Moroccan /ka-/, Syrian /b-/ may occur in embedded deontic clauses. While epistemic embedded clauses normally contain verbs with indicative prefixes in Moroccan, Egyptian, and Syrian, deontic clauses cannot embed indicative verb forms in Moroccan and Egyptian. The following sentences contain epistemic clauses with indicative verb forms (in boldface):

M3 كتظنّ بللي **كيعرفوا** هاد الشي؟
katḍənn bəlli **kayʿarfu** hād š-ši?
indic-you-think comp indic-they-know this the-thing?
Do you think ***they know*** *that?* (elicited)

E3 عارف انّ انا **باخاف** م الصرصار الصغيّر
ʿārif ʾinn ana **baxāf** mi ṣ-ṣurṣār iṣ-ṣuġayyar
knowing-m comp I **indic-am-afraid** from the-roach the-little
[He] knows ***I'm afraid*** *of the little cockroach*

S بتظنّ انه **بيعرف** الحكاية؟
bəṭẓənn ʾenno **byaʿref** l-ᵊḥkāye?
[indic-you-think comp-he **indic-he knows** the-story?]
Do you suppose ***he knows*** *the story?* (Cowell 1964:347)

However, only Syrian allows a /b-/-imperfective (or, in the case of Moroccan, /ka-/-imperfective) to be embedded in deontic subordinate clauses (example from Cowell 1964:347):

S نفرض انه ما **بيجي**
nəfroḍ ʾenno mā **byəži**
[we-suppose comp-he neg **b-he-come**]
Let's suppose he doesn't ***come*** *...*

Comparison of the /b-/ markers in the two preceding Syrian examples reveals that the first, /byaʿref/ *he knows* is durative (in this case, stative), while the second, /mā byəži/ *he's not going to come* is intentive future with respect to the main verb, /nəfroḍ/ *let's suppose*. Cowell gives a similar minimal pair (1964:347):

	(a)	(b)
S	وعدني انّه يرجع	وعدني انّه بيرجع
	waʿadni ʾenno yəržaʿ	waʿadni ʾenno byəržaʿ
	[promised-he-me comp-he he-return]	[promised-he-me comp-he b-he-return]
	He promised me to come back	*He promised me that he would come back*

The Egyptian /bi-/ imperfective corresponding to (b) above is ungrammatical:

E *وعدني انه بيرجع
* waʿadni innu biyirgaʿ
* promised-he-me comp-he indic-he-returns
* *He promised me that he is coming back*

However, Egyptian speakers do use future /ḥa-/ in this kind of context:

E5 وعدني انه حيرجع
waʿadni innu ḥayirgaʿ
promised-he-me comp-he fut-he-return
He promised me that he is coming back (elicited)

Table 8-4: Meanings of Syrian /b-/

Meanings of Syrian /b-/		
Syntactic Role	Mood	Example
main clause	indicative: durative, habitual, gnomic, performative	bišūfa kill yōm *He sees her every day* bhannīk *I congratulate you*[a]
following temporal verbs in compound phrases	indicative: stative, change of state	ibni ṣār byisbaḥ la-ḥālu *My son has started to swim by himself*
future marker	future, intentive	bukra byitṣālḥu *Tomorrow they'll make up* inšāḷḷa mā binsa *Hopefully I won't forget*
embedded clauses	modal future	nəfroḍ ʾenno mā byəži *Let's suppose he won't come*[b]
polite questions	modal future	btišrab šāy? *Would you [like to] drink some tea?*
conditional clauses	modal future	law kənt b-mḥallak, kənt bəbʾa bəl-bēt *If I were in your shoes, I'd stay home.*[c] ʾiza btəstannāni šī yōmēn yəmkən ʾəʳlaʿ maʿak *If you wait for me a couple of days I might go with you.*[d]

[a]Example from Cowell (1964:325-36).
[b]Cowell (1964: 347; translation mine).
[c]Cowell (1964:336).
[d]Cowell (1964:332).

Cowell notes that "the /b-/ prefix of a verb in the imperfect[ive] is not dropped after the hypothetical /kān/, as it is, usually, when /kān/ is used for past time reference" (1964:336). In the following example, /b-/ gives a modal sense to /əbʾa/ *I remain*; it is clear that /b-/ here indicates intentive rather than indicative mood (example from Cowell 1964:336):

S لو كنت بمحلّك، كنت ببقى بالبيت
law kənt ᵊb-mḥallak, kənt bəbʾa bəl-bēt
if was-I in-place-your, was-I b-I-remain in-the-house
If I were in your shoes, I'd stay home

Here too, Syrian /b-/ corresponds to Egyptian use of /ḥa/:

E5 لو كنت مكانك، كنت حاقعد في البيت
law kunt makānak, kunt ḥaʾʿud fi l-bēt
if was-I in-place-your, was-I fut-I-remain in-the-house
If I were in your shoes, I'd stay home (elicited)

Another distinctively Syrian use of /b-/ (as contrasted with Egyptian /bi-/) is its cooccurrence with temporal verbs. When /b-/ occurs in a verb phrase headed by temporal verbs (7.2), it adds a stative dimension to the verb phrase. Cowell's data include two contrasting examples of verbs embedded by /ḍall/ *to continue, remain*, the first with /b-/ and the second without (1964:356, 453):

S بتضلّ بتحكي وبتحكي
bə[t]ḍall ᵊbtəḥki w-ᵊbtəḥki
[indic-she-remains b-she-talks and-b-she-talks]
She keeps on talking and talking

S بيضلّ يحكي عن الحوادث الماضية
biḍall yəḥki ʿan əl-ḥawādes əl-māḍye
[indic-he-remains he-talk about the-events the-past]
He keeps talking about past events

In the first of the pair, the indicative /b-/ focuses attention on the stativity of the act of speaking, whereas in the second, the absence of /b-/ maintains focus on the temporal verb /biḍall/ *he keeps on*, and the habituality or iterativity of the act of speaking. The first sentence carries an element of stativity lacking in the second.

A Beiruti informant interprets the construction with a /b-/ imperfective as a circumstantial clause (/ḥāl/), providing the following pair of examples that contrast marked and unmarked imperfectives embedded by temporal verb /ṣār/ *to become, begin.* In the first, the /b-/

imperfective /byisbaḥ/ *he swims* focuses on the onset of a state, that of being able to or knowing how to swim, whereas in the second, the unmarked /yisbaḥ/ *he swim* focuses on the onset of an action:

L ابني صار بيسبح لحاله
ibni ṣār byisbaḥ la-ḥālu
son-my began-he b-he-swims for-self-his
My son has begun to swim by himself

L نزل ع البركة وصار يسبح
nizil ʿa l-birke w ṣār yisbaḥ
went-in-he to the-pool and began-he-he-swim
He went into the pool and started swimming (elicited)

The following examples from a Moroccan interview show a similar distinction. The verb /bqa/ (indicative /kaybqa/) *to remain, keep on* is followed in the first example by indicative /kayhəwwdu/ *they go down* and in the second by unmarked imperfective /yqūl/ *he say*:

M10 ما بقاوش كيهوّدوا عائلات
mā bqāwš kayhəwwdu ʿāʾilāt
neg remained-they indic-they-go-down families
Families no longer go down [to the beach]

M10 بحال مثلاً الانسان كيشرب الخمر كيبقى يقول شي كلمة قبيحة
b-ḥāl matalan l-ʾinsān kayšrab l-xmər kaybqa yqūl ši kəlma qbīḥa
like for-example the-person indic-he-drinks the-wine indic-he-remains he-say some word dirty
Like for instance [a] person drinks wine and keeps saying some dirty word

The use of the indicative with the perfective form /mā bqāwš/ *they no longer go* emphasizes the change of state in the same way that Levantine /b/ functions in the previously cited examples. In contrast, the use of the unmarked imperfective with /kaybqa/ *he keeps on* focuses on the habitual or iterative use of bad language.

El-Tonsi (personal communication) confirms that this distinction cannot be made in Cairene Arabic, where /bi-/ only occurs in verb phrases headed by /kān/ *to be*. However, he notes that it occurs in other regions outside Cairo, and one of Behnstedt's Alexandrian texts contains this pair of examples (1980:42; translation mine):

E قام يقول: احنا فين دلوقت؟
ʾām yiʾūl: iḥna fēn diwagti?
[got-up-he he-say: we where now?]
He up and says, Where are we now?

E قمت اني بنضرب بعيني
ʾumt ani biniḍrab biʿēni
[got-up-I indic-I-strike with-eye-my]
I started staring

In the first of the pair, the unmarked imperfective /yiʾūl/ he says represents a non-stative action, whereas the /bi-/-imperfective in the second constitutes a stative action. Non-Cairene /bi-/ thus appears to join Syrian /b-/ and Moroccan /ka-/ in adding a stative or change-of-state meaning not found in the unmarked imperfective.

Syrian /b-/ thus has two loci of meaning: future (intentive and modal) and durative (habitual/stative). The overlapping of /b-/ particles across several dialect areas and semantic fields suggests the possibility of two different origins. The future intentive meaning corresponds closely to Kuwaiti /b-/, whereas the durative and habitual meanings of /b-/ correlate with Egyptian /bi-/. It may be that Syrian /b-/ actually consists of two separate morphemes, each with its own origin, and that the phonological overlap of these two particles was, originally, mere coincidence.

8.5 Kuwaiti /čān/: Modal Auxiliary?

Kuwaiti /čān/ plays several roles in the mood system of this dialect. It combines with the perfective to produce a pluperfect, such as /čān tiʿibt/ *I had gotten tired* (speaker K1). At other times it occurs in narrative contexts indicating a kind of historical present (see 7.1.4). Elsewhere, /čān/ occurs in counterfactual conditional sentences (see 8.8).[7] This section briefly discusses the function of /čān/ as a modal auxiliary (approximately, *would*).[8]

[7]Ingham's description of /čān/ in Najdi suggests that this particle originated as a conditional marker (1994:139).

[8]Holes notes that Gulf speakers sometimes use the invariable /yikūn/ (3ms imperfective of *to be*) as a "periphrastic subjunctive" (1990:189). My Kuwaiti corpus does not have /yikūn/, but contains /kūn/ in what I interpret to be a

In the following, the particle /čān/ in the phrase /čān taʿṭīni/ *would you give me* clearly lends a modal meaning to the sentence, similar to the subjunctive of Egyptian and Moroccan (see 8.2):

K4 ... بناتج كلهم اعطيني اياهم. گلت لها، ابوي، چان تعطيني گصر عندج وايي اسكن انا ورايلي بعد؟

... banātič kilhum ʿaṭīni yāhum. gilt-laha, ʾubūy čān taʿṭīni gaṣər ʿandič w ayi ʾaskin ʾāna w rāyli baʿd?

girls-your all-them imper-give-me obj-them said-I to-her dear-my would you-give-me palace at-you and I-come I-live I and husband-my then?

[She said,] "All your girls, give them to me." I told her, "Dear, would you give me a palace there for me to come live with my husband as well?"

In his grammar of Gulf Arabic, Qafisheh translates /čān/ as *would* and provides several examples similar to the ones cited here (1975:226).

However, /čān/ has a narrower semantic range than, and is syntactically different from, the subjunctive in other dialects, which may express optative and hortative moods, polite questions, and potentiality.[9]

Of note here is that while other dialects mark the indicative form of the imperfective, Kuwaiti appears to be doing the opposite: developing a marked form for the subjunctive. In this respect the Kuwaiti verb system is closer to that of English, since the modal /čān/ functions similarly to the English modal verb "would." Superficially, Kuwaiti verbs bear certain affinities to Classical Arabic verbs: they lack

---

subjunctive sense:

K3 لو هو تعبان، لو فيه ويّا احد صاير كلام، شي، **كون** انت بتعطينَه بشرة حلوة، ويبة حلوة، نفس حلوة

lo huwa taʿbān, lo fī wiyya ʾaḥad ṣāyir kalām, šay, **kūn** intey btaʿṭīna bišra ḥilwa, wayba ḥilwa, nafs ḥilwa

if he tired, if there-is with anyone having-happened talk, thing, **kūn** you fut-you-give-him countenance sweet, meal tasty, disposition pleasant

If he is tired, if there has happened with anyone an argument [or] something, you ***should*** *give him a sweet countenance, a tasty meal, a pleasant disposition*

[9]Johnstone notes that the imperfective is most common in optative sentences (1967:142).

imperfective modal prefixes, and the imperfective third-person plural and second-person feminine singular retain final /nūn/, for example: /ygūlūn/ *they say*, /lā txallīn/ *don't let*. However, with an imperfective system that does not distinguish inflectionally between actual and possible, Kuwaiti may be innovating in a slightly different fashion by developing a modal particle, /čān/. Structurally, then, it is the Kuwaiti indicative and modal system that stands unique among the four dialects.

8.6 Commissive Mood: Marked Use of the Perfective

While the perfective normally represents a completed action, in certain marked, negated contexts it can represent an action that has technically not yet taken place, and the speaker, by using the perfective, indicates a commitment on his or her part that it never will. Palmer calls this the commissive mood (1986:115). This mood is more commonly expressed with the imperfective, except in negative oaths, in which the perfect or (in rare cases) the perfective may occur. In negative oaths, the action expressed by a perfective verb is not actually realized, as both speaker and audience undoubtedly know. However, what gives the oath its semantic and pragmatic force is precisely the tension between the realized and the unrealized: by expressing the event using a form normally reserved for realized actions, the urgency of the oath is clearly communicated. The following two examples contain commissive perfectives /mā ʿidti/ *you no longer* and /kal/ *(he) ate* respectively.

S2 ما عدت تسكني معنا!
mā ʿidti tiskəni maʿna!
neg returned-you you-live with-us!
You won't live with us any more!

Mitchell and El-Hassan note the following as "expostulatory usage of women" in Egypt (1994:31):

E انشا الله ما حدّ كل!
inšaḷḷa ma ḥaddı kal!
May nobody ever eat, then

This usage appears to be limited to the speech of women (the Syrian speaker is a young woman from a village in northern Syria) and may be dying out. I have found no examples of this use of the perfective in Moroccan or Kuwaiti.[10]

8.7 Conditional and Hypothetical Moods

This section explores the use of two different verb stems, the perfective and the imperfective, in the expression of conditional modality in the dialects. The primary concern here is with the conditional clause, or protasis, rather than the apodosis, except insofar as the latter helps us determine the modal nature of the former. While the unmarked mood of the perfective is indicative, in marked usage the perfective has a hypothetical mood.

Because formal Arabic stipulates the use of the perfective to indicate conditional mood with particles /ʾiḏā/ and /law/,[11] whereas most varieties of spoken Arabic permit the use of the imperfective or zero verb with conditional particles, it has been assumed that the perfective and imperfective have become more temporal and less aspectual, since these conditional sentences often refer to a non-past event (Holes 1995:177). However, close examination of conditional data reveals that speakers of most dialects choose between perfective and imperfective forms on the basis of modal and aspectual meanings, not temporal considerations.

8.7.1 Conditional Particles in the Dialects

Formal Arabic rules for the conditional dictate that the mood of the conditional as realis or irrealis is signalled through the choice of particle, /ʾiḏā/ for realis, /ʾin/ for hypothetical, and /law/ for irrealis. However, spoken Arabic does not follow these patterns. Conditional particles as described in the grammars show a range of variation and overlap of meanings. Egyptian, Syrian, and Kuwaiti all allow both perfective and imperfective forms of the verb, as well as non-verbal predicates, in conditional clauses. With the possible exception of Syrian,

---

[10]The apparent absence of the perfective as commissive in Moroccan is somewhat surprising, given that this dialect makes regular use of the perfective as a performative, as in /qbiltha/ *I accept it* (see also Caubet 1993ii:111-114).

[11]For a description of conditional usages in formal Arabic see Cantarino (1975iii:297-306, 311-326) or Wright (1898ii:6-17).

the dialects do not seem to rely upon the conditional particle to make an absolute distinction between possible and counterfactual sentences. Table 8-5 compares the conditional particles and their protases in the four dialects.

Table 8-5: Conditional Particles

Conditional Particles and Protases			
Dialect	ʾin	ʾiḏā and variants	law and variants
M	(unattested)	ʾīla, ʾīda + perfective	kūn, kurrāh, lūkān, ʾūka + perfective
E	ʾin (rural) + perfective	ʾiza + perfective, imperfective, or zero verb	law + perfective, imperfective, or zero verb
S	ʾin + perfective	ʾiza + perfective, imperfective, or zero verb	law + perfective
K	ʾin + perfective	ʾila, la, ʾiḏa + perfective or zero verb	lo + perfective or imperfective

The particle /ʾin/, found in proverbs in a number of dialects, occurs only once in my data, in Kuwaiti, but Behnstedt and Woidich report its use in rural dialects in the Egyptian Delta (1988:26). The use of /ʾiza/ as a reflex of formal /ʾiḏa/ is found in Egyptian and Syrian regions, but not in Morocco, where /ʾila/ is common, or Kuwait, where /ʾila/ is often elided to/la/. Educated Moroccan and Kuwaiti speakers commonly use /ʾida/ and /ʾiḏa/ respectively.

Moroccan speakers normally use the perfective in conditional clauses. The normal conditional particle is /ʾīla/:

M11 إلا هي ولدت الولد، خلّيها واجي عندي

ʾīla hiyya wəldat l-wəld xallīha w āži ʿndi

if she bore-she the-son leave-her and come to-me

If shegave birth to a male child, leave her and come back to me

Particles /kun/ *if* (variant /kunrāh/) and /lūkān/ *if only* function as irrealis conditional markers (Harrell 1962:168-9, see 8.7.2.2 for examples). Caubet also lists the expression /ʾūka ... ʾūka/ (heading both clauses)[12] with irrealis meaning (1993:206, translation mine):

M أوكا جات آمنة، أوكا مشينا للبحر معاها!

ʾūka žāt ʾāmīna, ʾūka mšīna l-əl-bḥar mʿāha!

if came-she Amina, if went-we to-the-sea with-her

If only Amina had come, we would have gone to the sea with her!

In Cairene, /law/ appears to be synonymous with /ʾiza/. El-Tonsi notes that conditional particles must be followed by a perfective verb, except in non-verbal sentences (including sentences whose predicate consists of a participle), or in "clauses that express an offer or proposal, i.e., what is in English *would/could*," in which the unmarked imperfective is often used (1982ii:80-1). The imperfective examples el-Tonsi gives all contain stative verbs, such as following /tiʾdar/ *you can* and /tiḥibb/ *you like*:

E اذا تقدر تيجي اهلاً وسهلاً

ʾiza tiʾdar tīgi ʾahlan wa sahlan

[if you-can you-come welcome]

If you can come, you're welcome [to]

E لو تحب تيجي اهلاً وسهلاً

law tiḥibb tīgi ʾahlan wa sahlan

[if you-like you-come welcome]

If you'd like to come, you're welcome [to]

However, in the following, /bitḥibbaha/ *you love her* must be preceded by perfective /kunt/ *you were*, suggesting that the verb /yiḥibb/ may appear in the imperfective in conditionals when it means *to like* or *to want*, but not when it means *to be in love with* (example from el-Tonsi 1982ii:82):

E اذا كنت بتحبّها اتجوّزها

ʾiza kunt bitḥibbaha ʾitgawwizha

[if were-you indic-you-love-her marry-her]

If you really love her, marry her

---

[12] A Moroccan informant from Meknas prefers /ʾūkān/ to /ūka/.

For Syrian, clauses with /ʾiza/ allow the use of imperfectives marked with either /b-/ or /ʿam/ (on the use of Syrian /b-/ in conditional sentences see Cowell 1964:336; this is intentive future /b-/, as shown in 8.4). Among Cowell's examples (1964:332):

S ان شا الله ما فيه مانع عندك اذا بروح هلق
nšāḷḷa mā fī mānеʿ ʿandak ʾiza brūḥ hallaʾ
[God-willing neg there-is objection at-you if b-I-go now
I hope you don't mind if I go now

According to Cowell, Syrian speakers generally reserve /law/ for use in irrealis conditionals, which generally take perfective verbs (1964:335).

Kuwaiti speakers use both /lo/ *if, even if* and /la/ *if, when*. However, while /la/ normally occurs with a perfective verb,[13] /lo/ often occurs with imperfective verbs or zero-verb, in contexts that are hypothetical but not necessarily irrealis.[14] Even the elderly Kuwaiti speaker K3, who regularly uses the perfective with /la/ meaning *when*, uses /lo/ with the imperfective. In the following sentence, the conditional clause headed by /lo/ contains the imperfective /nigdar/ *we are able* in a hypothetical (not irrealis) mood, while the result clause contains the perfective /ġanēna/ *we could manage, do*:

K3 لو نگدر نسوّي شي غنينا بروحنا
lo nigdar nsawwi šay ġanēna b-rūḥna
if we-are-able we-do thing managed-we with-selves-our
If we are able to do something, we could do with just ourselves

A young male Kuwaiti likewise uses /lo/ with zero-verb or imperfective verbs in stative conditionals, often meaning *even if*, as in the following:

K1 كل اربع وخميس ويمعة ما استثگلها، لو يومين اروح
kil ʾarbaʿ w xamīs w yimʿa mā astaṯgilha, lo yomēn arūḥ
every Wednesday and Thursday and Friday neg I-consider-heavy-it, if days-2 I-go
Every Wednesday, Thursday, and Friday, I don't consider it too tiresome, [even] if for two days, I go

---

[13]The use of /la/ to mean *when* parallels Classical Arabic use of /ʾiḏā/, see Cantarino (1975iii:297), Wright (1898ii:9).

[14]Ingham's description of and data from Najdi concur (1994:137).

In Kuwaiti, then, /lo/ is more likely than /ʾila/ to be followed by an imperfective verb.

In three of four dialects, then, both perfective and imperfective stems occur in similar conditional contexts (Moroccan being the exception). But the use of the imperfective in conditional clauses (which happens even in the most "conservative" dialects, see e.g. Ingham for Najdi 1994:131ff) has not affected the status of the perfective, and the verb /kān/ *to be* in particular, as the primary expression of hypothetical mood, as the following sections will show.

8.7.2 Hypothetical and Counterfactual /kān/

Palmer notes a high cross-linguistic frequency of past tense forms functioning modally as counterfactual (irrealis) mood markers (1986:210). Spoken Arabic follows this pattern as well: all four dialects contain reflexes of /kān/ that mark "hypothetical distance," that is, a position taken by the speaker that the condition is less likely to happen, or is counterfactual. In fact, /kān/ has developed into a conditional particle in several dialects, and acquired a counterfactual or irrealis meaning in certain conditional contexts, as the next sections will show.

8.7.2.1 /kān/ as Frozen Hypothetical Marker

Cowell notes the existence in Syrian of a frozen form /kān/ *was* that he calls "hypothetical /kān/." Two of his examples show /kān/ functioning more as a particle than a verb, forming a syntactic unit with /ʾiza/ *if* (1964:334). In the second example, the impersonal subject of /kān/ does not agree with that of the following verb, /laʾēt/ *you met*:

S اذا كان مالي احسن بتجيبي لي الحكيم
ʾiza kān māli aḥsan bətžībī-li l-ḥakīm
[if kān neg-I better fut-you-bring-for-me the-doctor]
If I'm not better you'll bring the doctor to (see) me

S اذا كان لقيت واحد ع الطريق هللي قال لك اسقيني خلّيه يشرب
ʾiza kān laʾēt wāḥed ʿ aṭ-ṭarīʾ halli ʾal-lak sʾīni, xallī yəšrab
[if kān met-you one on the-road rel said-he-to-you give-me-(water) let-him he-drink]
If you meet someone on the road who says to you "Give me water," let him drink

The following sentence shows a similar pattern. Here frozen /kān/ does not agree in gender with the subject, feminine /ḥaltu/ *his condition*:

S2 انا اذا اتجوّزت واحد غني ... بحبّ يكون عندي اربع ولاد، بنتين
وشابّين، امّا **اذا كان** يعني **حالته** وسط ... بحبّ يعني انّه ولدين
ʾana ʾiza itžawwazət wāḥid ġani ... bḥibb ykūn ʿandi ʾarbaʿ wlād, bintēn w šābbēn ʾamma **ʾiza kān** yaʿni **ḥāltu** wasaṭ ... bḥibb yaʿni ʾinnu waldēn
I if married-I one rich ... b-I-like be at-me four kids girls-two and boys-two, as-for **if was-it** that-is **circumstance-his** middle ... b-I-like that-is comp kids-two
If I marry a rich man ... I'd like to have 4 kids,2 girls and 2 boys, but ***if his circumstances are*** *modest ... I'd like to [have] 2 kids*

Ingham remarks that /kān/, /in-kān/, /čān/ and /in-čān/ all represent hypothetical conditional particles in Najdi (1994:139). Some of his examples contain pronoun suffixes marking the logical subjects of the sentences, indicating that these particles have become pseudo-verbs (see 5.3). In the following, /in-kān-kum/ *if you are* contains the suffixed object pronoun /kum/ *you*, which is the logical subject of the clause (1994:152):

N ان كانكم والمين ركّبتكم بالسيّارة ورحت بكم وان كان ما ولّمتم
رحت وخلّيتكم
in-kān-kum wālm-īn rakkab-t-kum bi-s-sayyārah u riḥ-t-ib-kum w in-kān ma wallam-tum riḥ-t u xallē-t-kum
if-kān-you ready-p put-I-you-p in-the-car and went-I-with-you-p and if-kān neg make ready-you-p went-I and left-I-you -p
If you are ready I will put you in the car and take you with me and if you are not ready I will go on and leave you

This frozen form of /kān/ as a hypothetical marker may be more common in the Najd than in Syria, however, since some of my Syrian and Lebanese informants find Cowell's thirty-odd-year-old examples strange. It is worth investigating the current use of frozen /kān/ in urban Syrian to compare with Cowell's examples.

In 7.2.2, it was argued that /kān/ sometimes occupies a topical sentence position. The analysis of hypothetical /kān/ as a topic is also supported by Haiman (1985:34), who believes that "the protasis of a conditional functions more like a topic or background state of affairs against which the apodosis is evaluated" (cited in Croft 1990:167). These frozen forms of /kān/ may have developed through this process: the topical use of /kān/ in conditionals probably helped give rise to the frozen form some Syrian and Gulf speakers use.

8.7.2.2 /kān/ with Perfective as Counterfactual (Irrealis) Mood

The verb /kān/ *to be* is frequently associated with counterfactual or irrealis mood, whether in direct or indirect conditional contexts. Examples from the four dialects show /kān/ (or Kuwaiti derivative /čān/) in indirect (implied) unreal conditional contexts. From Moroccan (Harrell 1962:185):

M كان خصكم تعطيوهم لي
kān xəṣṣkum taʿṭīwhum-li
[was-it necessary-for-you you-give-them to-me]
You all should have given them to me

From Egyptian (el-Tonsi 1982ii:25):

E كنت احب اجي لكن ماحدش عزمني
kunt ʾaḥibb āgi lākin maḥaddiš ʿazamni
was-I I-like I-come but no-one invited-he-me
I would have liked to come but no one invited me

My Syrian corpus includes a number of examples, among them:

S4 ما حابّها كنت من أول ما حبّيتها
mā ḥābb[h]a kint min ʾawwal mā ḥabbet[h]a
neg having-fallen-in-love-with-her were-you from first neg fell-in-love-with-you-her
You're not in love with her, you should have not fallen in love with her in the first place

From my Kuwaiti data:

K1 چان صرنا ضايعين
čān ṣirna ḏ̣āyʿīn
would became-we lost-p
We would have gotten lost

Several dialects have conditional particles that are derived from this association between /kān/ and the irrealis mood.

Moroccan speakers use /kūn/ or /kunrāh/ (/kurrāh/) followed by a perfective to represent irrealis or counterfactual mood in direct and indirect conditional contexts:

M3 كون جيتي كونراه تفيّكنا
kūn žīti kunrāh tfəyykna
kūn came-you kunrāh had-fun-we
If you had come we would have had fun (elicited)

Harrell's examples include (1962:169):

M كون غير قلتيها من قبيلا وهنّيتينا
kūn ġīr qultīha mən qbayla w hənnītīna
[kun only said-you-it from a-little-before and blessed-you-us]
you should have just said it a while ago and left us in peace

Feghali notes that Lebanese use /kūn/ (derived from /ykūn/, the imperfective of /kān/) in the same sense (1928:25; translation mine):

L لو كون شفته كنت هربت
law kūn šeftu kent hrebt
[if kun saw-I-him was-I fled-I]
If I had seen him, I would have fled

L لو كون جبتوه معكن كان ربح لكُن جميلة
law kūn žebtūh maʿkon kān rebeḥ-lkon žmile
[if kun brought-you-him with-you kān owed-he-you favor]
If you had brought him with you, he would have owed you a favor

Kuwaiti /čān/, derived from /kān/, marks counterfactual mood in the apodosis of conditionals:

K4 لو هي موصّلة لَه چان يا
lo ʾihiya mwaṣṣlat-la čān ya
if she having-brought-news-to-him čān came-he
If she had told him, he would have come

K3 انا لو اعرف اكتب واگرا چان يصير مسلسل ما ميش مثلَه
ʾāna lo ʾaʿarf ʾaktib w agra čān yiṣīr musalsil mā mīš mitla
I if I-know I-write and I-read čān he-become serial neg-there-is like-it

I, if I knew how to write and read, there would become a serial like no other

Finally, the imperative mood in Egyptian may be embedded by /kān/ to give a counterfactual reading:

E4 كنت تعالى
kunt taʿāla
were-you imper-come
You should have come

8.7.3 Habitual and Non-hypothetical Conditionals: Perfective

Ingham calls the use of Najdi /ʾila/ *if, when* "habitual" (1994:138). Moroccan and Kuwaiti speakers use /ʾila/ (Moroccan /ʾīla/) to mean *when*, normally followed by the perfective. Another type of habitual conditional involves the use of the particle /-ma/ with interrogatives in expressions meaning *whenever, wherever*, and *whatever*. These "habitual conditionals" normally take perfective verbs; however, they are not true conditionals but show the aspectual use of the perfective as a point in time.

8.7.3.1 /ʾīla/, /la/ *If, when*

The Moroccan and Kuwaiti conditional particle /ʾīla/ (and Kuwaiti variant /la/) may be used to mean *when* without a hypothetical sense. All my examples contain perfective verbs:

K3 بيت ط إلا صار الضحى يسوّون چاي
bēt ṭ ʾila ṣār əḍ-ḍəḥa yisawwūn čāy
house T if became-it the-mid-morning they-make tea
The T's, when it becomes mid-morning, they have tea

Moroccan speakers also use /ʾīla/ in this sense. Harrell cites the following example (1962:172):

M إلا جا راجلك في الليل، خلّيه حتى ينعس
ʾīla ža rāžlək fə-l-līl, xəllīh ḥətta ynʿəs
[if came-he husband-your in-the-night, let-him until he-sleep]
When your husband comes home tonight, leave him alone until he goes to sleep

Speakers of the central dialects, on the other hand, do not appear to use the corresponding conditional particle /ʾiza/ in this manner.

8.7.3.2 /-ma/ *-ever*

All four dialects share a construction that is a kind of habitual conditional: the particle /-ma/ suffixed to an interrogative particle to give the meaning *-ever*. This construction utilizes /-ma/ as a conditional marker and is normally followed by a perfective in Moroccan and Syrian (for Syrian, see Cowell 1964:338).

M9 فين ما مشينا انت معانا
fīn-ma mšīna, ʾinti mʿāna
where ever went-we you with-us
Wherever we went, you were with us

S3 لو شو ما عملت
law šu ma ʿamalt
if what ever did-I
Whatever I do ...

S2 كل ما جا واحد يخطبها بيجوا: هاي كانت حابّة فلان
kill ma ža wāḥid yəxṭəb[h]a, bīžu: hayy kānit ḥābbe flān
every ever came-he one he-ask-to-marry-her, indic-they-come: this was-she loving so-and-so
Every time someone comes to ask for her hand, they come: [saying] she was in love with so-and-so

S2 تاخد حيّالله مين ما قدّم لها
tāxud ḥayaḷḷa mīn ma qaddəm la[ha]
she-take whatever who ever presented-he to-her
She'll marry anyone who asks for her hand

In Egyptian, the habitual conditional with a perfective occurs most commonly with the particle /mahma/ *no matter how much.*[15]

E5 مهما عملت مش حيسامحني
mahma ʾamalt miš ḥaysamiḥni
however-much did-I neg fut-he-forgive-me
No matter what I do he'll never forgive me (elicited)

[15]The first syllable of /mahma/ , /mah/, is presumably a Classical variant of interrogative /mā/ (see Wright 1898i:274).

Kuwaiti speakers use /-ma/ conditionals with perfective and imperfective verbs. An elderly, uneducated Kuwaiti speaker uses an imperfective here:

K3 الحين تعالي، وين ما تدشّين وين ما تروحين
al-ḥīn taʿāley, wēn ma tdiššīn wēn ma trūḥīn
now come-f, where ever you-enter where ever you-go
Nowadays come [look], wherever you come and go [you see it]

8.7.4 Aspect and Mood in Conditional Sentences

Both aspect and mood appear to play a role in the choice of verb form in conditionals from all four dialects. Ingham's analysis of conditional sentences in Najdi makes a useful distinction between stative, punctual, and habitual conditionals (1994:133-); his analysis of Najdi Arabic serves as a useful comparative framework. The aspectual nature of the event is reflected by the choice of verb stem: the perfective often represents a punctual action, whereas the imperfective or a zero-verb marks a continuous or stative action or event.

At the same time, degree of hypotheticality plays an important role in determining verb stem. Cowell emphasizes the hypothetical nature of the use of the perfective with /ʾiza/ (1964:331-33), and the higher expectation created by the absence of the perfective. Non-perfective predicates often signal generalities, or that the speaker expects the condition to be fulfilled (see Cowell 1964:333). The more hypothetical the situation, the higher the tendency of the speaker to choose a perfective verb form, while zero-verb or the imperfective normally indicate a "non-hypothetical" conditional mood.[16]

The perfective is the true conditional mode, in the sense that there exists an equal possibility of the event happening and not happening, so it remains neutral or unmarked in this context. The use of the imperfective indicates a higher degree of speaker expectation or commitment to the possibility of it happening, and is marked in this context. The range of conditional choices the speaker makes may be represented as a continuum of hypotheticality, shown in Figure 3.

---

[16]The term "non-hypothetical conditional" is borrowed from Haiman, who uses it to designate a conditional whose protasis is factual (1985:33-4, cited in Croft 1990:167).

Figure 3 Continuum of Hypotheticality

Counterfactual: /kān/ with perfective	Punctual hypothetical: perfective	Stative hypothetical: imperfective or zero-verb

The speaker chooses from among zero-verbs, imperfectives, and perfectives according to the degree of hypotheticality and the aspect of the action. Non-hypothetical factive conditionals, or conditionals with a degree of expectation, tend to be stative and tend not to contain perfective verbs, except if the aspect is punctual. Less factive, more hypothetical clauses tend to be punctual and tend to contain perfective verb forms. Counterfactual conditionals usually contain, in addition to a perfective verb form, a reflex of /kān/ as well. It is as if the temporal distance signalled by /kān/ in these counterfactual conditionals indicated a kind of "hypothetical" distance, or speaker distance from a commitment to the truth of the conditional.

The following Syrian passage contains a two-part conditional with two different morphological forms: imperfective /mma yḥibbu/ *they are in love* and perfective /simʿu/ *they heard.* Both are governed by the particle /ʾiza/; the difference cannot then be temporal and must be modal or aspectual. The progressive indicative /mma yḥibbu/ gives the imperfective aspect of an action that takes place over a long period of time. By contrast, the perfective /simʿu/ *they heard*, gives a perfective aspect: a one-time, non-durative, completed event. The choice of verb form here is not temporal but aspectual.

S2 هلّق عنّا بالضيعة، اذا اتنين مّا يحبّوا بعضن وسمعوا كمان العالم فيهن يا لطيف! شغلة كبيرة

halla' ʿanna bi-ḍ-ḍēʿa -- ʾiza tnēn mma yḥibbu baʿḍon w simʿu kamān il-ʿālam fi[h]on, ya laṭīf! šaġle kbīre

now at-us in-the-village, if two prog they-love each-other and heard-they also the-world about-them O God! thing big

Now in our village, if two [young people] are in love, and everybody hears about them, God! [it's] a big deal

The next example is taken from a Kuwaiti folklorist's interview of an elderly woman about life in the old days. The use of the imperfective

/tḥaməl/ *she gets pregnant* here has nothing to do with time reference, marked past by the context; rather, the imperfective here signals a factive modality:

K4 اذا اهي ما تحمل ش يگولون عنها ؟
ʾiḏa ʾihiya mā tḥaməl š yigūlūn ʿanha?
if she neg she-gets-pregnant what they-say about-her?
If she wouldn't get pregnant what would they say about her?

By contrast, in the next example, the speaker uses a perfective verb in reference to the present. The aspect is punctual, hence the choice of the perfective:

K3 والصلاة، جاهلة ! علموها ! لا ما صلّت اليوم تصلّي باچر
wə ṣ-ṣala, yāhla! ʿallmūha! la mā ṣallit l-yōm tṣalli bāčir
and the-praying, kid! teach-p-her! if neg prayed-she today, she-pray tomorrow
As for praying, she's a kid! teach her! If she doesn't pray today, she'll pray tomorrow

If hypotheticality is signalled by the use of the perfective, then conditional sentences that set up an either/or choice with equal probabilities should normally contain a perfective verb. In the next example, whether the matchmaker gets the entire fee or not is contingent upon whether she works by herself or with another matchmaker. Both equally likely possibilities are marked with the perfective /kān/:

K2 ساعات يعطوني ميتين، من أهل الولد ميتين من اهل البنت ميتين،
ساعات يعطونني من اهل الـ — يعني مية وخمسين مية وخمسين،
اذا كان بروحي هذا زين، و **اذا كان** معي واحدة لا، اگسّمهم لميتين
حگي وميتين حگها
sāʿāt yaʿṭūnni mitēn, min ahl il-walad mitēn min ahl il-bint mitēn, sāʿāt yaʿṭūnni min ahl il -- yaʿni əmya w xamsīn əmya w xamsīn, **ʾiḏa kān** bi-rūḥi hāḏa zēn, w **iḏa kān** maʿi waḥda laʾ, ʾagsimhum l-mitēn ḥaggi w mitēn ḥaggha
times they-give-me 200, from family of-the-boy 200 from family of-the-girl 200, times they-give-me from family of-the -- that-is 100 and 50 and 100 and 50, **if was-it** by-self-my this good, and **if was-it** with-me one-f no, I-split-them to-200 for-me and 200 for-her

Sometimes they give me 200 [dinars], from the family of the boy 200 [and] from the family of the girl 200, sometimes they give me from the family of the -- that is, 150, 150 ***if it [is]*** *by myself that's good, and* ***if there [is]*** *a woman with me no, I split them, to 200 for me and 200 for her.*

The next passage, from Syria, contains a double conditional showing a modal difference. Both clauses in the following are stative; the first, /ʾiza ḥilwe/ *if she is pretty*, contains no verb, and the second, /ʾiza mā kānit mitʿallme/ *if she [was] not educated*, contains the verb /kānit/ *she was*. The meaning of the first clause would not change very much with the omission of /ʾiza/, and is thus marked by the speaker as being factive through the absence of /kān/, while the second, the "true" conditional, is clearly hypothetical, and contains /kān/:

S2 وهلق كتير ما عاد انّه الشباب ما عاد يهتمّوا مثلاً انّه مثلاً ياخدوا واحدة **اذا حلوة** كتير وكذا **اذا ما كانت** متعلّمة مستحيل يفكّر فيها الاّ يعني واحد كتير تافه

w hallaʾ ktīr mā ʿād ʾinnu š-šabāb mā ʿād yihtammu masalan ʾinnu masalan yāxdu waḥde **ʾiza ḥilwe** ktīr w kaza **ʾiza mā kānit** mitʿallme mustaḥīl yfakkir fī[h]a ʾilla yaʿni wāḥid ktīr tāfih

and now a-lot neg returned-3ms comp the-youth no longer they-care for-example comp for-example they-take one-f **if pretty** very and so-on **if neg was-she** educated impossible he-think about-her except that-is one very inane

Now, often, it's no longer that young people no longer care, for example, about marrying a girl ***if*** *[she's] very* ***pretty*** *and so forth,* ***if she's not*** *educated, [he] will never think of [marrying] her, except, that is, someone really inane*

The next set of examples illustrate the role of aspect in determining verb stem choice in conditional sentences. If the conditional event is punctual, it tends to be expressed with a perfective. If the conditional is stative, on the other hand, it tends to be expressed with a non-perfective, often zero-verb. The following sentences all contain punctual actions expressed by perfective verbs: in the first, /ʿaṭītīha/ *you gave it*, in the second, /gat/ *she came*, and in the third, /šiftha/ *I saw her*. The time references here include both future and non-specific non-past:

M9 الصدقة إيلا عطيتيها عطيتيها ما تقولش عطيت
ṣ-ṣadaqa ʾīla ʿṭītīha ʿṭītīha mā tqūlš ʿaṭīt
the-alms if gave-you-it gave-you-it neg you-say gave-I
Alms, if you give them, you give them, you don't say 'I gave'

E1 اذا جت منى خليها تروح تجيب الفستان
ʾiza gat muna xallīha trūḥ tigīb il-fustān
if she-came Muna have-her she-go she-bring the-dress
If Muna comes, have her go and get the dress

K2 اذا ما شفتها من بعيد، ما ادري عنها برّا
ʾiḏa mā šiftha min biʿīd, mā adri ʿanha barra
if neg saw-I-her from far neg I-know about-her outside
If I don't see her from a distance, I don't know anything about her [behavior] outside the house

In contrast, Egyptian, Syrian, and Kuwaiti speakers often express stative conditionals with zero-verb, as the following examples demonstrate. In the first, from Kuwait, the second conditional /lo fī/ *if there is* has a past time reference, even though the clause does not contain a perfective but rather the tenseless participle /ṣāyir/ *having occurred.*

K3 لو هو تعبان لو فيه ويّا أحد صاير كلام، شي
lo ʾuhu taʿbān lo fī wiyya ʾaḥad ṣāyir kalām, šay
if he tired if there-is with one having-occurred words, something
If he's tired, if there has occurred an argument with someone or something

The zero-verb in the next example hints at what this matchmaker knows, that many prospective grooms like the matches she picks for them. Hence she uses the zero-verb rather than /kān/ in the conditional clause:

K2 اذا هو له خاطر فيها، ادگ لهم تلفون، هه؟ ش رايكم في الولد؟
ʾiḏa huwwa la xāṭir fīha, ʾadigg-luhum telifōn, ha? š rāykum fi l-walad?
if he to-him fancy for-her, I-call to-them telephone, [asking] hmm? what do you think about the boy?
If he has a fancy for her I call them, and [say] hmm, what's your opinion of the boy?

The next speaker relates a frequently occurring event, her neighbors dropping in on her. The "condition" here, that she is not busy, is both habitual and expected:

S5 اذا ما عندك شي بدنا ندخل نشرب فنجان قهوة عندك
iza mā ʿandik ši bidna nidxul nišrab finjān ʾahwe ʿandik
if neg at-you thing desire-our we-enter we-drink cup of-coffee at-you
If you're not busy, we want to come in and drink a cup of coffee with you

The following Kuwaiti passage responds to the question, "What do you tell your clients about prospective brides?" The matchmaker's answer contains six stative conditionals, three headed by /ḥatta lo/ *even if* and three by /ʾiḏa/. Of these six clauses, five contain imperfectives /tʿarfīn/ *you know*, /aʿarf/ *I know* or /tṣīr/ *she is related to*, and one contains a tenseless perfect (participle) /dāxla/ *having entered.* In addition, the text contains one punctual quasi-conditional (a clause hypothetical in meaning but missing a conditional particle) so marked by the use of the perfective: /inti ʿaṭetīni raqam it-tilifōn/ *[if, let's say] you gave me the telephone number.*

K2 انا اگول لَه ما اعرف عن البنية —— **حتى لو تعرفين** ؟ —— **حتى لو اعرف** يعني مو **حتى لو اعرف** ، لا، يعني **اذا** يعني **تصير لي** ادخل دخلاتي وطلعاتي عليها وگاعدة معاهم لا، اشرح له، اگول له والله البنية بيت اوادم وخوش انسانة وعاجلة وبنية شريفة .. **اذا مو داخلة** معاها يعني مثلاً **انتي عطيتيني رقم التليفون** گلتِ لي والله بنت فلان انا ما اعرف عنها شي بس **اذا اعرف عنها** اي شي لا، اگول اللي ربّي يسألني عنّه
ʾāna ʾagūl-la mā ʾaʿarf ʿan lə-bnayya --- **ḥatta lo tʿarfīn?** --- **ḥatta lo ʾaʿarf** yaʿni mū **ḥatta lo ʾaʿarf** lā, yaʿni **ʾiḏa** yaʿni **tṣīr-li** ʾadxul daxlāti wa ṭalʿāti ʿalēha w gāʿda maʿāhum lā, ʾašraḥ-la, ʾagul-la waḷḷa l-bnayya bēt ʾawādim w xōš ʾinsāna w ʿājla w bnayya šarīfa ... **ʾiḏa mū dāxla** maʿāha yaʿni, maṯalan **ʾinti ʿaṭetīni raqam it-tilifōn** giltī-li waḷḷah bint flān ʾāna mā aʿarf ʿanha ʾay šay, bass **ʾiḏa aʿarf ʿanha** ʾay šay lā, ʾagūl illi rabbi yisʾalni ʿanna

I I-say-to-him neg I-know about the-girl --- **even if you-know**? --- **even if I-know** that-is neg **even if I-know** no, that-is **if** that-is **she-is-related-to-me** I-enter entries-my and exits-my on-her and sitting with-them no, I-explain-to-him, I-say-to-him by-God the-girl house of-good-people and good person and sensible and girl honorable ... **if neg having-entered** with-her that-is, for-example **you gave-you-me number of-the-telephone** said-you-to-me by-God daughter of-so-and-so I neg I-know about-her thing, but **if I-know** about-her any thing no, I-say rel lord-my he-asks-me about-it

*I tell him I don't know about the girl. --- **Even if you know?** --- **Even if I know**–I mean, not **even if I know**, no, **if she is a relative of mine** and I interact with her, come and go at her house, and sit with them, no, I explain to him, I say, the girl is from a good family, she is a nice girl, level-headed, and honorable ... **If I don't have any interaction** with her, that is for example **[if] you give me the telephone number** and tell me, [she's] the daughter of so-and-so, I don't know anything about her, but **if I know** anything about her no, I say what God will ask me about (what I will be responsible to God for).*

Moroccan presents an exception to this pattern, not allowing zero-verb conditional clauses. All of Harrell's conditional examples contain /kān/ (1962:170-71) as do Caubet's (1993:205), and mine:[17]

M6 شريت مگانة ديال الما، ما كتخدم غير إيلا كان الما

šrīt magāna dyāl l-ma, mā katəxdəm ġīr ʾīla kān l-ma

bought-I watch gen the-water neg indic-it-works only if was-it the-water

I bought a water[proof] watch, it only works if there's water

---

[17]The only Moroccan conditional I found with a zero-verb is the following:

M قال لها اجري أبنتي إيلا عندك شي شفرة

qāl-lha žri ʾā binti ʾīla ʿndk ši šəfra

said-he-to-her run O daughter-my if at-you some knife

He said to her, Run daughter, please, if you have a knife [bring it].

However, it is doubtful that this should even be classified as a conditional, since the expression /ʾīla mā/ is used as a polite request formula (Harrell 1962:171). While /mā/ is missing from this particular utterance, the sentence clearly expresses a polite request to bring the knife.

By way of concluding the discussion on conditionals, the analysis proposed here will be applied to several Syrian texts that happen to contain a number of conditional sentences. These passages may contain more information than at first meets the ear.

The following short sentence contains an imperfective verb, marked for low hypotheticality. The speaker herself has previously mentioned that she did learn the language (English). Having removed herself from the field of possible "subjects," the use of the imperfective suggests that being in a foreign country and not learning the language is in fact a regular occurrence, and further, serves to elevate her own achievement of learning English.

S5 لأن كتير صعب اذا واحد ما بيعرف لغة
la'in[n] ktīr ṣaʿb ʾiza wāḥid mā byaʿrif luġa
because very hard if one neg indic-he-knows language
Because it's very hard if one doesn't know [the] language

Three final passages all come from an interview with a young female Syrian informant. The topic of the first passage is marriage customs, specifically financial expectations and the right of the girl to choose whom she will marry. Talking in generalities, and not about a particular situation, the speaker uses /ʾiza/ repeatedly with zero-verb or pseudo-verbs (marked in boldface). The absence of /kān/ here gives her statements a degree of expectation of fulfillment, making them less hypothetical. Whether or not the groom buys gold jewelry for his fiancée, either situation can and does occur regularly. In contrast to these non-tensed forms, an *even if* clause contains the perfective verb /iʿtaraḍu/ *they objected*, showing both the non-stative nature of the verb and less speaker commitment to the regularity of parental objection.

S2 وع الاهل تجهيز العروس والعريس بيقدّم غرفة النوم والبيت طبعاً.
امّا ما بياخدوا من العريس أي شيء إلاّ **اذا هو بدّه** يقدّم لها لحاله
دهب او شي، ما بيفترضوا عندنا انّه لازم تلبّسها لازم ما تلبّسها
متل بعضها عندن **اذا معه** بيلبّسها، **اذا ما معه** مو مشكل. يعني
ما زال هي مختارته وعاجبها وبتحبّه وبيحبّها ما فيه مشكل عند
الاهل يعني، **حتّى لو اعترضوا** الاهل **اذا بدّها** غصباً عنّن بتاخده
لأنّها بتحبّه

w ʿa l-ahəl tažhīz il-ʿarūs w l-ʿarīs biqaddim ġərft in-nōm w l-bēt ṭabʿan. ʾamma mā byāxdu min l-ʿarīs ayy šēʾ ʾilla **ʾiza huwwe beddu** yqaddim-l[h]a la-ḥālu dahab ʾaw še, mā byiftirḍu ʿan[d]na ʾinnu lāzim tlabbis[h]a lāzim mā tlabbis[h]a, mitil baʿḍ[h]a ʿandon **ʾiza maʿu** bilabbs[h]a, **ʾiza mā maʿu** mū miškel. yaʿni ma zāl hiyye muxtārtu w ʿāžiba w bitḥibbu w biḥibb[h]a mā fī miškil ʿand il-ʾahəl yaʿni, **ḥatta law iʿtarḍu** l-ʾahəl, **ʾiza bedda** ġaṣban ʿannon btāxdu laʾinna bitḥibbu

and on-the-family trousseau of-the-bride and the-groom indic-he-presents room of-the-sleeping and the-house of-course. as-for neg indic-they-take from the-groom any thing except **if he he-wants** he-present-to-her for-self-him gold or thing, neg indic-they-assume at-us comp must you-dress-her must neg you-dress-her, like each-other at-them **if neg with-him** neg problem. that-is neg it-ceased she having-chosen-him and pleasing-her and indic-she-loves-him and indic-he-loves-her neg there-is problem at the-family that-is **even if they-objected** the-family **if she-wants** despite them indic-she-takes-him because-she indic-she-loves-him

*The family [of the bride] is responsible for the bride's trousseau, and the groom gives the bedroom and the house, of course. But they don't take anything [else] from the groom except **if he wants** to give her [something] himself, gold or something, they don't assume in our custom that (you) must give her [gold] to wear or not, it's all the same to them, **if he has** [the means], he gives her [gold] to wear, **if he doesn't have** [the means] it's not a problem. As long as she has chosen him and is happy with him and she loves him and he loves her, there's no problem with the family. **Even if they object, if she wants** [to marry him], she does, in spite of them, because she loves him.*

Later in the same conversation, this speaker discusses her thoughts on premarital sexual relations. Here she uses /ʾiza/ twice, once with /kān/ and once with the perfective /ḍallit/ *she remained*, in contrast to the previous passage which contained only zero-verbs with /ʾiza/. In this case, not only does /kān/ give a higher degree of hypotheticality, but it may also signal the speaker's own "distance" from the ideas she is expressing. While the speaker admits of the possibility of girls having pre-marital relations, she implies that this is not a normal course of events, and hints at her own ambiguous position vis-a-vis this behavior.

S2 بس يعني مو مشكل **اذا ضلّت** عزراء، يعني بإمكانها انّه تضلّ عزراء، بس ... يعني مو مشكل عندي **اذا كان عندها** علاقة جنسية او عندها صديق يعني شغلة عادية

bass ya'ni mū muškəl **'iza ḍallit** 'azrā', ya'ni b-'imkān[h]a 'innu tḍall 'azrā', bass ... ya'ni mū miškil 'andi **'iza kān 'and[h]a** 'alāqa žinsiyye 'aw 'and[h]a ṣadīq ya'ni šaġle 'ādiyye

but that-is neg problem **if remained-she** virgin, that-is in-possibility-her comp she-remain virgin, but ... that-is neg problem at-me **if was-it at-her** relationship sexual or at-her boyfriend that-is thing ordinary

But I mean it's not a problem ***if she remains*** *a virgin, I mean it's possible for her to remain a virgin ... It's not a problem in my opinion* ***if she has*** *a sexual relationship or [if] she has a boyfriend, that is, it's a normal thing*

Similarly, in the third excerpt, two verbs are governed by /'iza/: the perfective /šaṭṭet/ *she went too far* and /kānit/ *she was.* Both the "distancing" effect of the subject matter and the punctual nature of /šaṭṭet/ play a role in the choice of the perfective here:

S2 هلّق يعني صار شويّ العالم اتعوّدوا انّه يشوفوا اتنين ماشيين مع بعضن هيكي. بس كمان **اذا الواحدة شطّت** وهيك يعني **كانت** شوي **فلتانة** بعلاقتها كمان كتير بيزبلوها

halla' ya'ni ṣār šwayy il-'ālam it'awwdu 'innu yšūfu tnēn māšyīn ma' ba'ḍon hēki. bass kamān **'iza l-waḥde šaṭṭet** w hēk ya'ni **kānit** šwayy **faltāne** b-'alāqta kamān ktīr byizbilū[h]a

now that-is became-it a-bit the-people got-accustomed-they comp they-see two walking with each-other thus but comp also **if the-one-f went-too-far-she** and thus that-is **was-she** a-bit **loose-f** in-relationships-her also a-lot they-shun-her

Nowadays, everyone has somewhat gotten used to seeing two [youths] walking together in that way, but still, ***if a girl goes too far*** *and stuff and* ***[if] she's*** *a bit* ***too loose*** *in her relationships, they shun her a lot*

8.8 Summary

Of all the syntactic features examined in this study, modality shows the greatest range of variation from dialect to dialect. While Moroccan and Egyptian show essentially the same modal system, their indicative prefixes differ. Egyptian and Syrian appear to share the indicative marker /b(i)-/, but the range of meaning of Syrian /b-/ only partially overlaps with its Egyptian counterpart. Evidence suggests that Syrian /b-/ may have two sources: intentive /b-/, found in the Gulf, which Al-Najjar claims derives from the verb /ʾabi/ *I want* (1984:87-90), and another source, perhaps preposition /b-/, giving an indicative (continuous or habitual) meaning.

While Moroccan, Egyptian, and Syrian speakers have developed indicative markers, Kuwaiti seems to be headed in another direction by developing a non-indicative marker, /čān/, which has several functions, including a modal *would*, an irrealis conditional, and a narrative device that may signal non-progressive or non-present action. More research, and more contextualized data, are needed in this area.

In general, the use of the morphological tense forms in conditional sentences is not subject to temporal considerations, but rather reflects aspectual and modal factors. Speakers normally choose a perfective verb or /kān/ in punctual conditionals, a choice which contrasts with their consistent use of imperfective and zero-verbs in stative conditionals. These patterns show clearly the primacy of aspect–not tense–to the choice of verb form in conditional sentences. Finally, the association of /kān/ with counterfactual mood remains consistent across dialects.

9 Negation

9.0 Introduction

Of all the syntactic features examined in this study, only one major feature emerges as an isogloss separating eastern and western dialect areas: the use of /-š/ as a negative enclitic. The western dialects, Moroccan and Egyptian, combine variants of /mā/ with /-š/, while Kuwaiti and urban Syrian dialects use /mā/ and particles derived from it. Of course, the isogloss that separates east and west is difficult to locate and is surely not a continuous line: features do not disappear abruptly but rather fade out gradually, and the history and socio-sectarian diversity of the Levant have contributed to a rich patterning of dialects in the region, some of which use /-š/ in negation (Cowell 1964:383, Feghali 1928:220-21). Despite this surface-structure variation, however, all four dialects exhibit striking parallels in negative strategies and structures on the whole. Studying cross-dialectal patterns of negation can thus serve both to elucidate historical developments in spoken Arabic, and to demonstrate the importance of looking beyond surface structure to underlying strategies and pragmatic principles in studying the syntax of spoken language.

9.1 Overview of Negation in the Dialects

Grammars of the dialects vary in their treatment of negation, but all of them present negation in lists of particles and their possible uses. I will first present a brief overview of the most comprehensive treatments of negation in each dialect, then attempt to find parallels and pragmatic functions that can explain negation in the dialects with more precision and economy.

Harrell's *Reference Grammar of Moroccan Arabic* lists a "Basic Procedure" in which the split particle /mā - š/ is used, a separate category of "Negative Imperative" in which the same construction forms the prohibitive, "Additional Negative Forms," in which the /-š/ is omitted, a separate category of "Categorical Negative" in which the /-š/ is also dropped, and under "Non-Verbal Negation," he notes that "[n]ouns and adjectives are also sometimes prefixed with /mā/ and suffixed with /ši/" (1962:152-55). The presentation is a bit confusing, since a total of seven separate categories are given to detail three syntactic structures, and it appears that nouns and adjectives can be negated exactly as verbs. However, Harrell's analysis attempts to ascertain the various syntactic strategies that Moroccan Arabic uses, and his construction of 'categorical negation' as a distinct negating strategy with its own syntactic marking stands out as a significant contribution to the description of negation in Moroccan. In fact, this pragmatic function exists in all four dialects, as will be shown in 9.5.

Woidich (1968) examines in great detail every possible negative construction in Egyptian Arabic, resulting in a complete inventory of negation in Egyptian Arabic. His presentation is quite detailed, but no overall picture of negating strategies emerges.

Cowell classifies negation in Syrian Arabic according to four negative particles: /mā/, /mū/, /lā/, and the "negative copula" (1964:383-88). Cowell's streamlined approach describes the basic syntactic strategies in this dialect, making it useful for comparative studies. Cowell's distinction of the 'negative copula' as a separate syntactic category also has comparative value, and is adopted here as a subcategory of verbal negation.

Holes (1990) divides negation in Gulf Arabic into two categories, "sentence negation" and "constituent negation." Under the former, he lists /mā/ for perfective and imperfective verbs, /lā/ for imperatives, and /lā .. wila/ for coordinated clauses; under the latter, he includes /mū/ and its variants.[1] Holes also illustrates another unnamed negative structure in which /mā/ is prefixed to personal pronouns (1990:244). He makes several important observations on the pragmatic aspects of the various syntactic structures, most notably his distinction between sentence negation and constituent negation, and his analysis of /mū/ as the negation of a negative sentence proposition (such as, *It's not that I don't want to* 1990:72). Johnstone's cursory treatment of Kuwaiti records

---

[1]Holes lists /mūb/ as the primary negative particle for this category (1990:73); according to my data this is not commonly used in Kuwait, where /mū/ is preferred. The particle /mū/ has a feminine variant /mī/ which also does not occur in my data (Holes 1990:73-4).

"negation of adjectives and participles" by /mū/ and negation of "other nominal constructions" by /mā/; he also lists "negated forms of the personal pronouns" (1967:148).

What can be concluded from a preliminary comparison of these analyses? Features that appear to be common to two or more dialects include the fact that most of these dialects discriminate between a loosely 'verbal' category and a corresponding 'non-verbal' one that negates predicated structures. Moroccan and Egyptian dialects negate verbs with /mā - š/, urban Syrian and Kuwaiti with /mā/. Sentence predicates are negated in the western dialects with /miš/ or /māši/ while the eastern dialects normally use /mū/ or a variant thereof. Examples from each of the dialect regions illustrate these patterns. The first two sentences exemplify verbal negation in the western dialects:

M11 ما بغاش يدير لها السميّة ديك الساعة اللي زادت
mā bġāš ydīr-lha s-smiyya dīk s-sāʿa lli zādət
neg he-wanted-neg make-for-her the name that the-hour that she-was-born
He didn't want to give her a name at the time she was born

E1 ما شفتش الموديل دا قبل كدا
mā šuftəš il-mōdēl da ʾabl kida
neg saw-I the-style that before thus
I didn't see that style before

The following sentences illustrate predicate negation in these dialects, with /māši/ in Moroccan, and /miš/ in Egyptian:

M1 لطيفة ماشي ف الدار
laṭīfa māši fə-d-dār
Latifa neg in-the-house
Latifa's not home

E1 لا مش قديم
laʾ miš ʾadīm
no neg old
No, [it's] not old

The next Syrian passage contains both verbal negation, /mā btufruq/ *it makes no difference*, and non-verbal negation, /mū mʿallme/ *not educated*:

S2 امّا من قبل خلص، حلوة، يا لطيف! معلّمة مو معلّمة متل بعضها. ايه. هلّق كمان متل بعضها يعني واحد بيحبّ واحدة ولو كانت حابّة مو حابّة كمان ما بتفرق معه

ʾamma min qabəl xalaṣ ḥilwe yā laṭīf! muʿallme mū muʿallme mitil baʿḍ[h]a. ʾēh. hallaʾ kamān mitil baʿḍ[h]a yaʿni wāḥid biḥibb waḥde w law kānit ḥābbe mū ḥābbe kamān mā btufruq maʿu.

as-for from before that's-it pretty O-God! having-been educated neg having-been educated like each-other. yeah. now also like each-other it-mean one indic-he-loves one-f even if was-she having-loved neg having-loved also neg indic-it-differs with-him

Before, that [was] it, [if she's] pretty, wow! educated, not educated, it's all the same [to him]. Now too it's all the same, that is, [if] someone is in love with a [girl], whether she has had love affairs or not, also it makes no difference to him.

Likewise, this Kuwaiti sentence includes verbal negation /mā yiḥibbha/ *he doesn't love her*, and non-verbal negation /mū ḥilwa/ *not pretty*:

K3 ريّال عندَه مَرَة حريم ثنتين، واحدة حلوة بس هو ما يحبها، هاذيج مو حلوة بس يحبها

rayyāl ʿinda mara ḥarīm t̠intēn, waḥda ḥilwa bass hu mā yḥibbha had̠īč mū ḥilwa, bass yḥibbha

man at-him woman wives two one pretty but he neg he-loves-her that-one neg pretty but he-loves-her

A man has a wife, two wives, one is pretty but he doesn't love her, the other one is not pretty but he loves her

However, these unmarked forms of negation exist alongside other marked forms in which the use of these particles is reversed: that is, /mā - š/ and /mā/ can negate syntactic predicates, while /miš/ and /mū/ can negate verbs. The first two following sentences contain examples of the verbal particles /mā -š/ and /mā/ negating predicates, /mā maʿrūfš/ *[he is] unknown*, and /mā lāzim/ *must not*. The third and fourth examples contain the predicate negative particles /miš/ and /mū/ negating verbs, /miš tisallimi/ *[should] you not say hello*, and /mū yiyīni/ *he [better] not come to me.*

M3 حتّى ف المغرب ما معروفش
ḥtta f l-məġrib mā məʿrūfš
even in Morocco neg having-become-known
[He is] even in Morocco unknown

S2 قال انّه ما لازم نخبّره فجأةً
qāl ʾinnu mā lāzim nxabbru fažʾatan
said-he that neg must we-inform-him suddenly
He said, We mustn't inform him all of a sudden

E1 مش تسلّمي؟
miš tisallimi?
neg you-say-hello-f?
Shouldn't you say hello?

K1 خل بالك على محمد -- مو ييني!
xal bālak ʿala mḥammad -- mū yiyīni!
let attention-your to Muhammad -- neg he-comes-to-me!
Pay attention to Muhammad -- he [had better] not show up!

Do these contradictory examples, or marked forms of negation, render invalid the proposed schema of negation as verbal and non-verbal? If it can be assumed that the use of these negative particles in a variety of syntactic environments is not arbitrary, there must exist underlying principles guiding the choice of negating particle. I will begin by distinguishing between unmarked and marked usage, and demonstrate certain pragmatic principles which can account for both types of negation.

9.2 Three Strategies of Negation

It is significant that all four dialects have two basic particles of negation. These are: in Moroccan and Egyptian, (1) /mā - š/ and (2) variants of /miš/ in Egypt or /māši/ in Morocco; and in Syrian and Kuwaiti, (1) /mā/ and (2) /mū/ and variants. Both the syntax and pragmatics of these pairs correspond closely to one another from dialect to dialect, indicating that negation in all four dialects is of two standard types, which will be called Verbal Negation and Predicate Negation, in order to reflect their normal, unmarked usage. Table 9-1 summarizes the particles of each type.

Table 9-1: Particles of Negation

Particles of Negation		
	Verbal Negation	Predicate Negation
Moroccan	mā ... š(i)	māši
Egyptian	mā ... š(i)	miš
Syrian	mā	mū
Kuwaiti	mā	mū

The categories verbal and predicate negation have the additional advantage of reflecting Arabic sentence typology. Spoken as well as formal Arabic make use of two main sentence patterns, called by the medieval grammarians *the verbal sentence* (Arabic /al-jumla al-fiᶜliyya/) and *the nominal sentence* (/al-jumla al-ismiyya/). The former exhibits VSO typology and represents unmarked sentence order in formal Arabic (it is the normal structure for subordinate clauses such as relative clauses). Nominal sentences exhibit SVO order and reflect topic-prominent word order (see 10.1). While the claim has been made and repeated that modern spoken Arabic has all but lost its VSO typology, Chapter 10 will present evidence that refutes this claim. Both VSO and SVO typologies play prominent roles in spoken Arabic, and the fact that the dialects have different negating strategies for these two patterns offers one piece of evidence in support of this hypothesis.

The terms 'verbal' and ' predicate ' negation refer to the normal, unmarked negation of VSO and SVO typologies respectively. They are not meant to refer to absolute structural rules: while the verbal negation particles normally negate verbs and pseudo-verbs, and the predicate negation particles normally negate nominal sentences, data from all of the dialects include examples of marked negation patterns that violate these "rules," as I have shown. One possible explanation for these apparent violations is that sentences of the same syntactic type may not necessarily have the same underlying pragmatic structure. In fact, there exist few absolute syntactic restrictions on the use of negative particles with various sentence constituents, and purely formal syntactic analysis cannot completely explain negation in spoken Arabic.

In addition to the two standard particles, each of these dialects has a negative particle that will be called here, following Cowell, the "negative copula." The negative copula represents a special case within verbal negation, is distinguished by its combination of a verbal negation particle with a personal pronoun, and differs in structure and function from a negatively predicated sentence. For example, Egyptian Arabic allows both of the following:

E هو مش هنا
huwwa miš hina
He is not here

E ماهواش هنا
mahuwwāš hina
He is not here

The analysis that follows will show a pragmatic distinction between these two structures.

In addition to verbal negation and predicate negation, a third type of negation found cross-dialectally is a kind of emphatic negation I will call "categorical negation," adapting the term from Harrell. Like its syntactically more restricted counterpart in formal Arabic, *the /lā/ of absolute negation* /lā al-nāfiya li-l-jins/, categorical negation negates absolutely and categorically. Syntactically, categorical negation is marked in the western dialects by the absence of /-š/. While the eastern dialects have no counterpart to western /-š/, there exists evidence for this category in the use of negation in listing, for which all the dialects share a form of categorical negative listing, using the particle /lā/.

There thus exist three different types or strategies of negation shared by all four dialects: verbal, predicate, and catagorical negation. All of these negative strategies share essentially the same pragmatic functions across all four dialects, with minor regional variations that will be explored in the following sections.

9.3 Verbal Negation

The basic function of the particles of verbal negation /mā - š/ and /mā/ is to negate the imperfective and perfective verb forms. Examples from each dialect region:

M11 ما كتنوضش من الدار
mā katnūḍš mən d-dār
neg indic-she-gets-up from the-house
She doesn't leave the house

M9 ما شراشي كبير غير صغير
mā šrāši kbīr ġī[r] ṣġīr
neg bought-he big only small
He didn't buy a big one, only a small one

E3 ما بيعجبوش العجب
mā biyiʿgibūš il-ʿagab
neg indic-it-please-him-neg the-wonder
Nothing pleases him

E10 ما رفعتش ايدي
mā rafaʿtəš ʾīdi
neg raised-I hand-my
I didn't raise my hand

S6 لا ما بلحق
lā mā bəlḥaʾ
no neg will-I-catch-up
No, I won't have time

S4 قَللن ما حبّيتها
ʾal-lon mā ḥabbēt[h]a
said-he-to-them neg loved-I-her
He told them, I didn't fall in love with her

K1 كل اربع وخميس ويمعة ما استثگلها
kil ʾarbaʿ w xamīs w yimʿa mā astaṯgilha
every Wednesday, Thursday, and Friday neg I-consider-heavy-it
Every Wednesday, Thursday and Friday, I don't consider it too tiresome

K3 ما خلّوا شي ما خذوه
mā xallaw šay mā xaḏū
neg left-they thing neg took-they-it
They didn't leave anything they didn't take

All the examples cited above represent unmarked patterns of negation. The main exception to this rule is found in urban Egypt, where the future /ḥa- + imperfective/ is obligatorily negated with /miš/, which normally functions as the particle of predicate negation.[2]

E1 مش حيبقى حلو عليّ
miš ḥayib'a ḥilw ʿalayya
neg will-it-become pretty on-me
It won't look good on me

Dialects in southern Egypt and Morocco negate the future with /mā - š/. From an Egyptian movie:

E ما حنگولش!
mā ḥa ngulš!
neg fut we-say!
We won't tell!

In northern Morocco, negative /mā/ and future /māš/ collapse into /māš/:

M1 ماش ناكلشي وادا جيت نعندك
maš nākulši w-ida žīt n-ʿəndk
neg-will-I-eat and-if came-I to-at-you
I won't eat [even] if I come over

Syrian and Kuwaiti speakers negate future imperfectives with /mā/:

S ما حيزيد كتير
mā ḥa-yzīd ktīr
[it] isn't going to add much (Cowell 1964:384)

K3 ما بتيي
mā bityi
neg will-she-comes
She won't come

---

[2]This exception may be part of a larger historical process that negation in Egyptian appears to be undergoing, in which the syntactic environments of /miš/ appear to be expanding at the expense of /mā ... š/.

In the case of complex verb phrases, or verb phrases that consist of more than one constituent, such as compound verbs, the first linear element normally constitutes the focus of syntactically and semantically unmarked negation. In the western dialects, /mā/ and /-š/ enclose the focused element:

M10 ولد البلاد ما بقاش كيمشي البحر
wəld l-blād mā bqāš kaymši l-bḥar
boy of-the-town neg remained-he indic-he-go to-the-sea
The people of the town no longer go to the beach

E3 هي ما كانتش عارفة
hiyya mā kānitš ʿarfa
she neg was-she knowing
She didn't know

In the eastern dialects, /mā/ precedes the focused element. In compound verb phrases, this focused element may be a temporal verb, as /kān/ *was, used to* in the following Kuwaiti example, or a temporally embedded verb, like /yšūfu/ *they see* in the Syrian example:

K2 اوّل ما كان يشوفها
ʾawwel mā kān yšūfha
first neg was-it he-see-her
In the old days he didn't used to see her

S4 أبهاتنا وجدودنا كانوا ما يشوفوا العروس لليلة العرس
ʾabbahātna w ždūdna kānu mā yšūfu l-ʿarūs la-lēlt əl-ʿirs
fathers-our and grandfathers-our were-they neg they-see the-bride until-night of-the-wedding
Our fathers and grandfathers used not to see the bride until the wedding night

The syntactic flexibility of the western dialects permits other elements to be targeted when they constitute the semantic focus of negation. In the following minimal pair, the first sentence was uttered during a conversation about the next day's activities. Since it was a normal work day, the speaker's statement can be seen as a negation of a natural presupposition that he was physically going to work, hence the focus of negation on *going*.

M1 ما ماشيش نخدم غداّ
mā māšīš nəxdəm ġədda
neg going-m I-work tomorrow
I'm not ***going*** *to work tomorrow*

Later, I elicited the next sentence as a syntactically viable alternative, but with a focus on not *working*.

M1 ماش نخدمش غداّ
māš nəxdəmš ġədda
neg-will I-work tomorrow
I'm not ***working*** *tomorrow* (elicited)

In Moroccan, indirect and oblique objects may fall inside or outside the focus. The following minimal pair shows that indirect objects with the preposition /li/ *to* may fall inside or outside the scope of negation:

M5 ما تگولهاش ليّ
ma tgūlhāš liyya
neg you-say-it to-me
Don't tell it to me!

M1 ما تقولهاليش
ma tqūlhā-līš
neg you-say-it-to-me
Don't tell me it! or *Don't tell it to me!*

The next examples show prepositional phrases with /li/ and /fi/ contained within the scope of the negating particle:

M2 بنات اليوم ما يمكن ليهمش يديروا شي حاجة ويخافوا
bnāt l-yūm mā ymkən-lihumš ydīru ši ḥāža w yxāfu
girls of-today neg possible for-them they-do some thing and they-are-afraid
Girls of today, they can't do something and be afraid

M11 بشرط ما تشوف فيهاش
b-šarṭ mā tšūf-fīhāš
on-condition neg you-look at-her
On condition you don't look at her

Egyptian allows this type of variation as well. Here the preposition /bi/ and its object fall within the scope of /mā - š/:

E5 صراع ما تحسّ بوش
ṣirāʿ mā tḥiss būš
struggle neg you-feel it
A struggle you don't feel

College cafeteria food elicited the following comment from an Egyptian colleague containing the prepositional phrase /lu/ *to it*:

E الاكل دا ما يتغنّالوش
il-ʾakl da mā yitġanna-lūš
the-food that neg it-be-sung to-it
That food shouldn't be serenaded!

9.3.1 Negation of Pseudo-verbs

Cowell lists as possible foci of Syrian /mā/ "verbs and other verb-like expressions" (1964:384). This description applies to all four dialects, and the "other verb-like expressions" consist of pseudo-verbs, which are negated like verbs in all dialects, with /mā - š/ or /mā/:

M10 الحوت ما كاينشي بزّاف
l-ḥūt mā kāynši bəzzāf
the-fish neg there-is a-lot
Fish, there isn't a lot

E2 ما لوش حدّ
mā lūš ḥadd
neg at-him one
He doesn't have anyone

S2 ما فيه مجال يعني
mā fī mažāl yaʿni
neg there-is room it-mean
There's no way

K1 ما عليك
mā ʿalēk
neg on-you
Don't worry about it

Pseudo-verbs consisting of nominal and prepositional phrases are thus normally negated as verbs. The following section will examine another class of "verb-like expressions" that can at times function as pseudo-verbs: participles.[3]

9.3.2 Negation of Participles

Negation patterns involving participles reflect the partially verbal nature of this syntactic category. Participles are commonly predicated, and in such cases are negated with predicate negation. The following Moroccan, Egyptian, and Syrian examples contain participles /šārfa/ *having grown old*, /ʿarfa/ *having found out, knowing* and /ḥābbe/ *having fallen in love* with negated with predicate negatives /māši/, /miš/, and /mū/ respectively:

M9 ماشي شارفة بزّاف
māši šārfa bəzzāf
neg old a-lot
She isn't very old

E1 مش عارفة
miš ʾarfa
neg knowing (having-found-out)
I don't know

S2 واحد بيحب واحدة ولو كانت حابة مو حابة
wāḥid biḥibb waḥde w law kānit ḥābbe mū ḥābbe
one-m indic-he-loves one-f and if was-she having-loved neg having loved
A boy loves a girl, even if she's been in love or not been in love (or whatnot)

In this Kuwaiti passage, negation of the verbal phrase /mā tištəġəl/ *doesn't work* contrasts with the predicated participle /mū mitḥajjba/ *not veiled*:

K2 تسألني، هي تسألني، تگول لي يعني، نبي لَه چذي تدرس، نبي لَه مخلصة الدراسة، نبي لَه واحدة تشتغل ولاّ ما تشتغل، متحجّبة ولاّ مو متحجّبة

[3]For a discussion of the verbal characteristics of participles, see 6.4 and 7.3.

K2 tisʾalni, ʾihiya tisʾalni, tigul-li yaʿni nabī-la čiḏi, tadris, nabī-la mxallṣa d-dərāsa, nabī-la waḥda tištəġəl wəlla mā tištəġəl, mitḥajjba wəlla mū mitḥajjba
she-asks-me she she-asks-me it-means we-want for-him such she-studies we-want for-him having-finished studying we-want for-him one she-works or neg she-works veiled or neg veiled
She asks me, she [the mother] asks me, she says, you know, we want [to find] for him such-and-such, [a girl] who studies, we want [to find] him a girl who has finished her studies, we want a girl who works or doesn't work, veiled or not veiled

In the examples cited above, the participles all designate states. In other cases, participles carry more verbal meaning, often representing perfect aspect (see 6.4), and sometimes (in the case of active participles) taking syntactic objects. Hence it is not surprising that participles occasionally become more "verb-like," and that, in such cases, they may be negated with /mā/ in Syrian and Kuwaiti or /mā - š/ in Morocco and much of rural Egypt.[4] The following examples contain participles with verbal meaning and verbal negation:

M7 وحتّى انا من هاد الكوتشي ما نازلش!
w ḥtta ana mn hād l-kūtši mā nāzəlš!
and-even I from this the-carriage neg going-down!
I too am not getting out of this carriage!

S4 ما حابّها ، كنت من اوّل ما حبّيتها
mā ḥābb[h]a, kint min ʾawwal mā ḥabbēt[h]a
neg having-loved-her, were-you from first neg loved-you-her
You don't love her, you should from the start not have loved her

K1 ما گادر مرّة واحدة!
mā gādir marra waḥda
neg being-able time one
I couldn't all of a sudden

In this Syrian passage, the passive participle /maʿʾūl/ *reasonable* is negated with verbal /mā/ because it functions here as a pseudo-verb,

[4]Woidich's Egyptian examples containing /bāyin/ *seeming* and /fāḍil/ *remaining* negated with /mā - š/ are to be explained thus as well (1968:32).

syntactically embedding the non-finite verb /abruk/ *I sit*:

S5 بسّ دخلت انا كورس لغة بالجامعة، عملت بالاول، لأنّ ما باعرف ولا
كلمة، يعني ما معقول ابرك متل الجدبان
bass daxalt ana kūrs luġa bi-j-jām‘a, ‘əmilt bi-l-ʾawwal, laʾinn mā ba‘rif wala kilme, ya‘ni mā ma‘ʾūl abruk mitl ij-jidbān
but entered-I I course of-the-language at-the-university, did-I at-the-first, because neg indic-I-know neg a-word, it-mean neg reasonable I-sit like the-idiots
But I took a language course at the university, I did at first, because I didn't know a single word, I mean I couldn't just sit there like [an] idiot

Verbal negation of participles in Egypt seems in part to be a matter of geography. Behnstedt and Woidich draw an isogloss separating the negation of the active participle with /miš/ as opposed to /mā - š/ in southern Egypt: the former is used from Cairo to al-Minya, and the latter south of al-Minya (1985:111). However, they do not clarify whether participle negation with /mā - š/ is optional, as is the case in Moroccan Arabic, or obligatory. Examples from their rural Egyptian data include /mā xābirhūš/ *I don't know him/it* (1994:107) and /ma-ṣāyidš/ *I am not fishing* (1994:271).[5]

9.3.3 Verbal Negation of Predicates in Moroccan

It was noted above that verbal negation in the western dialects permits direct and oblique objects to be contained within the clitics /mā - š/ such that the semantic target of negation is focused. Moroccan differs slightly from Cairene Arabic in that it allows a comparatively broad range of syntactic structures, including non-verbal predicates, to be contained within the scope of the verbal negative /mā - š/:

M1 ما ف راسيش
mā f rāsīš
neg in-head-my-š
[It's] not in my head, i.e., *I don't know*

[5]I am grateful to Devin Stewart for providing references to these and subsequent examples of /mā - š/ negation in Behnstedt and Woidich (1994).

The next utterance came in response to a question about a Moroccan writer. The speaker, surprised at the question, denies the implied presupposition that the writer is well-known in Morocco:

M3 حتّى ف المغرب ما معروفش

ḥtta f l-məġrib mā məʿrūfš

even in Morocco neg known-š

[He is] even in Morocco not well-known

A hotel clerk in Fez replied in response to a telephone inquiry asking to speak to a guest (whom the caller presupposes is in his room):

M ما موجودش

mā muwžūdš

neg present-š

[He's] not here

Caubet designates this type of negation as marked, citing the following as a "polemic response" (1993ii:70, translation mine):

M —— اختك قبيحة ! —— لا، ما قبيحاش !

--- xtək qbīḥa ! --- la, mā qbīḥa š !

--- sister-your malicious! --- neg, neg malicious

--- *Your sister is malicious!* --- *No, not at all malicious!*

This kind of negation thus appears to be marked in Moroccan. Similar examples from rural Egypt, however, do not appear to be marked. Behnstedt and Woidich's glossary contains a number of examples in which non-verbal entities are negated with /mā - š/ in rural Egypt, among them the following pair, the first from the Fayyūm, and the second from the Delta (1994:100, 444; translations mine).

E علشان ماحاجاش تخشّه

ʿalašān mā-ḥagāš tixuššu

so-that neg-thing it-enter-it

So that nothing can enter it

E ونجيبوله بقى كماوي ، ما كماويش

wu nžibūlu baga kmāwi mā kmāwīš

[and we-bring-for-it chemicals neg chemicals]

... and so we get for it chemical fertilizer and whatnot (lit., and not chemical fertilizer)

In the other dialects, verbal negation of a nominal predicate represents marked usage. In the next two Cairene examples, the use of /mā - š/ to negate nominal predicates marks the denial of a presupposition. In the first sentence, the speaker has been called by the name *Sayyid,* but denies that this is his name. In the second, the speaker has been misunderstood, and seeks to correct the misunderstanding.

E ماسميش سيّد!

ma-smīš sayyid!

neg-name-my Sayyid!

*My name is **not** Sayyid!* [6]

E5 ما قصديش اقول كدا

mā ʾaẓdīš ʾaʾūl kida

neg intention-my I-say like-that

*I **don't** mean to say that*

Cowell gives several analogous Syrian examples, among them the following, in which verbal /mā/ negates the pronoun /huwwe/ *he*. Cowell's translation clearly indicates that this speaker is denying the presupposition that /huwwe/ *he* is responsible (Cowell 1964:385):

S ما هو المسؤول عن الحادث

mā huwwe l-masʾūl ʿan ᵊl-ḥādes

[neg he the-responsible for the-accident]

He's not the one responsible for the accident

My Kuwaiti corpus contains a single example of verbal /mā/ negating a nominal form, but I believe it is more accurately analyzed as the result of the interrogative /lēš/ attracting /mā/ to a pre-verbal interrogative position:

K2 اذا يعني واحد ولد دگّ لي تليفون وگال لي ابي اشك فيه، ليش ما امّه وليش ما اختَه دگّت لي تليفون وگالت لي؟

ʾiḏa yaʿni wāḥid walad dagga-li telifōn w gāl-li ʾabi ʾašikk fī, lēš mā umma w lēš mā ʾuxta daggat-li telifōn w gālət-li

if it-mean one boy called-he-to-me telephone and said-he-to-me I-want I-doubt in-him, why neg mother-his and why neg sister-his called-she-to-me telephone and said-she-to-me

[6]Devin Stewart provided this example from an Egyptian film.

If a boy calls me up and says to me, I want [you to find me a wife] I have doubts about him, why didn't his mother or why didn't his sister call me and tell me?

There is thus no evidence for marked verbal negation in Kuwaiti (with the exception of the negative copula; see 9.3.5).

9.3.4 Negation of the Imperative: The Prohibitive

The prohibitive constitutes a special case of verbal negation, in that some dialects use a different negating particle with this mood than they do with the indicative and subjunctive moods. The Moroccan and Egyptian dialects employ /mā - š/ to indicate the prohibitive, while Syrian and Kuwaiti normally use /lā/ rather than /mā/. However, there is a great deal of geographical overlap in the use of these two particles: while /mā/ is found across North Africa and into Syria, /lā/ is used in the prohibitive everywhere except Cairo, including the Egyptian Delta, and seems to be the only particle used in Kuwait:

K1 بسّ لا تحطّ لي فيه لا عود لا شي عشان لا يحسّون
bass lā tḥuṭṭ-li fī lā ʿūd lā šay lā hāda ʿašān lā yḥissūn
only neg you-put for-me in-it neg stick neg thing so-that neg they-feel
But don't put in it either a stick or anything else so they won't sense [what it is]

The distribution of /lā/ and /mā/ might be geographical in the Syrian and Egyptian areas. Speaker S2 is from a Christian village south of Aleppo, while S5 is from Aleppo:

S2 لا تاخدها كذا كانت حابّة
lā tāxid[h]a kaza kānit ḥābbe
neg you-take-her so-forth was-she having-loved
Don't marry her, and so forth, she has been in love (had love affairs)

S5 ما تقولي عن بلدنا كويّسة
mā tʾūli ʿan baladna kwayyse
neg you-say about town-our good
Don't say that our town is nice

A colleague reports that /lā - š/ is normally used in villages in the Egyptian Delta:[7]

E لا تشكيش

lā tiškīš

neg you-complain

Don't complain

Cairene speakers, on the other hand, use /mā - š/ exclusively:

E1 ما تدفعيش اكتر من ميتين

mā tidfaʿīš ʾaktar min mitēn

neg you-pay more than two-hundred

Don't pay more than two hundred

The coexistence of /lā/ and /mā/ as prohibitive particles should signal a distinction in pragmatic function, and indeed, Harrell found in his study of Moroccan that /lā/ carries a "morally admonishing" sense (1962:153). His analysis is supported by my data: the same speaker uttered the following pair of sentences, the first to a group of peers, the second to her husband. If it can be assumed that one takes more care to be polite with friends than with relatives, then her use of the /lā/ form with her husband and /mā/ with her peers suggests that /lā - š/ carries less imperative force than /mā - š/:

M9 سيروا لا تضحكوش عليّ

sīru lā tḍaḥkūš ʿliyya

go-p neg you-laugh-neg at-me

Go on, you shouldn't make fun of me!

M9 ما تضحكش عليّ

mā təḍḥakš ʿliyya

neg you-laugh at-me

Don't make fun of me!

Lack of sufficient contextualized examples makes it difficult to determine whether the same distinction holds true in other dialects that share both particles. The patterning of /mā/ and /lā/ across dialects indicates that further research into the prohibitive might yield insight into linguistic variation and the processes of change.

---

[7]Dwight Reynolds gave me this example from his fieldwork in the Delta.

9.3.5 The Negative Copula

All four dialects have a special negated copula form consisting of a personal pronoun combined with /mā - š/ or /mā/. Cowell calls this form in Syrian the "negative copula" (1964:387), this term fits analogous copulas in the other three dialects as well. I include in this category a parallel form consisting of the impersonal pronoun, /ḥad(d)(a)/ *one*, negated with the verbal particle to give the meaning *no one*. Table 9-2 lists the forms of the negative copula.

Table 9-2: The Negative Copula

The Negative Copula				
	Moroccan	Egyptian	Syrian	Kuwaiti
1s	mānīš	manīš	māni māli	māni
1p	māḥnāš	maḥnāš	māna mālna	miḥna
2ms	māntāš	mantāš	mānak mālak	mint mant
2fs	māntīš	mantīš	mānik mālik	minti
2p	māntumāš	mantūš	mānkon mālkon	mintu mantu
3ms	māhuwwāš	mahuwwāš	māno mālo	muhu
3fs	māhyyāš	mahiyyāš	māna māla	mihi
3p	māhumāš	mahummāš	mānon mālon	muhum
no one	(ḥətta wāḥəd)	maḥaddiš	māḥada	ma(ḥ)ḥad

Moroccan forms are taken from Harrell (1962:155-56), Syrian from Cowell (1964:387-88), and Kuwaiti adapted from Johnstone (1967:148; cf. Holes 1990:244), with several additional forms taken from my data. Cowell also notes the existence of a third Syrian stem, /mann-/ that shares the pronoun suffixes of /mān-/ and /māl-/; I have found this latter set common in Beirut.

In Moroccan, Egyptian, and Kuwaiti dialects, the negative copula shares not only syntactic, but also pragmatic characteristics. Syntactically, this form is marked by the use of verbal negation to negate a nominal form. Pragmatically, the contradictory force of the negative copula, which negates verbless sentences, stands in marked comparison to the neutral constructions in which a copulative sentence with a pronoun subject is negated with /miš, māši/ or /mū/. Contextualized examples illustrate that the negative copula in these three dialects marks the negation of a presupposition on the part of the interlocutor.

The context of the following Kuwaiti example is that a group of people are going downstairs, but the speaker has decided not to join them. His use of /māni/ *I am not* negates the presupposition that he will join the group. The second example is analogous, for the speaker does (or did) have a family, but it is not the people to whom she is speaking. However, she has been living with them, so they have assumed the role of her family; here, they are attempting to discipline her and she resists by negating their assumption that they have a right to do so.

K1 انا ماني نازل، ما عندي بنطرون
ʾāna māni nāzil, mā ʿindi banṭarōn
I neg-me descending, neg at-me pants
I am not going down, I don't have pants

K3 انتو مانتو هلي
ʾintu mantu hali
you-p neg-you family-my
You are not my family!

The speaker later mimics the petty way in which people argue about social status. The negative copula /mantu/ *you are not* represents the attempt of one party to deny the other the very status the former claims:

K3 حنا أصيلين إنتو مانتو أصيلين
ḥinna ʾaṣīlīn ʾintu mantu ʾaṣīlīn
we of-noble-origin you neg-you of-noble origin
We are of noble origin, you are not of noble origin

The Egyptian speaker of the following excerpt warns against taking her husband seriously, lest the other listeners believe what he tells them:

E3 هو ساعات بيكّلّم كلام يعني ماهوواش حقيقة جوّاه
huwwa sā‘āt biyikkallim kalām ya‘ni mahuwwāš ha’ī’a guwwā
he hours indic-he-speaks speech it-mean neg-it truth inside-him
Sometimes he just talks, it's not what he really feels inside

The next Egyptian speaker vigorously denies the claim made by one of her interlocutors that the /‘umra/ *minor pilgrimage* is an obligation for Muslims:

E8 العمرة ماهياش فرض، العمرة سنّة
il-‘umra mahiyyāš farḍ, il-‘umra sunna
the-umra neg-she obligation, the-umra practice-of-the-Prophet
The ‘umra (minor pilgrimage) is ***not*** *an obligation, the ‘umra is sunna (imitating the practice of the Prophet)*

Each of the next two Moroccan sentences represents the speaker's denial of a presupposition. The first, taken from the lyrics of a popular song, signals the speaker's feelings of alienation. The second carries the implication "*... so stop treating us as if we were!*"

M مانيش من هنا
manīš mən[h]na
neg-me from-here
I am not from here (Moroccan popular song)

M ما احناش دراري گالسين معاك
mā ḥnāš drāri gālsīn m‘āk
[neg-we children sitting with-you]
We aren't children sitting with you (Harrell 1962:155)

The pragmatic function shared by the negative copulas of all these dialects, then, seems to lie in contradicting a presupposition, by targeting the subject pronoun and emphatically negating the applicability of the predicate to the subject. In this sense it actually represents a marked usage of verbal negation, parallel to other instances of marked negation noted above (9.3.4).

Syrian dialects, however, present a more complex case. Analysis of the forms in Table 9-2 reveals that the Syrian negative copula has developed into a pseudo-verb, because its semantic subject is expressed in the form of an object pronoun, whereas the other dialects all exhibit the standard negative particles affixed to independent personal pronouns. This syntactic development parallels an apparent difference in pragmatic function. While the negative copula represents a pragmatically marked form in Moroccan, Egyptian, and Kuwaiti, the Syrian negative copula seems not to be pragmatically marked. A Damascene informant emphasizes that, of /mū/ and the negative copula, /mū/ represents the more "emphatic" or marked form. In my Syrian data, the use of /mū/ seems to be restricted to negating "subjectless" sentences, such as the first example below, or sentential subjects, as in the second example, in which /ḥada yfakkir fi[h]a/ *for anyone to think of her* functions as the subject of /mū mumkin/ *not possible* (mirrored in the English translation with the "dummy" subject *it*:

S2 اذا ما معه، مو مشكل
ʾiza mā maʿu mū miškəl
if neg with-him mū problem
If he doesn't have [money],[it's] not a problem

S2 مو ممكن بقى حدّ يفكر فيها
mū mumkin baqa ḥadd yfakkir fi[h]a
mū possible remained-it one he-think of-her
It is not possible anymore for anyone to think of [marrying] her

The negative copula, on the other hand, negates sentences that have a pronoun subject or topic, such as the following:

S2 اذا ما فكّرت بالمجتمع معناتها ماني من المجتمع
ʾiza mā fakkart bi-l-mužtamaʿ maʿnāt[h]a māni min il-mužtamaʿ
if neg I-thought of-the-society meaning-of-it neg-me from-the-society
If I don't think of society, that means I am not [part] of society

S6 انت مالك قدّ ام اليسر وبنتها
ʾinta mālak ʾadd ʾimm il-yusur w bint[h]a
you neg-you equal-to Umm al-Yusur and daughter-her
You're not up to the level of Umm al-Yusur and her daughter

The pattern that emerges in Syrian, then, is that sentences with pronoun subjects or topics are negated with the negative copula, while topicless sentences are negated with /mū/ (see also 9.4).

In addition to the Syrian negative copulas listed in Table 9-2, Cowell remarks that /māhu/ and /māhi/ are variants of the third person singular negative copula used in "some areas" (1964:388). In my data, these variants occur in the speech of an Aleppan informant:

S5 يعني، ريجن ماهو عايش متلكن!
ya'ni rēgan mā[h]u 'āyiš mitilkon
it-mean, Reagan neg-he living like-you
I mean, even Reagan isn't living like you!

S5 منطقة صناعية فيها البوينغ معامل الـ«بوينغ» منطقة كتير كتير غنية وماهي منطقة سياحية.
manṭ'a ṣinā'iyye fi[h]a l-bōing, ma'āmil il-bōing, manṭ'a ktīr ktīr ġaniyye, w mā[h]i manṭ'a siyāḥiyye
region industrial in-it the-Boeing factories of-the-Boeing region very very rich and not-3fs region tourist
[It's an] industrial region, it has Boeing, the Boeing factories, [it's] a very very rich region, it's not a tourist area

The impersonal negative copula is unmarked in all dialects, in the sense that there is no alternative word for *no one*. However, the meaning of *no one* itself is marked in a certain way: it is an example of categorical negation, which is a related form of marked negation (see 9.5) Typical examples of the impersonal negative copula from Egyptian and Kuwaiti include:

E5 ما حدّش بيتدخّل فيها
maḥaddəš biyitdaxxal fīha
neg-one indic-he-interferes in-it
Nobody interferes in it

K2 ماحد يدري عنها
maḥḥad yadri 'anha
neg-one he-knows about-her
Nobody knows about her

The one syntactic characteristic common to all of the data given in this section is that verbal negation particles /mā/ and /mā - š/ negate verbs and pseudo-verbs, but do not normally negate predicated structures. It may be concluded that, in general, verbal negation is the least marked negation strategy in these dialects. Its basic function is to negate a particular sentence element, rather than a predicate taken as a whole proposition, and as such may be contrasted with predicate negation, which is a strategy that negates an entire predicate as a single, embedded proposition.

9.4 Predicate Negation

The common particles of predicate negation are /mū/, in Syria and Kuwait, with variants /māhu/ (feminine /māhi/); /miš/, in Egypt, and /māši/ in Morocco. These particles negate predicated sentence constituents, including participles:

M9 ماشي شارفة بزّاف
māši šārfa bəzzāf
neg old a-lot
She isn't very old

E3 مش عايزة تطلع تاني
miš ʿayza tiṭlaʿ tāni
neg wanting-s she-come-out again
It doesn't want to come back out

S2 مو ممكن بقى حدّ يفكّر فيها
mū mumkin baqa ḥadd yfakkir fī[h]a
neg possible remained-it one he-think about-her
It's no longer possible that anyone will still think [to marry] her

K1 انا مو ماكل شي طول الظهر
ʾāna mū mākil šay ṭūl iḍ-ḍuhər
I neg having-eaten thing throughout the-afternoon
I hadn't eaten anything all afternoon

The subjects and verbs of the negated predicates may be elided, as in the following Moroccan and Syrian passages:

M10 ما كيهمّوش تبقى البلايا نقية او ماشي نقية
mā kayhəmmūš təbqa l-plāya nqiyya ʾaw māši nqiyya
neg indic-it-concerns-him it-remains the-beach clean or neg clean
It doesn't matter to him for the beach to remain clean or not clean

S6 انا قلت لك تقدّمي اجازة مو إذن
ʾana ʾilt-əllik tʾaddmi ʾižāze mū ʾizin
I said-I-to-you you-apply-for vacation neg permission
I told you to request vacation time, not time off

In marked predicated environments, this construction negates arguments that are predicated, whether they are verbal or nominal complements. The syntactic and semantic scope of the negation must be the entire predicate, and not just the verbal argument. The following examples are taken from contexts that are clearly predicated pragmatically.

In the next Moroccan example, the comment /māši yəddi mzyān/ *it's not that my hand is good* is made in response to the compliment /yəddk mzyān/ *your hand is good*. The thus speaker negates the entire proposition, as a predication.

M9 قال لي يدّك مزيان قلت له ماشي يدّي مزيان ربّي والجدود
qāl-li yəddk mzyān qult-lu māši yəddi mzyān, rabbi w ž-ždūd
said-he-to-me hand-your good said-I-to-him neg hand-my good Lord-my and the-ancestors
He told me, your hand is good. I told him, it's not that my hand is good, God and the ancestors [made it so]

A female Egyptian colleague uttered this remark in a casual conversation:

E مش برقص
miš barʾuṣ
neg indic-I-dance
I don't dance

Taking advantage of her linguistic training, I discussed with her possible motivations given the context. We concluded that /miš b-/ usually indicates a kind of categorical negation, a marked (but not emphatic) form of verbal negation. A similar example was heard from a teenage girl denying that she drinks (unhealthy) soft drinks:

E انا مش بشرب كوك
ʾana miš bašrab kōk
I neg indic-I-drink Coke
I don't drink Coke

Another speaker uses this construction to deny an assumption expressed by her interlocutor that she is refusing his request:

E1 انا مش بقول لأ ...
ʾana miš baʾūl laʾ
I neg indic-I-say no
I'm not saying no

El-Tonsi observes that female speakers tend to use this construction more than males, and that its occurrence is on the rise (personal communication). If /miš b-/ continues to spread, it may eventually lose its categorical status, perhaps the path that the Cairene future took from /mā ḥa - š/ to the now obligatory /miš ḥa-/.

The eastern dialects also use predicate negation as a marked form of negation with verbs. In the following Syrian passage, the use of /mū/ to negate the verb /byiži/ *it comes about* reflects its semantic predication, which is paraphrased in the English translation:

S2 الواحد بيمشي شوي شوي، مو بيجي ضربة واحدة
il-wāḥid byimši šwayy šwayy, mū byiži ḍarbe waḥde
the-one he-moves a-little a-little, neg he-comes blow one
One moves a little at a time, [it] isn't [the case that] it happens all at once

The meaning of the following sentence, that the speaker wishes to be left alone, is likewise reflected in the syntactic predication of /yiyīni/ *he come to me (show up)*:

K1 خل بالك على محمد مو ييني!
xal bālak ʿala Mḥammad -- mū yiyīni!
imper-keep attention-your to M -- neg he-comes-to-me!
Pay attention to M -- [it better not happen that] he show up!

Predicate negation is also used interrogatively to signal that the speaker presupposes and expects a positive answer to his or her question. In this case, the question is marked by a fronted particle of predicate negation, whether the question itself has an underlying verbal or predicated structure. In using predicate negation to frame a question, the speaker signals his or her own presupposition and requests confirmation or denial of that assumption. The following pair of Egyptian questions contrasts marked and unmarked uses of verbal negation. The first question clearly signals that the speaker had assumed her addressee had bought a suit and requests confirmation. Syntactically, it contrasts with the second question, in which normal (pragmatically unmarked) verbal /mā ... š/ negation is used:

E1 مش جبتي بدلة؟
miš gibti badla?
neg got-you suit
Didn't you get a suit?

E2 ما جبتهاش ليه؟
mā gibtihāš lē?
neg got-you-it why
Why didn't you bring it?

In the next example, the Moroccan speaker signals that he had assumed his addressee was at home and seeks confirmation or explanation:

M1 ماشي كنت ف الدار؟
māši kunti f d-dār?
neg were-you in the-house?
Weren't you in the house?

Similarly, this Syrian speaker signals his assumption that his friend had finished what he was doing:

Sn مو خلّص؟
mū xallaṣ?
neg finished-he?
Didn't he finish?

In all of the previous examples, the negated constituents function syntactically and pragmatically as single pieces of information, and as such, are negated as predicates. There are other syntactic consequences as well. When the verb contained in this proposition is imperfective, this type of negation has the effect of further embedding it, giving it a subjunctive meaning. In the Kuwaiti example above, /mū yiyīni/ may be loosely translated *it had better not be the case that he come to me*, reflecting the semantically subjunctive status of the verb /yiyīni/ *he come to me*, as well as the pragmatically predicated status of the negated clause. (Since Kuwaiti does not distinguish between main and embedded imperfective forms, syntactic embedding is not marked in this dialect.) Similarly, the embedded /mū tgūlīn/ *it's not (that) you'd say* in the following sentence contrasts with its corresponding verbal negation, /mā tgūlīn/ *you don't say/are not saying*:

K4 احنا وللّه شاليـنا يعني، مو تگولين جخّ كلّش، بس حلو

ʾiḥna waḷḷa šālēna yaʿni, mū tgūlīn jaxx killiš, bass ḥiləw

we by-God chalet-our it-means, neg you-say lavish very, but pretty

Well, our chalet, that is, not that you would say very lavish, but it's pretty

In Moroccan, Egyptian, and Syrian, syntactic embedding is grammatically marked through the use of the unmarked imperfective. Therefore, the embedded status of predicate-negated verbal clauses is clear. Examples from each of these dialects illustrate this point. In the first, the unmarked imperfective /yiktib/ *to write* is syntactically, pragmatically, and semantically embedded:

S4 اجا عم بيحكي لنا هوني وقلنا ناخدُه ع شيخ يكتب له، يعني التوفيق، مو يكتب له شي يعني

ʾija ʿam biḥkī-lna hōni w ʾəlna nāxdu ʿa šēx yiktib-lu, yaʿni t-tawfīʾ, mū yiktib-lu ši yaʿni

came-he prog indic-he-tells-us here and said-we we-take-him to sheikh he-write-for-him, it-means the-success neg he-write-for-him thing it-mean

He came and was telling us here, we thought to take him to a sheikh to write something for him, that is, [for] reconciliation, not [for the Sheikh] to write him something [bad]

In the next sentence as well, predicate negation particle /māši/ *it's not* embeds the verb /tšūf/ *you see*, which then assumes a subjunctive character.

M10 خصّك تهدر على كل شي هاد الحاجات، ماشي تشوف جوج

xṣṣək təhdar ʿla kull ši hād l-ḥāžāt, māši tšūf žūž

must-you you-talk about each thing this the-things, neg you-see 2

You must talk about all these things, [you mustn't] see [only] two

The following two sentences show a clear pragmatic and syntactic contrast. On the left is a prohibitive with normal verbal negation; on the right, an embedded subjunctive carrying the force of an imperative or reprimand to a small child:

En ما تروحش	E1 مش تسلّمي؟
mā truḥš	miš tisallimi?
neg you-go	neg you-say-hello-f?
Don't go	*Shouldn't you say hello?*

Predicate negation, then, represents an unmarked strategy for negating non-verbal predicates (with the possible exception of Moroccan). As a marked strategy, predicate negation negates a verbal argument as a whole, embedding it within a new overarching predicate structure.

9.5 Categorical Negation

As noted above, the normal patterns of negation in the western dialects include the enclitic /-š/, as either /māši/, /miš/, or /mā - š/. While the first two are morphologically fixed, the third, /mā - š/, is not, for in a number of cases /-š/ is omitted. Harrell identifies this omission in Moroccan Arabic as the 'categorical negative,' since the negated complement "refers to a whole category rather than to some specific item or member of a category" (1962:154). Harrell identifies both the syntactic and semantic features that identify this category in Moroccan, but he unnecessarily excludes some negative constructions that share these features. Egyptian Arabic, too, shares the omission of /-š/ in cases where the negation is absolute or unqualified, and all four dialects share the syntactic structures /wala/ *none, not any*, and /lā ... wala/ *neither ... nor*. With modification of Harrell's definition of "categorical" negation from negation of a "whole category" to absolute, unqualified negation, a coherent syntactic and pragmatic description of all these structures emerges. I will show that categorical or absolute negation exists at three levels in spoken Arabic: the verb phrase, a single sentence element, usually a noun phrase, and coordinated structures, by which I mean a list of entities that constitute a set (i.e., *this, that, and the other*).

9.5.1 Categorical Negation of the Verb Phrase

Categorical verbal negation is syntactically marked only in dialects whose unmarked verbal particle is /mā - š/. In Moroccan and Egyptian, this type of categorical negation is distinguished by the absence of the negative particle /-š/. In Moroccan speech, /š/ may be omitted from any verb phrase. Normally, /kāyn/ *there is* is negated as /mā kāynš/ *there isn't*, but here /-š/ is omitted, signalling a categorical negation of the existence of help or sympathy.

M2 اللي يعاونك ما كاين، واللي يحنّ فيك ما كاين
lli yʿāwnk mā kāyn w lli yəḥənn fīk mā kāyn
rel he-help-you neg there-is and rel he-take-pity in-you neg there-is
There's nobody to help you, nobody to take pity on you

In Egyptian, the use of categorical negation in verb phrases is more limited than in Moroccan. It occurs mainly in oaths and certain fixed expressions, such as /ʿumr .. mā/ *never* and /waḷḷāhi/ *by God!*

E10 عمره ما حس انه هو اجنبي
ʿumru mā ḥass innu huwwa ʾagnabi
life-his neg felt-he comp he foreign
Never has he felt that he was foreign

E3 طب والله ما كنت متصوّرة دي
ṭab waḷḷāhi mā kunt mitṣawwara di
well by-God neg was-I having-imagined this
Well, by God I never imagined this

Nouns functioning as pseudo-verbs may also be negated in this way:

E فارس ما زيُّه فارس
fāris mā zayyu fāris
knight neg like-him knight
A knight like no other knight [8]

E إلاّ ما حد جا زارنا
illa mā ḥadd ga zarna
Would you believe it–not a single person came to visit us!
(Badawi and Hinds 1986:33)

---

[8]Michael Cooperson supplied this example, from the film "al-Aragōz."

Moroccan particles /ʿamm(ə)r-/ *ever*, /gāʿ/ *at all*, /(ḥət)ta/ *any*, /(ḥət)ta ḥāža/ *anything*, /(ḥət)ta wāḥəd/ *anyone*, and /ġīr/ *only*, /ma/ *anything*, and /wālu/ *nothing*, all function in negative sentences as particles of categorical negation, semantically and syntactically. Harrell specifies that they may not occur with /-š/ (1962:153-54). Examples from my data include:

M1 راه حتّى شي حاجة ما كاينة
rāh ḥtta ši ḥāža mā kāyna!
look even any thing neg is
Look, there's nothing [amiss] at all

M9 ما عندي خاي ما عندي عمّي ما عندي تا شي واحد ماش ينوب عليَّ
mā ʿndi xāy mā ʿndi ʿammi mā ʿndi ta ši wāḥəd māš ynūb ʿliyya
neg at-me brother-my neg at-me uncle-my neg at-me even some one will he-act for-me
I don't have a brother, I don't have an uncle, I don't have anyone who would act on my behalf

M10 ما عندك ما تشوف
mā ʿndək ma tšūf
neg at-you what you-see
There's nothing for you to see

M11 گع ما تتخرج برّا
gāʿ mā tatxrəž bərra
at-all neg indic-she-goes-out outside
She never goes outside

M11 ما صابت والو غير الحيوط ف الدار بوحدها ناض شدّها الوجع
mā ṣābət wālu ġī[r] l-ḥyūṭ f d-dār bʷ-uḥdha, nāḍ šaddha l-wžaʿ
neg found-she nothing only the-walls in the-house by-herself rose-she grabbed-it-her the-pain
She didn't find anything but the walls in the house, [she was] by herself, [labor] pain overcame her

Syrian and Kuwaiti, on the other hand, lack /-š/, and hence verbal negation has no marked categorical form. However, these dialects share with Moroccan and Kuwaiti the two other types of categorical negation, discussed in the next two sections.

9.5.2 Categorical Negation of Single Sentence Elements

The particle /wala/ *not a, none, at all*, common to Egyptian, Syrian, and Kuwaiti speech, signals categorical negation in a number of environments.

En ما شفتش ولا حتّى كتاب
mā šuftəš wala ḥatta kitāb
neg saw-I not-a even book
I didn't see a single book

E2 ولا كأني واخدة حاجة!
wala ka'inni waxda ḥāga!
at-all as-if-I having-taken thing!
As if I took nothing at all!

S ما فيه ولا نتفة خبز بالبيت
mā fī w-lā nitfet xibəz bil-bēt
[neg there-is not-a scrap of-bread in-the-house]
There's not even a piece of bread in the house (Cowell 1964:391)

K4 ولا عمري تحكّيت
wala ʿumri tḥaččēt
neg life-my talked-I
Never did I say a word

K4 ولا حدّ يجيسَه!
wala ḥad yijīsa!
neg one he-touch-it!
Nobody touch it!

Moroccan speakers, on the other hand, use the categorical negating particles listed in 9.5.1, omitting the clitic /š/ in this case as well.

M2 راه حتّى شي حاجة ما كاينة
rāh ḥtta ši ḥāža mā kāyna
see-here even some thing neg there-is
Really, there is not a thing at all (to it)

9.5.3 Categorical Negation of Coordinated Structures

A third type of categorical negation, called here "categorical negation of coordinated structures," is recorded, but not identified as such, in the grammars of Moroccan (Harrell 1962:156), Egyptian (Mitchell 1956:46), Syrian (Cowell 1964:390), and Kuwaiti (Holes 1990:72). Coordinated structures may consist of lists of nouns or parallel clauses, which are negated with the conjunctions /lā ... wala/ or /lā ... lā/ *neither ... nor*. The following Egyptian example, typical of this construction in all four dialects, contains two verbs in parallel construction, coordinated by /lā ... wala/. The two phrases, /aʾdar ʾašūf farxa btindibiḥ/ *I can watch a chicken being slaughtered* and /aʾdar ʾašūf damm/ *I can look at blood*, are meant to be taken as a complete, closed set of acts that is "categorically" negated:

E8 انا لحدّ النهاردا لا اقدر اشوف فرخة بتندبح ولا اقدر اشوف دم
ʾana li-ḥadd in-naharda lā aʾdar ʾašūf farxa btindibiḥ wala aʾdar ʾašūf damm
I to-extent of-today neg I-can I-see chicken indic-it-is-slaughtered nor I-can I-see blood
I to this day can neither watch a chicken being slaughtered nor look at blood

The dialect grammars all describe this construction, but fail to point out that the use of particles /lā ... wala/ in negating coordinated structures is not syntactically obligatory. As the next three examples show, negative coordination may also be expressed as unmarked negation. In the first, the speaker lists two cities of origin among a number of possible alternatives before giving the correct information. Larache and Alcazr are not the only possible members of this set, they merely constitute representative members of the set:

M1 هو ماشي من العرايش وماشي من القصر، هو من طنجة
huwwa māši mn l-ʿrāyš w māši mn l-qṣar, huwwa mn ṭanža
he neg from Larache and neg from Alcazr, he from Tangiers
He's not from Larache and he's not from Alcazr, he's from Tangiers (elicited)

In the next passage, the speaker lists several activities that a family in mourning refrains from doing. It is not an exhaustive listing, but a partial, illustrative, list, as signalled by the use of /mā/ rather than /lā ... wala/.

S2 أهله ما عاد يحضروا افراح، ما عاد يشعلوا التليفزيون، ما عاد يسمعوا موسيقى، ما عاد يطلعوا مشاوير ...
ʾahlu mā ʿād yiḥḍaru ʾafrāḥ mā ʿād yšaʿʿlu t-tilvizyōn mā ʿād yismaʿu musīqā mā ʿād yiṭlaʿu mšāwīr
family-his neg he-remained they-attend weddings neg he-remained they-turn-on the-television neg he-remained they-listen-to music neg he-remained they-go-out outings
His relatives no longer go to weddings, no longer turn on the television, no longer listen to music, no longer go out ...

A parallel example occurs in my Kuwaiti data:

K2 ما يلبسون ملوّن ما يروحون عزايم ما يسوّون افراح ...
mā yilbisūn məlawwan, mā yruḥūn ʿazāyim, mā ysawwūn afrāḥ
neg they-wear colored, neg they-go invitations, neg they-hold weddings
They don't wear colored (clothes), they don't accept social invitations, they don't hold weddings ...

These unmarked negated structures coordinated by /w/ *and* stand in contrast to categorical negation with /lā ... wala/, which signals a closed set of acts or entities that is completely negated or denied. The speaker in the next example does not want anyone to know he is having an alcoholic drink, and so requests that it be served without *any* of the typical decorations associated with such drinks:

K1 بسّ لا تحطّ لي فيه لا عود لا شي لا هادا عشان لا يحسّون
bass lā tḥuṭṭ-li fī lā ʿūd lā šay lā hāda ʿašān lā yḥissūn
only neg you-put for-me in-it neg stick neg thing neg this so-that neg they-feel
But don't put in it either a stick or anything at all so they won't realize [what it is]

S2 فيه بنات ما بيهمّن لا أهلن لا المجتمع لا كذا
fī banāt mā bihimmon lā ʾahlon lā l-mužtamaʿ lā kaza
there-is girls neg indic-it-concern-them neg family-their neg the-society neg so-forth
There are girls who don't care, not about their family or society or anything

Categorical negation of coordinated structures frequently involves double negatives, in which the verb is negated along with the listed items, whether they be nouns or clauses:

M11 ما صابت مسكينة لا ما تاكل لا فاش تكمّط داك الولد
ma ṣābət mskīna lā mā tākul lā fāš tgəmməṭ dāk l-wəld
neg found-she poor neg what she-eat neg rel she-wrap that the-child
She found, poor dear, neither a thing to eat nor anything to wrap the child in

S2 امّي كمان ما عندها لا شغلة ولا عملة
ʾimmi kamān mā ʿand[h]a lā šaġle wala ʿamle
mother-my also neg at-her neg business nor work
My mother, too, doesn't have any kind of job

K4 لا سوّى زين لا لنفسَه ولا حكّ عيالَه
lā sawwa zēn lā li-nafsa wala ḥagg ʿyāla
neg did-he good neg for-himself nor for kids-his
He did not do right, neither for himself nor his kids

This type of categorical negation extends in some dialects to the negative copula, in which the morpheme /ma-/ is replaced with /la-/. Examples from Lebanese (Feghali 1928:216, translation mine) and Kuwaiti:

L مانّو صاحبي ولانّي صاحبه
mannu ṣāḥbi w-lanni ṣāḥbu
[neg-he friend-my nor-I friend-his]
He is not my friend, neither am I his friend

K3 كلّه واحد، لاني بزايدة ولا بناقصة
killa wāḥid, lāni b-zāyda wala b-nāqṣa
all-of-it one, neg-me having-increased nor having-lost
It's all the same, I've neither gained nor lost

Negative listing and categorical negation of coordinated structures thus contrast semantically in that categorical negation is exhaustive, including all possible members of an implied closed set, while unmarked verbal or predicate negation contains illustrative examples of an open-ended set.

9.6 Summary

Analysis of negation patterns in the four dialect regions has revealed that all of them utilize three basic strategies of negation: verbal, predicate, and categorical negation, each of which shares certain syntactic and pragmatic features. The two most basic negating strategies, verbal and predicate negation, have both unmarked and marked usages. Egyptian and Syrian make use of marked verbal negation in which verbal particles negate predicate structures. Kuwaiti seems to restrict marked verbal negation to the negative copula, a special form of verbal negation that is marked in all dialects except Syrian.

Some languages have a special negative form that performs the function of denying a presupposition or a proposition (Chinese is one, Li and Thompson 1981). In the case of Arabic, it appears that the two basic unmarked negation strategies, verbal and predicative, share that function in the following manner: each is used as the marked form of negation for the other category. Thus, negation of verbs with the predicate negative /mū/, /miš/, or /māši/ constitutes marked negation, the negation of the verb phrase as a predicated proposition. Likewise, negation of a predicate with verbal negation, /mā/ or /mā - š/, constitutes marked negation, lending verbal force to participles and nominal phrases functioning as pseudo-verbs.

The two dialects that use /-š/ exhibit an interesting syntactic divergence: while Moroccan allows a wide range of sentence components to be contained within the particles /mā/ and /-š/, Egyptian exhibits the opposite trend: /miš/ is becoming increasingly inseparable into its component parts. The increasing frequency noted by el-Tonsi of the construction /miš + indicative imperfective/ suggests that it may eventually replace the normative /mā + indicative imperfective + š/, in the same way, probably, that /miš + future/ replaced /mā + future + š/ (a construction still prevalent in southern Egyptian dialects, see Behnstedt and Woidich 1985, 1994). Further evidence of this trend is found in Behnstedt's and Woidich's isogloss of the negation of the active participle with /miš/ as opposed to /mā - š/ in southern Egypt; the former is used from Cairo to al-Minya, and the latter south of al-Minya (1985:111). Moreover, while participles retain their verbal characteristics in Egyptian, they never seem to be negated verbally in Cairene Arabic, nor is the future. In a number of constructions, then, Cairene speakers favor predicate negation over verbal negation, a phenomenon which points to a process of historical change.

Within the broad framework proposed here, much work remains to be done. The Syrian region in particular needs further syntactic and pragmatic study, having a number of regional variants that it has not been possible to examine in depth here. The complex patterns of negation in all areas bear watching for future developments.

10 Sentence Typology

10.0 Introduction

Variations in Arabic word order are often attributed to a rather vague "emphasis." Thus Wright says of the difference between /zaydun māta/ *Zayd died* and /māta zaydun/ *died Zayd*, that the former implies or expresses a contrast between /zayd/ and another (unnamed) person, whereas in the latter the "logical emphasis rests almost solely on the verb" (1898ii:255). Two problems undermine this analysis: in constructions of the former type, *Zayd* is not necessarily contrastive, and the term "logical emphasis" is too vague. A clearer explanation of the types of contrast and emphasis signalled by changes in word order will be sought here. As Ingham notes, "the term 'emphatic' is much abused in linguistics as a blanket term for undetermined distinctions" (1994:148).[1]

In 7.2.2, it was proposed that /kān/ and other temporal verbs sometimes occupies a sentence position called *topic*, which will be defined here in greater detail. The analysis of negation in Chapter 9 distinguished between predicate-complement and verbal negation, reflecting an underlying pragmatic distinction in argument structure. Here I will argue for a parallel distinction in sentence typology, and propose that sentence structure in spoken Arabic is best analyzed as being of two distinct, equally basic types: topic-prominent and subject-prominent, each type having its own discourse function.

The term *topic* is used here, following the literature, in two different senses. At the sentence level, topic is used in a technical sense to refer to a particular pragmatic function in a particular type of sentence structure, the topic-comment sentence, in which the topic position is syntactically defined as sentence-initial (see further 10.2). At the discourse level, topic refers in a non-technical sense to any one of a number of subjects under discussion in any given conversation. Here I use *topic* to mean sentence topic in the technical sense, while *discourse topic* will refer to the non-technical meaning of a subject under discussion.

---

[1]An important and welcome exception to this trend is Caubet's (1993) detailed functional approach to sentence typology in Moroccan Arabic.

10.1 Sentence Typology

Language typology, being concerned with universal laws and patterns, began with the study of the relative order of sentence constituents verb (V), subject (S), and object (O), arranged into permutations of SVO, VSO and others.[2] Even though typologists themselves warn that not all languages can be classified according to this system (Comrie 1981:32, 82), this taxonomy has been adopted by some Arabists as a construct within which Arabic may be situated. Grand'Henry (1976:85) and Rosenhouse (1984a:49), among others, have remarked that in general, both SVO and VSO are found in the dialects. Verb-initial sentences from my data include:

M11 مشى داك العبد عندها
mša dāk l-ʿabd ʿndha
went-he that the-slave to-her
The slave went to her

E6 كان عادل إمام راكب في الطيّارة هو ويسرا
kān ʿādil ʾimām rākib fi ṭ-ṭayyāra huwwa w yusra
was-he Adil Imam riding in the-plane he and Yousra
Adel Imam was riding in a plane, he and Yousra

S1 شافها صاحب المحلّ، «يا ابن الكلب»!
šāf[h]a ṣāḥib l-maḥall, ya ʾibn il-kalb!
saw-he-it owner of-the-shop, O son of-the-dog!
The shop owner saw it (and said), You s.o.b.!

K2 يگعد الولد، تدشّ البنية
yigʿəd il-walad, tidišš lə-bnayya
sits-he the-boy, enters-she the-girl
The boy sits, the girl enters

Subject-initial sentences include:

M10 السي عبد الحافظ كيقول لي، امشي البحر
s-si ʿabd l-ḥāfiḍ kayqūl-li mši l-bḥar
Mister Abdelhafid indic-he-says-to-me go the-sea
Abd al-Hafid says to me, go to the beach

---

[2]Led by Greenberg et al. (1978); see also Croft (1990).

E3 فالانبوبة فضيت
fa-l-ʾambūba fiḍyit
and-the tank emptied-she
So the gas tank ran out

S5 الجار ما بيعرف شي عن جاره أبداً
ij-jār mā byaʿrif šī ʿan jāru ʾabadan
the-neighbor neg indic-he-knows thing about neighbor-his at-all
(A) neighbor doesn't know anything about his neighbor at all

K2 البنية طبعاً تستحي
lə-bnayya ṭabʿan tistəḥi
the-girl of-course is-shy-she
The girl, of course, is shy

Often, however, verb-initial sentences show no independent subject, the syntactic subject being marked only as inflection on the verb itself. In each of the following examples, the subject is marked on the verb, and no independent subject appears in the sentence.

M6 شدّ واحد الدرّي مجهول ما عندوش الورقة د الهوية
šadd wāḥd əd-dərrī məžhūl mā ʿndūš l-wərqa d l-huwwiyya
grabbed-he one the-boy unknown neg at-him the-paper of the-identity
He grabbed one unknown kid who didn't have his identity card

E6 قالت له، انت حضرتك تعرفني؟ قال لها أيوه
ʾalit-lu, ʾinta ḥaḍritak tiʿrafni? ʾal-laha ʾaywa
said-she-to-him, you sir you-know-me? said-he-to-her yes
She said to him, you, sir, Do you know me? He told her, yes

S4 جابتها من مصر من هنيك لَهون وبركت معن هوني خمستعش نهار لَصار العرس
jābit[h]a min maṣər min hənīk la-hōn, w barkit maʿon hōne xamstaʿš nhār la-ṣār l-ʿərs
brought-she-her from Egypt from there to here and stayed-she with-them here 15 days until-became-it the-wedding
She brought her from Egypt, from there to here, and she stayed with them here for two weeks until the wedding took place

K2 گعدنا، سألها وسألتَه، سلام، مع السلامة، طلعنا
ga'ədna, w sa'alha w sa'əlta, salām, ma' s-salāma, ṭala'na
sat-we, asked-he-her and asked-she-him, bye, good-bye, left-we
We sit, he asks her, she asks him, good-bye, good-bye, we leave

Verb-initial sentences that lack independently expressed subjects are classified here as having VSO typology.

Several studies on modern dialects postulate a typological development from VSO-prominent Old Arabic or Classical Arabic to the SVO-prominent modern dialects. Feghali, assuming that pre-verbal pronoun subjects occur in the dialects more frequently than in Classical Arabic, explains this 'development' by means of semantic shift: Classical /'ana katabtuhu/ *I'm the one who wrote it* came eventually to mean *I wrote it* (1928:85; see also Ingham's discussion of similar statements, 1994:38, and Fassi-Fehri 1988:127). This purported development is seen as evidence of a major break between written or formal varieties of Arabic on one hand and spoken or informal ones on the other. However, no frequency studies of modern Arabic have yet been undertaken to either support or challenge this assumption. Both VSO and SVO are common enough in all varieties of Arabic to be considered "basic;" a thorough study of word order typology in all varieties and registers of Arabic would be necessary to show if or how the basic typologies of Arabic have changed over time. Until such a study is conducted, the discussion must remain limited to indirect evidence.[3]

The investigation of sentence typology presented here has three related aims. First, evidence will be adduced in support of the claim that the dialects retain VSO as a basic word order. Second, it will be argued that a functional approach to sentence typology that distinguishes between subject-oriented and topic-oriented typologies gives a more complete description of sentence construction in spoken Arabic than a structural approach that relies on subject-oriented analysis alone. Finally, the basic discourse functions of word order typologies characteristic of spoken Arabic will be examined.

---

[3]See Khan (1988:30) for a study of word order in Classical Arabic, discussed in 10.1.2.

10.1.1 Structural Evidence for the Primacy of VSO

Arabic shares with other VSO languages a number of corollary typological patterns that are statistically typical of verb-initial languages. These patterns include the post-nominal position of adjectives and genitives, and the use of prepositions rather than postpositions (Croft 1990:203). Longacre classifies languages with this typology as "strong VSO" types (1995:332).

Typologists use several kinds of evidence in determining the markedness of alternative grammatical forms (Croft 1990:70-72). One kind of evidence they consider is the relative number of morphemes each one contains, assuming that–other factors notwithstanding–the marked structure contains as many or more morphemes in comparison to the unmarked (Croft 1990:73). According to this criterion, VSO sentences in Arabic stand unmarked with respect to SVO, because the latter contains two separate subject markings, one a subject marker on the verb, and the other the overt subject noun or pronoun.

Relative clause structure also typically shows VSO order, especially indefinite relative clauses, which are almost always headed by a verb or pseudo-verb. Eid (1983:288) and Fassi-Fehri (1988:124-6) point out that definite relative clauses in Egyptian and Moroccan only allow an initial subject pronoun if it contrasts with another possible referent. Normally, relative clauses show VS order, two instances of which occur in this Syrian example:

S2 كان فيه واحد ماتت امّه —— مات ابوه أول شي. —— إيه. كان فيه واحد مات ابوه

kān fī wāḥid mātit ʾimmu. --- māt ʾabū ʾawwal ši. --- ʾēh. kān fī wāḥid māt ʾabū

was there-is one-m died-she mother-his. --- died-he father-his first thing. --- yeah. was there-is one-m died-he father-his

There was a [guy] whose mother died. --- His father died first. --- Yeah. There was a guy whose father died

When a relative clause contains SVO order, it is usually possible to point to a pragmatic motivation. In the following Egyptian passage, the occurrence of the pronoun /hiyya/ *it* in the second relative clause parallels the use of the definite relative pronoun /illi/ in the first, and may be motivated by the speaker's desire to mark the specificity of the indefinite noun /tamsiliyya/ *serial*:[4]

E4 فيه تمثيليّة اللي كانوا بيجيبوها في التليفزيون اللي هي بتقول حبكت ياعمدة؟

fī tamsiliyya illi kānu biygibūha fi t-tilivizyōn illi hiyya bitʾūl ḥabakit ya ʿumda?

there-is serial rel were-they indic-they-bring-it in the-TV rel she she-says was-necessary-she O mayor?

There's a serial that they used to show on TV that says, Is it really necessary, Mayor?

10.1.2 Typological Frequency and Discourse Type

Typologists also rely on frequency as a measure of markedness: if a particular construction occurs more often than an alternative one, it is likely to be unmarked in comparison to that alternative (Croft 1990:84-5). However, the frequency of VSO and SVO in Arabic main clauses is not readily answerable, because the frequency of both typologies varies from text to text and from context to context. If patterns can be established correlating the frequency of a given word order with a particular type of text, it may be that Arabic has more than one basic word order, one for each type of discourse.

Discourse analysts distinguish primarily between language as an "expression of content," which they call *transactional*, and language as expression of "social relations and personal attitudes," which they designate *interactional* (Brown and Yule 1983:1). Transactional situations tend to be primarily information-giving, and much of the information is "new," in the discourse sense, whereas the discourse topic tends to remain constant. Narratives, which constitute one type of transactional language, often revolve around the actions of a particular entity or group. In such cases, when the discourse topic remains stable, one might expect VS word order to dominate. On the other hand, narratives also contain descriptive passages that break the recounting of events to focus on a particular discourse topic. In conversation, which is often primarily interactional, the discourse topic is likely to

---

[4]The use of the definite relative pronoun in this passage is discussed in 3.1.

shift many times, often with each change of speaker. Since people tend to talk about themselves, a higher percentage of independent pronoun subjects should also occur in this type of language. The passages in this section, taken from the four dialect regions, support the notion that word order variation varies with the type of language use.

In the following descriptive passage, a Moroccan informant discusses problems caused by the influx of summer tourists into his quiet beachfront town. He introduces a number of discourse topics, /l-plāya/ *the beach*, /n-nās/ *people*, and several unspecified individuals, referred to as /l-āxur/ *another [person]*. The passage is primarily descriptive rather than narrative, and SV order predominates:

M10 [الپلايا] تبدّلت، على حسب الناس ما بقتشي النوع د الاحترام، ما بقاوش النوع ديال – النوع ديال – واحد نوع الانسجام، الناس ما كتفهمشي بعضها، ما كتفهم شَي ... الاخُر كياكل هنا الآخر كياكل الكوّر الاخُر كيسيّب الزبل هنا الاخُر كينعس بوحده ...

[l-plāya] tbəddlət, ʿla ḥasab n-nās mā bqatši n-nūʿ d l-əḥtirām, mā bqāwš n-nūʿ dyāl - n-nūʿ dyāl - waḥd nūʿ l-ənsižām, n-nās mā katfahəmš baʿḍha, mā katfhəm šay ... l-āxur kayākul hna, l-āxur kayākul l-kuwwar, l-āxur kaysəyyəb z-zbəl hna, l-āxur kaynʿas b^w-uḥdu ...

[The beach] changed, on account of the people are no longer the type that have respect, are no longer the type -- the type -- the type that gets along, people don't understand each other, don't understand at all ... one eats here, the other eats watermelon, the other throws garbage here, the other sleeps by himself ...

The following Egyptian passage shows a clear jump from transactional narrative to interactional language within the narrative. The first four main clause verbs, /kān/ *he was*, /kānu/ *they were*, /ʾal-laha/ *he said to her*, and /ʾalit-lu/ *she said to him*, are all clause-initial, and no independent pronoun subject appears either before or after the verb. However, as soon as the narrator begins to quote the actors, subject-initial word order predominates. The shift from VS to SV order occurs at the exact points at which the transactional (here, narrative) nature of the passage gives way to an internal, interactional dialogue (SV in bold).

E6 كان عادل إمام راكب في الطيّارة هو ويسرا. كانوا نازلين فقال لها حمد الله ع السلامة. قالت له **انت حضرتك تعرفني ؟** قال لها أيوه، **مش انت كنتي في المعهد ؟**

kān ʿādil ʾimām rākib fi-ṭ-ṭayyāra huwwa w yusra. kānu nazlīn, fa-ʾal-laha ḥamd-illa ʿa-s-salāma. ʾalit-lu, **ʾinta ḥaḍritak tiʿrafni?** ʾal-laha ʾaywa, **miš ʾinti kunti fi-l-maʿhad?**

Adel Imam was riding in [a] plane, he and Yousra. They were exiting, and he said, Welcome home. She said to him, ***You, sir, do you know me?*** *He told her, Yes,* ***weren't you at the Institute?***

The next narrative passage begins with two SVO sentences, as the Syrian speaker introduces the characters, /rfīʾu/ *[her husband's] friend,* /ʾəmmu/ *his mother,* and /bint ʾaxūha/ *her niece.* Once these characters are identified and established as discourse topics, the focus shifts to the actions of the characters and VS word order predominates:

S4 هادا رفيقه متزوج، امّه مصرية، وقامت راحت خطبت له بنت اخوها. جابتها من مصر من هنيك لَهون، وبركت معن هوني خمستعش نهار لَصار العرس. من بعد ما اخدها، قال ما بقى بيحبها، قال ما بقى بدي ادخل ع البيت. اجى عم بيحكي لنا هوني وقلنا ناخده ع شيخ يكتب له، يعني التوفيق، مو يكتب له شي يعني.

hāda rfīʾu mitzawwej, ʾimmu məṣriyye, w ʾāmit rāḥit xaṭbit-lu bint axū[h]a. jābit[h]a min maṣər min hənīk la-hōn, w barkit maʿon hōne xamstaʿš nhār la-ṣār l-ʿərs. min baʿd ma axad[h]a, ʾāl mā baʾa biḥibb[h]a, ʾāl mā baʾa bəddi idxul ʿa l-bēt. ʾija ʿam biḥkī-lna hōni w ʾilna nāx̆du ʿa šēx yiktib-lu, yaʿni t-tawfīʾ, mū yiktib-lu ši yaʿni.

Him, his friend [was] married, his mother is Egyptian, and she went and got him engaged to her niece. She brought her from Egypt, from there to here, and she stayed with them here for two weeks until the wedding took place. After he married her, he said he didn't love her any more, he said I don't want to go back in the house. He came and was telling us here, and we thought to take him to a sheikh to write him [a spell], that is, for success [of the marriage], not to write him anything [bad], that is.

The next Syrian joke shows clearly that VS order predominates in the narration of events. In this text, thirty main and subordinate clauses exhibit verb-initial order (clause-initial verbs are highlighted in boldface). Only seven clauses exhibit SV (or, in the case of 4, OV) typology: (1) constitutes a circumstantial clause (Arabic /ḥāl/) that describes a state, and has obligatory SV order, while (2), (3), (4), (5), and (7) indicate shifts of discourse topic from one character or set of characters to another. The SV word order of (6) echoes that of the preceding clause, (5), the repetition here being a narrative device.

S2 **كان** فيه واحد **مات** ابوه. (١) هو بالجيش، **فجابوا له** للضابط تبعه، **قالوا له** انه (٢) هادا مات بيّه، يعني انه **خبّره**. **راحوا خبّروه**، **قالوا له** طوني، **مات** بيّك. **تفاجأ** هادا و **وقع** بالارض **ومرض**. المهم **عالجوه** وكذا، بعد فترة، **ماتت** امّه. **اجوا** لعند الضابط **خبّروه** انه (٣) لطوني **ماتت** امّه . (٤) هادا شو بدّه يعمل؟ **خاف** كتير **وقال** انّه **ما لازم نخبّره** فجأةً وكذا **لازم نعمل له** شي مقدّمة لحتّى **ما ينصدم** متل هاديك المرّة **ويمرض**. بعدين **راحوا جمّعوا** العساكر كلياتهن و **صفّوهن**: استَعد! استَريح! وكذا. **قال** الضابط تبعهن (٥) اللي ميّتة امّه يقدّم خطوة، (٦) اللي ميّتة امّه قدّم خطوة. بعدين **قال له** (٧) طوني - قدّم خطوة! انّه **ماتت** امّه. **قال** لطوني قدّم خطوة!

kān fī wāḥid **māt** ʾabū. (1) huwwe bi-ž-žēš, fa-**žābū-lu** la-ḍ-ḍābiṭ tabaʿu, **qālū-lu** ʾinnu (2) hāda māt bayyu, yaʿni ʾinnu **xabbru**. **rāḥu xabbrū, qālū-lu** ṭōni, **māt** bayyak. **tfāža'** hāda w **wuqaʿ** bi-l-ʾarḍ w **miriḍ**. il-muhimm **ʿālžū** w kaza, baʿd fatra, **mātit** ʾimmu. **ižu** la-ʿand iḍ-ḍābiṭ, **xabbrū** ʾinnu (3) la-ṭōni mātit ʾimmu. (4) hāda šu biddu yaʿmul? **xāf** ktīr w **qāl** ʾinnu **mā lāzim nxabbru** fažʾatan w kaza **lāzim niʿmil-lu** ši muqaddime la-ḥatta **mā yinṣidim** mitil hadīk il-marra w **yumraḍ**. baʿdēn **rāḥu žammʿu** l-ʿasākir killayāton w **ṣaffū[h]on:** istāʿid! istāriḥ! w kaza. **qāl** iḍ-ḍābiṭ tabaʿon (5) illi mayyte ʾimmu yqaddim xaṭwe. (6) illi mayyte ʾimmu qaddam xaṭwe. baʿdēn **qāl-lu**, (7) ṭōni, qaddim xaṭwe! ʾinnu **mātit** ʾimmu. **qāl** la-ṭōni qaddim xaṭwe!

*There **was** a guy whose father **died**. (1) He was in the army, so they **brought** [the news] to his officer, and **told him** (2) that [guy's] father died; meaning, **give him** the news. They **went** and **told him**, they **said**, Tony, your father **died**. He **got a shock** and **fell** to the ground and **got sick**. Anyway, they **treated** him and so forth. After a while, his mother **died**. They **came** to the officer and **told him** that (3) Tony's mother died. (4) What should that [officer] do? He **became** very **afraid**, and **said**, we **mustn't tell him** suddenly so that he **won't go into shock** like that last time and **get sick**. Then they **went** and **gathered** all the soldiers and **lined them up:** "Attention! At ease!" and so forth. Their officer **said**, (5) "[Anyone] whose mother has died, [must] step forward," (6) [The ones] whose mother had died stepped forward. Then he **said**, (7) "Tony, step forward!," [meaning] that his mother **had died**. He **told** Tony, step forward!*

The next passage constitutes part of a narration of matchmaking procedure in Kuwait. VS order predominates throughout this description of a typical visit to a prospective bride's house. Word order shifts from VS to SV just four times, when the central discourse topic shifts among the various characters involved (SV clauses are highlighted in boldface).

K2 تگول لي انشا الله، واعديهم اي يوم نيي ونروح معاچ ونشوف البنية. ادگّ حكّ اهل البنية واگول ترى اليوم بييوا – بنييكم انشا الله، امّه واختَه والولد معانا. يگعد الولد، تدشّ البنية، يا امّا يايبة عصير يا امّا بارد يا امّا يعني أي شي، چاي، تدخل البنية ويشوف. **هو گاعد** ، **انا اگول لَه** هادي البنية ترى شوفها، يشوفها، انشا الله، اذا يعني فيه، اسألها، تبيها، ما تبيها، اسألها على الشي اللي تبيه، يسألها. **البنية طبعاً تستحي** ، مو شكل يعني واحدة بعد تيي تركض چذي، تستحي. يسألها، وين تشتغلين، شنو دارسة. **امّا انا اگول لها** بعد **انت** اسأليه. تسألَه. فيه يعني بنات يگدرون يسألون فيه بنات يستحون، ما يسألون. تسألَه. گعدنا وسألها وسئلتَه، سلام، مع السلامة، طلعنا طلعنا. **انا طبعاً انا** اسأل الولد بالسيّارة اگول لَه عجبتك البنية وليدي ولاّ ما عجبتك؟

tgul-li inšaḷḷa, wāʿdīhum ay yōm niyi w nrūḥ maʿāč w nšūf lə-bnayya. adigg ḥagg ahal lə-bnayya w agūl tara l-yōm bīyu -- binyīkum inšaḷḷa, umma w uxta w l-walad maʿāna. yigʿəd il-walad, tidišš lə-bnayya, ya umma yāyba ʿaṣīr, ya umma bārid, ya umma yaʿni ay šay, čāy, tidxal lə-bnayya w yšūf. **huwwa gāʿid, ʾāna agul-la** hāḏi l-bnayya, tara šūfha, yšūfha, inšaḷḷa. ʾiḏa yaʿni fī, isʾalha, tabīha, mā tabīha, isʾalha yaʿni ʿala š-šē lli tabī, yisʾalha. **lə-bnayya ṭabʿan tistəḥi**, mū šikil yaʿni, waḥda baʿd tiyi tarkaḏ̣ čiḏi, tistəḥi. yisʾalha, wēn tištəġlīn, šənnu dārsa. **ʾamma ʾāna agul-lha** baʿd **inti** siʾəlī. tisʾala. fī yaʿni banāt yigədrūn yisəʾlūn, fī banāt yistəḥūn, mā yisəʾlūn. tisʾala. gaʿədna, w saʾalha w saʾəlta, salām, maʿ s-salāma, ṭalaʿna, ṭalaʿna. **ʾāna ṭabʿan ʾāna ʾasʾal** il-walad bi-s-sayyāra, ʾagūl-la ha, š ʿəjibtak lə-bnayya wlīdi wəlla mā ʿəjibtak?

[The boy's mother] says, okay, make an appointment with them which day we'll come and we'll go with you and see the girl. I call the girl's family and say, Look, today they're coming -- we'll come, God willing, his mother and his sister and the boy with us. The boy sits, the girl comes in bringing either juice or a soda, or anything,tea, the girl enters and he sees. ***He's sitting, I tell him*** *this is the girl, look at her, he sees her, okay, if there is, [I say] ask her, [see if you] want her or don't want her, ask her what you want, he asks her.* ***The girl, of course, is shy,*** *it's not nice, after all, for a girl to come running, she's shy. He asks her, Where do you work? What have you studied?* ***As for me, I tell her****, now* ***you*** *ask. She asks. There are girls who are able to ask, there are girls who are shy, they don't ask. She asks him. We sit, he asks her, she asks him, good-bye, good-bye, we go out.* ***I, of course, I ask*** *the boy in the car, I say, Did you like the girl, my son, or didn't you like her?*

The next Kuwaiti text contains several dialogue passages. Here, too, VS and SV word order alternates with the genre of language use. VS passages, most of them narrative, are numbered (1) in the text, whereas SV passages, descriptive and interactional, are numbered (2).

K3 (٢) ريّال عنده مَرَة حريم ثنتين، واحدة حلوة بس هو ما يحبها، هاذيچ مو حلوة بس يحبها. نزين. (١) گامت المرا هاذي چان تگول (٢) انا ليش حلوة انا، ما يحبني وهاي الكريهة يحبها. انا اروح حگ المطوّع اسوّي له شي علشان يحبّني. (١) راحت حگ واحد مطوّع يعني، گالت له (٢) رايلي عنده مرا وانا ما يحبني وهاذيچ كريهة ويحبها، (١) وابيك تسوي لي شي عشان يحبني. يگول لها، روحي ييبي لي شعر مال سبع. نزين، (٢) سبع وين فيه؟ گولي مثل بالحديقة مال – حديقة حيوانات. (١) راحت هناك. زين. وين تگدر على السبع تاخذ منّه الشعر؟ گامت ش تسوّي، كل يوم تشتري فخوذ لحم وتروح تعطيها للحارس مالَه. تشتري كل يوم هالفخوذ اللحم وتعطيه الحارس وتتگرّب شوية كل يوم تگرّب شوية كل يوم تگرّب. خذت شهر شهرين، وين — كل يوم تتگرّب. لين توالفت ويّا السبع. گام السبع ياكل ويتمسح عليها. ذاك اليوم والله استعدت حطت لها مگص في مخباطها. يات حگ الحارس حگ السبع. (٢) هو غمض ياكل، ويتمسح عليها چذي، (١) گصي گصي الشعر حطيه بمخباطچ روحي حگ المطوع. گالت له كا يبت لك. گال شلون يبتي؟ يعني (٢) ها سبع، (١) شلون گدرتي تاخذين منّه شلون؟ گات والله سويت هالكيت هالكيت وخذت منه.

(2) rayyāl ʿinda mara ḥarīm ṯintēn waḥda ḥilwa bass hu mā yḥibbha, haḏīč mū ḥilwa, bass yḥibbha. nzēn. (1) gāmat il-mara hāḏi čan tgūl, (2) ʾāna lēš ḥilwa ʾāna, mā yḥibbni w hāy l-karīha yḥibbha. ʾāna arūḥ ḥagg lə-mṭawwaʿ ʾasawwī-la šay ʿalašān yḥibbni. (1) rāḥat ḥagg wāḥid mṭawwaʿ yaʿni, gālat-la (2) rayli ʿinda mara w āna mā yḥibbni w haḏīč karīha w yḥibbha, (1) w abīk tisawwī-li šay ʿašān yḥibbni. yigul-laha, rūḥī yībī-li šaʿar māl sibiʿ. nzēn, (2) sibiʿ wēn fī? gūli miṯil bi-l-ḥadīqa māl – ḥadīqat ḥaywānāt. (1) rāḥat hināk. zēn. wēn tigdar ʿala s-sibiʿ tāxiḏ minna š-šaʿar? gāmat š tsawwi, kil yōm tištiri fxūḏ laḥam w trūḥ taʿṭīha li-l-ḥāris māla, tištiri kil yōm ha-l-fxūḏ il-laḥam taʿṭī l-ḥāris w titgarrab šwayya kil yōm tigarrab šwayya, kil yōm tigarrab. xaḏat šahər šahrēn, wēn – kil yōm titgarrab. lēn twālifat wiyya s-sibiʿ. gām is-sibiʿ yākil w yitmassaḥ ʿalēha. ḏāk l-yōm waḷḷah istaʿaddat

ḥaṭṭat-laha magaṣṣ fi mixbāṭha. yāt ḥagg il-ḥāris, ḥagg is-sibiʿ. (2) hu ġammaḏ yākil, w yitmassaḥ ʿalēha čiḏi, (1) gəṣṣi gəṣṣi š-šaʿar ḥuṭṭī bi-mixbāṭič rūḥi ḥagg lə-miṭawwaʿ. gālat-la ka yibt-lak. gāl šlōn yibtey? yaʿni (2) ha sibiʿ (1) šlōn gədartey tāxḏīn minna šlōn? galt waḷḷa sawwēt halkēt halkēt w xaḏt minna.
(2) *A man is married, has two wives, one is pretty but he doesn't love her, the other one isn't pretty but he loves her.* (1) *This woman up and says,* (2) *why, [if] I am pretty, doesn't he love me, and that ugly one, he loves her? I'm going to the religious master to do something to him so that he'll love me.* (1) *She went to such a man and said to him,* (2) *My husband has [another] wife and he doesn't love me, and that one is ugly, but he loves her.* (1) *I want you to do something for me so that he will love me. He tells her, Go get me a hair from a lion. Well, (2) where is there a lion? Say in the garden of -- in a zoo.* (1) *She went there. Well, where can she get [close enough] to the lion to get the hair from him? She up and what did she do? Every day she would buy legs of meat, and she'd go give them to the guard of [the lion]. She would buy every day those legs of meat and give it to the guard and get a little closer, every day she'd get a little closer, every day she'd get closer, She took a month, two months, eventually, every day she'd get closer, until she became on friendly terms with the lion. The lion started eating and rubbing against her. One day by God she got ready, she put a scissors in her pocket. She came to the guard, to the lion.* (2) *[The lion] closed his eyes, eating and rubbing against her so,* (1) *Cut! Cut the hair!*[5] *Put it in your pocket! Go to the religious master! She told him, here it is, I brought [it] to you. He said, how did you get [it]?* (2) *That's a lion,* (1) *how did you get [the hair] from it, how? She said, well, I did such and such and took [it] from him.*

While these few examples hardly suffice to constitute proof, a consistent pattern has begun to emerge. The plot-focused parts of narratives usually center on one or two discourse topics which vary little from sentence to sentence. Moreover, other discourse topics which

---

[5]On the use of the imperative in bedouin narrative style, see Palva (1977).

are introduced into the narrative must usually be introduced as new entities or information, and marked as such (see section 1.5). On the other hand, in conversational or interactional discourse, the change of speaker often necessitates a change of discourse topic, since each speaker tends to talk about himself or herself, or the conversation moves from one discourse topic to another. Therefore, it is reasonable to expect different patterns and frequencies of word order to emerge in narrative texts and conversational texts. The assumption that dialects have normalized SVO order may be based largely on transactional, conversational texts in which it is natural that the topic of discourse would shift frequently.

It is worth noting that Khan's study of Classical Arabic syntax supports this analysis. His count of SV in narrative and expository texts reveals a significant difference in frequency: 45 clauses out of 550 lines of an expository text constitute SV structure, whereas an equivalent length of narrative text contains no SV clauses at all (1988:30).[6]

If both VSO and SVO represent basic typologies, each one unmarked in its own context, is one context less marked than another? Longacre argues that "[i]f storyline clauses in narrative discourse in a given language are VSO, then that language should be classified as a VSO language" (1995:333). Whether or not he is right, VSO typology can be shown to be prominent in spoken Arabic narratives, and remains a basic word order of the language.

Structural typology cannot take the analysis beyond this point. Functional typology, on the other hand, investigates not only the syntactic roles of constituents, such as subject, object, and verb, but also semantic and pragmatic roles. Semantic roles are identified by the "logical" role of the entity in the action, such as agent, patient, and receiver. Pragmatic roles involve the status of the information carried by a sentence

---

[6]Khan also remarks that VSO sentences in Classical Arabic are usually headed by a perfective verb, and further, that SV sentences tend to be descriptive (1988:30). The same is true for the dialects, as our examples have shown. This tendency reflects a universal pattern that Hopper and Thompson (1980) call "transitivity," by which they mean the degree of "effectiveness" of verbal action as expressed not only in the verb, but in the entire clause. High transitivity is associated with punctual, telic verbs, object marking, and other features, all of which tend to co-occur in foregrounded clauses in discourse.

constituent as perceived by the speaker and presented to the interlocutor, and it is at this level that explanation will be sought for the variations in spoken Arabic word order.

10.2 Topic-Prominent and Subject-Prominent Sentence Structures

Li and Thompson challenge the "assumption ... that the basic sentence structure should be universally described in terms of subject, object, and verb" (1976: 461). They argue that in some languages, "the notion of topic may be as basic as that of subject" (1976:459), and propose a typology that classifies languages into topic-prominent, subject-prominent, both topic- and subject-prominent, and neither topic- nor subject-prominent. According to their theory, then, some languages may incorporate both topic-prominent and subject-prominent structures. There is considerable evidence that spoken Arabic is one of these languages.

Both traditional and modern analyses of Classical Arabic support a distinction between topic-oriented and event-oriented typologies. Traditional Arabic grammatical terminology separates SV and VS orders, called /al-jumla al-ismiyya/ *noun-initial sentences* and /al-jumla al-fiʿliyya/ *verb-initial sentences*, respectively. In sentences headed by nouns (not necessarily subjects), 'new information' is called /xabar/, usually translated as *predicate*, but etymologically meaning *a piece of information, news* (the subject here being called /al-mubtadaʾ/ *the primary or basic [part]*).[7] The Arabic term /xabar/ describes the predicate of noun-initial sentences only, whereas the terminology used for verb-initial sentences derives from the Arabic word for verb, /al-fiʿl/ *the action*. Arabic terminology thus distinguishes between topic-prominent, given-new information packaging,[8] and event-prominent, or verb-initial packaging. VSO word order, as seen by Arab grammarians, does not follow the same information packaging principles as noun-initial

[7]The term /mubtadaʾ/ *starting point* echoes a metaphor used by psycholinguists Gernsbacher and Hargreaves for the process of cognitive processing: first, "laying a foundation," then "mapping" information onto it (cited by Payne 1995:450).

[8]Given-new, also called theme-rheme, refers to the linear order of presentation of information in a sentence. Given (old, known, or shared) information leads, and new information follows (Chafe 1976).

sentences. Moreover, Khan points to a syntactic and distributional congruence between SV word order and topic-prominent information packaging in Classical Arabic texts (1988:29-30). He lists a number of specific discourse functions of SV word order in Classical Arabic, which show a high degree of correspondence to Li and Thompson's topic-prominent functions (Khan 1988:32-40; see further 10.2.1).

It is well-known that topic-comment structure commonly occurs in spoken Arabic. However, discussions of topic-comment structure (e.g., Harrell 1962:160-61, Cowell 1964:429) tend to focus on sentences with fronted or dislocated nouns, such as *Ahmad, I know (him).* The view taken here holds all SV sentences, not merely those with explicit topics distinct from subjects, to be topic-prominent.

Li and Thompson's approach to sentence typology thus provides a powerful theory of sentence typology in Arabic, one that coincides with analyses of other varieties of the language, and helps to account for the motivations behind the patterns of both noun-initial and verb-initial typologies in different environments.

10.2.1 Spoken Arabic as a Topic-Prominent Language

Li and Thompson list a number of characteristics which, taken together, tend to characterize topic-prominent languages (1976:461-64). These characteristics include: (1) the topic is syntactically distinct from the subject, and the verb agrees with the subject but not the topic; (2) sentence construction with dummy subjects tend not to occur in topic-prominent languages; and (3) topic-prominent languages tend to make limited and/or specialized use of passive constructions. Examples from the dialects will show that spoken Arabic shares these properties with other topic-prominent languages (but in the case of the passive, only partly so).[9]

The topic position in Arabic is sentence-initial, as it is in other topic-prominent languages. Since subjects may also be sentence-initial,

---

[9]However, Li and Thompson also list other properties which are not shared by Arabic, among them that topic-prominent languages tend to be verb-final (1976:490). The fact that Arabic shares some properties but not others, and some properties to a greater extent than others, may perhaps be explained by the fact that Arabic incorporates both topic-prominent and subject-prominent typologies.

a noun in that position sometimes fulfills two roles at once, that of grammatical subject, and that of pragmatic topic. However, many sentences contain sentence-initial topics that do not fill the syntactic role of subject.

The following examples contain sentence-initial nouns that are topics, but not subjects. In the first, the topic, /martu/ *his wife*, cannot be the subject of the main verb, /hərbu/ *they fled.*

M11 مرته، منين دخل الشهر ديالها، هربوا عليها
martu, mnīn dxal š-šhər dyālha, hərbu ʿalīha
wife-his, when entered-it the-month gen-hers, fled-they from-her
His wife, when her month (to give birth) came, they deserted her

In the next passage, the two topics, /l-ʿāʾila/ *the family* and /l-ʿazri/ *the young single man*, are singular, whereas the subjects, /ʿāʾilāt/ *families* and /l-ʿzāra/ *(the) young single men*, are plural:

M10 العائلة، اللي كيقول الإنسان، ما بقاوش كيهوّدوا عائلات، العزري،
حتى العزارى ديال ولاد البلاد ما بقاوش كيهوّدوا
l-ʿāʾila, lli kayqūl l-ʾinsān, mā bqāwš kayhawwdu ʿāʾilāt, l-ʿazrī, ḥtta l-ʿazāra dyāl wlād l-blād mā bqāwš kayhawwdu
the-family, rel indic-he-says the-person, neg remained-they indic-they-descend families the-bachelor even the-bachelors gen sons of-the-town neg remained-they indic-they-descend
The family, what one calls [the family], families no longer go, the young single man, even local young single men no longer go

The speaker in the following passage is a female addressing a group of women and pointing to her husband, the only male present. The masculine gender of /ʿārif/ *he knows* clearly does not agree with the sentence-initial pronoun /ʾana/ *I*. The only plausible grammatical analysis, then, is that /ʾana/ *I* represents the sentence topic, whereas the unexpressed subject of the main clause, *he*, is indicated by the masculine singular gender of /ʿārif/ *he knows*.

E3 أنا، عارف انّ انا باخاف م الصرصار الصغيّر
ʾana, ʿārif ʾinn ana baxāf mi ṣ-ṣurṣār iṣ-ṣuġayyar
I knowing-m comp I indic-am-afraid of the-roach the-little
Me, he knows I'm afraid of the little cockroach

The underlying structure of the next sentence is equational, the subject being /aktar ši/ *the most common thing*, and the predicate /kibbe/ *kibba.* While /niḥna/ *we* is coreferent with the verb /mnaʿmlu/ *we make it*, its relationship to the main clause cannot be subject because of the intervening /ʾaktar ši/ *most [common] thing*, but can only be a topic position.

S2 نحنا اكتر شي منعمله يعني كبّة مقلية
niḥna ʾaktar ši mnaʿmlu yaʿni kibbe maqliyye
we most thing prog-we-do-it it-means kibbe fried
We, the thing we make most, that is, is fried kibbe

The fronted topic in the following, /killuhum/ *all of them*, does not represent the subject of the sentence, which is an omitted /ʾāna/ *I*.

K1 كلهم زعلان عليهم
killuhum zaʿlān ʿalēhum
all-of-them angry at-them
All of them, [I was] angry at them

Topics must be definite; subjects, on the other hand, may be either definite or indefinite. Arabic sentences follow this principle by definition: in formal Arabic, syntactic restrictions prohibit sentence-initial indefinite subjects, and in spoken Arabic, they are rare.

Among Li and Thompson's criteria for topic-prominence is that the "verb determines *subject* but not *topic*" (1976:462). In the following sentences, the topics do not fulfill subject roles, and in some cases, the sentence-initial topic has no syntactic referent in the sentence it heads. The topic of the first sentence, /d-drāri ṣ-ṣġār/ *little kids*, is plural, and as such, has no syntactic relationship to the main clause, although it does have an obvious semantic one, in that the masculine singular pronouns in *to him* and *he says* refer to *a kid*.

M2 الدراري الصغار ديال دروكا تتگول ليه ها بوعو تيگول لك فينَ هو
d-drāri ṣ-ṣġār dyāl drūka tatgūl-lih ha būʿu taygūl-lik fīna huwwa
the-kids the-young gen now indic-you-say to-him here monster indic-he-says to-you where he
Little kids of today, you tell him, there's a monster, and he tells you, where is it?

The topic of the following is /ʾana/ *I*, whereas the subject of the verb /kān/ *was* is /ʿēn samaka/ *plantar's wart*:

E3 طب أنا كان في رجليّ من تحت عين سمكة وسع كدا
ṭab ʾana kān fi riglayya min taḥt ʿēn samaka wisʿ kida
well I was-it in legs-my from below plantar's wart wideness of-so
Well, I, there was in my feet on the bottom a plantar's wart this big

The topic of the next sentence is /ʾinta/ *you*, while the subject is /is-safīne/ *the ship*:

S1 انت بيجوز تغرق السفينة بوجود واحد متلك ع ها السفينة
ʾinta bižūz tiġraʾ is-safīne bi-wužūd wāḥid mitlak ʿa ha-s-safīne
you you indic-it-is-possible-for it-sink the-ship with-existence of-one like-you on this-the-ship
You, the ship might sink with the presence of one like you on this ship!

The topic of the following, /ḥinna/ *we*, has no syntactic relationship to the rest of the sentence:

K3 اول حنا وعليّ!، المرا چسوة الگيظ وچسوة الشتا. بس
ʾawwal ḥinna, w ʿalayya!, il-mara čiswat il-gēḏ̣ w čiswat lə-šta. bass
first we, and upon-me!, the-woman clothing of-the-summer and clothing of-the-winter. only
In the old days, we, I swear! the woman [had] the summer outfit and the winter outfit. That's all.

The dialects share with other topic-prominent languages the absence of dummy subject constructions (Li and Thompson 1976:467). Dummy subjects function as place-holders for an empty syntactic subject position, such as English *It* in sentences like *It's snowing*. Spoken Arabic does not require a dummy subject, as the following examples show:[10]

[10]The Egyptian pronoun /huwwa/ *he*, it in sentences such as /huwwa l-ʾustāz mā gāš?/ *Didn't the teacher come?* is not a true dummy pronoun but rather functions as an interrogative particle that signals a presupposition on the part of the speaker. For a discussion of the functions of this pronoun, see Eid (1992).

M10 ماشي مزيان تخرج هايدا ف الليل
māši mzyān txrəž hāyda fə-l-līl
neg good you-go-out thus in the-night
It's not good to go out like that at night

E3 صعب انّها تسيب عمر وتنزل
ṣaʿb innaha tisīb ʿumar wi tinzil
difficult that-she she-leave and she-go-down
It is difficult for her to leave Omar and go out

S2 مستحيل هوني عندنا واحد يقبل انّه ياخد بنت ما تكون عزراء
mustaḥīl hōni ʿan[d]na wāḥid yiqbal innu yāxud binət mā tkūn ʿazrāʾ
impossible here at-us one he-accept that-he he-take girl neg she-be virgin
It is impossible here in our country for one to accept to marry a girl who is not a virgin

K2 مو شكل يعني واحدة بعد تيي تركظ چذي
mū šikil yaʿni waḥda baʿd tiyi tərkaḏ čiḏi
neg form it-mean one-f as-well she-comes she-runs like-that
It's not right, that is, [that] a girl after all come running like that

Lastly, Li and Thompson note that topic-prominent languages often do not have a passive voice, or have passives with special meanings (1976:467). While the passive voice occurs in spoken Arabic, in many cases, speakers prefer a topicalized construction using a dummy subject *they*, as in this sentence:

S4 العريس ايديه بيطلسوا له اياهن طلس بالحنّا، العروس بيرسموا لها اياهن رسم
il-ʿarīs ʾidēh biṭləsū-lu yāhon ṭaləs bi-l-ḥinne, il-ʿarūs birsimū-l[h]a yāhon rasəm
the-groom hands-his they-blot for-him obj-them blotting with-henna, the-bride they-draw for-her obj-them drawing
The groom, his hands, they blot henna on them for him, the bride, they draw designs on hers

Often, the Arabic imperfective passive carries a gerundive meaning loosely rendered by *-able*, as these examples show:

M1 هاد الربيع ما كيتنكلش
hād ər-rbīʿ mā kaytənkəlš
this the-grass neg indic-it-is-edible
This grass (green stuff) is inedible

E9 السرير دا ما بيتنامش عليه
is-sirīr da mā byitnamš ʿalē
the-bed that neg indic-it-can-be-slept on-it
This bed cannot be slept in

En الاكل دا ما يتغنّى لوش!
il-ʾakl da mā yitġanna-lūš
the-food this neg it-is-sung to-it
This food should not be sung to!

S1 هالطقس ما بينطلع فيه
ha ṭ-ṭaʾs mā binṭiliʿ fī
this the-weather neg be-gone-out in-it
(This weather) can't be gone out in

G هالبيت ما ينّام فيه
ha l-bēt mā yinnām fīh
[this-the-house neg it-is-slept in-it]
This house can't be slept in (Holes 1990:182)[11]

Ingham recognizes the similarity of Arabic sentence patterns to Li and Thompson's description of topic-prominent languages, but stops short of recognizing Arabic as a topic-prominent language because of Li and Thompson's claim that the topic is not syntactically related to the rest of the sentence (Ingham 1994:36). However, Li and Thompson's analysis is based largely on Chinese, the structure of which differs from that of Arabic in important ways, including the fact that Chinese is a low anaphoric language that makes limited use of referent pronouns (Li 1997). Arabic, on the other hand, is a high anaphoric language that requires a high degree of reference among various sentences parts signalled by referent or resumptive pronouns. To my knowledge, it has not been established that topic-prominent sentence structure requires a

[11]Since Holes does not state the country of origin of his examples, this example may not be specifically Kuwaiti.

low degree of anaphoric reference, or that a language with a high frequency of anaphoric pronouns cannot be a topic-prominent language. Even so, it is not difficult to find examples of topic-prominent sentences in which the topic has no direct syntactic relationship with the rest of the sentence. In addition to the Moroccan and Kuwaiti examples cited above, Cowell's Syrian examples include (1964:429):

S هالبيضات الدزينة بخمسين قرش
ha-l-bēḍāṭ ᵊd-dazzīne b-xamsīn ʿərš
these-the-eggs the-dozen for-50 piastre
These eggs are 50 piastres a dozen

S انا المغامرات كانت بين عمر السبعتعش والعشرين
ana, l-ᵊmġāmarāt kānet bēn ʿəmr ᵊṣ-ṣabaṭaᵊš wə l-ʿəšrīn
I the-adventures were-they between life of-the 17 and the-20
[For] me, the age of adventures was between 17 and20

A final piece of evidence supporting the analysis of SV sentences as topic-prominent is found in a situation in which a Kuwaiti speaker catches herself and "corrects" a misstep. The speaker describes here how she goes about making contact between the two families when trying to arrange a marriage. Several people are involved: the prospective bride and groom and both of their mothers, in addition to the matchmaker herself. The speaker first structures the sentence VSO, then changes her mind about the information packaging, ostensibly because the number of participants involved may cause confusion about the narrative. The speaker "corrects" the original VS word order, /tirjaʿ tigul-li umm lə-bnayya/ to SV /umm lə-bnayya tirjaʿ tigul-li/ *the girl's mother comes back and says to me*, clarifying the topic of the sentence:

K2 نگول حگ اهل البنت الولد چذي چذي، ولد فلان بن فلان، يشتغل چذي، تگول انشا الله ام احمد. نعطيها ونگول لها. تگول - **ترجع تگول لي امّ البنية - ام البنية ترجع تگول لي** يا امّ احمد انت تعرفينَه؟

ngūl ḥagg ahl əl-bint il-walad čiḏi, čiḏi, wild flān bən flān, yištiġil čiḏi, yištiġil čiḏi, tgūl inšaḷḷa ʾumm aḥmad. naʿṭīha w ngul-lha. tgūl -- **tirjaʿ tgul-li ʾumm lə-bnayya -- ʾumm lə-bnayya tirjaʿ tgul-li** ya umm aḥmad, ʾinti taʿrfīna?

we-say to the-family of-the-girl the-boy such such, son of-so-and-so son of-so-and-so, he-works thus, she-says alright Umm Ahmad. we-give-her and we-tell-her. she-says -- **she-returns she-says-to-me mother of-the-girl -- mother of-the-girl she-returns she-says-to-me,** O Umm Ahmad you you-know-him?
We say to the girl's family, The boy is such-and-such, son of-so-and-so son of so-and-so, he works such-and-such. She says alright, Umm Ahmad. We give her [the information] and tell her. She says, ***the girl's mother comes back and tells me, the girl's mother comes back and tells me,*** *Umm Ahmad, do you know him?*

Spoken Arabic thus shares several features with the topic-prominent languages Li and Thompson describe. The following sections explore the functions of sentence topic as Chafe (1976) defines it.

10.2.2 Temporal Frame as Topic

The sentence position of topic is difficult to define beyond a rather vague "what the sentence is about,"[12] but Chafe identifies the function of the topic as establishing "a *spatial*, *temporal*, or *individual* framework within which the main predication holds" (1976:50-51, emphasis mine). Many examples cited in the previous section contain topics that establish an individual framework for their sentences. This section will explore Chafe's concept of temporal framework as it is syntactically realized in spoken Arabic.

In 7.2.2, I argued that temporal verbs, especially /kān/ *to be*, can be topicalized, on the basis that they sometimes lie outside the main clause, showing no direct syntactic relationship to it. Examples cited therein contain the verbs /kān/ *to be* and Syrian /ṣār/ *to become* with subject agreement differing from that of the main verb. Moreover, temporal frames as sentence topics are not limited to informal registers of Arabic. Khan's study of extraposition in Classical Arabic contains a number of examples similar to the ones cited in 7.2.2, such as the following, in which the temporal verbs /kānat/ *was* and /ʾaṣbaḥtu/ *I became in the morning* precede the perfective particle /qad/, which heads the verb phrase it modifies (Khan 1988:9):

---

[12]See Tomlin (1995) for criticism of the vagueness of the term *topic*.

CA كانت اليهود قد أعجبهم إذ كان يصلّي قِبَل بيت المقدس.

kānat il-yahūdu qad ʾaʿjabahum ʾid̠ kāna yuṣallī qibala bayti l-maqdisi

The Jews–he pleased them, since he prayed towards the temple (in Jerusalem)

CA اصبحت قد حلّت يميني

ʾaṣbaḥtu qad ḥallat yamīnī

In the morning my oath was discharged

It is interesting to note that these Classical examples, and several additional ones from the Syrian region in particular, contain topics that combine both a temporal frame and an individual one. Of Khan's examples, the topic in the first consists of the phrase /kānat il-yahūd/ *the Jews were*, and in the second, /ʾaṣbaḥtu/ *I became in the morning.*

Parallel examples from Syrian include the following pair. In the first example, the use of feminine /ṣārit/ *she became* rather than masculine /ṣār/ is unusual in two respects. First, this syntactic structure, in which the syntactic subject is indefinite and sentence-final, normally attracts a masculine verb. Second, the syntactic subject of the clause is masculine singular, /mantūž/ *that which is produced*. What motivates the speaker to use /ṣārit/ rather than /ṣār/? I believe it is to give the sentence a topical frame with both temporal and individual referents: the change in circumstances signalled by the verb *it became*, and the generic educated young woman, *she.*

S2 هلّق وقت بتكون متعلّمة وكذا وصارت عندها منتوج وبتطلع بتشتغل

halla' waqt bitkūn mitʿallme w kaza w ṣārit ʿand[h]a mantūž w btiṭlaʿ btištiġil

now time indic-she-is educated-f and so-forth and became-she at-her produced and indic-she-goes-out indic-she-works

Now, when she is educated and so forth and she has come to be productive and she goes out and works

Similarly, in the second sentence of the following passage, the verb /kānit/ *she was* contains both temporal and individual topic frames, past time reference and *she*, in reference to /l-māšṭa/ *the "dressing woman" [for brides]*, mentioned in the first sentence:

S4 هالماشطة هاي مَرَة كانت تشتغل بالحمام ... كانت اول يجيبوا لها ياها تحنّي لها اجريها

ha-l-māšṭa hāy mara kānit tištiġil bi-l-ḥammām ... kānit ʾawwal yijību-l[h]a yāha tḥannī-l[h]a ijrē[h]a

that-dressing-woman this woman was-she she-work in-the-bathhouse ... was-she first they-bring for-her obj-her she-puts-henna-for-her legs-her

This "dressing woman" [was] a woman who used to work in the bathhouse ... In the old days they used to bring her to her [the bride] to henna her legs for her

I have heard similar patterns in Egypt, though infrequently. In the following example, the syntactic structure of the sentence should trigger a neutralized, masculine singular verb /kān / *it was*. Instead, the verb /kān/ is conjugated for person, providing a topic that combines both past time reference and person.

E5 كنت لازم اشوفه

kunt lāzim ašūfu

was-I necessary I-see-him

I had to see him (elicited)

These examples, and those cited in 7.2.2, show that temporal verbs can function to set a topic frame for sentences in two ways, either as a temporal frame alone, or, when conjugated for person, as a temporal and individual topic frame.

10.2.3 Topical Circumstantial Clauses (/ḥāl/)

Using Chafe's definition of topic as a "spatial, temporal, or individual framework within which the predication holds" (1976:50-51), I have claimed that topic in Arabic includes nouns and temporal verbs. Adverbs, too, often occur sentence-initial position, in which case their function in providing a frame for the sentence fits in with Chafe's definition of the function of sentence topic. The ordering of information in a sentence such that topical elements are sentence-initial, and new information sentence-final, can apply not only to the main clause constituents subject, verb, and object, but also to adverbial clauses, including the large and heterogeneous Arabic class called circumstantial clauses (/al-jumla al-ḥāliyya/).

As defined in formal Arabic, circumstantial clauses "describe the state or condition" of a main sentence subject or object (Wright II:330). Circumstantial clauses may be syndetic, signalled by /wa/ (literally *and*), or asyndetic.[13] In discussing circumstantial clauses in Syrian, Cowell places more emphasis on the temporal nature of these clauses than on their descriptive nature (1964:531). Rosenhouse notes that circumstantial clauses in the dialects (unlike in formal Arabic) may precede the main clause. She attributes this difference to a vaguely defined semantic shift: in the dialects, "there is a heavier stress put on the subordinate part, so that it becomes as important (psychologically) as the main clause" and is "more deeply connected" to the sentence (1978:229). A more precise linguistic description for the sentence-initial position of these clauses is "frame-setting," or topicality. When circumstantial clauses occur in sentence-initial position, they function to give a temporal and descriptive frame within which the action of the main verb takes place.

The following Egyptian example demonstrates this point. The clause /wə humma mašyīn/ *while they were leaving*, provides the situational frame within which the focused event, forgetting the bag, takes place.

E6 آه، وهمّ ماشيين نسي شنطته معاها
ʾāh, wə humma mašyīn nisi šanṭitu mʿāha
Oh, and they leaving forgot-he bag-his with-her
Oh yeah, when they were leaving he forgot his briefcase with her

Two examples from Morocco contrast the topicality of the circumstantial clause in sentence-initial position with the focus of new information of the sentence-final position. The first example sets up the frame, /w ḥna ṭālʿīn/ *as we were going up*, for the important event, seeing Khadija. In the second, the temporal frame is provided by the adverb /yūmayn/ *two days*, while the circumstantial clause provides new information, that he was angry.

[13]For an extensive description of circumstantial clause structures in Egyptian Arabic, see Woidich (1991).

M1 واحنا طالعين ف العقبة شفنا خديجة
w ḥna ṭālʿīn f l-ʿəqba šəfna xadīža
and we going-up in the-hill saw-I Khadija
As we were going up the hill we saw Khadija

M2 يومين وهو غضبان
yūmayn w huwwa ġəḍbān
two-days and he angry
For two days he was angry

A major variation in the structure of the circumstantial clause occurs in Syrian speech. In this variation, the subject of the circumstantial clause may be extraposed, or fronted, resulting in a topical pronoun subject followed by a topical circumstantial clause headed by /w-/ *and*. It is significant that the extraposed subjects consist of highly individuated personal pronouns, suggesting that the highly individuated nature of the subject attracts this kind of syntactic movement, lending it syntactic and pragmatic prominence. The following examples show extraposed /ʾint/ *you* and /ʾana/ *I* heading their respective clauses. While each clause as a whole provides a topical frame for the following sentence, the pronoun subject plays a special role in linking the two:

S انت ورايح خدني
ʾint w-rāyiḥ xidni
[you and coming take-me]
Pick me up on your way (Cowell 1964:532)

S انا وجايي وحاملها بصدري، قام قال لي ...
ʾana w-jāye w-ḥāmilha b-ṣidri, ʾām ʾal-li
[I and coming and carrying-it on-chest-my, got-up-he and said-he-to-me]
While I was coming and carrying it on my chest, he up and told me ... (Grotzfeld 1965:101, translation mine)

This pattern does not seem to occur regularly in other dialects, although a sentence-final circumstantial clause with subject fronting /ḥna wu ṣġayyarīn/ *when we were young* occurs in a text from Upper Egypt (Behnstedt and Woidich 1988iii:264, translation mine):

E زمان بدري كنا عنسرگوا منّيهم الزبادي حنا وصغيّرين

E zamān badri kunna ʿanisirgu minnīhum iz-zabādi ḥna wu ṣġayyarīn
time early were-we indic-we-steal from-them the-yoghurt we and young-p
In early times, we would steal their yoghurt, when we were young

10. 3 Variation in Word Order: Information Packaging

The previous sections have demonstrated that both VS and SV typologies are well established in the dialects. However, these two word orders do not account for all sentence typologies found in spoken Arabic. Even a relatively small body of data is sufficient to show that almost any basic constituent may begin an Arabic sentence, even, at times, an indefinite predicate. These non-VS, non-SV types of sentences represent marked forms of topic-prominent or subject-prominent sentences.

Discourse theory on information packaging helps explain the range of word order typologies in spoken Arabic, because it proposes principles that speakers use to present information in a way accessible to their interlocutors. Chafe summarizes "packaging phenomena" that affect way nouns are presented in discourse (1976:28):

> (a) the noun may be either *given* or *new*; (b) it may be a *focus of contrast*; (c) it may be *definite* or *indefinite*; (d) it may be the *subject* of its sentence; (e) it may be the *topic* of its sentence; and (f) it may represent the individual whose *point of view* the speaker is taking, or with whom the speaker empathizes.

The remainder of this chapter will explore the ways in which these features affect sentence structure in spoken Arabic. I will add to the ones Chafe lists a function that may be syntactically expressed in Syrian dialects, one that I will call *resumptive topic*. By resumptive topic, I mean a topic that the speaker assumes is known to the interlocutor, but that the former believes needs to be recalled or resumed. A resumptive topic is not new, but is often in some sense unexpected, hence its position is sentence-final (also called "right-dislocated").

It was noted previously that topics must be chosen from information that is given, that is, entities that can be assumed by the speaker to be known to his or her interlocutor, whether because they belong to the permanent registry (meaning that they are universally known), or because they are present in the conversational registry (meaning that they have been mentioned or alluded to in the conversation at hand, Chafe 1976:26). One of the main organizing principles of information packaging is that new information tends to follow old information. Thus new information, expressed by an indefinite noun or predicate, tends to gravitate toward the end of a sentence or clause. Formal Arabic syntax adheres closely to this discourse principle: the normal word order for a copulative sentence with an indefinite subject (/mubtadaʾ/) is predicate-subject (/xabar muqaddam/), indicating a strong propensity against an indefinite noun assuming a place at the head of a sentence.

It is important to distinguish Chafe's "focus of contrast" from another kind of focus, focus of new information. Nouns that represent focus of contrast do not constitute new information, since only known entities can be contrasted. Moreover, unlike new information, which occupies sentence-final position, the focus of contrast does not have one definable sentence position, because it occupies a marked position with respect to its normal, unmarked one. I will show that, in VSO typology, the unmarked position of object is post-verbal, whereas objects that are contrastive may occupy pre-verbal position (OVS). Subjects that are contrastive, on the other hand, can occupy clause-final position (VOS).

The following sections investigate the information packaging strategies of various marked word orders and nominal marking that occur in spoken Arabic. The discussion will begin with subject-initial structures, then turn to object-initial sentences, and finally, consider two object marking strategies that fulfill specific pragmatic roles.

10.3.1 Right-Dislocated Subjects: New Information

Among the common word order typologies in Arabic is the right-dislocation (moving to the end of the sentence) of indefinite subjects, resulting in VOS word order. These indefinite subjects cannot function as topics, because their sentence-final position signals that they contain new information. In the following Egyptian and Kuwaiti examples, the indefinite subjects lie as close as possible to the end of their sentences, allowing the indefinite subjects to be focused as new information:

E2 جا لي الساعة تلاتة وجع في ودني فظيع
gā-li s-sāʿa talāta wagaʿ fi widni faẓīʿ
came-it-to-me the-hour three pain in ear-my horrible
At three o'clock I got this horrible pain in my ear

K2 أگول لها يعني يوم الفلاني بييچ بالساعة الفلانية بييچ واحد يسأل
ʾagūl-lha yaʿni yōm il-flāni biyyīč b-s-sāʿa l-flāniyya biyyīč wāḥid yisʾal
I-say-to-her it-mean day the-such-and-such fut-he-come-to-you at the-hour the-such-and-such fut-he-come-to-you one he-ask
I tell her that is the day such-and-such will come to you at the hour such-and-such will come one [who will] ask

10.3.2 Pronoun Subject Position

In spoken Arabic, the pronoun subject of a verb is obligatorily marked on the verb as a prefix, suffix, or circumfix, indicating gender and/or number. An independent pronominal subject may be optionally expressed as an additional subject marker in verbal sentences. The position of this independent pronoun subject vis-a-vis the verb is also variable, since it may precede the verb or follow it. The various combinations of these two options result in three possible cases: (a) no independent pronoun appears, (b) an independent pronoun precedes the verb, and (c) an independent pronoun follows the verb. These three cases all have quite specific pragmatic functions.

No independent pronoun subject is expressed in cases where the discourse topic remains stable. The following exchange is taken from a conversation about a /tayyēr/ *woman's suit* that speaker E1 had bought and then taken to the cleaner. There are a number of places in which the subject pronoun /huwwa/ *he*, referring to the suit, could be inserted in this conversation. The fact that this subject pronoun does not occur in this passage reflects the fact that the discourse topic has not changed, and in the absence of a change of topic, no pronoun is necessary.

E1 — فجبته، بس من – يظهر من التعليق أو ايه –
— ماكانش مكوي؟ — مكوي و كل حاجة، بس شكله كدا فيه –
— قديم؟ — لا مش قديم لان الموديل بتاعه حلو قوي يعني ما شفتش الموديل دل قبل كدا

E1 --- fa-gibtu, bass min - yiẓhar min it-taʿlīʾ ʾaw ʾēh -
--- mā kanš makwi? --- makwi wi kull ḥāga, bass šaklu kida fī -
--- ʾadīm? --- laʾ miš ʾadīm liʾinn il-modēl bitāʿu ḥilw ʾawi, yaʿni mā šuftəš il-modēl da ʾabl kida
--- so-got-I-it, but from - it-appears from the-hanging or what -
--- neg was-it ironed? --- ironed and every thing, but form-its like-that in-it -
--- old? --- no neg old because the-style gen-it pretty very it-means neg saw-I the-style that before this
--- *So I got it, but from - it seems from hanging or whatever -*
--- *Wasn't [it] ironed?* --- *[It was] ironed and everything, but it looked like it had -*
--- *[Was it] old?* --- *No [it was] not old because its style is very pretty, that is, I hadn't see that style before that*

Similarly, the next Moroccan example contains only two subject pronouns, and both occur at the point of topic switches, marked as (1) and (2) in the text. (1) /huwwa/ *he* occurs when the topic changes from the husband, the subject of the verb /ṣifəṭ/ *he sent*, to /l-ʿabd/ *the slave*; (2) /hiyya/ *she* appears at the topic switch from *the slave (him)* to *the wife (her)*. In contrast, the second mention of the wife has no pronoun, because she remains the discourse topic.

M11 صيفط العبد (١) هو الاول گال له سير إيلا (٢) هي ولدت الولد
خلّيها وآجي عندي. ولدت البنت، ادبحها وادبح البنت وآجي.
ṣifəṭ l-ʿabd (1) huwwa l-uwwəl gāl-lu sīr ʾīla (2) hiyya wəldat l-wəld xəllīha w āži ʿndi. wəldat l-bənt, dbaḥha w dbaḥ l-bənt w āži
sent-he the-slave (1) he the-first said-he-to-him go if (2) she bore-she the-son leave-her and come-ms to-me. bore-she the-girl slay-her and slay the-girl and come
He sent the slave (1) *first, he told him, go, if* (2) *she bore [a] son, leave her and come back. (If) she bore [a] girl, slay her, slay the girl, and come*

When an independent subject pronoun occurs, it may precede or follow the verb, and the speaker's choice of sentence position reflects the pragmatic role of the pronoun in the information structure of the sentence. A pre-verbal independent pronoun subject fulfills a different pragmatic role than a post-verbal subject. In the former case, the underlying SV sentence typology is topic-prominent, and the pronoun fulfills the role of topic. In the latter case, the VOS typology represents a marked form of subject-prominent or VSO typology, and the pronoun usually acts as a focus of contrast, such as a contrast in expectations, or the sudden, unexpected (re)appearance of a known entity.

Examples from all four dialects document the focus of contrast signalled by VOS typology with pronoun subject. In the first passage, the post-verbal pronoun subject signals a contrast between the older generation, whose marriages were arranged, and the young generation nowadays, who arrange their marriages /hinnin/ *they (themselves)*.

S4 يعني عادات الاولية، أبهاتنا وجدودنا، كانوا ما يشوفوا العروس للَيلة العرس. هلّق هالجيل هالموجود ، بيخطبوا بعضن **هنن**

yaʿni ʿādāt il-ʾawwaliyye, ʾabbahātna w jdūdna, kānu mā yšūfu l-ʿarūs la-lēlt l-ʿərs. hallaʾ ha-j-jīl ha-l-mawjūd buxṭbu baʿḍon **hinnin**

it-mean the-customs of-the-previous-ones, fathers-our and grandfathers-our, were-they neg they-see the-bride until-night of-the-wedding. now this-the-generation the-present indic-they-get-engaged each-other-they **they**

The customs of the previous [generations], *our fathers and forefathers, they used not to see the bride until the wedding night. Now, this present generation,* ***they*** *get engaged* ***themselves***

The following Egyptian sentence is taken from a narrative of a movie plot. The speaker has just reported an ominous dialogue between the two main characters, a man and a woman, and now describes the ensuing events. When the discourse topic shifts from the man to the woman, the speaker uses a post-verbal pronoun subject, /hiyya/ *she*, to contrast *his* actions to *hers*:

E6 جه تاني يوم، جه الصبح، ما كانتش **هي** في البيت

geh tāni yōm, geh iṣ-ṣubḥ, mā kānitš **hiyya** fi l-bēt

came-he second day, came-he the-morning, neg was-she **she** in the-house

He came the next day, came in the morning, ***she*** *was not at home*

In the next passage, a Kuwaiti interviewer asks the matchmaker if she and her partner (the referents of plural *you* in the translation) set the fee for their services, or if they have a sliding scale according to the customer's means. In her reply, the matchmaker first specifies a sliding scale, then stipulates that the customers–not she and her partner–decide how much they will pay. The post-verbal repetition of the subject /uhuma/ *they* functions to contrast the customers with the matchmakers:

K4 — نزين، الحين، هل مثلاً مقررين ش كثر السعر ولاّ حسب كل واحد ومادّته؟

K2 — كل واحد ومادّتَه، على حسب كل واحد ومادّتَه. بس الوگت الحالي هذا الحين گاموا يقررون **هم**

--- nzēn, al-ḥīn, hal maṯalan mqarrərīn š kiṯir is-siʿr wəlla ḥasab kill wāḥid w māddita?

--- kill wāḥid w māddita, ʿala ḥasab kill wāḥid w māddita. bass il-wagt il-ḥāli hāḏa l-ḥīn gāmu yqarrirūn **ʾuhuma**

--- okay now ques for-example having-decided-p what amount the-price or according-to each one and material-worth?

--- each one and material-worth, according-to each one and material-worth. but the-time the-present this, now got-up-they they-decide **they**

--- *Okay, now, have [you] decided how much the price is, or is it according to each one and his material worth?*

--- *Each one and his material worth, according to each one and his material worth. But at the present time now [the customers] have started to decide* ***themselves***

In the next example, the post-verbal /ʾāna/ *I* singles out the Moroccan speaker, creating a contrastive distance between him and a situation he wants nothing to do with:

M7 واش بغيتي ندير لك انا؟

w-aš bġīti ndīr lək **ʾāna**?

and-what wanted-you I-do for-you **I**?

What do you want ***me*** *to do for you?*

Another form of contrastive focus is the indication of unexpectedness or surprise. The immediately preceding Moroccan example hints at unexpectedness as well as contrastive distance, giving a sense of astonishment: *You want* ***me*** *to do something?* This kind of focus of contrast indicates surprise on the part of the speaker. The post-verbal pronoun in the following Syrian example likewise indicates both a contrast between /ʾana/ *I* and /ʾintu/ *you*, and astonishment on the part of the speaker at her neighbors' unexpected visit:

S5 تصوّري، انا اكون باركة الصبح، يندقّ الباب، هلّق شلون جيتوا انتو؟!

tṣawwari, ʾana [a]kūn bārke iṣ-ṣubuḥ, yindaʾʾ il-bāb, hallaʾ šlōn jītu ʾintu?!

imagine-f, I i-be sitting-f the-morning, it-be-knocked the-door, now how came-you-p you-p?!

Imagine, I would be sitting in the morning, there would be a knock at the door, now, how did ***you*** *get here?!*

It may therefore be claimed that the occurrence and position of independently-expressed pronoun subjects is variable in spoken Arabic, according to the informational role played by the subject: a pre-verbal pronoun subject serves mainly as a sentence topic, which I argue is grammaticalized in Arabic, while a post-verbal pronoun subject supplies either contrastive or unexpected reference.

10.3.3 Object-Initial Sentences

Object-initial sentences consist of two types, one a marked form of topic-prominent sentence structure, and the other a marked form of subject-prominent structure. These two types differ syntactically in that the topic-prominent type contains a place-holding or resumptive pronoun that marks the original post-verbal position of the object. The fronted object in this case functions like other topics, to set the frame for the rest of the sentence. By contrast, sentence-initial objects in the latter type leave behind no trace pronoun. This difference in syntactic structure seems to parallel a difference in pragmatic function: while objects that have resumptive pronouns are topical, objects without resumptive pronouns are highly contrastive. Examples of both types are examined in the next two sections.

10.3.3.1 Topic-prominent OV: Object as Topic

A large percentage of object-initial sentences show topic-comment structure; that is, the object is fronted, or moved to the sentence-initial position, and a resumptive pronoun marks its original place in the sentence. The sentence-initial position of the object in this case marks the syntactic object as taking the role of sentential topic. These examples contain objects as topics, all of them functioning as the frame for the rest of the sentence:

M2 الطحين تنغربلوه
ṭ-ṭḥīn tanġarblūh
the-flour indic-we-sift-it
The flour, we sift

E1 الفستان جبته
il-fustān gibtu
the-dress got-I-it
The dress, I got

S1 وشّك ما بشوفه نهائياً
wiššak ma bšūfu nihāʾiyyan
face-your neg indic-I-see-it at-all
Your face I don't (want to) see (it) at all

K4 الاسهم مالوت الجمعية حوّلهم باسمه
al-ʾashum mālōt lə-jamʿiyya ḥawwalhum b-isma
the-stocks gen the-association transferred-them in-name-his
The stocks of the association he transferred in his name

10.3.3.2 Subject-Prominent OV: Contrastive Function

In contrast to the preceding topic-prominent, object-initial sentences, the following sentences are subject-prominent, object-initial. They show object extraposition or fronting, not topicalization, as demonstrated by the absence of a resumptive pronoun marking the object position after the verb. They also exhibit a clear contrastive function not present in topic-prominent sentences.

In the first Moroccan example, the man has just asked for a knife, and is told that the only one available is the one used for feast slaughtering. His reply emphasizes that this specifically is the one he wants, contrasting it to other possible members of the set of *knives*. The placement of /hādīk/ *that one* indicates that it is singled out for contrast, and this interpretation is borne out by an informant's paraphrase of the sentence by means of a relative clause: /hādīk lli bġīt/ *that's the one I want* (and not any other).

M9 قال لها ، هاديك بغيت انا، آراها باش ندبح
qāl-lha, hādīk bġīt āna, ʾārāha bāš nədbaḥ
said-he to-her, that-one want-I I, give-here-it so-that I-slaughter
He said to her, that one I want, give it here so I can slaughter

In the next passage, the object /žūž d l-ʿyālāt/ *two wives* precedes its verb, /ədda/ *he took*, and contrasts with the *one wife* /l-mra/ the man had previously:

M11 واحد الراجل عندُه المرا تتولد غير البنات، ما عندهاش الولد. ناض
گال لها أنا خصّني الولد. ناض تجوّج مرا اخرى، تجوّج واحد المرا
اخرى، وجوج د العيالات ادّى
wāḥəd r-rāžəl ʿndu l-mra tatəwləd ġi[r] l-bnāt, mā ʿndhāš l-wəld. nāḍ gāl-līha ʾāna xəṣṣni l-wəld. nāḍ tžəwwəž mra x^{w}ra, tžuwwəž wāḥəd l-mra x^{w}ra, w žūž d l-ʿyālāt ədda
one the-man at-him the-wife indic-she-bears only the-girls, neg at-her the-son. got-up-he said-he-to-her I necessary-for-me the-son. got-up-he married-he wife other, married-he one the-wife other, and two gen the-wives took-he
[There was] a man who had a wife who [kept] having only girls; she had no son. He up and told her, I need a son. He up and married another woman, and two wives he took.

In the Syrian play "Wādi al-Misk," a female character becomes angry at her boss (who is also her father) for rejecting her request for time off. He told her to apply for /ʾižāze/ *vacation time*, and she wants /ʾizin/ *[special] permission [to miss work]*. Here, /ʾizin/ *permission* contrasts tacitly with /ʾižāze/ *vacation time* in the context of the play:

S6 إذن ما بتعطيني
ʾizin mā btaʿṭīni
permission neg indic-you-give-me
Permission you won't give me

Cowell calls this construction object-verb inversion, remarking that it occurs in "certain kinds of exclamations with the elative" (1964:439). His examples contain superlative noun phrases, which in these cases represent objects contrasted in the absolute to everything else:

S اعجب شي الله ما خلق!
ʾaʿžab šī ʾaḷḷa mā xalaʾ
[more-marvelous thing God neg created]
A more marvelous thing God has never created!

S اجنن من هيك عمري ما شفت!
ʾažnan mən hēk ʿəmri mā šəft!
[crazier than such life-my neg saw-I]
Crazier than that I've never seen!

The next passage, from Kuwait, mentions two groups of girls, one with fair complexions and one with dark complexions. In the second sentence, the speaker singles out dark complexioned girls as being less desirable as brides, fronting the object /is-sumur/ *dark-skinned ones*:

K2 هالايام هاذي كلّه يبون البيض ما يبون السمر. السمر حيل ما يبون
ha l-iyyām hāḏi killa yabūn il-bīḍ, mā yabūn is-sumur, is-sumur ḥēl mā yabūn
this-the-days these always-it they-want the-white-p neg they-want the-dark-p . the-dark-p very neg they-want
These days, they always want light-skinned [girls], they don't want dark-skinned ones. Very dark-skinned they don't want

This kind of variation in word order further supports the distinction between topic-prominent and subject-prominent sentence structures, because object-fronting and subject extraposition perform different pragmatic functions. When the syntactic object is fronted without a resumptive pronoun, its function is contrastive, whereas a fronted object in topic-comment structure plays the role of non-contrastive sentence topic. Similarly, pre-verbal pronoun subjects are topical, while post-verbal pronoun subjects are contrastive. For both subjects and objects, then, a reversal from unmarked to marked word order parallels a shift in function.

10.3.4 Predicate-Subject Inversion

Predicate-subject inversion falls under the rubric of topic-prominent typology. This inversion can be either marked or unmarked, depending in part on the relative "weight" of the constituents. Inversion is common when the sentence consists of a short predicate and a sentential subject, and follows Hawkins' (1994) "heaviness principle:" that longer or morphologically 'heavier' constituents tend to follow shorter or morphologically 'lighter' ones. At the same time, fronted predicates do not represent new information, but rather topics, or frames within which the subject clauses are to be assessed. Moroccan, Egyptian, and Syrian examples of predicate fronting include:

M10 ماشي مزيان تخرج هايدا ف الليل
māši mzyān txrəž hāyda f-l-līl
neg good she-leave like-that in the-night
It's not good to go out like that at night

E3 صعب انّها تسيب عمر وتنزل
ṣaʿb innaha tisīb ʿumar wi tinzil
hard comp-she she-leave Omar and she-go-out
It is difficult for her to leave Omar and go out

S2 مستحيل يفكر فيها
mustaḥīl yfakkir fī[h]a
impossible he-think about-her
It's impossible for him to think about [marrying] her

In other contexts, inverted predicate-subject order may fulfill a contrastive function, as suggested by the following Moroccan example. The inverted order here signals the denial of a tacit assumption (projected by the speaker onto her listeners) that there no longer remain true believers. In this sentence, stress falls on the inverted predicate, indicating a contrastive function (unmarked order here would be /l-mūminīn bāqyīn/ *(the) believers remain*, in which *believers* would function as topic):

M9 لا باقيين المومنين باقيين المومنين
lā bāqyīn l-mūminīn, bāqyīn l-mūminīn
no remaining-p the-believers remaining-p the-believers
No, there remain believers, there remain believers.

Inverted predicate-subject structure occurs with some frequency in Syrian speech. Cowell calls it predicate-subject inversion, and notes that the inversion

> gives the impression that the subject was at first suppressed (to be "understood" from context), then restored later as an afterthought. Its effect is to put relatively more emphasis on the predicate, less on the subject (1964:419).

Cowell's definition indicates that these inverted subjects contain given, not new, information. In normal, topic-initial word order, these "subjects" would constitute the topics as well. The inversion of the word order functions to reinvoke or resume a topic that is given but not active, not present in the immediate discourse registry–Cowell's "afterthought." It is also worth noting that my narrative data contain no examples of this construction, and that all of Cowell's examples are interactional in genre, among them (1964:419):

S والله ذكية، هالبنت
walḷa zakiyye ha-l-bənt
[by-God intelligent that-the-girl]
That girl is certainly intelligent

S كان كاتب لي عنوانه هون بواشنطن هو
kān kātəb-li ʿənwāno hōn b-wašᵊnṭon huwwe
[was-hehaving-written-for-me address-his here in-Washington he]
He'd written me his address here in Washington

This particular resumptive function of inverted predicate-subject word order, well-documented for Syrian, parallels in function another "resumptive topic" construction involving the Syrian object-marker /la-/, examined in the next section.

10.4 Syrian Object-Marker /la-/: Resumptive Topic[14]

Of the four dialect areas under investigation here, the Syrian region is distinguished by use of the preposition /la-/ to mark certain right-dislocated objects (objects shifted to sentence-final position). This construction contains a resumptive or place-holding pronoun marking the syntactic position from which the marked object has been dislocated.

[14]As a preposition, /la-/ has another meaning, *to, direction toward*. Here I am concerned only with /la-/ as an object-marker.

In such clauses, the verb phrase contains an object pronoun, which is then followed by a coreferent full noun object complement marked with /la-/. In the bedouin joke (excerpt repeated here from 1.5), the verb /ʾāl/ *he said* is followed first by a pronoun object /lu/ *to him*, then followed by the same object component, expressed this time as a full noun marked with /la-/, /la-l-garsōn/ *to the waiter*. The waiter here is a known entity, because his existence can be inferred from that of /l-maṭʿam/ *the restaurant*. Hence he does not represent a new topic, but rather one that is recalled into active registry. In addition, /la-/ assigns the waiter discourse topic (but not sentence topic) status, and alerts the listener to the fact that the waiter plays an important role in the joke.

S2 فيه واحد بدوي فات ع المطعم، قال له للگارسون، انطيني بوظة
fī wāḥid badwi fāt ʿa l-maṭʿam, qāl-lu **la**-l-garsōn, inṭīni būẓa
there-is one bedouin entered-he into the-restaurant said-he-to-him **la**-the waiter, give-me ice-cream
There was a bedouin who went into a restaurant and said to the waiter, Give me some ice cream

Since this /la-/ can mark both direct and indirect objects (a combination only possible in this particular case), its function must be both syntactic and pragmatic.

Cowell designates this construction as topic-comment inversion, and remarks that /la-/ often marks human inverted topics (1964:434-5). Khan (1984) reviews this construction in Semitic, and concludes that it marks individuated nouns only. Levin (1987) observes that this "definite object marker" occurs in contexts with an emphasis or emotional content, such as wonder, impatience, or disapproval. What is the motivation for the inverted word order? And why should there be an emotional content associated with this construction?

Objects marked with /la-/ are always definite, representing given rather than new information. In the following, the speaker must assume that his interlocutor knows Muhammed:

S3 شفته لمحمد اليوم؟
šiftu la-mḥammad il-yōm?
saw-you-him **la**-Muhammed today?
Did you see Muhammed today?

Since /la-/ marks highly individuated entities, it functions neither as a new topic, nor a contrastive topic marker. Rather, this kind of object marking fulfills a specific pragmatic function of recalling or reinvoking a topic into active registry. In doing so, the speaker assumes that the listener knows the topic and can identify the specific referent, but feels the need to reinvoke the topic, perhaps because it has not been active in the conversational registry, or perhaps because the speaker believes that the interlocutor has forgotten about it. In the immediately preceding example, the speaker assumes that Muhammed is not present in the interlocutor's active conversational registry, and therefore needs to be reinvoked. This phrasing may be contrasted with another equally possible construction that signals the speaker's belief that Muhammad is still within active discourse registry:

S شفت محمد اليوم؟
šift mḥammad il-yōm?
saw-you Muhammad today?
Did you see Muhammad today? (elicited)

Cowell's designation of this construction as an inverted topic-comment does not match the function of /la-/ as it occurs in my data. This type of construction is typically found in narratives with verbs that take two object complements, such as /ʾāl/ *to say* and /ʿaṭa/ *to give*, in which /la-/ usually occurs in subject-prominent VSO typology (not topic-prominent typology). The tendency of /la-/ to occur in narrative contexts is a natural consequence of its pragmatic function. /la-/ marks highly individuated topics in general, often human beings, or entities with textual prominence, which often constitute discourse topics. Since subject-prominent typology normally focuses on events, the speaker needs pragmatic and syntactic help in managing discourse topics (discourse topic contrasting with sentence topic).

The following joke demonstrates another dimension of the recall or resumptive (discourse) topic-marking function of /la-/. After introducing the main characters, /t-tūme/ *the garlic* and /ž-žəbse/ *the watermelon* in the first sentence, the speaker reinvokes them in the second, in this case not because they have been forgotten, but to specify their respective roles as addresser and addressee. Here, /la-/ marks both the indirect object position of /t-tūme/ *the garlic* and also its status as discourse topic.

S2 فيه مرّة الجبسة والتومة ماشيين مع بعضن، قالت لها الجبسة للتومة روحي يا لطيف شو ريحتك طالعة، روحي روحي ما بدي امشي معك. قالت لها التومة بعدين، احسن مو كل واحد جا دق لي ع طيزي بروح معه!

fī marra ž-žəbse w ət-tūme māšyīn maʿ baʿḍon. qālit-l[h]ā ž-žəbse **la**-t-tūme, rūḥi ya laṭīf šu rīḥtik ṭālʿa, rūḥi rūḥi mā biddi imši maʿik. qālit-lha it-tūme baʿdēn, ʾaḥsan mū kill wāḥid ža daqq-əlli ʿa ṭīzi brūḥ maʿu!

there-is time the-watermelon and the-garlic walking with each-other, said-she-to-her the-watermelon **la**-the-garlic, go O God what odor-your coming-out, go-f go-f neg desire-my I-walk with-you. said-she-to-her the-garlic then, better neg every one came-he knocked-he on ass-my indic-I-go with-him!

One time the watermelon and the garlic were walking together, the watermelon said to the garlic, go away, you stink, go, go, I don't want to walk with you. The garlic then said to her, [that's] better--[at least] not everyone who comes and knocks on my ass I go off with!

The emotional content noted by Levin in his study of Palestinian Arabic can be seen as a natural consequence of the recall. Levin points out that teachers use this construction to reprimand students who have apparently not done their homework. By "recalling" the book, the teacher signals that the student has forgotten about the book–or perhaps, sarcastically, that he or she has pretended to forget about it–as his example shows (1987:35; translation mine):

P انت فتحته للكتاب؟

inti fataḥto **la**-l-ktāb?

you opened-you-it **la**-the-book?

Did you [even] open the book?!

Levin observes that some speakers also use this construction to express "sorrow and pity" (1987:34-5). In this example, the speaker's "recall" of the tree to the attention of the children indicates that they have indeed forgotten about it, hence their destructive behavior toward it:

P انزلوا! كسّرتوها للشجرة!
inzalu! kassartūha **la**-š-šažara!
get-down-p! broke-you-it **la**-the-tree!
Get off! You have broken the tree!

This and similar instances of resumptive topic parallel in form and function the ethical dative, whose function is to provide the means to express a point of view other than the speaker's (see further 10.5)

Two unusual cases of /la-/ from my data, apparent performance errors, further clarify the pragmatic functions of resumptive /la-/. The first passage, about a party given by the wife of the president of the university, contains a rather complex clause containing /la-/ marking the *subject* of the subordinate clause, a syntactic error. Although this construction has been judged by a native informant to be a performance error, it offers a unique perspective on the pragmatic function of this construction. *The president's wife* is highly individuated (definite, specific, textually prominent, and has high social status), and this prominence is one reason for the attraction of /la-/. The second reason has to do with the speaker's desire to reinvoke or recall the topic of the president's wife, which has been superseded in the immediately preceding clause by other events (see full text in Appendix 2). The resumptive function of /la-/, together with the highly individuated status of *the president's wife*, have taken momentary precedence over its syntactic restrictions:

S5 مشان هيك حطّينا لها سكرتيرة خصوصية بدها تخبّرها خلال
يومين مشان تعرف تحكي عربي مشان تاخدها ع الزيارة، يعني
ع العزيمة يللي عاملة النا ايّاها **لمرة رئيس الجامعة**
mišān hēk ḥaṭṭēnā-l[h]a sikirtēra xṣūṣiyye bəd[h]a txabbr[h]a xilāl yōmēn mišān taʿrif tiḥki ʿarabi mišān tāxd[h]a ʿa z-ziyāra, yaʿni, ʿa l-ʿazīme lli ʿāmilt-əlna yāha **la-mart raʾīs ij-jāmʿa**
because-of thus put-we-for-her secretary private desire-her she-tell-her during days-two in-order she-know she-speak Arabic in-order she-take-her to the-visit it-mean to the-party rel having-arranged-for-us obj-it **la-wife of-president of- the-university**

For that reason we arranged a private secretary who will call her in the next two days so that she can talk to her in Arabic so that she can take her to visit, that is, to the party that ***the president of the University's wife*** *is having for us*

The second unusual case contains an OVS structure with a clause-initial /la-/ phrase, /la-ṭōni/ *Tony*:

S2 اجوا لعند الضابط خبّروه انّه لطوني ماتت امّه

ižū la-ʿand iḍ-ḍābiṭ xabbrū ʾinnu **la**-ṭōni mātit ʾimmu

came-they to-at the-officer informed-they-him comp **la**-Tony died-she mother-his

They came to the officer and informed him that Tony's mother had died

The importance of this particular example lies in the sentence-initial position of /la-ṭōni/ *Tony's.* /Normally, la-/ occurs in or near sentence-final position (hence Cowell's identification of it as an inverted comment-topic construction). A Lebanese informant finds this sentence unusual because of the fronted position of /la-ṭōni/, preferring instead /mātit ʾimmu la-ṭōni/ *Tony's mother died.* If indeed it constitutes a performance error, what prompted the shift in the normal word order?

The answer may lie in conflicting information packaging needs on two different narrative levels. First, the speaker is telling the joke to an audience, and she must package the information in a way accessible to them. Tony is the main topic in this joke, and as such, the speaker wants to organize the sentence around him. On the other hand, the narrative logic within the joke has a different organizing imperative involving the speakers within the text. These speakers (*they* in the text) need to package Tony as a resumptive topic for the officer in charge, because Tony is an entity in the officer's permanent registry, but in need of recall. The two packaging imperatives clashed, resulting in the unusual word order of a fronted /la-/ phrase.

In addition to its object-marking function, then, /la-/ acts as an information packaging device that recalls or reinvokes a highly individuated entity from either the permanent or the conversational registry into discourse topic. Syrian Arabic thus stands unique among these dialects in possessing a syntactic means to mark resumptive topics.

10.5 The Ethical Dative: Point of View and Empathy

The final pragmatic consideration Chafe lists as relevant to the packaging of nouns is that of point of view or empathy (cited in 10.3). All four dialect areas under investigation here make use of a syntactic feature, called the "ethical dative," whose function it is to highlight a certain point of view, indicate the speaker's empathy, or elicit empathy on the part of the hearer. Mitchell and El-Hassan, in their study of educated spoken Arabic of Egypt, Jordan, Syria and Lebanon, note the widespread use of this construction in Egypt and the Levant (1994:107-9).

The term *ethical dative* is commonly used to refer to prepositional phrases headed by /l(i)-/ that are not complements, but rather indicate some sort of involvement of the marked person(s). Cowell's definition of it as indicating "an assumed relevance or interest of the statement" to involved parties explains one aspect of this function (Cowell 1964:483). A more precise statement of the function of this dative replaces "assumed" with "invoked," because the speaker controls and exploits this device. Rather than indicating "assumed relevance or interest," the ethical dative reflects the speaker's attempt to *invoke* the relevance of the statement by indicating a particular point of view and eliciting the listener's empathy.[15] Examples of this construction in all four dialects demonstrate its function (dative constructions in boldface).

The first example, from Morocco, contains the speaker's expression of empathy for the victim and his invoking of the listener's empathy as well. Here /lu/ *for him* obviously does not imply that the victim's face was broken at his request or for his benefit, but that it happened *to* the victim. The use of /la-/ here invokes the victim's point of view, and by extension, the listener's empathy:

M1 شوف هادا، **مهرّس له** وجهه
šūf hāda, **mharrəs-lu** wəžhu
see that, **having-been-broken-for-him** face-his
Look at that one, his face has been broken ***for him***

The next example, from Egypt, shows the speaker using an ethical dative to solicit the listeners' emotional involvement in the drama of

[15] This analysis of the ethical dative was inspired in part by the work of Kuno (1976) on ways in which empathy affects syntax in English and Japanese.

the events he describes. By including the listener in his own action of watching his brother, /la'ēt-lak/ *I found for you*, the speaker invites the listener to share his point of view:

E9 **فلقيت لك** اخويا محمود اوّل الاهلي ما حطّ جون بيقفز في السقف
ونسي نفسه ويلفّ في الصالة

fa-**la'ēt lak** 'axūya maḥmūd da 'awwal il-'ahli ma ḥaṭṭ gōn biyi'fiz fi s-sa'f w nisi nafsu w yiliff fi ṣ-ṣāla

so-**found-I for-you** brother-my Mahmoud that first the-Ahli nom put-he goal indic-he-jumps in the-roof and forgot-he self-his and he-run-around in the-room

So I found ***for you*** *my brother Mahmoud, as soon as the Ahli team scored a goal, he jumps to the ceiling and forgot himself and is running around the room*

In this Syrian passage, the speaker uses the ethical dative to solicit agreement with the speaker's point of view in condemning modern (as opposed to traditional) marriage:

S4 بس اوّلي ما يشوف العروس ورأساً **تلاقي لك** تصير المفاهمة
وتجيهن ولاد ... هلّق **بتشوفي لك** بيعرفوا بعضن بيعاشروا بعضن
سنة وسنتين وبعدين وقت اللي بيتزوّجوا بيقللك صار اختلافات
معها

bass 'awwali mā yšūf il-'arūs w ra'san **tlā'ī-lik** tṣīr il-mufāhame w tjī[h]on wlād ... halla' **bitšūfī-lik** bya'rfu ba'ḍon bi'āšru ba'ḍon sine w sintēn w ba'dēn wa't illi bitjawwazu bi'il-lak ṣār ixtilāfāt ma'[h]a

but first neg he-see the-bride and directly **you-find for-you** it-become the-understanding and 3fs-come-to-them kids ... now indic-**you-see for-you** indic-they-know each-other indic-they-consort-with each-other year and years-two and then time rel indic-they marry indic-he-says-to-you became-it differences with-her

But in the old days, [the groom] wouldn't see the bride and you would find ***for yourself*** *there would be [mutual] understanding, they'd have children ... Now, you see* ***for yourself*** *they know each other and consort with each other for a year and two years, then when they get married, he tells you, there have occurred differences with her*

In the next Syrian example, the speaker solicits the listener's empathy for his need for household help (example from Cowell 1964:483):

S بتعرف لي شي بنت بتقعد صانعة؟

bta‘rif-li šī bint bti’‘od ṣān‘a ?

[**indic-you-know-for-me** some girl indic-she-sits maid]

*Do you know [**for me**] any girl who would work as a maid?*

Finally, this Kuwaiti sentence contains an ethical dative that reveals the speaker's urgency that his drink not be identifiable as alcoholic:

K1 بسّ لا تحطّ لي فيه لا عود لا شي لا هادا عشان لا يحسّون

bass **lā tḥuṭṭ-li** fī lā ‘ūd lā šay lā hāda ‘ašān lā yḥissūn

but neg **you-put-for-me** in-it neg stick neg thing neg this so-that neg they-feel

*But **don't put** in it either a stick or anything **for me** so they won't realize*

10.6 Summary

I have argued in this chapter that the sentence structure of spoken Arabic retains both VSO and SVO word orders as basic typologies. These two typologies fulfill different discourse functions, and tend to predominate in different discourse genres. Using the framework of Li and Thompson (1976) and evidence from the dialects, I proposed that Arabic be classified as a language with both subject-prominent and topic-prominent typologies, the former associated with VSO typology and the latter with SVO. VSO represents the dominant typology in event narration, while SVO functions as a topic-prominent typology that is used to describe and converse, contexts in which discourse topics either shift around, or are taken as a frame within which a main sentence predication holds.

Beyond the two basic typologies, a number of marked sentence structures, such as OVS, VOS, and predicate-subject (verbless), were also examined, with the goal of identifying their pragmatic functions. Adopting Chafe's types of information packaging, and adding to them resumptive topic, a function found in Syrian, I found that the inversion of unmarked word orders often results in either a focus of contrast or one of several kinds of topicalization (new topic, contrastive topic, or resumptive topic). Thus object-initial word orders, inverted from the normal object-final VSO, indicate a contrastive topic or contrastive focus. Subject pronouns in post-verb position fulfill a different function than pre-verbal subject pronouns: the former represent a focus of contrast, while the latter represent (non-contrastive) sentence topics.

The four dialects examined here all appear to share these information packaging strategies. They also share a construction called the ethical dative, which is seen as invoking a particular point of view in an attempt by the speaker to elicit empathy from the listener.

One area of syntactic divergence has been explored here. Syrian grammaticalizes a resumptive topic function that does not seem to be syntactically marked in other dialects. The object-resumptive topic marker /la-/ marks highly individuated direct and oblique objects and recalls them into active discourse registry. The marking of individuation in this case parallels other cases in which Syrian speakers accord syntactic attention to (partly) individuated nouns, such as the indefinite-specific article (1.4), indefinite-specific relative clauses with /illi/ (3.1) and unstressed demonstratives (4.2).

As I argued to be the case for other syntactic structures examined in this study, speaker control plays an important role in the realization of sentence structure. The speaker's perception of a state or event determines its portrayal as topic-focused, event-focused, and the framing of entities as new topics, resumptive topics, contrastive topics, or new information.

Conclusions

This overview of the syntax of four Arabic dialects has raised as many questions as it has answered. The most basic question I sought to answer, to what extent do the dialects share a common syntax, may now be more narrowly specified and focused, as the similarities and differences uncovered here point in several promising directions. A number of tentative conclusions and suggestions for further research may be proposed.

Individuation and Syntactic Marking

It has been emphasized throughout this study that the syntax of spoken language reflects not only formal, structural rules, but also speaker-controlled continua. Adapting the work of Khan (1984, 1988) and others, I have proposed a continuum of individuation that helps explain many kinds of syntactic variation in spoken Arabic. Individuation continua undoubtedly affect the syntax of many, if not all, languages. But even if the effect of individuation on syntax is indeed a language universal principle, its language-specific applications still remain to be compared and contrasted. Arabic dialects differ in the number of morphosyntactic markings they employ to mark individuation on nouns, and certain dialects tend to mark individuation on nouns more than others. I will review the findings of the present study on the syntactic features affected by the continuum of individuation, first with a broad overview of shared features, and then with dialect-specific observations and hypotheses.

In Chapter 1, the continuum of individuation was shown to explain variation in the use of definite and indefinite articles. Chapter 2 argued that individuation can help explain patterns of agreement marking and the choice of genitive exponents over a genitive construct phrase. Speakers choose between collective and individuated plural agreement to reflect their perception of the noun's identity. They also choose between the construct state and the genitive exponent on the basis of several kinds of motivating factors, ranging from formal structural ones to pragmatic factors. These pragmatic considerations seem to be shared by most of the dialects. In Chapter 3, it was argued that the occurrence of the definite relative pronoun on clauses modifying indefinite head nouns is also motivated by the partial individuation of that noun, and Chapter 4 showed that the patterned use of demonstrative articles and pronouns reflects in part the degree of individuation of the noun they modify. In Chapter 8, it was suggested that the mood marking on imperfective verbs may be affected by the degree of individuation of the nouns they modify, such that individuated nouns tend to occur with indicative marking, while non-specific nouns may attract unmarked (subjunctive) imperfectives.

The features of spoken Arabic most affected by this continuum may be plotted along the original model as follows:

Figure 4: Individuation and the Syntax of Spoken Arabic

Unindividuated	Partly individuated	Individuated
+ construct genitive	± indef-specific article	+ definite article
- article	± relative pronoun	+ plural agreement
+ collective agreement	± plural agreement	+ relative pronoun
+ neutralized agreement	± genitive exponent	+ genitive exponent
- indicative mood	± new-topic article	+ indicative mood
- resumptive pronoun (rel)	± quantifier	

Nouns that are more individuated tend to be marked with the definite article, a definite relative pronoun if modified by a relative clause, and modified with a genitive exponent (within the bounds of other constraints, such as inalienable possession, 2.4). Moroccan speakers tend to use the definite article to mark even a partial degree of individuation in nouns, in contrast to the behavior of speakers from other areas (1.6). At the opposite end of the continuum, unindividuated nouns tend to be indefinite, and if modified by a genitive, it tends to be expressed as a construct phrase. Cross-dialect variation is evident in the choice of the genitive exponent to express partly or unindividuated nouns: while Moroccan and Kuwaiti speakers make this choice regularly, Egyptian and Syrian speakers tend to use the genitive exponent to modify specified or individuated nouns only (2.4). Partly individuated nouns take a wide range of markings, and it is in this middle range that speakers exercise the greatest control over syntactic structure. Syntactic markers that signal partial specification or individuation include the indefinite-specific article /ši/ in Moroccan and Syrian (1.4), and the "new-topic" article /wāḥid/, in all four dialects (1.5). Evidence suggests that Egyptian, Syrian, and Kuwaiti speakers use the dual suffix /-ēn/ as a kind of new-topic article as well, since it tends to occur only with nouns that have some degree of individuation (2.1).

In modifying plural nouns, speakers from all regions choose between collective (feminine) and individuated (plural) agreement marking to highlight the degree of individuation of the noun (2.2). Unindividuated nouns tend to take neutralized agreement in Egyptian; that is, in noun-adjective phrases containing relational (/nisba/) and classificational adjectives, the adjective often shows masculine singular agreement regardless of the gender of the noun (2.3). Agreement neutralization occurs in limited environments in the Syrian and Kuwaiti regions; no evidence of agreement neutralization has been found in Moroccan data.

The motivation behind unexpected patterns in the relativization of indefinite nouns also seems to lie with the individuation continuum. The definite relative pronoun /illi/ normally modifies definite nouns only; its occurrence in indefinite relative clauses poses a problem for the description of spoken Arabic syntax. This problem is solved by the individuation continuum: while indefinite, non-specific head nouns are modified by indefinite relative clauses with no relative pronoun, an indefinite but specific noun may be modified by a "definite" /illi/ clause. Speakers from all four dialect regions can use the definite relative pronoun /illi/ to partly define or specify indefinite nouns (3.1).

Several pieces of evidence indicate that temporal nouns such as *day, hour,* and *time* tend to have a naturally low individuation in all dialects. These temporal nouns regularly occur in two low-individuated constructions across dialects. First, they may be modified with a non-gendered demonstrative pronoun, /dīk/. Expressions such as /dīk in-nahār/ *the other day* are attested in all four areas, except for urban Egypt and Syria (4.3). Second, all dialects share a relative construction in which these temporal nouns are nominalized rather than relativized, as demonstrated either by the absence of resumptive reference within the /illi/ clause in Moroccan, Syrian, and Kuwaiti, or the use of nominalizer /ma/ instead of the relative pronoun /illi/ (3.4).

Nominal marking phenomena in the dialects thus indicate that speaker control plays an important role in the syntactic realization of noun modification. Within this framework, however, variation can be seen among the dialects. Greater syntactic attention is accorded to marking individuation in Syria and Morocco: while Moroccan and Syrian speakers have at their disposal an indefinite-specific article, /ši/, Egyptian and Kuwaiti speakers have no such article. Moroccan and Syrian speakers also make use of indefinite-specific relative pronouns, /ma/ in Moroccan and /mīn/ in Syrian.

Of particular note is the absence in Egyptian speech of several kinds of individuating nominal marking. All dialects except Egyptian have non-gendered, unstressed demonstrative articles that play a role in the marking of discourse topics and other salient entities (4.2). Egyptian speakers lack both an anaphoric demonstrative article and an indefinite-specific article. Moreover, Egyptians tend to favor agreement neutralization of adjectives (masculine singular adjective forms) when modifying unindividuated noun phrases. Perhaps additional synchronic and diachronic research will shed light on whether or not these patterns result from syntactic levelling involving several different types of nominal marking.

The Verb System

The analysis of aspect in the dialects has distinguished between formal and lexical aspect. Lexical aspect a property not of verb itself but of verbal meaning, since many Arabic verbs have a range of meanings, e.g., /nām/ *to sleep* or *go to sleep* or /rāḥ/ (M /mša/ *to set out to go* or *to go (from one point to another)* (6.1). It is helpful to distinguish between telic and atelic meanings, especially in predicting the meaning of the active participle: telic verbal meanings result in a perfect reading for the participle, while atelic verbs of state and motion result in a stative, progressive reading. I have argued here that the three verb stems, perfective, imperfective, and participle, correspond to the three major types of formal aspect in language: perfective, imperfective, and perfect

(6.2). Evidence from all four dialect areas attests to the primacy of aspect to the verb system of spoken Arabic, especially in the choice of verb forms in narrative contexts (6.5). Moreover, the narrative use of certain translocative verbs, called here narrative contour verbs, show surprising parallels across the four dialect regions (6.5).

The most basic meaning of the participle in spoken Arabic is a resultant state, which corresponds to cross-linguistic definitions of perfect aspect. The progressive state meaning often given by participles of motion can be shown to derive from the resultant one (6.4). The participle carries no tense or time reference; rather, its time reference is established through context, adverbs, and temporal verbs (7.3).

The dialects also share strategies of time reference and narrative temporal framing. Time reference in the dialects may be established in a number of ways. The most basic reference point is the moment of speech, but that point may be fairly easily shifted both grammatically, through the use of adverbs and temporal subordination, and contextually, through tense neutralization (7.1). In all dialects, a group of verbs called here temporal verbs, whose core member is the verb /kān/ *to be*, takes as its primary function establishing time reference, especially of non-punctual events and states (7.3).

The choice of verb form in conditional clauses ranges from perfective to imperfective or zero-verb (representing the present tense of *to be*) in copulative sentences. The use of imperfective and zero-verb in conditional clauses is not primarily related to time reference, but to aspect and mood. Aspectually, perfective verbs tend to occur in non-stative conditionals, in which the event is one-time or action viewed as a (to-be-) completed whole. Imperfective and zero-verb, on the other hand, occur in stative conditionals. Modally, the use of perfective verb forms in conditional sentences indicates a relatively high degree of hypotheticality of the condition itself. However, some cross-dialect variation can be discerned in the use of non-perfective verb forms. While Moroccan speakers appear to maintain the use of perfective verbs in most, if not all conditional clauses, Egyptian speakers use zero-verb and certain stative imperfectives in stative conditionals, and Syrian and Kuwaiti speakers make regular use of imperfective verbs and null copula or zero-verb in stative and low-hypothetical conditionals or conditional sentences in which the expectation of fulfillment is relatively high (8.7). While unmarked use of the perfective indicates a realized, factual mood, in conditional contexts, the perfective fulfills the opposite function, indicating counterfactual, irrealis mood. It is the markedness of the usage that makes this role reversal work: the marked usage is the exact opposite of the unmarked.

The same kind of reversal of markedness holds true for negation patterns as well. All dialects have three basic strategies of negation: verbal (9.3), predicate (9.4), and a marked "categorical negation," which indicates the categorical or absolute negation of an entity or set (9.5). The two basic unmarked negation strategies, verbal and predicate, also function as the marked form of negation for the other category. Thus, negation of verbs with the predicate negative Moroccan /māši/, Egyptian /miš/, or Syrian and Kuwaiti /mū/, constitutes marked negation, the negation of a predicated proposition or presupposition. Likewise, the negation of a predicate with verbal negation, Moroccan and Egyptian /mā - š/ and Syrian and Kuwaiti /mā/, constitutes marked negation, lending verbal force to a participle or a nominal phrase functioning as a pseudo-verb. Both unmarked and marked negation patterns show strong parallels across the dialects.

Sentence Typology

A number of dialect studies assume that the unmarked word order in spoken Arabic is SVO. I have argued here that these dialects, like formal registers of Arabic, make use of both SVO and VSO sentence typologies in a principled manner, and that word order in Arabic is properly treated as being of two different typological types, topic-prominent (SVO) and subject-prominent (VSO). These typologies, recognized by the Arab grammarians, do not merely represent a convenient way to notate surface structures, but rather reflect two different information packaging options: one based on topic-prominent information found in contexts demanding the management of multiple discourse topics, and another in which the narration of ordered events is the primary organizing principle (10.2). Other variations in word order common in spoken Arabic, such as OVS, fronting, and predicate-subject inversion, have been shown to follow similar patterns across dialects, and constitute information packaging devices that signal functions of new information, contrastive subject, object, and topic, and resumptive topic (10.3, 10.4).

Cases of Individual Dialect Variation

Only in a few cases does the syntax of one dialect follow a unique pattern not found in the others.

In the area of sentence typology, Syrian grammaticalizes a resumptive topic function that does not seem to be marked in other dialects. The object/resumptive topic marker /la-/ marks highly individuated direct and oblique objects (10.4). The marking of individuation in this case parallels other cases in which Syrian speakers accord syntactic attention to individuated nouns, the indefinite-specific article and the anaphoric demonstrative article.

In addition to the regular /illi/ clause, Moroccan dialects show relativization strategies not found elsewhere. A relative pronoun /fāš/ may be used to relativize non-human nouns of low individuation (3.6). At the same time, Moroccan speakers generally do not use resumptive pronouns to mark the syntactic position of the relativized noun with /illi/ (except in negative sentences). Taken together, these two strategies suggest that Moroccan may be shifting from a relativizing strategy that relies heavily on case-marking to one in which case marking plays a less significant role. The one area in which a large number of divergent developments emerge is verbal morphosyntax. Moroccan and Egyptian dialects exhibit parallel imperfective categories and functions, even though their lexical markers diverge. However, the mood systems of Syrian and Kuwaiti dialects depart substantially both from each other and from the western dialects. Syrian in particular makes use of a greater number of mood markers than any of the other three dialects, while Kuwaiti has fewer modal categories. The Syrian verbal prefix /b-/ fulfills two functions, one a future intentive modal marker and the other a stative indicative one. The former is shared with Kuwaiti future intentive /b-/, while the latter parallels indicative Egyptian /bi-/, suggesting the possibility of cross-dialect contact and borrowing (8.4).

Isoglosses

Very few syntactic isoglosses emerge from this comparative study. In contrast, several features occur in geographically broken patterns, such as the indefinite-specific article /ši/, found in Morocco and Syria, but not in Egypt or Kuwait,[1] and the anaphoric demonstrative article /ha/ (M /hād/) in Morocco, Syria, and Kuwait, but not Egypt (4.2).

The single syntactic isogloss separating eastern and western dialect regions that emerges from this study is the use of the negative enclitic /-š/. The western dialects, Moroccan and Egyptian, negate with /-š/, whereas the eastern dialects, Syrian and Kuwaiti, do not.

The rather transparent origin of the negative enclitic /-š/ is assumed to be the word /šay'/, *thing* (pronounced in most varieties of spoken Arabic as /še/ or /ši/): in parts of Morocco and Egypt, and in certain contexts, the negative clitic /-š/ retains the pronunciation /-ši/ and sometimes /šay/ (Harrell 1962:152). The origin of this negation pattern can be reconstructed along the following lines:

ما اعرف شيء
mā aʿrif šay'
not know-I (a) thing
I do not know at all

Originally, then, /mā - š/ must have been an emphatic form, motivated by the pragmatic function "categorical negation" that I have argued is part of the negative repertoire of Arabic speakers. The hypothetical example above must then have shifted semantically from *I don't know at all* to *I don't know*, and the previous unmarked form, without /-š/, became marked as categorical. The shift of a given form from emphatic

[1]Since it is not found in Egypt, the indefinite-specific article /ši/ in Morocco and Syria must either have developed independently, or be of common origin, that is, be traceable to dialects of Old (pre-Classical) Arabic. Other patterns of nominal marking common to all four areas, such as the "new topic" article /wāḥid/ one, demonstrative articles, the non-gendered use of demonstrative pronouns in modifying nouns of low individuation, also suggest a common origin for the dialects. These and many other features explored in this study support the notion that the modern dialects have descended from older dialects, and not from what we know as Classical Arabic. The range and detail of parallel syntactic structures and strategies described here have obvious negative implications for the likelihood of pidginization as proposed by Versteegh (1984).

or marked to non-emphatic or unmarked is a well-attested process of historical change.

The distribution of /-š/ suggests that it spread by means of dialect contact and borrowing throughout the region that it now occupies. The fact that negative /-š/ is not found in the urban dialects of greater Syria indicates that the spread of /-š/ occurred before the prolonged and intense political ties between Syria and Egypt beginning in the Ayyūbid period. The fact that Shiʿite and Druze dialects of the Levant also use /-š/ suggests that this particle was already in use at the time of their migration from Fatimid Egypt. It thus seems probable that the use of /-š/ as a negative particle spread throughout the Fatimid Caliphate during the tenth century, and continued to spread thereafter throughout North Africa and followed emigrants from there to the rural and mountain regions of greater Syria.

The history of /-š/ before the tenth century is probably untraceable; however, it may be concluded with some degree of certainty that this feature had already undergone some development before it began to spread. If verbal negation with /-š/ originated as an emphatic or categorical negation strategy, coexisting with non-emphatic negation without /-š/, then at some point, this pragmatic distribution must have reversed itself, and /-š/ gradually lost its emphatic status. Because /-š/ fulfills the same functions in both Morocco and Egypt, it is unlikely that this reversal took place independently across such a large geographic area. It seems more likely that /-š/ had already lost its emphatic status at the time when it spread throughout Fatimid North Africa.

It is also worth noting that Moroccan retains greater usage of the (now marked) form of negation without /-š/, and that Cairene Arabic restricts the contexts in which the marked form of negation occurs.

Suggestions for Further Study

All of the features examined here merit further attention, both to expand the framework to encompass data from other dialects and to test the analyses proposed. In addition, several features may be singled out as deserving of more intensive study than has been possible here.

In the area of definite and indefinite marking, more synchronic research is needed in the dialect areas that retain the nunation or /tanwīn/

suffix /-in/ to substantiate the hypothesis that this suffix fulfills a pragmatic function of marking indefinite-specific nouns.

This study has suggested that further sociolinguistic attention to agreement patterns may uncover a role for agreement in signaling social status. Speakers' use of collective and individuated plurals for humans may, at times, reflect their perception of the social prominence of various social groups, and by extension, their own relative status.

The development of mood markers for the indicative mood is widespread among the dialects, but is not necessarily an inevitable path of development. Kuwaiti may be developing in a different direction, increasingly marking non-indicative moods with the frozen particle /čān/ (8.5). Cross-dialect research into dialects that mark subjunctive or non-indicative moods is needed to establish both synchronic systems and diachronic patterns of development of modal marking in spoken Arabic.

The two typological features of word order and negation appear to be parallel in structure. The principled use of verbal and predicate negation strategies may mirror the patterning of VSO and SVO word order and topic-prominent and subject-prominent typologies. Within this general framework, Cairene Arabic appears to be in the process of losing its verbal negation strategy. Compared to rural Egyptian and Moroccan patterns, in which verbal negation with /mā - š/ retains a role in negating non-topical structures, the Cairene use of /mā - š/ is restricted, and is losing ground to predicate negation with /miš/. Both the processes of change and possible implications for underlying VSO sentence typology in Cairene should be explored further.

Finally, during my research, I made note of several morphosyntactic structures that seem to exhibit distribution patterns following an approximate (but not always absolute) east-west division. Further research into the distribution of these features may be worth pursuing.

Pronunciation patterns of the feminine active participle followed by a pronoun object differ in the eastern and western regions examined here.[2] In Syrian and Kuwait, feminine /-t/ is pronounced on the participle

---

[2]This isogloss is not geographically contiguous, however, since the

when suffixed (5.4). This feature may be related to the pronunciation of the /tanwīn/ suffix /-in/ on participles, found today in some areas of the Arabian Peninsula (Ingham 1994). The distribution of this feature may thus contribute to the diachronic study of the /tanwīn/ suffix.

The use of /yā-/ to mark the direct object in double-object pronoun constructions is found in the two eastern dialects but not the two western ones. Thus Syrian and Kuwaiti speakers use /yā-/ to mark the direct object of ditransitive arguments:

S, K عطيني اياهم
ʿaṭīni yāhum
give-me obj-them
Give me them

Moroccan and Egyptian speakers, on the other hand, must mark the indirect object with /li-/:

E, M جابهم لي
gāb-hum (M žāb-hum) -li(ya)
brought-he-them to-me
He brought them to me

Comparative constructions in spoken Arabic include the familiar elative patterns with /ʾafʿal/, and alternatively, regular adjectives paired with the "comparative" prepositions /min/ *than* and /ʿan/. The former is prevalent in Egyptian, Syrian, and Kuwaiti dialects:[3]

E1 التايير احلى من البدلة
it-tayyēr ʾaḥla min il-badla
the-two-piece-dress prettier than the-suit
The dress is prettier than the suit.

S4 كان يرجّعها بحالها، اشرف
kān yrajjiʿ[h]a bi-ḥālha ašraf
was-he he-return-her in-condition-her more-noble
He should have returned her as she was,[it would've been] nobler

---

pronunciation of feminine /t/ on the participle in Libyan follows eastern, not western, patterns (see examples in Mitchell 1952) .

[3]Cowell's extensive list of /ʾafʿal/ words suggests that this morphological pattern may be more productive in the eastern dialects than the western ones (1964:311-12).

K4 اهي اشوى منّي بعد
ihiy ʾašwa minni baʿd
she better from-me
She's even better than me

Moroccan speech, on the other hand, exhibits "limited use of the comparative form as a superlative" (Harrell 1962:205); I have found no examples of this type of construction in my Moroccan data. Moroccan speakers do make use of the alternative comparative construction, in which any adjective may be made comparative by means of prepositions /min/ or /ʿala/ *than* :

M9 باقة صحيّحة عنّي
bāqa ṣḥayyḥa ʿanni
has remained-f healthy-diminutive than-me
she's still a little healthier than me

Egyptian speakers also make use of this construction, with preposition /ʿan/:

E2 سألت واحدة كبيرة شوية عشان تبقى فاهمة عننا
saʾalt waḥda kibīra šwayya ʿašān tibʾa fahma ʿannina
asked-I one-f old-f a-bit so-as she-be having-understood-f than-us
I asked a woman who was a bit older because she would have a better understanding

Finally, the frequency of two particular morphological patterns appears to vary from region to region. First, the morphological diminutive (the /fuʿayyil/ pattern and variants) is highly productive in Moroccan (the immediately preceding Moroccan example contains one, /ṣḥayyḥa/ *a bit healthy*; see also Harrell 1962:81), less common but present in Kuwait, limited to certain fixed expressions in Egypt, and quite restricted in the Syrian area. Second, the Levantine dialects show a more productive use of the stative participle form /faʿlān/ with a perfect meaning, such as Lebanese /inte ḍaʿfān/ *you have lost weight.*[4] The /faʿlān/ pattern is limited to certain stative lexical items in Egypt and Morocco.

These features represent only a few of the many morphosyntactic features deserving of comparative study.

---

[4]See also, e.g., /faʿlān/ forms reported from eastern Syria by Behnstedt (1990).

Postscript

This project originally began, in part, in response to the claim that Arabic dialects are mutually unintelligible, and that the only language Arabs have in common is the formal register. Over the course of many years studying Arabic here and abroad, I have often heard such statements as, "I don't understand Moroccans/Kuwaitis/Egyptians when they speak;" "Moroccans speak French, not Arabic;" and "Why don't Syrians speak "/ʿarabi/" *Arabic* like us?" While during this century speech communities in many parts of the world have found themselves in a position to take advantage of increased contact with other dialect communities via mass communication and travel, all-but-closed borders (and sometimes attitudes) in the Arab world have prevented an similar increase in interdialectal contact. Now, after echoes of the voices of Arab nationalists Sāṭiʿ al-Husari, Gamāl Abd al-Nasser, Michel ʿAflaq, and others have almost died, modern technology has begun to find away around–or above–these barriers. In the last eight years, between the time that a primitive version of this study was presented as a doctoral dissertation and the time that I finished reworking it for publication, the rapid spread of satellite television and the appearance of multinational broadcasting networks such as the ART Movie and Entertainment Network, MBC in London, and Al-Jazīra in Qatar have begun to make their impact on the Arabic speech community by offering programming in a number of varieties and registers of Arabic. My Egyptian colleague Abbas el-Tonsi can now watch Moroccan movies at home in Cairo, and reports that, as a result, he has come to understand a great deal of the Moroccan dialect. Such developments, if they continue, will undoubtedly affect spoken Arabic over the long term, as larger "virtual" speech communities take their place beside local ones. A greater degree of consensus on what constitutes "Arabic"–now the subject of heated debates and disagreements–may emerge as a result. This trend will not decrease the need for studies of spoken Arabic; if anything, it should increase interest in, and lessen apprehension surrounding, such projects.

Appendix 1: Informants

Morocco

M 1 male, 40, educated, originally from Tetouan, lived abroad for 20 years.
M 2 female, 60's, uneducated, Marrakesh.
M 3 male, 35, Ph.D., has lived extenstively in the U.S and France.
M 5 female, mid-20's, college graduate, works outside the home, Rabat.
M 6 male, 20's, university graduate, linguistics major, Rabat.
M 7 comedy routine from Moroccan television, recorded July 1988.
M 9 female, 60-70's, illiterate, originally from near Chaoun, of the Jbāla ("mountain Arabs"), has lived for some time in Larache.
M 10 male, late 20's, high-school education, Larache.
M 11 female, 50-60's, uneducated, rural Beni Mellal area.

Egypt

E 1 female, 30's, university educated, fluent English, Cairo.
E 2 female, 30's, university educated, fluent English, Cairo.
E 3 female, late 40's, educated, from Simbilawēn, a Delta town.
E 4 male, early 30's, educated, Cairo.
E 5 male, 40's, educated, Arabic teacher, Cairo.
E 6 male, 14, in middle school, Cairo.
E 8 female, 50's, educated, Cairo.
E 9 male, 30's, educated, writer, Cairo.
E10 *ʿAla N-Naṣya*, "On the Street Corner" Cairo radio program, 12/9/89.

Syria

S 1 female, 21, Alawite, from a northwestern Syrian town, studying in the University of Damascus.
S 2 female, 20, Christian, from a village south of Aleppo, studying in the University of Damascus.
S 3 male, mid 30's, Ph.D., Damascus, living abroad.
S 4 husband and wife, late 50's, limited education, Aleppo.
S 5 female, 50's, educated, Aleppo, has lived abroad.
S 6 *Wādi al-Misk*, an old Durayd Laḥḥām play

Kuwait

K 1 male, 20's, post-secondary education.
K 2 female, 40-50's, secondary education.
K 3 female, 60-70's, illiterate, lived for some time in Bahrain.
K 4 female, early 40's, secondary education, works outside her home.

n indicates sentences taken down as field notes.

Appendix 2: Texts

Morocco

Text A: A Jummāni Joke[1] (M6)

(١) هادي نكتة عليه هو: هو حسّ بأن عباد الله تيگولوا عليه النكت بزّاف، وديرونجَته هاديك القضية يعني، وما عجبوش الحال. (٢) مشى شكا، گالوا ليه اَ ودّي أش غَ تدير، واحد القضية : اللي لقيتيه تيعاود شي نكتة ، خد كتاب واكتبها، وانت اكتبها . (٣) داك الشي اللي دار نيت، اللي لقاه تيگول له أشنو دار الجُمّاني، گولها ليّ، تيكتبها. (٤) تا جمعهم كاملين ويقطع داك الكتاب (٥) گال ليهم دابا قلّبوا ما تگولوا.

(1) hādi nukta ʿlīh huwwa: huwwa ḥəss biʾanna ʿibād ḷḷāh taygūlu ʿlīh n-nukat bəzzāf, w dīrunžātu hādīk l-qaḍiyya yaʿni, w mā ʿžbūš l-ḥāl. (2) mša ška, gālū-līh, ʾa wəddi ʾaš ġa tdīr, wāḥəd l-qaḍiyya: lli lqītīh tayʿāwd ši nukta xud ktāb w ktəbha, w ənta ktəbha. (3) dāk š-ši lli dār nīt, lli lqāh taygūl-lu ʾašnu dār ž-žummāni, gūlha liyya, tayktibha, (4) ta žmaʿhum kāmlīn w yiqṭaʿ dāk l-ktāb, (5) gāl lihum dāba qallbu ma tgūlu.

(1) Here is a joke about him: He felt that people were telling a lot of jokes about him and this disturbed him, that is, and he didn't like it. (2) He went and complained. They told him, my friend, what will you do? one thing: whoever you find telling a joke, take a book and write it down, and you write it down. (3) That's exactly what he did, whoever he found saying "What did Jummani do?," [he told him] tell me, and he would write it down. (4) Until he gathered them all, and he tears up the book. (5) He told them, now look for something to say!

---

[1]Al-Jummāni is a Moroccan Juḥa-like character, the subject of many popular jokes.

Text B: The Mother-in-Law (M2)[2]

... (١) وانا عندي شي ناس ضيفان بغيت نحط لهم داك الغطار ديال السفّا باش ياكلوه. (٢) آيوا خفت تاني من عگوزتي باش تخاصم ولاّ تگول ليّ شي حاجة. (٣) خويت هاديك — داك السطيّل كلهو في هاداك — العصيدة — اللي ولّت بحال العصيدة، (٤) خويتها ف السطيّل وعاود صيفطت شريت سميدة اخرى وعاود صاوبت سفّا اخرى وحطّيت السفّا هي هاديك وسكتّ. (٥) كانت خارجة الوالدة اللي جات عندي هي وعمتي وخفت باش تلقى عگوزتي هاداك الشي تخاصم عليّ ولاّ شي كنت تنخاف منها بزّاف. (٦) گلت للوالدة ها العار، تالله إيلا ما هاد السطيّل ادّيه عليّ شوفي فين تديريه ولاّ فين تلوحيه ولاّ فين ... (٧) ها عگوزتي تنوّت، گالت دابا وهادي شوف اش عطت لامّها ولاّ ش مخّرت ولاّ ش دارت ولاّ ... (٨) هاد الناس د زمان كانوا صعوبة بزّاف، تكرفصنا. (٩) صبحت تتعيّرني، تتگول لك إيوا هكا وياكلوا الناس، ياكلوا ويشربوا وحيت يكونوا خارجين تعطى لهم المسايل يشدّوها تا هي. (١٠) يا لالّة نعلي الشيطان، راه حتى شي حاجة ما كاينة. (١١) إيوا، وتتبقى تتخاصم وتتبقى تت — واحنا تنساعدوا الايام.

(1) ... w ana ʿndi ši nās ḍīfān bġīt nḥəṭṭ lihum dāk l-ġəṭār dyāl s-sffa bāš yāklūh. (2) ʾīwa xəft tāni mən ʿgūzti bāš txāṣm wəlla tgūl liya ši ḥāža. (3) xwīt hādīk -- dāk s-sṭiyyəl kullahuwa f hādāk -- l-ʿṣīda -- lli wəllat b-ḥāl l-ʿṣīda, (4) xwītha f s-sṭiyyəl w ʿāwd ṣifṭt šrīt smīda x^{w}ra, w ʿāwd ṣāwəbt sffa x^{w}ra w ḥəṭṭīt s-sffa hiyya hādīk w skətt. (5) kānt xārža l-wālida lli žāt ʿndi hiyya w ʿammti w xəft bāš təlqa ʿgūzti hādāk š-ši txāṣm ʿliyya wəlla ši kənt tanxāf mnha bəzzāf.. (6) gult lə-l-wālida ha l-ʿār, təḷḷāh ʾīla mā hād s-sṭiyyəl ddīh ʿliyya šūfi fīn tdīrīh wəlla fīn tlūḥīh wəlla fīn ... (7) ha ʿgūzti tnuwwāt, gālt dāba w hādi šūf aš ʿṭat l-ummha wəlla š məxxrāt wəlla š dārt wəlla .. (8) hād n-nās d zmān kānu ṣuʿūba bəzzāf, tkərfəṣna. (9) sbḥat tatʿayyərni tatgūl-lik ʾīwa hāka w yāklu n-nās, yāklu w yšərbu w ḥīt ykūnu xāržīn təʿṭa lihum l-məsāyəl yšəddūha ta hiyya. (10) ya lalla nəʿli š-šīṭān, rāh ḥtta ši ḥāža mā kāyna. (11) ʾīwa, w tatəbqa tatxāṣm w tatəbqa tat -- w ḥna tansāʿdu l-ʾiyyām.

---

[2]The recording begins here, in the middle of a narrative about how the speaker's mother-in-law made her early married life difficult. This portion recounts an incident in which the speaker ruined the sweet couscous she was making for guests and tried to cover up the waste for fear of being chastised.

(1) ... *when I had some guests to whom I wanted to serve that platter of sweet couscous to eat.* (2) *Well, I got scared again of my mother-in-law that she would pick a fight with me or say something to me.* (3) *I emptied that other -- that pail all of it in that -- mush -- what had become like mush,* (4) *I emptied it in the pail and then sent and bought more semolina and then made another sweet coucous and served the sweet couscous, this other one, and said nothing.* (5) *My mother, who had come over, she and my aunt, was on her way out, and I was afraid that my mother-in-law would find that thing [and] pick a fight with me or something, I was very afraid of her.* (6) *I told my mother, here's a scandal, for God's sake, this pail, take it from me, see where you can put it or throw it out or where ..* (7) *Here my mother-in-law has suspected (something), she said, Now, this one, see what she gave to her mother or what she stole or what she did or ...* (8) *Those people of old were a great difficulty. We had a rough time of it.* (9) *She began to criticize me, she says, well, so that's it, people eat, they eat and drink and when they are on their way out, stuff is given them and they take it too.* (10) *Madam, curse the devil, look, there is nothing at all [going on].* (11) *Well, she kept on picking fights and kept on -- and we would get through the days.*

Text C: Part One of a Moroccan Folktale (M11)

(١) حاجيت لك على واحد الراجل عنده المرا تتولد غير البنات، ما عندهاش الولد. (٢) ناض گال لها، انا خصني الولد. (٣) ناض تجوّج مرا اخرى، تجوّج واحد المرا اخرى وجوج د العيالات ادّى. (٤) هاديك عندها سبعة دالولاد، هاديك ادّاها عاد باش تولد. (٥) ناضت هاديك مولت سبعة كانت حاملة غادي تولد تا هي. (٦) منين دخل الشهر ديالها، هربوا عليها، (٧) گالت له وا نوض آ الراجل ، المرا غادي تولد تاني بنت اخرى دابا نوض نخويوا عليها هنا ونخلّيوها تدبّر راسها. (٨) نوض نخويوا البلاد ونمشيوا لواحد البلاد اخرى ونخليوها هنا ف الدار بوحدها. (٩) ناضوا بناتها گالوا لها امّي عاطيالنا البنت بالضهر گاع ما تتشوف فينا. (١٠) گال لها اعطيني أ بنتي غادي نمشي ندّي گفّا د الرماد، (١١) واحدة تهزّ گفّا د النخالة ف ضهرهم منين يهزّوا الرحيل وتتبعهم امّهم بالامارة ف

الطريق. (١٢) احنا غادي نمشيوا البلاد اللي ما تعرفيهاش، غادي تتبعي غير ديك الرماد والنخالة حتى لديك البلاصة فين غادي نحطوا وتبعينا. (١٣) البنات مشاوا مع باهم، هزوا الرحيل ديالهم، مشاوا ف الليل. (١٤) الصباح ناضت مسكينة ما صابت والو غير الحيوط ف الدار بوحدها. (١٥) ناض شدّها الوجع، بقات غادية يالله يالله يالله يالله حتى قرّبت حداهم، تابعة غير ديك الطريق — التعليمة ديال الطريق. (١٦) وصلت بحال اللي وصلت لهاد القبور جاها الوجع تمّا. (١٧) تمّا نعست مسكينة وولدت. (١٨) خرجوا لها الحوريات والملايكات وولّدوها. (١٩) گالوا لها وا عيّطي حسنتي يا رزقتي إيلا عاطية شي ف الدنيا شي صدقة غادي تجي لك دابا. (٢٠) ما صابت مسكينة لا ما تاكل لا فاش تكمّط داك الولد، وزاد لها الولد. (٢١) إيوا فرحت ملّي زاد لها الولد وجات عل الطريق قريبة توصل للراجل فاين مشى. (٢٢) قريبة توصل ليه، وولدت ف الطريق، بحال اللي جات لهاد القبور هادو حداكم، وولدت. (٢٣) گال لك مشاوا الناس گالوا آ فلان، واحد المرا هاكيفاش هاكيفاش راها ولدت ف القبور. (٢٤) مشى العبد دياله تسوّق وداز عليها، راه ولدت وولدت الولد. (٢٥) گال له كيفاش، گال له ولدت الولد. (٢٦) گال له ايلا ولدت الولد نردّها. (٢٧) گال لك مشى ادّى أ لالّة تفصيلة، القفطان بالجلاّبة بالشربيل، تكشيطة كاملة، وفرح وادّى الغيّاطة والطبل ومشى لعندها. (٢٨) صيفط بعدا العبد هو الاوّل گال له سير، إيلا هي ولدت الولد خلّيها واجي عندي. (٢٩) ولدت البنت، ادبحها وادبح البنت واجي. (٣٠) مشى داك العبد عندها، گال لها، گال لك سيدي شنو ولدت؟ گالت له ولدت بنت. (٣١) گال لها گولي لي اش ولدت، راه إيلا ولدت البنت غ ندبحك وندبحها. (٣٢) تا شافته زايد لها بالموس، گالت له اهدا، ولدت الولد، العزري اللي ولدت. (٣٣) مشى أ لالّة ركب ومشى عنده، گال له راه ولدت الولد. (٣٤) جاب لها التكشيطة، جاب لها الغيّاطة، جاب الطبّالة. (٣٥) جابوا غسّلوا لها ولبّسوها ولبّسوا وهزّوا داك الولد وادّاها للدار، گالت له المرا، هي اللي ما نشوفشي فيها. (٣٦) ناضوا بناتها فرحانين وتيخدموا ودبحوا ويعرض على الناس، والغيوط والطبل، بحال اللي گلت انت عاد مروّحها عروسة، فرحان بداك الولد.

(1) ḥāžīt-lək ʿla waḥd r-rāžəl ʿndu l-mra tatəwləd ġī[r] l-bnāt, mā ʿndhāš l-wəld. (2) nāḍ gāl liha, ʾana xəṣṣni l-wəld. (3) nāḍ tžəwwəž mra xʷra, tžəwwəž wāḥəd l-mra xʷra w žūž d l-ʿyālāt ədda. (4) hādīk ʿndha səbʿa d l-wlād, hādīk ddāha ʿād baš təwləd. (5) nāḍət hādik mūlat səbʿa kānt ḥāmla, ġādi təwləd ta hiyya. (6) mnīn dxal š-šhar dyālha hərbu ʿlīha, (7) gā[l]t lu wa nūḍ ʾā r-rāžəl, l-mra ġādi təwləd tāni bənt xʷra, dāba nūḍ nxwīw ʿlīha hna w nxəllīwha tdəbbər rāsha. (8) nuḍ nəxwīw l-blād w nəmšīw l-wāḥəd l-blād xʷra w nxəllīwha hna f əd-dār bʷ-uḥdha. (9) nāḍu bnātha gālu-lha mmʷi ʿaṭyā-[l]na l-bənt b-ḍ-ḍhar, gāʿ mā tatšūf fīna. (10) gāl-lha ʿṭīni ʾa bənti ġādi nəmši nəddi gʷffa d ər-rmād, (11) wāḥəda thəzz gʷffa d nəxxʷala f ḍharhum mnīn yhəzzu r-rəḥīl w ttbəʿhum ᵘmmhum b-l-imāra f t-ṭrīq. (12) ḥna ġādi nəmšīw l-blād lli mā təʿrfīhāš, ġādi ttəbʿi ġī[r] dīk ər-rmād w n-nəxxʷāla ḥtta l-dīk l-blāṣa fīn ġādi nḥəṭṭu w təbʿīna. (13) l-bnāt mšāw mʿa bʷāhum, həzzu r-rəḥīl dyālhum, mšāw f l-līl. (14) ṣ-ṣbāḥ nāḍət məskīna mā ṣābt wālu ġī[r] l-ḥyūṭ f d-dār bʷ-uḥdha. (15) nāḍ šəddha l-wžəʿ, bqāt ġādya yāḷḷāh yāḷḷāh yāḷḷāh yāḷḷāh ḥtta qərrbāt ḥdāhum, tābʿa ġī[r] dīk ṭ-ṭrīq -- t-təʿlīma dyāl ṭ-ṭrīq. (16) wəṣlāt b-ḥāl lli wəṣlāt l-hād l-qbūr, žāha l-wžəʿ təmma. (17) təmma nəʿsāt məskīna w wəldat. (18) xəržū-liha l-ḥūriyyāt w l-malāykāt w wəlldūha. (19) gālū-lha wa ʿəyyṭi ḥasanati ya razaqati ʾīla ʿāṭya ši f-d-dənya ši ṣadaqa ġādi tžī-lək dāba. (20) mā ṣābət məskīna lā ma tākul lā fāš tgəmməṭ dāk l-wəld, w zād-lha l-wəld. (21) ʾīwa fərḥāt məlli zād-lha l-wəld, w žāt ʿəl ṭ-ṭrīq qrība təwṣəl lə-r-rāžl fayn mša. (22) qrība təwṣəl līh, w wəldat f ṭ-ṭriq, b-ḥāl lli žāt l-hād l-qbūr hādu ḥdākum, w wəldat. (23) gāl-lək mšāw n-nās gālu ʾa flān, wāḥəd l-mra hākīfāš hākīfāš hākīfāš rāha wəldat f l-qbūr. (24) mša l-ʿabd dyālu tsəwwəq w dāz ʿlīha, rāh wəldat w wəldat l-wəld. (25) gāl-lu kīfāš, gāl-lu wəldat l-wəld . (26) gāl-lu [i]la wəldat l-wəld nrəddha. (27) gāl-lək mša ədda ʾa lalla təfṣīla, l-qəfṭān b-ž-žəllāba b-š-šərbīl, təkšīṭa kāmla w fraḥ w ədda l-ġəyyāṭa w ṭ-ṭbəl w mša l-ʿndha. (28) ṣīfəṭ baʿda l-ʿabd huwwa l-uwwəl gāl-lu sīr, ʾila hiyya wəldat l-wəld, xəllīha w āži ʿndi. (29) wəldat l-bənt, dbəḥha w dbəḥ l-bənt w āži. (30) mša dāk l-ʿabd ʿndha, gāl-lha, gāl-lək sīdi šnu wlədti? gā[l]t-lu, wlədt bənt. (31) gāl-lha gūlī-li ʾaš wlədti, rāh ʾīla wlədti l-bənt ġa ndəbḥək w nədbəḥha. (32) ta šāftu zāyd liha b-l-mūs gā[l]t-lu hda, wlədt l-wəld, l-ʿazri lli

wlədt. (33) mša ʾa lalla rkəb w mša ʿndu, gāl-lu rāh wəldat l-wəld. (34) žāb-lha t-tkšīṭa, žāb-lha l-ġəyyāṭa, žāb ṭ-ṭəbbāla. (35) žābu ġəsslū-lha w ləbbsūha w ləbbsu w həzzu dāk l-wəld w əddāha l-d-dār, gā[l]t-lu l-mra, hiyya lli mā nšūfši fīha. (36) nāḍu bnātha fərḥānīn w tayxədmu w dəbḥu w yʿrəḍ ʿla n-nās, w l-ġyūṭ w ṭ-ṭbəl b-ḥāl lli gulti nti ʿād mrəwwəḥha ʿrūsa, fərḥān b-dāk l-wəld.

(1) I tell you a story about a man whose wife bears only girls, she has no son. (2) He up and said to her, I need a son. (3) He up and married another woman, he married one other woman; two wives he took. (4) That one had seven children, the other one he married then so she could have [a son]. (5) That one who had seven was pregnant, was going to give birth, she too. (6) When her month arrived, they deserted her, (7) [the other wife] said, get up, man, the woman is going to have another girl again, now let's leave her here and let her take care of herself. (8) Get up and let's leave this place and go to another place and leave her here in the house by herself. (9) Her daughters up and said to her, Mother, the girl [the second wife] ignores us, she doesn't pay attention to us at all. (10) [The father] said, Give me, my daughter, I am going to walk and take a basket of ashes, (11) one [daughter] will carry a basket of chaff on their backs when they set out, and their mother [can] follow them by the signs on the road. (12) [They told the mother] We are going to leave and go to the place that you don't know; you will follow only these ashes and chaff until that place where we will alight, and you follow us. (13) The girls left with their father, they set off, leaving at night. (14) In the morning, she got up, poor thing, didn't find a thing in the house except the walls, [she was] all alone. (15) Her labor pains took hold, [but] she kept going, kept going, kept going, until she got close to them, following only that road -- that marking on the road. (16) She arrived [to a place near them], as if she arrived at that cemetery over there, the labor pains set in there. (17) There she lay down and gave birth. (18) The houris (beautiful spirits) and the angels came to her and helped her give birth. (19) They told her, Call out 'my good deed(s), my reward(s),' if you have given anything, any alms in this life it will come back to you now. (20) She didn't find anything, poor dear,

neither to eat nor to wrap the child in, and the child was born to her. (21) Well, she was overjoyed when the son was born to her, and she came on the road near to where her husband went. (22) She was close to reaching him, and gave birth on the road, as if she had come to that cemetery there by your house, and gave birth. (23) They say that people went and told him, So-and-so, a woman of such-and-such description gave birth in that cemetery. (24) His slave went shopping, and passed by her. She had given birth, and she had borne a son. (25) He said, How? [The slave] said, She had a son. (26) He said, If she had a son I'll take her back. (27) They say that he went and took, dear lady, fine clothing, the caftan, with the dress and the shoes, a whole ensemble, and was so happy, and took the flutists and the drums and went to where she was. (28) But he sent the slave first, he told him, go, if she bore [a] son leave her and come to me. (29) [If] she had a daughter, slay her and slay the girl and come. (30) That slave went to her, and told her, my master asks what you bore? She told him, I bore a girl. (31) He said, tell me what you bore, look, if you had [a] girl, I will slay you and slay her. (32) Until she saw him heading toward her with the knife, [then] she said calm down, I bore [a] son, [a] young man is what I had. (33) He went, dear lady, and got on [his riding beast] and went to [his master], he told him, she bore [a] son. (34) He brought her the ensemble, he brought her the flutists, he brought the drummers. (35) They brought and washed her and dressed her and dressed and carried the boy and took her to the house [because] the [other] wife said to him, Her I do not want to see. (36) Her daughters were very happy, they [were] serving [the guests], they slaughtered, [the father] invites people, and the flutes and the drums, it was as if you'd say he had just taken her as a bride, [so] happy with that son.

Text D: About the Larache Beach (M10)

(١) اليپلايا، ف الحقيقة، ش عنقول لك، اليپلايا مزيانة وعيّانة. (٢) مزيانة بالنسبة — مزيانة — تبدّلت، على حسب الناس ما بقاتشي النوع د الاحترام، ما بقاوش النوع ديال — النوع ديال - واحد نوع الانسجام، (٣) الناس ما كتفهمش بعضها، ما كتفهم شي وكتـ— (٤) الآخُر

كياكل هنا، الآخر كياكل الكوّر، الآخر كيسيّب الزبل هنا، الآخر كينعس بوحده، (٥) خصّه يستغلّ، خصّه يگلس ف ديك البلاصة بوحده، خصّه يعوم بوحده، خصّه كدا ما — (٦) يعني لأن كيخصّه — يتمنّى الپلايا تكون كلها دياله، فهمتِ، كيخصّه تكون الپلايا دياله كلها. (٧) عاود تاني حتى ديك الحيوية ديال الانسان اللي كيجي تمّا البحر ما بقاتشي كيمّا كانت، (٨) ودابا كتشوف بزّاف د الناس ولاد البلاد ما بقاوش كيمشيوا البحر نهائياً، ولاد البلاد. (٩) غير البرّاني هو اللي كيمشي، ولد البلاد ما بقاش كيمشي البحر. (١٠) دابا البرّاني كيكون له — ولد البلاد كله كيمشي قند [ا]خُر — بحال مثلاً شي بلاصة بعيدة على البحر د العرايش ... (١١) ميامي؟ لا، المسألة هاديك ميامي حال قريبة، لا، كي[ف] بحال دابا مثلاً قدّام الحبس، فين مصيطرو، فين الما جديد، فين كتصيب الموضع بوحدك تمّا، ما كاينشي الناس بزّاف. (١٢) وتاني عاود تاني تمّا ف الپلايا كيوقع بزّاف ديال الحاجات اللي كتمسّ كتقيس الشخصية د الانسان، (١٣) بحال مثلاً الانسان كيشرب الخمر كيبقى يـ — كيبقى يقول شي كلمة قبيحة، كيقول شي مسائل قبيحة اللي كتـ — (١٤) كيكون الانسان گالس مع — هو والمرا دياله، كيسمع ديك الشي، كيتغدّد. (١٥) كيتغدّد وكينفجر وكيضطرّ — وكيطلع بالزربة باش يمشي بحاله، ما يبقاش يجي لديك البلاصة. (١٦) عاود تاني ملّي كتجيهم يبغيوا يگلسوا ف شي قهوة يريّح فيها شي شويّش ويشرب شي آتاي ولاّ قهوة ولاّ ما أو موناضا، كيجي واحد خور عاود تاني سكران، ويجي ويتكبّ له على البلاصة فين گالس هو والمرا دياله وولاده. (١٧) ش كيدير، كينوض يتخاصم معاه، كيجيوا البوليس كيجيوا هادا و — طاق طاق، ها هي ما بقاتشي، عاود تاني كيتصالحوا. (١٨) إيوا مثلاً السيّد كينعس هو والمرا دياله گالسين ف البحر هاكّا كيجي واحد خور سلگوط كيجي كيتكّى عليهم وكيضحك عليهم وكيسيّب عليهم الرملة كدا — (١٩) يعني بزّاف د الحاجات اللي كتخلّي الانسان ديما ما يبقاش يهوّد للبحر. (٢٠) حنا مثلاً، عزري ماشي بحال مجوّج. (٢١) العائلة ... ما بقاوش كيهوّدوا عائلات، العزري، حتى العزارى ديال ولاد البلاد ما بقاوش كيهوّدوا، قلال، (٢٢) وانت كتلاحظ هاد القضية هادي، كتشوف هاد الناس بزّاف.

(1) l-plāya, f l-ḥaqīqa, š ʿanqul-lk, l-plāya mzyāna w ʿayyāna. (2) mzyāna b-n-nisba - mzyāna - tbəddlət, ʿla ḥasab n-nās mā bqatši n-nūʿ d l-əḥtirām, mā bqāwš n-nūʿ dyāl - n-nūʿ dyāl - waḥd nūʿ l-ənsižām, (3) n-nās mā katfəhəmš baʿḍha, mā katfhəm šay w kat - (4) l-āxur kayākul hna, l-āxur kayākul l-kuwwar, l-āxur kaysəyyəb z-zbəl hna, l-āxur kaynʿas b^w-uḥdu, (5) xəṣṣu ystaġəll, xəṣṣu ygləs f dīk l-blāṣa b^w-uḥdu, xəṣṣu yʿūm b^w-uḥdu, xəṣṣu kāda mā - (6) yəʿni liʾanna kayxəṣṣu - ytmənna l-plāya tkūn kullha dyālu, fhəmti, kayxəṣṣu tkūn l-plāya dyālu kullha. (7) ʿāwd tāni ḥtta dīk l-ḥayawiyya dyāl l-ʾinsān lli kayži təmma l-bḥar mā bqātši kimma kānt. (8) w dāba katšūf bəzzāf d n-nās wlād l-blād mā bqāwš kaymšīw l-bḥar nihāʾiyyan, wlād l-blād. (9) ġī[r] l-bərrāni huwwa lli kaymši, wəld l-blād mā bqāš kayəmši l-bḥar. (10) dāba l-bərrāni kayku[n]-lu -- wəld l-blād kullu kayəmši qənd xūr - b-ḥāl matalan ši blāṣa bʿīda ʿla l-bḥar d l-ʿrāyš ... (11) mīyāmi? la, l-məsʾala hādīk mīyāmi ḥāl qrība, la, ki-b-ḥāl dāba matalan qəddām l-ḥabs, fīn mṣīṭrū, fīn l-ma ždīd, fīn katṣīb l-mūḍaʿ b^w-uḥdək təmma, mā kāynši n-nās bəzzāf. (12) w tāni ʿāwd tāni təmma f l-plāya kayəwqaʿ bəzzāf dyāl l-ḥāžāt lli katməss katqīs š-šaxṣṣiyya d l-ʾinsān, (13) b-ḥāl matalan l-ʾinsān kayšrab l-xmər kaybqa y -- kaybqa yqūl ši kəlma qbīḥa kayqūl ši masāʾil qbīḥa lli kat -- (14) kaykūn l-ʾinsān gāls mʿa -- huwwa w l-mra dyālu, kaysmaʿ dīk š-ši, kaytġaddəd. (15) kaytġaddəd w kaynfažər w kayḍṭərr -- w kayṭlaʿ b-z-zərba baš ymši b-ḥālu, mā ybqāš yži l-dīk l-blāṣa. (16) ʿāwd tāni məlli katžihum yəbġīw ygəlsu f ši qahwa yrayyəḥ fīha ši šwəyyəš w yšrab ši ʾātāy wəlla qahwa wəlla ma ʾaw mūnāḍa, kayži wāḥəd xūr ʿāwd tāni skrān, w yži w ytkəbb-lu ʿla l-blāṣa fīn gāls huwwa w l-mra dyālu w wlādu. (17) š kaydīr, kaynūḍ ytxāṣəm mʿāh, kayžīw l-būlīs kayžīw hāda w - ṭāq ṭāq, ha hiyya mā bqātši, ʿāwd tāni kaytṣālḥu. (18) ʾīwa matalan s-siyyd kaynʿas, huwwa w l-mra dyālu gālsīn f l-bḥar hakka kayži wāḥəd xūr səlgūṭ kayži kaytəkka ʿlīhum w kayḍḥak ʿlīhum w kaysəyyib ʿlīhum r-ramla kāda - (19) yəʿni bəzzaf d l-ḥāžāt lli katxəlli l-ʾinsān dīma mā yəbqaš yhəwwəd l-l-bḥar. (20) ḥna matalan, ʿazri māši b-ḥāl mžəwwəž. (21) l-ʿāʾila ... mā bqāwš kayhəwwdu ʿāʾilāt, l-ʿazri, ḥtta l-ʿzāra dyāl wlād l-blād mā bqāwš kayhəwwdu, qlāl, (22) w ənta katlāḥəḍ hād l-qaḍiyya hādi, katšūf hād n-nās bəzzāf.

(1) The beach, really, what am I going to tell you, the beach is good and bad. (2) Good, because -- [it's] good, [but] it changed, on account that people are no longer the type that [have] respect, they no longer the type of -- the type of -- a type of harmony, (3) people don't understand each other, they don't understand at all, and they -- (4) The other [person] eats over here, the other one eats watermelon, the other one throws trash here, the other one is lying down by himself, (5) He has to take over [the space], he has to sit in that place by himself, he has to swim by himself, he has to do this and that, not -- (6) That is, because he has to -- he wishes the beach were all his, you understand? He has to have the beach to himself, all of it. (7) Then again even that liveliness of the person who comes there to the seashore is no longer as it was. (8) Now you see a lot of people native of the town no longer go to the seashore at all, the natives of the town. (9) Only the outsider is the one who goes; the native of the town no longer goes to the seashore. (10) Now the outsider has -- the native of the town all go to another spot -- like for instance some place far from the shore of Larache ... (11) Miami? No, the thing is, that [spot], Miami, is a nearby situation, no, like now for instance in front of the prison, where Msitro is, where l-Ma Jdid is, where you find [a] spot by yourself there, there aren't a lot of people. (12) And then again there at the beach there happen a lot of things that infringe, that touch the personal space of the person. (13) Like for instance [a] person drinks wine, he keeps on -- he keeps on saying a nasty word, he says some bad things that -- (14) [A] person is sitting with -- he and his wife, he hears that stuff, he gets upset. (15) He gets upset and he explodes and he is forced to -- and he gets up in a hurry to leave, to no longer come to this place. (16) Then again when it occurs to them that they'd like to sit in a cafe and [so that he can] relax awhile and drink tea or coffee or water or a soft drink, another one comes along then drunk, and comes and throws up on the place where he is sitting he and his wife and kids. (17) What does he do, he gets up to fight with him, the police come and [people] come and -- rap! rap! here the [fight] is no longer, then they smooth things over. (18) Or for instance, [a] man lies on [the beach], he and his wife are sitting on the shore like so, another guy, a jerk comes along and "leans on" them [bothers them], teases

them, throws sand on them and so on -- (19) [There are] many things which make [a] person constantly no longer want to go to the shore ... (20) We, for instance, a young single guy is not like a married man. (21) The family ... families no longer go down [to the beach], the young single guy, even the young single men native to the town no longer go down, rarely. (22) And you notice this problem, you see these people a lot.

Egypt

Text A: A Pain in the Ear (E8, E2)
(i) E8

(١) طب انا اقول لكو على حاجة بقى! (٢) في يوم سوسو السنة اللي فاتت قبل ما تسافر يمكن ما يجيش شهر، كان خمستاشر أو عشرة ايام، قامت تعبانة الصبح قوي (٣) بتقول جا لي الساعة تلاتة وجع في ودني فظيع، (٤) وقعدت كتير، بتاع ساعتين، وبعدين ع الساعة خمسة زي ما تقولي استكنّ أو هي تعبت فعينها غفلت. (٥) في ستة ونص ونزلت راحت الشغل. (٦) لقيتها راجعة م الشغل بدري وقالت لي انا تعبانة قوي هنروح للدكتور. (٧) فعلا رحنا الدكتور. (٨) فرحنا، وبتقول له ودني حصل كذا كذا. (٩) فبيشوف ودنها كدا، لقيناه راح جايب بنص كدا وراح مدخلها جوّه ودنها وراح مطلع وحاطط في قطنة، لقيت حشرة! (١٠) يعني هي زي الدبانة كدا، ما بين الدبانة والدودة. (١١) ولها زي ديل يعني، كانت لسه حية تصوري دي اللي دخلت في ودنها وهي نايمة. (١٢) ديل رفيّع كدا. (١٣) فبيقول لها، ايه دا، انت كنت قاعدة تحت شجرة ولاّ حاجة؟!

(1) ṭab ʾana aʾul-luku ʿala ḥāga baʾa! (2) fi yōm sūsu s-sana lli fātit ʾabl ma tsāfir yimkin mā yigīš šahr kān xamasṭāšar ʾaw ʿašar tiyyām, ʾāmit taʿbāna ṣ-ṣubḥ ʾawi, (3) bitʾūl gā-li s-sāʿa talāta wagaʿ fi widni faẓīʿ, (4) wi ʾaʿadit kitīr , bitāʿ saʿtēn, wi baʿdēn ʿa s-sāʿa xamsa zayy ma tʾūli istakanna, ʾaw hiyya tiʿbit fa-ʿenha ġiflit. (5) fi sitta w nuṣṣ wi nizlit rāhit iš-šuġl. (6) laʾetha ragʿa mi š-šuġl badri wi ʾālit-li ʾana taʿbāna ʾawi hanrūḥ li-d-duktūr. (7) fiʿlan ruḥna d-duktūr. (8) fa-ruḥna, wi bitʾul-lu widni ḥaṣal kaza kaza. (9) fa-biyšūf widnaha kida, laʾenā rāḥ gāyib binṣ kida wi rāḥ midaxxalha guwwa widnaha wi rāḥ miṭallaʿ wi ḥāṭiṭ fi ʾuṭna, laʾēt ḥašara! (10) yaʿni hiyya zayy id-dibbāna kida, ma bēn id-dibbāna wi d-dūda. (11) wi laha zayy dēl yaʿni, kānit lissa ḥayya tṣawwari di illi daxalit fi widnaha wi hiyya nayma. (12) dēl rufayyaʿ kida. (13) fa-biʾul-laha, ʾēh da, ʾinti kunti ʾaʿda taḥt šagara walla ḥāga?!

(1) Well, I'll tell you about something! (2) One day Susu, last year before she left maybe less than a month, it was fifteen or ten days, she woke up in the morning feeling very poorly, (3) saying, I got at three o'clock a horrible pain in my ear , (4) and she sat up for a long time, around two hours, and then about five o'clock as if you'd say [the pain] settled down a bit, or she got tired and her eyes closed. (5) [She got up] at six o'clock and went to work. (6) I found her coming back from work early, and she said, I'm feeling very poorly, we're going to the doctor. (7) Indeed, we went to the doctor. (8) So we went, and she tells him, my ear, such and such happened. (9) So he examines her ear a bit, [suddenly] we found him bringing a tweezer, and he went and pulled out and put in a piece of cotton, I found an insect! (10) I mean, it [was] somewhat like a fly, between a fly and a worm. (11) And it has something like a tail, it was still alive, imagine, this is what went in her ear while she was sleeping. (12) A skinny little tail. (13) So he says to her, What's this? Were you sitting under a tree or something?!

(ii) E2

(١) انت عارف بقى، ما هي دخلت و — ما هو الألم اللي صحّاني. (٢) هي جت ومشيت ودخلت في ودني وانا نايمة، فانا صحيت ع الالم. (٣) هي دخلت دخلت لحدّ عند الطبلة، مش عارفة تعدّي فقاعدة تخبط في طبلة ودني عشان تعدّي تكمّل بقى المشوار بتاعها. (٤) مش عايزة تطلع تاني!

(1) ʾinta ʿārif baʾa, māhi daxalit wi -- māhu l-ʾalam illi ṣaḥḥāni. (2) hiyya gat wi mišyit wi daxalit fi widni w ana nayma, fa-ʾana ṣḥēt ʿa l-ʾalam. (3) hiyya daxalit daxalit li-ḥadd ʿand iṭ-ṭabla, miš ʿarfa tʿaddi f-ʾaʿda tixbaṭ fi ṭablit widni ʿašān tiʿaddi tikammil baʾa l-mišwār bitaʿha. (4) miš ʿayza tiṭlaʿ tāni!

(1) You know, [the insect] entered and -- it was the pain that woke me. (2) It came, kept going, and entered my ear while I was asleep, and I awoke from the pain. (3) It entered, entered until the [ear] drum, [it] couldn't pass and so it was sitting [there] hitting at my eardrum in order to pass and finish its journey. It [didn't] want to come back out!

Text B: On the Expression "Is it necessary tonight, Mayor?" (E4)

(١) يعني هو ما فهمش عشان ما سمعهوش قبل كدا لكن انا اقول لك حاجة. (٢) فيه موقف مثلا — انا فاهم انت تقصد إيه. (٣) مثلا فيه تمثيلية اللي كانوا بيجيبوها في التليفزيون اللي هي بتقول حبكت يا عمدة؟ الليلة؟! (٤) انت عارف حبكت يا عمدة ليه؟ (٥) بقول لك فيه لفظ فيه جملة بتقول حبكت يا عمدة، الليلة. (٦) هو كان — هو متجوّز اتنين. (٧) عشان يعني انا فاهم المعنى اللي انت بتقوله. (٨) متجوّز اتنين. فكل واحدة يعني لمّا يروح ينام مع التانية، ضرتها يعني تزعل. (٩) فهي الواحدة منهم لما يروح ينام مع مراته التانية تروح مخبطة عليه، وتعالَ مش عارف إيه حصل إيه، — انا ما شفتش بس سمعت. (١٠) بتقول له — يقول لها حبكت؟ الليلة؟ تقول له أيوه، تعالَ. (١١) هي ليلتها، ليلة التانية، انت فاهم؟ (١٢) يعني ينام مع التانية، وهي عايزاه الليلة. (١٣) يقول لها حبكت الليلة؟ الليلة يا عمدة.

(1) yaʿni huwwa mā fihimš ʿašān mā simʿūš ʾabl kida lākin ʾana aʾul-lak ḥāga. (2) fī mawqif masalan -- ʾana fāhim yaʿni ʾinta tuʾṣud ʾēh. (3) masalan fī tamsiliyya illi kānu biygibūha fi t-tilivizyōn illi hiyya bitʾūl ḥabakit yā ʿumda? il-lēla?! (4) ʾinta ʿārif ḥabakit yā ʿumda lēh? (5) baʾul-lak fī lafẓ fī gumla bitʾūl ḥabakit yā ʿumda, il-lēla? (6) huwwa kān -- huwwa miggawwiz itnēn. (7) ʿašān yaʿni ʾana fāhim il-maʿna illi ʾinta bitʾūlu. (8) miggawwiz itnēn. fa kull waḥda yaʿni lamma yirūḥ yinām maʿa t-tanya ḍurritha yaʿni tizʿal. (9) fa-hiyya l-waḥda minhum lamma yirūḥ yinām maʿa mrātu t-tanya trūḥ mixabbaṭa ʿalēh, wi taʿāla miš ʿārif ʾēh ḥaṣal ʾēh, -- ʾana mā šuftūš bass s[i]miʿt. (10) bitʾul-lu -- yiʾul-laha ḥabakit? il-lēla? tiʾul-lu ʾaywa, taʿāla. (11) hiyya lēlitha, lelt it-tanya, ʾinta fāhim? (12) yaʿni yinām maʿa t-tanya, wi hiyya ʿayzā il-lēla. (13) yiʾul-laha ḥabakit il-lēla?! il-lēla ya ʿumda.

(1) He didn't understand because he hadn't heard it before, but I'll tell you something. (2) There is a situation -- I understand what you mean. (3) For instance there is this serial that they used to show on TV that says "Is it really necessary, Mayor? Tonight?!" (4) Do you know "Is it really necessary, Mayor, tonight?!" why? (5) I'm telling you, there is an expression, there is a sentence that says "Is it really necessary, Mayor, tonight?" (6) He was -- he [was] married to two [women]. (7) Because I mean I understand the meaning you are saying. (8) [He was] married to two [women]. And each one, when he would go sleep with the other one, the other wife, her co-wife, that is, would get angry. (9) So each one of them, when he would go and sleep with his other wife, would go and knock on his [door] and [say] "Come here," I don't know what, [something] happened -- I didn't see it, but I heard [about it]. (10) She says to him -- he says to her, "Is it really necessary? Tonight?" She says to him, "Yes, come." (11) It is her night, the night of the other [wife], do you understand? (12) He sleeps with the other one, and she wants him [that] night. (13) He tells her, "Is it really necessary tonight?" Tonight, Mayor.

Text C: A film plot (E6)

(١) كان عادل إمام راكب في طيّارة هو ويسرا، كانوا نازلين فقال لها حمد الله ع السلامة. (٢) قالت له انت حضرتك تعرفني؟ (٣) قال لها أيوه، مش انت كنت في معهد البحوث كذا وكذا، فايه، قالت له انت طيّب ايش عرّفك؟ (٤) قال لها باقرب للخواجه مش عارف جاك ولا جيم. (٥) فقالت له آه، دا اللي عامل معايا كتاب، عمل معايا كتاب وكدا هوت. (٦) فإيه، آه، وهمّ ماشيين نسي شنطته معاها. (٧) فإيه، ما كانتش تعرف عنوانه، فهي في يوم إيه -- شالتها عندها أول ما روّحوا. (٨) فيوم لقت قطّة جوّا الدولاب بعد الـ -- (٩) قامت إيه، جاية وحاطّة الشنطة، شنطة امّه، مكانها وقافلة على القطّة الدولاب. (١٠) فقامت إيه، القطّة ديت اختفت هي والشنطة. (١١) وبعد كدا هوت جاية تدوّر ع الشنطة ما لقتهاش، ومش عارفة وزعلت وكدا هو. (١٢) فيوم كان عادل إمام بيضايقها فإيه، جا لها الشغل وكدا هوّ، قالت له فيه موقف حصل مش قادرة اقول لحضرتك.

(١٣) قال لها إيه هو؟ قالت له الشنطة اللي حضرتك سبتها لي ضاعت. (١٤) قال لها — فكان — هي بيقول لها انّ فيها اوراق مهمة بس هي ما كانش فيها. (١٥) فايه، قالت له قالت له ان الشنطة اللي حضرتك قلت لي فيها اوراق مهمة ضاعت. (١٦) قال لها الصراحة كنت باكدب عليك لأن ما كانش فيها اوراق تهمّني وكدا هوت. (١٧) قالت له امّال كان فيها ايه؟ (١٨) قال لها كان فيها شوية اوراق كدا عن ملك امّي وحاجات عادية. (١٩) فقالت له انا آسفة جدّاً وكدا هوت. (٢٠) جه تاني يوم جه الصبح ما كانتش هي في المكتب. (٢١) قام حاطط لها شنطة، نفس الشنطة المطابقة للّي كانت في الدولاب. (٢٢) جت سألت السكرتيرة قالت لها مين اللي جاب الشنطة دي هنا؟ ... (٢٣) قالت لها الاستاذ فهمي فكدا فجه هو بعد شوية فإيه، قالت له انت ازاي حضرتك قدرت تجيب الشنطة دي؟ (٢٤) قال لها، دي مش الشنطة التانية، دي شنطة زيّها. (٢٥) بس إيه، انا اشتريتها من نفس الراجل اللي انا اشتريت منه. (٢٦) فإيه، جت السكرتيرة قالت له تشرب إيه؟ قال لها قهوة مضبوط. (٢٧) فعملت له القهوة، جاي يشربها، قعد يشرب عادي وكدا هوت. (٢٨) في الآخر، بعد ما خلّصوا كلام عن حكاية الشنطة وكدا هو، هي جاية تقول له ع الله تكون القهوة عجبتك. قال لها كويسة. (٢٩) بعد ما مشي جاية تشوف في الفنجان لقت القهوة زي ما هي. (٣٠) بس هو فعلاً كان بيشرب بس القهوة ايه، يعني هي ما كانتش عارفة ايه اللي رجّعها.

(1) kān ʿādil ʾimām rākib fi ṭayyāra huwwa w yusra, kānu nazlīn fa-ʾal-laha ḥamdilla ʿa s-salāma. (2) ʾalit-lu ʾinta ḥaḍritak tiʿrafni? (3) ʾal-laha ʾaywa, miš ʾinti kunti fi maʿhad il-buḥūs kaza w kaza, fa-ʾēh - ʾālit-lu ʾinta ṭayyib ʾēš ʿarrafak? (4) ʾal-laha baʾrab li-l-xawāga miš ʿārif žāk walla žim. (5) fa-ʾalit-lu ʾā, da lli ʿāmil maʿāya ktāb, ʿamal maʿāya ktāb wi kida huwwat. (6) fa-ʾēḥ, ʾā, wi humma mašyīn, nisi šanṭitu maʿāha. (7) fa-ʾēh, mā kānitš tiʿraf ʿinwānu, fa-hiyya fi yōm ʾēh - šālitha ʿandaha ʾawwal ma rawwaḥu. (8) fa-yōm laʾit ʾuṭṭa guwwa d-dulāb baʿd il -- (9) ʾāmit ʾēh, gayya wi ḥaṭṭa š-šanṭa, šanṭit ʾummu, makānha wi ʾafla ʿa l-ʾuṭṭa d-dulāb. (10) fa-ʾāmit ʾēh, l-ʾuṭṭa diyyat ixtafit hiyya wi š-šanṭa. (11) wi baʿd kida huwwat gayya tdawwar ʿa š-šanṭa mā laʾithāš, wi miš

ʿarfa wi ziʿlit wi kida ho. (12) fa-yōm kān ʿādil ʾimām biydāyiʾha fa-ʾēh, ga-lha š-šuġl wi kida huwwa, ʾalit-lu fī mawqif ḥaṣal miš ʾadra ʾaʾūl li-ḥaḍritak. (13) ʾal-laha ʾēh huwwa? ʾalit-lu š-šanṭa lli ḥaḍritak sibtahā-li ḍāʿit. (14) ʾal-laha -- fa-kān -- hiyya biyʾul-laha ʾinni fīha ʾawrāʾ muhimma wi kida bass hiyya mā kānš fīha. (15) fa-ʾēh, ʾalit-lu, ʾalit-lu ʾinn iš-šanṭa lli ḥaḍritak ʾult-ili fīha ʾawrāʾ muhimma ḍāʿit. (16) ʾal-laha iṣ-ṣarāḥa kunt bakdib ʿalēki laʾinn mā kanš fīha ʾawrāʾ tihimmini wi kida huwwat. (17) ʾalit-lu ʾummāl kān fīha ʾēh? (18) ʾal-laha kān fīha šwayyit ʾawrāʾ kida ʿan milk ʾummi wi ḥāgāt ʿadiyya. (19) fa-ʾalit-lu ʾana ʾasfa giddan wi kida huwwat. (20) geh tāni yōm geh iṣ-ṣubḥ mā kanitš hiyya fi l-maktab. (21) ʾām ḥāṭiṭ-laha šanṭa, nafs iš-šanṭa il-muṭabqa li-lli kānit fi d-dulāb. (22) gat saʾalit is-sikirtēra ʾālit-laha mīn illi gāb iš-šanṭa di hina? ... (23) ʾālit-laha il-ʾustāz fahmi fa-kida, fa-geh huwwa baʿd šwayya fa-ʾēh, ʾālit-lu ʾinta izzāy ḥaḍritak ʾidirt tigīb iš-šanṭa di? (24) ʾal-laha di miš iš-šanṭa it-tanya, di šanṭa zayyaha. (25) bass ʾēh, ʾana štaretha min nafs ir-rāgil illi ʾana štarēt minnu. (26) fa-ʾēh, gat is-sikirtēra ʾālit-lu tišrab ʾēh? ʾal-laha ʾahwa maẓbuṭ. (27) fa-ʿamalit-lu l-ʾahwa, gayy yišrabha, ʾaʿad yišrab ʿādi w kida huwwat. (28) fi l-ʾāxir, baʿd ma xallaṣu kalām ʿan ḥikāyit iš-šanṭa wi kida ho, hiyya gayya tʾul-lu ʿal aḷḷa tkūn il-ʾahwa ʿagabitak. ʾal-laha kwayyisa. (29) baʿd ma miši gayya tšūf fi l-fingān laʾit il-ʾahwa zayy ma hiyya. (30) bass huwwa fiʿlan kān biyišrab bass il-ʾahwa ʾēh, yaʿni hiyya mā kānitš ʿarfa ʾēh illi raggaʿha.

(1) Adel Imam was riding in an airplane, he and Yousra, they were deplaning, and he said, welcome home (thank God for your safe arrival). (2) She said, Do you know me, sir? (3) He said, yes, didn't you use to work in the Research Institute Such-and-Such? So -- she said to him, but how do you know? (4) He told her, I am a relative of Mister I don't know who, Jack or Jim. (5) So she told him, Yeah, that's who did a book with me, he did a book with me and stuff. (6) So, oh yeah, when they were leaving, he forgot his briefcase, [leaving it] with her. (7) So, she didn't know his address, so she one day -- she took the briefcase with her when they went home. (8) One day she found a cat inside the closet after the -- (9) She up and comes and puts the briefcase, his mother's briefcase, in its place and she shuts the cat in

the closet. (10) Then the cat up and disappeared, it and the briefcase. (11) After that she comes looking for the briefcase [but] didn't find it, and she doesn't know [where it is], and she's upset and so on. (12) So one day Adel Imam was annoying her, so then he came to her place of work and so on. She told him, there is a situation that happened that I can't tell you about. (13) He said, what is it? She told him, the briefcase that you left for me got lost. (14) He told her -- it was -- she, he tells (told) her that there are important papers and stuff but there really weren't. (15) So she told him, she told him that the briefcase that you told me had important papers in it got lost. (16) He told her, in all honesty, I was lying to you because it didn't have any papers that were important to me, and so forth. (17) She said to him, But then what was in it? (18) He told her, It had some papers about my mother's inheritance and ordinary stuff. (19) So she told him, I'm very sorry, and so forth. (20) He came the next day, came in the morning, she wasn't in the office. (21) He up and put a briefcase for her [to find], just like the briefcase that had been in the closet. (22) She came and asked the secretary, Who brought that briefcase here? (23) [The secretary] told her, Mr. Fahmi. Then he came after a while and she asked him, how were you able to bring this briefcase? (24) He said, this isn't the other briefcase, this is a briefcase just like it. (25) But I bought it from the same guy I bought [the other one] from. (26) Then the secretary came and asked him, what would you like to drink? He said, coffee with medium sugar. (27) So she made him the coffee, he comes to drink it, he keeps drinking it, normal, and so on. (28) Finally, after they finished talking about the problem of the briefcase and stuff, she comes and tells him, I hope you liked the coffee. He said, it [was] good. (29) After he left, she comes looking at the cup, and found the coffee just as it was [originally]. (30) But he was really drinking, but the coffee, that is, she didn't know what returned it [to its original state].

Syria

Text A: A Year in the USA (S5)

(١) بعدا اختلطت كتير مع مرة رئيس الجامعة هونيكي. (٢) رئيسة الجامعة عاملة لنا عزيمة من أول ما جيت، كمان، (٣) وعزمتني عليها وبعتوا لي سكرتيرة خصوصية مشان تحكي معي عربي تترجم لي بالعربي لأني انا وقت رحت ما بعرف انكليزي أبداً أبداً — انا لغتي الاصلية فرنسي — (٤) وبعتوا — دقوا لي تليفون قال نحن — بالاول بعتوا لي الكرت، بعد يومين تلاتة دقّوا تليفون (٥) قال سكرتيرتها لمرة رئيس الجامعة دقّت تليفون قال نحن — حكت مع محمد لأني انا ما بعرف انكليزي — (٦) حكت معاه وحدة، قالت عزمنا المدام. (٧) قال لها وصلنا الكرت. (٨) قالت له بس نحن منعرفها انه ما بتعرف انكليزي. (٩) مشان هيك حطّينا لها سكرتيرة خصوصية بدها تخبّرها خلال يومين مشان تعرف تحكي عربي مشان تاخدها ع الزيارة، يعني ع العزيمة اللي عاملة لنا ياها لمرة رئيس الجامعة. (١٠) ورحنا هونيك كلّن نسوان دكاترة ومن كل دول العالم، يعني، فرنساويين ... وحياة الله، انا كتير كتير انبسطت وقت رحت لهنيكي. (١١) ايه، يعني لأن الحياة الـ عشتها، جيراننا يقولوا لي انتو عايشين يعني ريغن ماهو عايش متلكن، وحياة الله عم بقللك. (١٢) انبسطنا كتير، اخدنا بيت كتير كويس. (١٣) منطقة الـ اخدنا فيها كتير كويسة وغنية كتير وبيت الـ اخدناه كتير كويس، اولاً ما بيت للايجار. (١٤) المنطقة كلّها هونيك ما بيأجّروا لحدا أبداً أبداً، أبداً أبداً. (١٥) واذا بدّه حدا من بيناتن، يعني مغلقة تقريباً المنطقة الـ سكنّا فيها، ما بيدخل لها إلاّ اصحاب المنطقة بالذات، فيه — بالمدخل هادا فيه حرس. (١٦) يعني ماهو مين ما كان بيدخل هالمنطقة، ما فيه اجانب أبداً أبداً. (١٧) يعني نحن لمّا اجّرتنا البيت، اجّرتنا البيت لأن عن طريق عميد الـ — كلية العمارة اجّرتنا ايّاه. (١٨) ومن بعد ما بعتت رسالة لكلّ الجيران عم تشرح لن مين نحن واشّو وضعنا واشّو شغل جوزي واشّو نحن بالواحد، عم بقللك، المرا كذا، الولاد، رنا الكبيرة عم تدرس عمارة، الاصغر دينا بالعاشر، (١٩) يعني كاتبة لن تفاصيل عنّا طويلة عريضة لأنّ تركت النا

رسالة بالبيت مشان نقرا اللي باعتتن للجيران. (٢٠) بقى من وقت الـ وصلنا، — مو باعتة للجيران هالرسالة؟ — ووافقوا انّه تأجّرنا البيت، عادت اجّرتنا البيت، كلّن صاروا يدقّوا تليفونات يسلّموا علينا، وبعدها اجوا شربوا قهوة عندنا. (٢١) وواحدة من بيناتن عملت عزيمة ع السهرة، يعني، المسا بعد العشا الساعة تمانية، عملت سهرة لكلّ الجيران عرّفتن علينا. (٢٢) وصاروا بقى كلّ واحد يعزمنا ونحن بالـ — بعدها عزمناهن واجوا لعندنا وصار كتير فيه يعني — (٢٣) تصوّري انا اكون باركة الصبح يندقّ الباب هلّق شلون جيتوا انتو؟ (٢٤) يدقّوا الباب يقولوا لي ايش عم بتساوي، اذا ما عندك شي بدنا ندخل نشرب فنجان قهوة عندك. (٢٥) عم بقللك —بعدها هنن، قلت الن — قال اشهي فكرتك عن أميركا؟ قلت له والله كتير كتير اتغيّرت فكرتي عن أميركا من وقت اللي كنت انا بسوريا ووقت الـ جيت لأميركا. (٢٦) قال شلون تغيّرت؟ قلت له، نحن منعرف ان الجار ما بيعرف جاره، انا هون لقيت غير شي. (٢٧) قال لا، ما تفترضي هاي أميركا. نحن هوني منطقة غير أميركا. (٢٨) قال مضبوطة فكرتك انت. اطلعي برات هالمنطقة بتلاقي نفس الشي، الجار ما بيعرف شي عن جاره أبداً أبداً. (٢٩) عم بقللك هولي يكونوا عم بيمشّوا كلابن يكونوا عم بيتمشّوا بالشارع يدقّوا الباب عليّ ويقولوا عندك مانع نشرب قهوة؟ أقللن لا ييه! (٣٠) تعلّمت اللغة، تعلّمت اللغة من جيراننا، قدّ ما احكي معن واضطرّ احكي معن، تعلّمت منن اللغة. (٣١) بس دخلت انا كورس لغة بالجامعة، عملت بالأول، لأن ما بعرف ولا كلمة، يعني ما معقول ابرك متل الجدبان. (٣٢) لأن كتير صعب اذا واحد ما بيعرف لغة. (٣٣) عملت كورس لغة انا بالاول، بعدها لقيت حالي قدّ ما عم بنزل وبروح وبجي معن صار عندي پراتيك كتير كويس. (٣٤) يعني ما بقى بتفرق معي يعني اني اخد كمان مثلاً كورس تاني. (٣٥) انبسطت، كتير انبسطت. قلت الن يعني انا الحقيقة الحياة الـ عشتها هونيكي حياة دالاس وداينستي يعني.

(1) baʿda ixṭalaṭit ktīr maʿ mart raʾīs il-jāmʿa hōnīki. (2) raʾīst ij-jāmʿa ʿāmlit-əlna ʿazīme mən awwal ma jīt kamān, (3) w ʿazamitni ʿalē[h]a w baʿatū-li sikirtēra xṣūṣiyye mišān tiḥkī maʿi ʿarabi ttarjim-li bi-l-ʿarabi

la'inni 'ana wa't rəḥt mā ba'rif 'inglīzi 'abadan 'abadan -- 'ana luġti il-'aṣliyye ferensi -- (4) w ba'atu -- da''ū-li talifōn 'āl niḥna - bi-l-'awwal ba'atū-li l-karət, ba'd yomēn tlāte da''u talifōn (5) 'āl sikirtērt[h]a la-mart ra'īs ij-jām'a da''it talifōn 'āl niḥne -- ḥakit ma' mḥammad la'inni 'ana mā ba'rif 'inglīzi -- (6) ḥakit ma'ā wāḥde, 'ālit 'azamna l-madām. (7) 'al-l[h]a wəṣəlna l-karət. (8) 'ālit-lu bass niḥna mna'rif[h]a 'innu mā bta'rif 'inglīzi, (9) mišān hēk ḥaṭṭēnā-l[h]a sikirtēra xṣūṣiyye bəd[h]a txabbr[h]a xilāl yōmēn mišān ta'rif tiḥki 'arabi mišān tāxd[h]a 'a z-zyāra, ya'ni, 'a l-'azīme lli 'āmilt-əlna yāha la-mart ra'īs ij-jām'a. (10) w rəḥna honīk killon niswān dakātra w min kill duwal il-'ālem, ya'ni frensāwiyyīn ... w ḥyāt 'aḷḷah, 'ana ktīr ktīr inbasaṭət wa't rəḥt la-hnīki. (11) ēh, ya'ni, la'inn il-ḥayāt il 'išt[h]a, jīrānna y'ūlū-lna 'intu 'āyšīn -- ya'ni rēgan mā[h]u 'āyiš mitilkon, w ḥyāt 'aḷḷah 'am ba'il-lik. (12) 'inbasaṭna ktīr, 'axadna bēt ktīr kwayyis. (13) manṭi't il 'axadna fī[h]a ktīr kwayyse w ġaniyye ktīr w bēt il 'axadnā ktīr kwayyis, 'awwalan mā bēt lə-l-'ījār. (14) il-manṭ'a killa hōnīk mā bi'ajjru la-ḥada 'abadan 'abadan, 'abadan 'abadan. (15) w 'iza bəddu ḥada mən bēnāton, ya'ni muġlaqa ta'rīban, mā byidxil-l[h]a 'illa 'aṣḥāb il-manṭ'a bi-z-zāt, fī -- bi-l-madxal hāda fī ḥaras. (16) ya'ni mā[h]u mīn ma kān byidxul ha l-manṭ'a, mā fī 'ajānib 'abadan 'abadan. (17) ya'ni niḥna lamma 'ajjaritna l-bēt, 'ajjaritna l-bēt la'innə 'an ṭarī' 'amīd il -- killiyyit il-'amāra 'ajjaritna yyā. (18) w mən ba'd ma ba'atit risāle la-kill ij-jīrān 'am tišraḥ-lon mīnon niḥna w 'eššu waḍə'na 'eššu šuġl jōzi w 'eššu niḥna bi-l-wāḥid, 'am ba'il-lik, l-mara kaza, il-wlād, rana l-kbīre 'am tidrus 'amāra l-'aṣġar dīna bi-l-'āšir -- (19) ya'ni kātibt-əlon tafāṣīl 'anna ṭawīle 'arīḍa la'inn tarkit-əlna risāle bi-l-bēt mišān ni'ra lli bā'itton li-j-jīrān. (20) ba'a min wa't il wṣəlna, -- mū bā'te li-j-jīrān ha r-risāle? -- w wāfa'u 'innu t'ajjirna l-bēt, 'ādit 'ajjaritna l-bēt -- killon ṣāru ydi''u talifōnāt ysallmu 'alēna, w ba'da 'iju širbu 'ahwe 'an[d]na. (21) w wāḥde min benāton 'əmlit 'azīme 'a-l-- sahra, ya'ni, l-masa ba'd l-'aša s-sā'a tmānye, 'əmlit sahra la-kill ij-jīrān 'arrafiton 'alēna. (22) w ṣāru ba'a kill wāḥid yi'zimna w niḥna bi-l -- ba'da 'azamnāhon w 'iju la-'an[d]na w ṣār ktīr fī ya'ni -- (23) tṣawwari, 'ana 'akūn bārke iṣ-ṣubuḥ, yinda'' il-bāb, halla' šlōn jītu 'intu? (24) ydi''u l-bāb y'ūlū-li 'ēš 'am bitsāwi, 'iza mā 'andik ši bid[d]na nidxul nišrab finjān 'ahwe 'andik. (25) 'am ba'il-lik -- ba'd[h]a hinnin,

ʾilt-ilon -- ʾāl ʾešš[h]i fikərtik ʿan ʾamērka? ʾilt-lu waḷḷa ktīr ktīr itġayyarit fikərti ʿan ʾamērka min waʾt illi kint ʾana bi-sūriya w waʾt il jīt la-ʾamērka. (26) ʾāl šlōn tġayyarit? ʾilt-lu niḥa mnaʿrif inn ij-jār mā byaʿrif jāru, ʾana hōn laʾēt ġēr šī. (27) ʾāl lā, mā tiftərḍi hāy ʾamērka. niḥna hōne manṭʾa ġēr ʾamērka. (28) ʾāl maẓbūṭa fikərtik ʾinti. ṭlaʿi la-barrāt ha-l-manṭʾa, bitlāʾi nafs iš-ši, ij-jār mā byaʿrif ši ʿan jāru ʾabadan ʾabadan. (29) ʿam baʾil-lik, hōle ykūnu ʿam bimaššu klābon, ykūnu ʿam bitmaššu bi-š-šāriʿ, ydiʾʾu l-bāb ʿaleyy w yʾūlū-li ʿandik māniʿ nišrab ʾahwe? ʾaʾil-lon lā yīh! (30) tʿallamt il-luġa, taʿallamt il-luġa min jīrānna, ʾadd mā aḥkī maʿon w aḍṭarr aḥkī maʿon taʿallamt minnon il-luġa. (31) bass daxalt ʾana kūrs luġa bi-j-jāmʿa, ʿamilt bi-l-ʾawwal, laʾinn mā baʿrif wala kilme, yaʿni mā maʿʾūl ʾabruk mitl ij-jidbān. (32) laʾin[n] ktīr ṣaʿb ʾiza wāḥid mā byaʿrif luġa. (33) ʿəmilət kūrs luġa ʾana bi-l-ʾawwal, baʿd[h]a laʾēt ḥāli ʾadd ma ʿam banzil w barūḥ w baji maʿon ṣār ʿandi prātīk ktīr kwayyis. (34) yaʿni mā baʾa btifriʾ maʿi yaʿni ʾinni ʾāxud kamān masalan kūrs tāni. (35) ʾinbasaṭət, ktīr inbasaṭət. ʾilt-ilon yaʾni ʾana l-ḥaʾīʾa yaʿni l-ḥayāt il ʿišt[h]a hōnīke ḥayāt dālās w dāynasti yaʿni.

(1) What's more, I mixed [socialized] a lot with the wife of the president of the university there. (2) The [wife of the] president of the university arranged for us a luncheon when I first arrived too, (3) and she invited me to it and sent me a private secretary to speak with me in Arabic to translate for me in Arabic because when I went I didn't know English at all -- my original [foreign] language is French -- (4) and they sent -- they called me on the phone and said we -- first they had sent the card, two or three days later they called. (5) The secretary of the university president's wife telephoned saying we -- she talked with Muhammad because I didn't know English -- (6) A woman talked with him who said, we have invited [your] wife. (7) He said, we received the card. (8) She said, but we know she doesn't know English. (9) For that reason we have assigned for her a private secretary who will call within a couple of days because she can speak Arabic in order to take her to the visit, that is, to the luncheon that the wife of the president of the university has arranged for us. (10) We went, and there all of them were wives of doctors and from all the countries of the world, you know, French ... I swear to God, I had a very very good time when I

went there. (11) Yeah, because the life I lived, I mean, my neighbors used to tell me, you are living -- Reagan isn't living like you are, I swear to God, I'm telling you. (12) We had a very nice time, we got a very nice house. (13) The area where we took the house was very nice and very rich, and the house that we got was very nice: first of all, it wasn't a rental house. (14) [In] the whole region over there they don't rent to anyone at all, at all, ever, ever. (15) And if someone wants [to rent, it must be] someone from among them, that is, [it's] practically closed off, no one enters it except for the people who live in the area in particular, there is -- in that entrance there is a security guard. (16) I mean, not just anyone can enter that area; there are no foreigners at all at all. (17) I mean, we, when she rented us the house, she rented us the house because -- by way of the dean of the School of Architecture she rented it to us. (18) After she sent a letter to all the neighbors explaining to them who we were and what we were, one by one, I'm telling you, the wife is such-and-such, Rana the oldest is studying architecture, the youngest, Dina, is in the tenth [grade], (19) that is, she had written all sorts of details about us, [we know] because she left a [copy of] the letter in the house so that we could read what she had sent to the neighbors. (20) So, from the time we arrived, -- hadn't she sent the neighbors that letter? and they agreed that she could rent us the house, she then rented us the house -- all of them started calling on the telephone to say hello to us, and then they came and had coffee at our house. (21) One of them had a party, in the evening, after supper, at eight o'clock, she had a party for all the neighbors and introduced them to us. (22) They started, you know, every one [started] inviting us while we were -- after that we invited them and they came to our house and there started to be a lot of, you know -- (23) Imagine, I would be sitting in the morning, there would be a knock [at] the door, now, how did you get here? (24) They would knock at the door and say to me, What are you doing? If you don't have anything [aren't busy], we'd like to come in and have a cup of coffee [with] you. (25) I'm telling you -- Then they, I told them -- [One] said, What is your opinion about America? I told him, well, my opinion about America has changed a lot from the time that I was in Syria [to] the time I came to America. (26) He said, How has it changed? I told him, We know that [a] neighbor doesn't know his neighbor, [but] I found here something else. (27) He said, no, don't suppose that this is America. We here are an area other than America. (28) He said, your idea is correct. Go outside of this area and you find the same thing, a neighbor doesn't know a thing about his neighbor at all at all. (29) I'm telling you, those [people] would be walking their dogs, they would be taking a stroll in the road, they would knock at the door and say, Do you have any objection if we [come in] to drink some coffee? I'd say to them, Why, no! (30) I learned the language, I learned the language from my neighbors, [from] the amount that I would talk with them and be forced to talk with them I learned the language from them. (31) But I took a language course at the university, I did [that] first, because I didn't know a single word, it wasn't reasonable to stay like idiots. (32) I mean, it's very difficult if one doesn't know a language. (33) I took a language course first, after that I found myself from the amount that I was going out and coming and going with them I got very good practice. (34) I mean, it was no longer important to me to take another course. (35) I had a very good time, a very good time. I told them, really, the life I led in America is the life of "Dallas" and "Dynasty."

Text B: Modern Marriage (S4, husband speaks first)[1]

(١) يعني عادات الاولية - أبهاتنا وجدودنا - كانوا ما يشوفوا العروس لليلة العرس. (٢) هلّق هالجيل هالموجود بخطبوا بعضن هنن، ما بدّن مين يخطب لن يعني. (٣) وبيشوفوا بعضن وبيعاشروا بعضن لا بدّه يتعب الاب ولا بدّها تتعب الام. (٤) وبيرتفقوا مع بعضن. ايه. (٥) تغيّر يعني الدقّة الاولية تغيّرت. —— (٦) ويقولوا يعني انّ الرجّال ما يعني يشوف العروس ولا تشوفه يعيشوا اكتر من هلّق. —— (٧) كان ما فيه، كان ما فيه تفكير متل هلّق. —— (٨) يعني هلّق بيخطبوا وبتخطبي بتروح وبتيجي و بعدين بياخدها جمعتين تلاتة شهر - يقِللك انا حبّيتها انا ما حبّيتها. (٩) بس أولي ما يشوف العروس ورأساً تلاقي لك تصير المفاهمة

[1]The text contains a number of ellipses because in certain places, both husband and wife are speaking at the same time, and some phrases are unclear.

وتجيهن ولاد وهاي وما يصير أبداً طالع خلافات. (١٠) هلّق بتشوفي لك بيعرفوا بعضن بيعاشروا بعضن سنة او سنتين وبعدين وقت اللي بيتجوّزوا، بيقللك صار اختلافات معها، وزعلت منه وزعل مني، ما تفاهمنا مع بعضنا. ... —— (١١) بفرط الحب مع بعضن، بيكرهوا بعضن، يعني يكونوا رغبانين ببعضن بس يتجوّزوا، بيقعدوا، بيعودوا بيكرهوا بعضن، ايه، هيك بيصير. (١٢) ... هادا رفيقه متزوّج. امّه مصرية، وقامت راحت خطبت له بنت اخوها. (١٣) جابتها من مصر من هنيك لهون، وبركت معن هوني خمتعش نهار لصار العرس. (١٤) من بعد ما اخدها، قال ما بقى بحبّها، قال ما بقى بدي ادخل ع البيت. (١٥) اجا عم بيحكي لنا هوني وقلنا ناخده ع شيخ يكتب له، يعني التوفيق، مو يكتب له شي يعني. (١٦) ما صبر عليها، طلّقها ورجّعها على بلدها. —— (١٧) بعتها ع مصر. —— (١٨) لك ايه، اسّه ما صار لك جمعة، عشرة ايام ما صار لك ... —— (١٩) بركت - اجت معه من مصر لهون، بركت خمستعش نهار بين ما صار العرس - —— (٢٠) بنت خاله هي. —— (٢١) خمستعش نهار لوقت ما يعني ياخدوا لها اغراض وهيك، بعدين ساووا العرس. (٢٢) برك معها تلات تيام نهار التلات تيام عند المسا قال لن ما حبّيتها، بدّي اعيفها. (٢٣) لك يا ابني جبنالك بنت خالك وتبهدلنا مع خالك، وهاي، قال لهن ... —— (٢٤) خجلة يعني. —— (٢٥) خلال خمستعش نهار كانت في مصر. (٢٦) قطع لها وبعت لها، طلّقها وبعتها. —— (٢٧) قليل اصل، كان يرجّعها بحالها اشرف. —— (٢٨) ما حابّها كنت من اول ما حبّيتها، من اول مو على - وبركت خمستعش نهار عنده من دون ما يتجوّزها. (٢٩) والغدا بغداه والفطور بفطوره والعشا بعشاه، وتعا فلان وتعا علاّن. (٣٠) وبعدين وقت اللي اخدها تلات تيام قال لن ما حبّيتها.

(1) yaʿni ʿādāt il-ʾawwaliyye - ʾabbahātna w jdūdna - kānu mā yšūfu l-ʿarūs la-lēlt l-ʿərs. (2) hallaʾ ha-j-jīl ha-l-mawjūd b[y]uxṭbu baʿḍon hinnin, mā bəd[d]on mīn yuxṭub-lon yaʿni. (3) w bišūfu baʿḍon w biʿāšru baʿḍon, lā bəddu yitʿab il-abb w lā bədda titʿab il-ʾimm. (4) w birtifʾu maʿ baʿḍon. ēh. (5) tġayyar yaʿni d-daʾʾa l-awwaliyye tġayyarit. --- (6) w yʾūlū yaʿni ʾinn ir-rijjāl mā yaʿni yšūf il-ʿarūs w lā tšūfu, yʿīšu

aktar min halla'. --- (7) kān mā fī, kān mā fi tafkīr mitil halla'. --- (8) ya'ni halla' byuxəṭbu w btuxəṭbi bitrūḥ w btiji w ba'dēn byaxd[h]a jimi'tēn tlāte šahr, y'il-lak 'ana ḥabbēt[h]a 'ana mā ḥabbetha. (9) bass 'awwali mā yšūf il-'arūs w ra'san tlā'ī-lik tṣīr il-mufāhame w tjīon wlād w hayy w mā yṣīr 'abadan ṭāli' xilāfāt. (10) halla' bitšūfī-lik bya'rfu ba'ḍon bi'āšru ba'ḍon sine w sintēn w ba'dēn wa't illi bitjawwazu, bi'il-lak ṣār ixtilāfāt ma'ha, w z'ilt minnu w zi'il minni, mā tfāhamna ma' ba'ḍna. ... --- (11) b[y]ufruṭ il-ḥubb ma' ba'ḍon, bikrahu ba'ḍon, ya'ni ykūnu raġbānīn b-ba'ḍon, bass yitjawwazu bi''ədu, bi'ūdu bikrahu ba'ḍon, ēh, hēk biṣīr. (12) ... hāda rfī'u mitzawwej, 'əmmu məṣriyye, w 'āmit rāḥit xaṭbit-lu bint axū[h]a. (13) jābita min maṣər min hənīk la-hōn, w barkit ma'on hōne xamsta'š nhār la-ṣār l-'ərs. (14) min ba'd ma axad[h]a, 'āl mā ba'a bḥibb[h]a, 'āl mā ba'a bəd[d]i idxul 'a l-bēt. (15) 'ija 'am biḥkī-lna hōni w 'ilna nāxdu 'a šēx yiktib-lu, ya'ni t-tawfī', mū yiktib-lu ši ya'ni. (16) mā ṣabar 'alē[h]a, ṭalla'ha w rajja'ha 'ala balad[h]a. --- (17) ba'at[h]a 'a maṣər. --- (18) lak, ē, 'issa mā ṣār-lak jim'a, 'ašr tiyyam mā ṣār-lak ... --- (19) barkit - 'ijit ma'u min maṣər la hōn, barkit xamsta'š nhār bēn ma ṣār l-'ərs. --- (20) bint xālu hiyye. --- (21) xamsta'š nhār la-wa't ma ya'ni ta yāxdū-l[h]a ġrāḍ w hēk, ba'dēn sāwu l-'ərs. (22) barak ma'ha tlat tiyyām, nhār it-tlat tiyyām 'and l-masa 'āl-lon mā ḥabbet[h]a, bəddi a'īf[h]a. (23) lak yā 'ibni jibnā-lak bint xālak w tbahdilna ma' xālak, w hayy, 'āl-lon ... --- (24) xajle ya'ni. --- (25) xilāl xamsta'š nhār kānit fi maṣər. (26) 'aṭa'-l[h]a w ba'at-l[h]a, ṭalla'[h]a w ba'at[h]a. --- (27) 'alīl 'aṣəl, kān yrajji'[h]a bi-ḥālha ašraf. --- (28) mā ḥābb[h]a kint min 'awwal mā ḥabbet[h]a, min 'awwal mū 'ala - w barkit xamsta'š nhār 'andu min dūn ma yitjawwaz[h]a. (29) w əl-ġada b-ġadā w əl-fṭūr b-fṭūru w il-'aša b-'ašā w ta'a flān w ta'a 'illān. (30) w ba'dēn wa't illi axad[h]a tlat tiyyām 'āl-lon mā ḥabbet[h]a.

(1) The customs of the old [generations]--our fathers and forefathers--they used not to see the bride until the night of the wedding. (2) Now, this present generation arrange their own marriages, they don't want anyone to arrange for them, that is. (3) And they see each other and get to know each other, neither the father need wear himself out nor the mother need wear herself out. (4) And they form their own friendships.

Yeah. (5) It changed, that is, the old pattern changed. --- (6) And they say, you know, that the man wouldn't see the bride nor she see him but they [the marriages] would survive longer than nowadays. --- (7) There didn't used to be, didn't used to be thinking like there is today. --- (8) That is, now they get engaged and you get [them] engaged and [the bride-to-be] comes and goes and then he marries her, two weeks, three, a month, he tells you I love her, I don't love her. (9) But in the old days he wouldn't see the bride and right away you find there would come to be mutual understanding and they'd have children and all that and there wouldn't be--there wouldn't at all arise disagreements. (10) Now you see that they know each other, they interact with each other for a year or two years and then when they get married, [they] tell you, Disagreements with her have arisen, and I'm mad at him, and he's mad at me, we couldn't get along. ... --- (11) Love with each other falls apart, they hate each other; that is, they would desire each other but as soon as they get married, they stay [together awhile, then] they turn around and hate each other, yeah, that's what happens. (12) ... This one, his friend [was] married, his mother is Egyptian, and she went and got him engaged to her brother's daughter. (13) She brought her from Egypt, from there to here, and she stayed with them fifteen days (two weeks) until the wedding took place. (14) After he married her, he said, I don't love her any more, he said, I don't want to go back in the house. (15) He came and talked to us here, and we thought to take him to a shaykh to write him something--that is, to make the marriage work, not something [bad]. (16) He didn't give her a chance, he divorced her and sent her back to her country. --- (17) He sent her [back] to Egypt. --- (18) Look here, now it hasn't even been a week, you haven't even been [married] ten days ... --- (19) She stayed - she came with him from Egypt to here, she stayed fifteen days until the wedding took place. --- (20) His cousin, she is. --- (21) Fifteen days until, that is, so that they could buy her things and so forth, then they had the wedding. (22) He stayed with her three days, on the evening of the third day he told them I don't love her, I want to get rid of her. (23) Look here, son, we brought you your cousin, do you want to shame us before your uncle, and such, he told them ... --- (24) [It's] an embarrassment, that is. --- (25) Within fifteen days she was in Egypt. (26) He bought her a ticket and sent [it] to her, he divorced he and sent her [back]. --- (27) [He is] poorly bred (doesn't know how to behave properly), he should have sent her back as she was [before marrying her, it would have been] more noble. (28) You aren't in love with her, you should have not loved her from the beginning, from the beginning, not [after] - and she stayed two weeks at his house without him marrying her ??? (29) And [her] lunch is his lunch (they have lunch together), [her] breakfast is his breakfast, [her] dinner is his dinner, and come one, come all [to the wedding]. (30) And then when he married her three days and he told them, I didn't love her.

Text C: Love in a Conservative Society (S2)

(١) هلّق متل عندنا نحنا الحب بالضيعة كتير- يعني كان بالبداية بالاول شغلة كبيرة وهيك. (٢) هلّق صايرين البنات مّا يطنشوا ، ما عاد مّا يهمّن يعني. (٣) بالاول كانوا يشوفوا اتنين ماشيين مع بعضن: يا لطيف ، جريمة. (٤) هلّق بتلاقي هالجيل الطالع انه الشاطرة ياللا .- بدن يطلعوا، اهلي مو مشكلة ، خليني احب وانبسط وهاي متل بعضها . (٥) هلّق عندنا بالضيعة - اذا اتنين مّا يحبوا بعضن وسمعوا كمان العالم فيهن يا لطيف! شغلة كبيرة، (٦) انه كل ما جا واحد يخطبها بيجوا ، بيجوا : هاي كانت حابة فلان هاي كانت تطلع معه، هاي كانت تتمشى معه هاي كانت حقيرة هاي كانت كذا - (٧) يعني ما بيخلوا مثلاً بيحاولوا بشتى الوسائل اللي بيكونوا سامعين منشان يعطلوا انه العريس - ايه، لا تاخدها كذا كانت حابة كانت - (٨) هلّق يعني صار شوي العالم اتعودوا انه يشوفوا اتنين ماشيين مع بعضن هيكي، (٩) بس كمان اذا الواحدة شطّت وهيك يعني كانت شوي فلتانة بعلاقتها، كمان كتير بيزبلوها. (١٠) وهلّق كتير ما عاد ان الشباب ما عاد يهتموا مثلا انه مثلا ياخدوا واحدة اذا حلوة كتير وكذا اذا ما كانت متعلمة، مستحيل يفكر فيها الاّ يعني واحد كتير تافه يعني. (١١) يعني ما بتاخد اللي بتشتهيه ببالها، يعني. (١٢) اما هلّق وقت بتكون متعلمة وكذا وصارت عندها منتوج وبتطلع بتشتغل، صار يعني

بتلاقي غير مجال انه تلاقي شريك حياتها المناسب الكويس وهيك. (١٣) اما من قبل خلص – حلوة – يا لطيف! مُعلمة مو مُعلمة ، متل بعضها. ايه. (١٤) هلّق كمان متل بعضها يعني واحد بيحب واحدة ولو كانت حابة مو حابة، كمان ما بتفرق معه يعني اذا كان عندها كمان علاقة مع غيره متل بعضها معه. (١٥) يعني منضلّ بالضيعة لهلّق انه ما فيه كمان هالزيادة يعني هالعلاقات المفضوحة وهيك. (١٦) بتضلّ الواحدة متحفّظة يعني انه ما يسمعوا كتير — يعني نسبة كبيرة من العالم، (١٧) لأنه بيضلّ الواحدة إلها عدوّينها وإلها محبينها وكذا، لأن بيعطّلوا مستقبلها، ايه، حبّت وحبّت وخبّصت ودفترها مشقشق وكذا (١٨) يعني من هالحكي هادا ، ما بيخلّوه ، يعني بيحاولوا بشتى الوسائل انه يبعدوه. (١٩) طبعاً اللي بيكرهوها. اما اللي بيحبوها، ايه كويسة وايه كل العالم بتحب وكل العالم بتعشق وكل العالم – (٢٠) يعني ما عاد فيه مشكلة. ... (٢١) انا من النوع يعني بفكر انه بالمجتمع، لأنه انا من المجتمع، اذا ما فكرت بالمجتمع معناتها ماني من المجتمع. (٢٢) يعني الواحد بيمشي شوي شوي مو بيجي ضربة واحدة مثلاً، (٢٣) هالمجتمع متعصب متحجب كذا بيجي مرة واحدة بتحبي بتطلعي بتفوتي بتنامي مع الـ بتحبيه. (٢٤) هاي الشي بيرفضه المجتمع وخاصة نحنا عندنا بلاد يعني بلدنا متعصبة بيقولوا عنها إسلامي ومحافظة. (٢٥) يعني ما بتسمح بهالشي وخاصة لهلّق فيه محلات مثلاً متعصبين بشكل، مستحيل انه الشاب يحكي مع البنت. (٢٦) بالبيت مثلاً فيه هوني بالشام محلات مستحيل تدخلي ع البيت قبل ربع ساعة لحتى يشوفوا «اتستّروا يا حريم واتضبضبوا!» وكذا لحتى يحسن انه مثلاً الواحد يدخل ع البيت. (٢٧) واذا – مستحيل يبيّنوا شعرن مثلاً ع العالم: هادا شو؟! (٢٨) بيقبل الاب مثلاً او المجتمع انه واحدة هيكي تطلع وتفوت وتكون الها علاقات، كتير مع الشباب وتحكي مع الشباب وبنفس الوقت بيعرفوا انه عندها علاقة جنسية؟! (٢٩) طبعاً هاي مشكلة كبيرة ومستحيل انه حدي يفكر فيها يعني.

(1) halla’ mitil ʿan[d]na niḥna l-ḥubb bi-ḍ-ḍēʿa ktīr -- yaʿni kān bi-l-bidāye bi-l-ʾawwal šaġle kbīre w hēk. (2) halla’ ṣāyrīn il-banāt mma yṭannšu mā ʿād mma yhimmon yaʿni. (3) bi-l-ʾawwal kānu yšūfu tnēn māšyīn

maʿ baʿḍon, ya laṭīf, žarīme. (4) hallaʾ bitlāqi ha-ž-žīl ṭ-ṭāliʿ ʾinnu iš-šāṭra, yaḷḷa -- biddon yiṭlaʿu, ʾahli mū miškle xallīni ḥibb w ənbiṣiṭ w hayy mitil baʿḍ[h]a. (5) hallaʾ ʿan[d]na bi-ḍ-ḍēʿa, ʾiza tnēn mma yḥibbu baʿḍon w simʿu kamān il-ʿālam fīon, ya laṭīf! šaġle kbīre (6) ʾinnu kill mā ža wāḥid yəxṭəb[h]a bižu, bižu: hayy kānit ḥābbe flān hāy kānit tiṭlaʿ maʿu, hayy kānit titmašša maʿu hayy kānit, hayy kānit ḥaqīra hayy kānit kaza -- (7) yaʿni mā bixallu masalan biḥāwlu b-šatta l-wasāʾil illi bikūnu sāmʿīn minšān yʿaṭṭlu ʾinnu l-ʿarīs -- ʾēh, lā tāxid[h]a kaza kānit ḥābbe kānit -- (8) hallaʾ yaʿni ṣār šwayy l-ʿālam itʿawwdu ʾinnu yšūfu tnēn māšyīn maʿ baʿḍon hēki. (9) bass kamān ʾiza il-waḥde šaṭṭit w hēk yaʿni kānit šwayy faltāne b-ʿalāqt[h]a kamān ktīr byizbilū[h]a. (10) w hallaʾ ktīr mā ʿād ʾinnu š-šabāb mā ʿād yihtammu masalan ʾinnu masalan yāxdu waḥde ʾiza ḥilwe ktīr w kaza, ʾiza mā kānit mitʿallme mustaḥīl yfakkir fī[h]a ʾilla yaʿni wāḥid ktīr tāfih. (11) yaʿni mā btāxud illi btišthī b-bāl[h]a, yaʿni. (12) ʾamma hallaʾ, waqt bitkūn mitʿallme w kaza w ṣārit ʿand[h]a mantūž w btiṭlaʿ btištiġil, ṣār yaʿni bitlāqi ġēr mažāl ʾinnu tlāqi šarīk ḥayāt[h]a il-munāsib il-kwayyis w hēk. (13) ʾamma min qabəl xalaṣ, ḥilwe - ya laṭīf! muʿallme mū muʿallme, mitil baʿḍ[h]a. ʾēh. (14) hallaʾ kamān mitil baʿḍ[h]a yaʿni, wāḥid biḥibb waḥde w law kānit ḥābbe mū ḥābbe, kamān ma btufruq maʿu, yaʿni ʾiza kān ʿand[h]a kamān ʿalāqa maʿ ġēru mitil baʿḍ[h]a maʿu. (15) yaʿni minḍall bi-ḍ-ḍēʿa la-hallaʾ ʾinnu mā fī kamān ha l-- -ziyāde yaʿni, ha l-ʿalāqāt l-mafḍūḥa w hēk. (16) bitḍall il-waḥde mitḥaffẓa yaʿni, ʾinnu mā yismaʿu ktīr - yaʿni nisbe kbīre mn il-ʿālam. (17) laʾannu biḍall il-waḥde ʾil[h]a ʿaduwwīn[h]a w ʾil[h]a muḥibbīn[h]a w kaza laʾann biʿaṭṭlu mustaqbal[h]a, ʾēh, ḥabbit w ḥabbit w xabbṣit w daftər[h]a mšaqšaq w kaza. (18) yaʿni min ha l-ḥaki hāda, mā bixallū, yaʿni biḥāwlu b-šatta l-wasāʾil ʾinnu yibʿədū. (19) ṭabʿan illi bikrahū[h]a. ʾamma lli biḥibbū[h]a, ʾēh kwayyse, w ʾēh w kill il-ʿālam bitḥibb w kill il-ʿālam btəʿšaq w kill il-ʿālam -- (20) yaʾni mā ʿād fī miškle. ... (21) ʾana min in-nōʿ yaʿni bfakkir (ʾinnu) bi-l-mužtamaʿ laʾinnu ʾana mn il-mužtamaʿ, ʾiza mā fakkart bi-l-mužtamaʿ maʿnāta māni mn əl-mužtamaʿ. (22) yaʿni l-wāḥid byimši šwayy šwayy, mū biži ḍarbe waḥde masalan, (23) ha l-mužtamaʿ mutaʿaṣṣib mutaḥajjib kaza, byiži marra waḥde bitḥibbi btiṭlaʿi bitfūti bitnāmi maʿ il bitḥibbī. (24) hay š-še birfuḍu l-mužtamaʿ, w xāṣṣa niḥna ʿanna bilād yaʿni baladna mutaʿaṣṣiba biqūlu ʿan[h]a ʾislāmi w muḥāfiḍa. (25) yaʿni mā btismaḥ bi-ha š-še w xāṣṣa la-hallaʾ fī maḥallāt masalan mutaʿaṣṣibīn bi-šakəl, mustaḥīl ʾinnu š-šābb yiḥki maʿ əl-binət. (26) bi-l-bēt masalan fī hōnī bi-š-šām maḥallāt mustaḥīl tidxili ʿa l-bēt qabəl ribəʿ sāʿa la-ḥatta yšūfu "tsattaru yā ḥarīm w əḍḍabəḍbu" w kaza la-ḥatta yiḥsun ʾinnu masalan il-wāḥid yidxul ʿa l-bēt. (27) w ʾiza - mustaḥīl ybayynu šaʿron masalan ʿa l-ʿālam: hāda šu?! (28) byiqbal il-ʾab masalan ʾaw il-mužtamaʿ ʾinnu waḥde hēki tiṭlaʿ w tfūt w tkūn ʾila ʿalāqāt ktīr maʿ iš-šabāb w tiḥki maʿ əš-šabāb w b-nafs il-waqt byaʿrfu ʾinnu ʿand[h]a ʿalāqa žinsiyye?! (29) ṭabʿan hayy miškle kbīre w mustaḥīl ʾinnu ḥadi yfakkir fīha yaʿni

(1) [For] us, love in the village [is] very -- it was at first in the past a big deal and stuff. (2) Now, girls have begun to pay no mind, they no longer care, that is. (3) In the past [people] would see a couple walking together: God! what a crime. (4) Now you find [with] this rising generation, that the smart girl [says] go for it -- they want to go out: my family is not a problem, let me love and have a good time and stuff, it's okay. (5) Now, in our village, if a couple are in love and everyone hears about them, God! it's a big deal. (6) Every time someone comes to ask for her hand they come [saying], this girl was in love with so and so, she used to go out with him, she used to walk around with him, she was despicable, she was such and such -- (7) They don't let for example -- they try in all sorts of ways, the ones who have heard [something], so as to prevent the [prospective] groom -- don't marry her, she was involved with someone, she was -- (8) *Now everyone has gotten somewhat used to seeing a couple walking together like that. (9) But as well, if a girl crosses the line and stuff, that is, if she is a bit loose in her relationships, they also shun her quite a bit. (10) Now often it is no longer the case that the guys no longer care for example that they marry a girl if she is very pretty and so forth, if she is not educated, no way will he think about [marrying] her, except someone who's quite inane, that is. (11) That is, she won't marry the man she really wants. (12) As for now when she is educated and so forth and has become productive and goes out and works, she has started finding other ways to meet [a] good, appropriate life-partner. (13) As for before, that's it -- if she's pretty - wow! educated, uneducated,*

it's all the same. (14) Now, too, it's all the same, that is, a boy loves a girl, even if she has had a love affair and whatnot, also, it doesn't make any difference to him, and also if she had a relationship with someone else it's okay with him. (15) We remain in the village until today [such] that there is not this increase, that is, these explicit relationships and the like, (16) a girl still behaves with reserve, that is, [so] they don't hear a lot [about what she does] -- that is, a substantial number of people, (17) because one still has her enemies and her friends, and so forth, because they ruin her future, for sure, [saying] she has had love relationships and she has messed things up and her record is blotted (torn) and so forth. (18) You know, stuff like that, they don't leave him alone, that is, they try by every means to get him away [from her]. (19) Of course, those who dislike her [do that]. As for those who like her, [they say, she's] good, sure, everyone falls in love, everyone gets infatuated, everyone ... (20) That is to say, there's no longer a problem ... (21) I am the type that thinks about society because I am of the society, if I don't think abut society that means I'm not of the society. (22) I mean, one has to go slowly, not come all at once for example -- (23) This society is morally strict, veiled, [and] so forth, it comes about all at once [that] you love and you go out and come in and sleep with the one you love[?] (24) This thing society rejects, especially [since] we have a country, that is our country is morally strict, they say about it Islamic and conservative. (25) That is, it doesn't permit this thing and especially until now there are places in Damascus for instance [they are] so strict, it's impossible for a guy to talk to a girl. (26) In the house, for example, there are areas here in Damascus [where it's] impossible for you to enter the house for a quarter of an hour so that they can see [the women are hidden] "cover up, women and get out of the way!" and so forth, so that one is able for instance to enter the house. (27) And if -- it's impossible for them to show their hair for example to people: "What is this?!" (28) Does the father accept, or society, that a girl can come and go and have lots of relationships with guys and talk with guys and at the same time they know that she has a sexual relationship?! (29) Of course, this is a big problem, and it's impossible for anyone to think about [marrying] her, that is.

Kuwait

Text A: On Matchmaking (K2, Interviewer K4)

––– (١) شوفي ام احمد ، بنسألچ احنا عن شلون تعلّمت الخطبة. ––– (٢) تفضلي، اسألي. ––– (٣) شلون تعلمتيها ، من منِّه اخذتيها ، شلون اكتسبتيها؟ ––– (٤) والله اكتسبتها من واحدة تخطب ، خطّيبة تخطب، سنين وانا اروح وايي معاها، علّمتني الخطبة شلون. ––– (٥) شلون طريگتها؟ ––– (٦) طريگتها ان ام الولد اخت الولد تدگ لچ تلفون تگول لچ ولله يا ام فلان نبي حگ وليدنا بنيّة. (٧) تگول لها انشالله. تسألني، هي تسألني، تگول لي يعني، نبي له چذي، تدرس، نبي له مخلصة الدراسة ، نبي له واحدة تشتغل والا ما تشتغل، متحجبة والا مو متحجبة. (٨) اگول لها عطيني شنو يشتغل ولدچ، يشتغل والا ما يشتغل. تگول لي يشتغل. (٩) اگول لها شنو شهادته، اسألها شنو شهادته، تگول والله – اللي تگول مخلص الثانوية، واللي تگول مخلص الجامعة، واللي تگول مخلص من برّا، واللي تگول ما عندَه شهادة. (١٠) المهم، نگول انشالله ، على الطلب اللي تبينَه. (١١) ندوّر له بنية. ناخذ اسمَه الكامل، اسم الولد الكامل وشغلَه، المعلومات اللي عندنا كلها، ندگ حگ اهل البنية، ردّي علي بعد ثلاثة ايام واردّ عليچ. (١٢) ندوّر لَه بنية اللي تناسب لَه. (١٣) نگول حگ اهل البنت الولد چذي، چذي، من – ولد فلان ابن فلان، يشتغل چذي، يشتغل چذي، تگول انشالله ام احمد، نعطيها ونگول لها. (١٤) تگول – ترجع تگول لي ام البنية، ام البنية ترجع تگول لي يا ام احمد انت تعرفينَه؟ (١٥) اگول لها لا والله انا ما اعرفَه، الام داگة لي تليفون تگول ابيچ تخطبي حگ ولدي، شكل ما انت ما اعرفچ انا ما اعرفَه، ما اعرف عنهم اي شي. (١٦) لمّا اييبَه لكم، تسألون – اهي تسأل – تسألون عنَّه ويسأل عنكم. (١٧) دگّينا حگ ام الولد، گلنا لها لگينا لچ بنيّة، بنت فلان من بنتَه؟ تسألني نفس اللي سألتَه. (١٨) تسألني بنت فلان ابن فلان، اگول لها، وتاخذ اسمها الكامل تگول حگ ولدها. (١٩) تگول ام احمد، لأ خل انا اروح اشوفها اوّل. (٢٠) انا ما ارضى، اگول لها لأ، اول خلّي الولد ييي يشوف البنيّة ويطالعها بدون انت، يعني، انت معاه واختَه ما

يخالف، بس الولد لازم ييي ويّاكم. (٢١) ما ارضى اخلّيها تيي بروحها. (٢٢) المهم، ييي – تگول لي انشالله، واعديهم اي يوم نيي ونروح معاچ ونشوف البنيّة. (٢٣) ادگ حگ اهل البنيّة واگول ترى اليوم بييوا – بنييكم انشالله، امّه واختَه والولد معانا. (٢٤) يگعد الولد، تدشّ البنية، يا امّا يايبة عصير، يا امّا بارد، يا امّا يعني اي شي، چاي، تدخل البنية ويشوف. (٢٥) هو گاعد، انا اگول لَه هاذي البنية، ترى شوفها، يشوفها، انشالله. (٢٦) إذا يعني فيه، اسألها، تبيها، ما تبيها، اسألها يعني على الشي اللي تبيه، يسألها. (٢٧) البنيّة طبعاً تستحي، مو شكل يعني، واحدة بعد تيي تركض چذي، تستحي. (٢٨) يسألها، وين تشتغلين، شنّو دارسة. (٢٩) امّا انا اگول لها بعد انت اسأليه. تسألَه. (٣٠) فيه بنات يعني يگدرون يسألون، فيه بنات يستحون، ما يسألون. (٣١) تسألَه، گعدنا، وسألها وسألتَه، سلام، مع السلامة، طلعنا، طلعنا. (٣٢) انا طبعاً انا اسأل الولد بالسيارة، اگول لَه هه، ش عجبتك البنيّة وليدي ولاّ ما عجبتك؟ (٣٣) ساعات يردّون علي يعني في نفس الكلام، يگول والله ام احمد عجبتني البنيّة وشوفي ردّ البنيّة بعد شنّو، وساعات لا والله، يگول يصير خير. (٣٤) هاذا اللي يگول لچ يصير خير، اعرف انّه ما يبي البنية، ايه، واللي يگول لچ والله سئلي البنية شوفي ايش گالت عني، ش رايها فيني، هاذا اعرف انهو يعني لَه خاطر بالبنية، امّا هالبنية لها – الها راي. (٣٥) المهم، يگطونني في بيتي وارجع ادگ لهم تليفون، بنفس الوگت ادگ حگ اهل البنت تليفون اذا هو لَه خاطر فيها، ادگ لهم تليفون، هه؟ ش رايكم في الولد؟ (٣٦) گالت الام طبعاً يعني الحين ما نگدر نردّ عليچ بهالدگيگة هاذي، حتى لو البنية لها خاطر، ما نگدر نردّ عليچ. (٣٧) صبري لنا يومين ثلاثة احنا نردّ عليچ الجواب. (٣٨) اصبر يومين ثلاثة، هَم تدگ لي تليفون الام وتگول لي والله البنية عجبها الولد وان شالله السؤال، نبي نسأل عنّه وهاذا ويسألون عنّه. ... —— (٣٩) بس اول يگولون بالخطبات الاولية مو چذي؟ —— (٤٠) الحين احنا خطباتنا الحين هاذا چذي. —— (٤١) اول يگول لچ يعني تمدحها، تلگينها يعني مو حلوة مو جميلة وتحطها بالسما لأن اول ما كان يشوفها مو چذي؟ —— (٤٢) ايه، ما كان يشوفها، اول ما كان يشوفها، عورا، عميا، عريا، اهو وحظّه،

ييبونها مكمكمة، مكمكمة في عبايتها، ماحد يدري عنها شنهي اهي. بس الحين لأ، كل شي ع المكشوف.

--- (1) šūfi umm aḥmad, bnisʾəlič iḥna ʿan šlōn tʿallamti l-xəṭba. --- (2) tfaḏḏli sʾili. --- (3) šlōn tʿallamtīha, mən minna ʾaxaḏtīha, šlōn ktasabtīha? --- (4) waḷḷa ktasabtha min waḥda txaṭəb, xaṭṭība txaṭəb, əsnīn w āna ʾarūḥ w ayi mʿāha, ʿalləmatni l-xəṭba šlōn. --- (5) šlōn ṭarīgətha? --- (6) ṭarīgətha ʾinna ʾumm əl-walad, ʾuxt əl-walad tdigg-lič telifōn tgul-lič waḷḷah ya umm flān, nabi ḥagg wlīdna bnayya. (7) tgul-lha inšāḷḷa. tisʾalni, ʾihiya tisʾalni, tigul-li yaʿni nabī-la čiḏi, tadris, nabī-la mxallṣa d-dərāsa, nabī-la waḥda tištəġəl wəlla mā tištəġəl, mitḥajjba wəlla mū mitḥajjba. (8) ʾagul-lha ʿaṭīni šinu yištiġil wildič, yištiġil wəlla mā yištiġil. tigul-li yištiġil. (9) ʾagul-lha šinu šahādta, ʾasʾalha šinu šahādta, tgūl waḷḷah - illi tgūl mxəllaṣ iṯ-ṯānawiyya, w illi tgūl mxəllaṣ il-jāmʿa, w illi tgūl mxəllaṣ min barra, w illi tgūl mā ʿinda šahāda. (10) il-muhimm, ngul-lha inšāḷḷa, ʿala ṭ-ṭalab illi tabīna. (11) əndawwir-la bnayya. nāxəḏ ʾisma l-kāmil, ʾism il-walad il-kāmil, wə šuġla, il-maʿlūmāt illi ʿindna killaha, ndigg ḥagg ahl əl-bnayya, rəddi ʿalay baʿd ṯalāṯ tayyām w arədd ʿalēč. (12) ndawwir-la bnayya lli tnāsib-la. (13) ngūl ḥagg ahl əl-bint il-walad čiḏi, čiḏi - min - wild flān bən flān, yištiġil čiḏi, yištiġil čiḏi, tgūl inšāḷḷa ʾumm aḥmad, naʿṭīha w ngul-lha. (14) tgūl - tirjaʿ tgul-li ʾumm lə-bnayya, ʾumm lə-bnayya tirjaʿ tgul-li ya umm aḥmad, ʾinti taʿrfīna? (15) ʾagul-lha lā waḷḷa, ʾāna mā aʿrfa, il-ʾumm dāggat-li telifōn tgūl ʾabīč txaṭbi ḥagg wildi, šikil ma ʾinti mā aʿrfič, ʾāna mā aʿrfa, mā aʿrəf ʿanhum ʾay šay. (16) lamma ayība lukum, tsəʾlūn - ʾihiya tisʾəl - tsəʾlūn ʿanna w yisʾal ʿankum. (17) daggēna ḥagg umm il-walad, gilnā-lha lgēnā-lič bnayya, bint flān, mən binta? təsʾalni nafs illi səʾəlta. (18) təsʾalni, bint flān bən flān, ʾagul-lha, w tāxəḏ ʾismha ik-kāmil tgūl ḥagg waladha. (19) tgūl umm aḥmad, laʾ, xal ʾāna arūḥ ʾašūfha ʾawwal. (20) ʾāna mā ʾarḏa, ʾagul-lha laʾ, ʾawwal xalli l-walad iyyi yšūf lə-bnayya w yṭāliʿha bidūn ʾinti, yaʿni ʾinti maʿā w uxta mā yxālif, bass il-walad lāzim yiyi wiyyākum. (21) mā ʾarḏa axallīha tiyi b-rūḥha. (22) il-muhimm, yiyi - tgul-li inšaḷḷa, wāʿdīhum ʾay yōm niyi w nrūḥ maʿāč w nšūf lə-bnayya. (23) ʾadigg ḥagg ahal lə-bnayya w agūl tara l-yōm bīyu - binyīkum inšaḷḷa, ʾumma w ʾuxta w l-walad maʿāna. (24) yigʿəd il-walad, tidišš lə-bnayya, ya ʾumma yāyba ʿaṣīr, ya ʾumma bārid, ya ʾumma yaʿni ʾay šay, čāy, tidxal lə-bnayya w yšūf. (25) huwwa gāʿid, ʾāna agul-la hāḏi l-bnayya, tara šūfha, yšūfha, inšaḷḷa. (26) ʾiḏa yaʿni fī, ʾisʾalha, tabīha, mā tabīha, ʾisʾalha yaʿni ʿala š-še lli tabī, yəsʾalha. (27) lə-bnayya ṭabʿan tistəḥi, mū šikil yaʿni, waḥda baʿd tiyi tərkaḏ̣ čiḏi, tistəḥi. (28) yisʾalha, wēn tištəġlīn, šənnu dārsa. (29) ʾamma ʾāna agul-lha baʿd ʾinti siʾəlī. tisʾəla. (30) fī banāt yaʿni yigədrūn yisəʾlūn, fī banāt yistəḥūn, mā yisəʾlūn. (31) tisʾəla, gaʿədna, w səʾalha w səʾəlta, salām, maʿ s-salāma, ṭalaʿna, ṭalaʿna. (32) ʾāna ṭabʿan ʾāna ʾasʾal il-walad bi-s-sayyāra, ʾagūl la ha, š ʿəjibtak lə-bnayya wlīdi wəlla mā ʿəjibtak? (33) sāʿāt yrəddūn ʿalayy yaʿni fi nafs il-kalām, ygūl waḷḷa ʾumm aḥmad, ʿəjibatni lə-bnayya w šūfi radd lə-bnayya baʿd šənu, w sāʿāt lā waḷḷa, ygūl inšaḷḷa yṣīr xēr. (34) hāḏa lli ygul-lič yṣīr xēr, ʾaʿrəf ʾinna mā yabi l-bnayya, ʾeh, w illi ygul-lič waḷḷa siʾli l-bnayya šūfi ʾeš gālit ʿanni š rāyha fīni, hāḏa aʿrəf ʾinnahu yaʿni la xāṭir b-l-bnayya, ʾamma ha l-bnayya lha - ʾilha rāy. (35) il-muhimm, yigəṭṭūnni fi bēti w arjaʿ w adigg luhum telifōn, b-nafs il-wagt ʾadigg ḥagg ahl əl-bint telifōn ʾiḏa huwwa la xāṭir fīha, ʾadigg-luhum telifōn, hah? š rāykum fi l-walad? (36) gālat il-ʾumm ṭabʿan yaʿni l-ḥīn mā nigdar nrədd ʿalēč bi-hād d-digīga hāḏi, ḥatta lō l-bnayya laha xāṭir, mā nigdar nrədd ʿalēč. (37) ṣəbri-lna yōmēn ṯalāṯa ʾiḥna nrədd ʿalēč il-jawāb. (38) ʾaṣbir yōmēn ṯalāṯa, ham tdigg-li telifōn il-umm w tgul-li waḷḷa l-bnayya ʿajabha l-walad w inšaḷḷa s-suʾāl, nabi nisʾal ʿanna w hāḏa w yisʾəlūn ʿanna. ... --- (39) bass ʾawwal ygūlūn bi-l-xəṭbāt il-ʾawwaliyya mū čiḏi? --- (40) al-ḥīn ʾiḥna xəṭbātna l-ḥīn hāḏa čiḏi. --- (41) ʾawwal ygul-lič yaʿni timdaḥha, tilgēnha yaʿni mū ḥilwa mū jamīla w tḥuṭṭha bi-s-səma liʾanna ʾawwal mā kān yšūfha mū čiḏi? --- (42) ʾēh, mā kān yšūfha, ʾawwal mā kān yšūfha, ʿōra, ʿamya, ḥōla, ʿarya, ʾuhuwa w ḥaḏḏa, yiyībūnha mkamkama, mkamkama fi ʿbāyətha, māḥḥad yadri ʿanha šini ʾihiya. bass al-ḥīn laʾ, kill ši ʿa l-makšūf.

--- *(1) Look, Umm Ahmed, we want to ask you about how you learned matchmaking.* --- *(2) Please go ahead and ask.* --- *(3) How did you learn it, from whom did you take it, how did you acquire it?* --- *(4) Well, I learned it from a woman who makes matches, a professional matchmaker who makes matches, for years I used to come and go with her. She taught me how matchmaking is [done]. --- (5) How is the way [to do it]? --- (6) The way to do it is that the boy's mother, the boy's sister calls you on the phone and says, Umm So-and-So, we want for our son a wife (girl). (7) You tell her, Okay, God willing. She asks me, she asks me, she says, We want for him such and such, (a girl who is) studying, we want for him someone who has finished her studies, we want for him a girl who works, or doesn't work, veiled or not veiled. (8) I tell her, Give me (information on) what his job is, I tell (ask) her (if) he works or doesn't work, she tells me he works. (9) I say, What degree does he hold? I ask her what his degree is, she says, well - [there is one] who says he has finished secondary school, [one] who says he has finished university, [one] who says he has graduated from a school abroad, and [one] who says he has no degree. (10) Anyway, the important thing is, we tell her, Okay, God willing, whatever request you want. (11) We look for a girl for him. We take his full name, the full name of the boy and his job, the information that we have, all of it, about him, we call the girl's family, [saying], Get back in touch with me in three days and I'll give you an answer. (12) We look for a girl who is suitable for him. (13) We say to the girl's family, The boy is such and such, from - the son of so-and-so son of so-and-so, he works as such and such, she says, Okay, Umm Ahmed. We give her (the information) and tell her (all that). (14) She says, she comes back and tells us, the mother of the girl comes back and tells me, Umm Ahmed, do you know him? (15) I tell her, No, I don't know him. The mother has called me on the phone saying, I want you to find a bride for my son; the same way I don't know you, I don't know him, I don't know a thing about them. (16) When I bring him to [meet] you, you can inquire - [the girl's mother] inquires - you can inquire about him and he can inquire about you. (17) We have called the mother of the boy and told her we have found for you a girl, daughter of so-and-so, Daughter of whom? She asks me the same [things] that I had asked [the girl's family]. (18) She asks me, Daughter of so-and-so son of so-and-so, I tell her, and she takes [the girl's] full name to tell her son. (19) She says, Umm Ahmed, no, let me go and see her first. (20) I refuse, I tell her, No, first let the boy come and see the girl and take a look at her without - You, that is, you [can come] with him and his sister, that's okay, but the boy must come with you. (21) I refuse to let her come alone. (22) Anyway, he comes - She tells me, Okay, make a date [for] which day we will come, and I'll go with you and we'll see the girl. (23) I call the girl's family and say, Look, today they're coming - we're coming, God willing, his mother and his sister and the boy with us. (24) The boy sits, the girl comes in, either bringing juice or bringing a cold drink, or anything, tea, the girl enters and he sees [her]. (25) He is sitting [there], I tell him, This is the girl, go ahead, take a look at her. He looks at her, okay. (26) If, that is, there is [positive reaction, I say], Ask her, if you want her or whatnot, ask her about the thing you want. He asks. (27) The girl, of course, is shy, it's not seemly, that is, [for] a girl after all to come running like that, she's shy. (28) He asks her, Where do you work, what have you studied. (29) As for me, I tell her, Then you ask. She asks. (30) There are girls, that is, who can ask, and there are girls who are too shy and don't ask. (31) She asks, we sit, he asks her and she asks him, good-bye, good-bye, we leave, that's that. (32) I, of course, I ask the boy in the car, I say, Hmm? Did you like the girl, son, or didn't you like her? (33) Sometimes they answer me in the same words, saying, Well, Umm Ahmed, I liked the girl, see what the girl's reply is, and sometimes by God he says, Hopefully it will work out for the best. (34) The one that tells you hopefully it will work out for the best, I know that he doesn't want the girl, and the one who tells you, Well, ask the girl, see what she said about me, what her opinion of me is, that one, I know that he likes the girl; as for the girl, she has an opinion [too]. (35) Anyway, the important thing is, they drop me off at my house, and I go back and call them, at the same time I call the girl, if he likes her, I call them and [ask], What is your opinion of the boy? (36) The mother of the girl says, Of course, now, we can't answer you right this very minute, even if the girl likes the boy, we can't answer you. (37) Be patient with us two or three days and we'll give you an answer. (38) I give them two or three days, again the mother calls me and says, Well, the girl likes the boy, and now [it's time] to ask [about him], we want to ask about him and all that, and they ask about him. ... --- (39) But in the old days they say with the old matches it [wasn't] like that. ---*

(40) Now, us, our matchmaking now, this is the way it is. --- (41) In the old days [they] tell you she [the matchmaker] would praise her, you would find her [to be] not pretty, not beautiful, and she would raise her up to the sky (exaggerate in praising her) because in the old days [the groom] didn't used to see her, isn't that right? --- (42) Yeah, he didn't used to see her, in the old days he didn't used to see her, cross-eyed, blind, lame, [it was up to] him and his luck, they would bring her wrapped up, wrapped up in her abaya (cloak), no one knew anything about her, what she [was]. But now no, everything is out in the open.

Text B: In the Old Days (K3)

(١) لا، اكو الحين حبيبتي، ما تدرين انت بنتي، اكو ناس الحين غير الاول. الاول المرا تصبر. (٢) تعرفين ليش تصبر؟ أول تصبر [ا]لا طلّگها، تغربل ويّا عيالها، هه، إن مات رايلها تغربل. (٣) مو مثل الحين، البنت تشتغل، المرا تشتغل، مثل ما الريّال يدخّل معاش اهي تدخّل معاش. ما تصبر عل - هاذا. (٤) حنّا زمن أول عيوز مربوطة، المفاتيح بمخباط، تصكّ. العيايز يصكّون اول على الچنة ويصبرون، هه، أول غير. (٥) أول المرا چسوة الگيظ وچسوة الشتا. بس. (٦) ... الحين تعالي وين ما تدشّين وين ما تروحين ذيچ العيوز ... : آه! يغربل راح السكّر گال چذي والطبيب الثاني گال چذي وذا. (٧) و شوي وگالت ما شفت الچبرا؟ صحارة التفاح هالكبر، أ - بـ بـ بـ - والگيظ وچذ د -د -د - بس بال وتشكّي ومرض. (٨) هذا حنّا، العيايز والشباب، وي! ما شفت أثاث بيت فلان؟ وي! والله بيسوّي احسن منّي. (٩) ما شفت ذا - هالموديل؟ والله خذتَه بتسعين ... الحين موديل واثاث. والعيايز على التشكّي والبال والأكل. (١٠) أول حنّا - وعلي! المرا چسوة الگيظ وچسوة الشتا. بس. تصبر العيوز أول. ... (١١) الحين العيوز دْرَيولها واجف، دريوِلها واجف وهذا، هي من تصبح، اليوم چاي الضحى هني وباچر چاي - (١٢) أول لا، العيوز ... تربي هالياهل وتمهدَه وتغسّلَه تبابيه، هه، والچنة تطبخ تخوم تغسّل تسوّي. (١٣) الحين عيوز تيوّد الياهل؟ ما تيوّدَه والله ما تتصوّر - درَيوِلها واجف. (١٤) الحين اهي تاخذ من الشؤون مية دينار، شوفيها هندية،

فليبينية، سايگ، ثلاثة. (١٥) اهي تاخذ من الشؤون، هه، ليش؟ فلانة عندها انا باسوّي مثلها، فلانة سوّت چذي وفلان سوّى چذي. (١٦) الاخو يحسد الخو، والاخت تحسد الاخت. الحين الناس كل واحد يطالع الثاني.

(1) lā, ʾaku l-ḥīn ḥabībti, mā tadrīn inti binti, ʾaku nās al-ḥīn ġēr l-awwal. l-awwal il-mara taṣbir. (2) taʿrfīn lēš taṣbir? ʾawwal taṣbir la ṭallagha tġarbal wiyya ʿyālha, hah, ʾin māt rāyilha tiġarbal. (3) mū mitil al-ḥīn, il-bint tištiġəl, il-mara tištiġəl, mitil ma r-rayyāl ydaxxil maʿāš, ʾihi tdaxxil maʿāš. mā taṣbir ʿal - hāḏa. (4) ḥinna zaman ʾawwal ʿayūz marbūṭa l-mafatīḥ b-mixbāṭ, tṣəkk. il-ʿayāyiz yṣikkūn ʾawwal ʿala l-čanna w yṣəbrūn, hah, ʾawwal ġēr. (5) ʾawwal l-mara čiswit lə-gēḏ w čiswit lə-šta. bass. (6) ... al-ḥīn taʿāley wēn mā tdiššīn wēn mā trūḥīn, ḏič al-ʿayūz ... : ʾāh! yiġarbal rāḥ is-sikkar gāl čiḏi wi ṭ-ṭabīb iṯṯāni gāl čiḏi w ḏa (7) w šwayy w gālt mā šifti l-čabra, ṣaḥārt it-tuffāḥ ha l-kubur ʾa b - b - b - b - w l-gēḏ čiḏ - d - d - d - d - bass bāl w tišikkey w maraḏ. (8) hāḏa ḥinna l-ʿayāyiz. w iš-šabāb, wī! mā šifti ʾaṯāṯ bēt flān? wī! waḷḷa biysawwi ʾaḥsan minni. (9) mā šifti ḏa - ha l-mōdēl? waḷḷah xaḏtha b-tisʿīn ... al-ḥīn mōdēl w ʾaṯāṯ, wi l-ʿayāyiz ʿala t-tišikkey w l-bāl wi l-ʾakəl. (10) ʾawwal ḥinna - w ʿalayya! l-mara čiswat l-gēḏ w čiswat lə-šta. bass. taṣbir l-ʿayuz ʾawwal. ... (11) al-ḥīn l-ʿayūz, drēwilha wājif, drēwilha wājif w haḏa, hiya min tiṣbaḥ, il-yōm čāy iḏ-ḏəḥa hni, w bāčir čāy - . (12) ʾawwal lā, l-ʿayūz ... trabbi ha l-yāhil w tmahda w tġassla, ʾitbābīh, hah, w il-čanna tiṭbax, txōm, tġassil, tsawwi. (13) al-ḥīn ʿayūz tyawwid il-yāhil? mā tyawwida, waḷḷa mā tiṣawwar - drēwilha wājif. (14) al-ḥīn ʾihi tāxiḏ mn iš-šuʾūn myət dīnār, šūfīha hindiyya, filipiniyya, sāyig ṯalāṯa. (15) ʾihi tāxiḏ mn iš-šuʾūn, hah, lēš? flāna ʿindaha, ʾana basawwi miṯilha, flāna sawwat čiḏi w flān sawwa čiḏi. (16) l-ʾuxu yiḥasid il-xu w il-ʾuxət tḥasid il-ʾuxt, al-ḥīn in-nās kil wāḥid yṭāliʿ iṯ-ṯāni.

(1) No, there are now my dear, you don't know, you are [like] my daughter, there are people now not like the old days. In the old days, the woman would endure. (2) Do you know why she would endure? In the old days she would endure lest [her husband] divorce her, she would flounder with her kids. If her husband died she would flounder.

(3) Not like now, the girl works, the woman works, just like the man brings home a salary, she brings home a salary. She doesn't put up with - that. (4) We in the time of the old days the mother-in-law, the keys [were] tied in [her] breast pocket, she would close [the door]. The mothers-in-law would lock the daughters-in-law in in the old days, and they would endure, hmm, in the old days, it was different. (5) In the old days, the woman had only the [one] outfit for the summer and the [one] outfit for the winter. That's all. (6) ... Now, come [look], wherever you come, wherever you go, that old woman ... : Oh! [God] blast, the diabetes has gone [up], [the doctor] said this and the second doctor said that, and so forth. (7) And then [the old woman] says, Didn't you see the Chabra Market? The box of apples is this big blah blah blah and the summer is such blah blah blah - just worries and complaints and illness. (8) That's us the old women. And the young people, Oh! Didn't you see the furniture in so-and-so's house? Oh! By God he wants to do better than me. (9) Didn't you see that - that style [furniture]? Well, I got it for ninety [dinars] ... Nowadays [everything is about] styles and furniture, and the old women are into complaining and worries and food. (10) In the old days, we - I swear! - the woman [had one] clothing outfit for the summer and one outfit for the winter. That's all. The old woman used to endure. (11) Now, the old woman, her driver is standing by, her driver is standing by and all that, from the time she wakes up, today [she has] midmorning tea here, tomorrow tea [there] -. (12) In the old days no, the mother-in-law (old woman) ... she raises that child, she cradles him, she washes him, she coddles him, hah, and the daughter-in-law cooks, cleans the house, washes, does [housework]. (13) Nowadays does an old woman hold the child? She doesn't hold him. By God she can't imagine [doing anything herself] - her driver is standing by. (14) Now, she takes from the [Bureau of Social] Affairs 100 dinars, see her, an Indian, a Filipino, a driver, three [servants]. (15) She takes from the [Bureau of Social] Affairs, hah, why? So-and-so has, I want to do like her, so-and-so did thus and so-and-so did thus. (16) The brother envies the brother and the sister envies the sister, nowadays, people, everyone looks to the other [to see what they are doing].

Text C: A Romeo and Juliet Story (K3)

(١) شوفي. بنية ويّا ولد يدشّون في بغداد. (٢) ها مو بعيد، هاذا من عندچ الحين يمكن خمسة وثلاثين سنة. (٣) البنية مسيحية و، هه، هالصبي [ا]هله من اهل الزبير. يسمّونهم - --- يعني ناس طيّبين. --- (٤) هذيلا يدرسون البنت. البنت تحب الولد الولد يحب البنت. زين. (٥) ياوا، خلّصوا. خلّصوا الجامعة مال بغداد، ياوا. (٦) هاذي البنت في البصرة، الولد بن الزبير. (٧) والولد تمّ - مسيحيين، ما يخلّو - يشوفونه يحب بنتهم، بنتهم تحبّه، يروح وييي عليها، گالوا شلون؟ (٨) گالوا يللاخلْنا نتزوج. زين. (٩) ياوا، يا الولد خطبها من ابوها. ابوها وافگ، گال الا هي تبّيك وتحبك ما يخالف. نزين. (١٠) [ا]هل الولد ما رضَوا، مسيحية! شلون تاخذ مسيحية؟! ما رضَوا. لا، ما تاخذها. زين. (١١) هذيلا ش گالوا، بس ما دام [ا]هلك مو راضين بعد انت لا تيي لنا. بعد شلون تيي لنا؟ اول تيي وتروح علينا ليش بنت - البنت تبيك وانت تبيها بتتزوجون. (١٢) الحين [ا]هلك مو راضين تتزوج بنتنا شلون تيي لنا، ما يصير. يودّوا الولد. (١٣) البنت تحبَه، تمّت طاحت مريضة. (١٤) الولد ييي يطوف، كل يوم يروح وييي على الباب وتصگّه. (١٥) يگول عساني اراكم ولاّ ارى من يراكم مثل يگول --- (١٦) امرّ على الابواب - --- (١٧) امشي على الابواب من غير حاجةً عساني اراكم ولاّ ارى من يراكم. والبنت مريضة بالبيت. زين. (١٨) يوم واحد بعد الولد على العادة طايف، لگى الجنازة، إلاّ البنت! من كثر ما تحب الولد ماتت عليه. (١٩) الولد گوم گط روحَه ويّاها، موّت روحَه. گال بس خلص. (٢٠) گالوا هاذا شغلكم انتو يا الاهل حرام. خسرتو ولدكم. هاذا الحب اول.

(1) šūfi. bnayya wiyya walad, yidiššūn fi baġdād. (2) ha mū bʿīd hāḏa min ʿindič al-ḥīn yumkən xamsa w ṯalāṯīn sana. (3) lə-bnayya masīḥiyya wa, hah, ha lə-ṣbayy hala min ahal iz-z[u]bēr. ysammūnhum - --- yaʿni nās ṭayybīn. --- (4) haḏēla yidirsūn il-bint. il-bint tḥibb il-walad il-walad yḥibb il-bint. zēn. (5) yāw, xallaṣaw. xallaṣaw il-jāmʿa māl baġdād, yāw. (6) hāḏi l-bint fi l-baṣra, il-walad bən iz-zubēr. (7) w il-walad tamm -- masīḥiyyīn, mā yixallu -- yišūfūna yiḥibb binthum, binthum tḥibba, yirūḥ wi yiyi ʿalēha, gālu šlōn? (8) gālu yaḷḷa xalna

nitzawwaj. zēn. (9) yāw, ya l-walad xaṭabha min abūha. abūha wāfag, gāl ʾila hiya tabbīk w tḥibbak mā yxālif. nzēn. (10) hal il-walad mā riḏ̣aw, masīḥiyya! šlōn tāxiḏ masīḥiyya?! mā riḏ̣aw. lā, mā tāxiḏha. zēn. (11) haḏēla š gālaw, bass ma dām halak mū rāḏ̣īn baʿd ʾinta lā tyī-lna. baʿd šlōn tyī-lna? ʾawwal tyi w trūḥ ʿalēna lēš bint - il-bint tabbīk w inta tabbīha btitzawwajūn. (12) al-ḥīn halak mū rāḏ̣īn titzawwaj bintna šlōn tiyī-lna, mā yṣīr. yawwidaw il-walad. (13) il-bint tḥibba tammat ṭāḥat marīḏ̣a. (14) il-walad yiyi yṭūf, kil yōm yirūḥ w yiyi ʿala l-bāb w tṣikka. (15) yigūl ʿasāni arākum walla ara man yarākum miṯil yigūl --- (16) ʾamurru ʿala l-ʾabwāb --- (17) ʾamši ʿala l-abwāb min ġēri ḥājatan ʿasāni arākum wella ʾara man yarākum.[1] wi l-bint marīḏ̣a bi-l-bēt. zēn. (18) yōm wāḥid baʿd il-walad ʿala l-ʿāda ṭāyif, liga l-jināza, ʾilla l-bint! min kiṯir mā tḥibb il-walad mātat ʿalē. (19) il-walad baʿd gūm, gəṭṭ rūḥa wiyyāha, mawwat rūḥa. gāl bass xalaṣ. (20) gālu hāḏa šuġulkum ʾintu ya l-ʾahal ḥarām. xasartu waladkum. hāḏa l-ḥabb ʾawwal.

(1) See [now]. A girl and a boy, they go to Baghdad. (2) This [was] not long ago, from where you are now perhaps 35 years ago. (3) The girl is Christian, and huh, that boy, his family is from al-Zubayr [tribe]. Their name is - --- In other words, good people. --- (4) Those [people] [used to let] girls study. The girl loves the boy, the boy loves the girl. Okay. (5) They came, they finished. They finished the University of Baghdad, they came [back]. (6) This girl is in Basra, the boy is of the al-Zubayr. (7) The boy kept -- [the girl's family were] Christian, they wouldn't let -- they see him in love with their daughter, their daughter loves him, he comes and goes [visiting] her, they said, How [can we allow this]? (8) [The boy and girl] said, Let us get married. Fine. (9) They came [to do this], the boy came and asked for her hand from her father. Her father agreed; he said, If she wants you and loves you that's all right. (10) The boy's family did not approve, [She's] a Christian! How can you marry a Christian?! They did not

---

[1]The speaker quotes here with less than perfect accuracy a line of Classical Arabic poetry. Dwight Reynolds reports that the line comes from a song performed by simsimiyya musicians in Port Saʿīd, Egypt, and attributed to Shaykh Juyūšī, whose zāwiya lies in the Muqaṭṭam Hills outside Cairo.

approve. No, don't marry her. Okay. (11) Those people [the girl's family], what did they say, That's it, as long as your family hasn't approved of your marrying our daughter, how can you come to our house [to see her]? (12) Now, your family has not approved your marrying our daughter how can you come to our [house], it's not done. They prevented the boy [from seeing the girl]. (13) [But] the girl loves him: she went and fell ill. (14) The boy comes wandering, every day he goes and passes by the door, they close it [in his face]. (15) Like they say, "Perhaps I might see you or see someone who sees you." --- (16) "I pass by the gates" --- (17) "I pass by the gates without purpose, [hoping] perhaps I might see you or see someone who sees you." (18) One day, again, as was his habit, the boy [was] wandering around, he found the funeral - it was the girl! She loved the boy so much, she died over him. (19) The boy then, get up! He did away with himself along with her, killed himself. He said, that's it, it's all over. (20) They said, This is your doing, you, family [of the boy], for shame. You lost your son. That is love in the old days.

References

ʿAbd al-ʿāl, ʿAbd al-Munʿim. 1968. *Lahjat Šamāl al-Maġrib: Ṭaṭwān wa mā Ḥawlahā.* Cairo: Dār al-Kitāb al-ʿArabī.

ʾAbū Ḥākima, ʾAḥmad Muṣṭafā. 1984. *Tārīx al-Kuwayt al-Ḥadīṯ.* Kuwait: Ḏāt al-Salāsil.

Ambros, Arne. 1977. *Damascus Arabic.* Afroasiatic Dialects, 3. Malibu: Undena Publications.

Anderson, Lloyd. 1982. "The 'Perfect' as a Universal and as a Language-Specific Category." *Tense-Aspect: Between Semantics and Pragmatics*, ed. Paul J. Hopper, 227-64. Amsterdam/Philadelphia: John Benjamins.

Anttila, Raimo. 1989. *Historical and Comparative Linguistics.* Current Issues in Linguistic Theory, 6. Amsterdam/Philadelphia: John Benjamins.

Badawi, El-Said, and Martin Hinds. 1986. *A Dictionary of Egyptian Arabic.* Beirut: Librairie du Liban.

Bakkala, Muhammad Hassan. 1983. *Arabic Linguistics: An Introduction and Bibliography.* UK: Mansell.

Barlow, Michael, and Charles A. Ferguson, eds. 1988. *Agreement in Natural Language: Approaches, Theories, Descriptions.* Palo Alto: Center for the Study of Language and Information.

Behnstedt, Peter. 1978. "Zur Dialektgeographie des Niledeltas." *ZAL* 1:64-92.

_______. 1980. "Zum ursprünglichen Dialekt von Alexandria." *ZDMG* 130:35-50.

_______. 1989. "Christlich-Aleppinische Texte." *ZAL* 20:43-89.

_______. 1990. "Mʾaḏḏamiiye: ein neuer qeltu-Dialekt aus Syrien." *ZAL* 22:44-66.

Behnstedt, Peter, and Manfred Woidich. 1985. *Die ägyptisch-arabischen Dialekte.* 2 vols. Beihefte zum Tübinger Atlas des vorderen Orients, series B, 50/1, 2. Wiesbaden: Ludwig Reichert Verlag.

_______. 1987. *Die ägyptisch-arabiscen Dialekte: Texte, Teil 1.* Beihefte zum Tübinger Atlas des vorderen Orients, series B, 50/3. Wiesbaden: Ludwig Reichert Verlag.

_______ . 1988. *Die ägyptisch-arabiscen Dialekte: Texte, Teil 2.* Beihefte zum Tübinger Atlas des vorderen Orients, series B, 50/3. Wiesbaden: Ludwig Reichert Verlag.

_______ . 1994. *Die ägiptisch-arabiscen Dialekte: Glossar Arabisch-Deutsch.* Beihefte zum Tübinger Atlas des vorderen Orients, series B, 50/4. Wiesbaden: Ludwig Reichert Verlag.

Belnap, Kirk. 1991. "Grammatical Agreement Variation in Cairene Arabic." Unpublished Ph.D. dissertation, University of Pennsylvania.

Bishai, Wislon B. 1962. "Coptic Grammatical Influence on Egyptian Arabic." *JAOS* 82:285-89.

Blanc, Haim. 1964. *Communal Dialects in Baghdad.* Cambridge MA: Harvard University Press.

_______ . 1970. "Dual and Pseudo-dual in the Arabic Dialects." *Language* 46:42-57.

Blau, Joshua. 1960. *Syntax des Palästinensischen Bauerndialekts von Bīr Zēt, auf Grund der Volkserzählungen aus Palästina von Hans Schmidt und Paul Kahle.* Beitrage zur Sprach- und Kulturgeschichte des Orients, 13. Waldorf-Hessen.

_______ . 1965. *The Emergence and Linguistic Background of Judeo-Arabic: A study of the origins of Middle Arabic.* London: Oxford University Press.

_______ . 1966-67. *A Grammar of Christian Arabic, Based Mainly on South-Palestinian texts from the First Millennium.* 3 vols. Louvain: Imprimierie Orientaliste.

Bloch, Ariel. 1965. *Die Hypotaxe im damaszenisch-Arabischen, mit Vergleichen zur Hypotaxe im Klassisch-Arabischen. AKM* 35 (4).

_______ . 1986. *Studies in Arabic Syntax and Semantics.* Wiesbaden: Otto Harrassowitz.

Bloch, Ariel, and Heinz Grotzfeld. 1964. *Damaszenisch-Arabische Texte. AKM* 35 (2).

Brown, Gillian and Yule, George. 1983. *Discourse Analysis.* Cambridge: Cambridge University Press.

Bybee, Joan, Revere Perkins, and William Pagliuca. 1994. *The Evolution of Grammar: Tense, Aspect, and Modality in the Languages of the World.* Chicago: University of Chicago Press.

Bybee, Joan , John Haiman, and Sandra A. Thompson, eds. 1997. *Essays on Language Function and Language Type.* Amsterdam/Philadelphia: John Benjamins.

Bynon, T. 1977. *Historical Linguistsics.* Cambridge: Cambridge University Press.

Cantarino, Vincente. 1975. *Syntax of Modern Arabic Prose.* 3 vols. Bloomington: Indiana University Press.

Cantineau, J. 1946. *Les Parles Arabes du Ḥōrān.* Paris: Librarie C. Klincksieck.

Caubet, Dominique. 1983. *La Détermination en Arabe Marocain.* Laboratoire de Linguistique Formelle, Collection ERA 642. Paris: Université Paris, Département de Recherches Lingustiques.

_______. 1993. *L'Arabe Marocain.* 2 vols. Études Chamito-Sémitiques. Paris-Louvain: Éditions Peeters.

_______. 1995. "ža, Élément Narratif dans le Récit Familier en Arabe Marocain." *Dialectologia Arabica. A Collection of Articles in Honour of the Sixtieth Birthday of Professor Heikki Palva,* ed. Tapani Harviainen, Asko Parpola, and Harry Halén, 41-48. *Studia Orientalia 75.* Helsinki: The Finnish Oriental Society.

Chafe, Wallace L. 1976. "Givennness, Contrastiveness, Definiteness, Subjects, Topics, and Point of View." *Subject and Topic,* ed. Charles N. Li, 25-56. New York: Academic Press.

Cohen, David. 1970. *Etudes de Linguistique Semitique et Arabe.* The Hague: Mouton.

Comrie, Bernard. 1976. *Aspect.* Cambridge: Cambridge University Press.

_______. 1981. *Language Universals and Linguistic Typology: Syntax and Morphology.* Chicago: University of Chicago Press.

_______. 1985. *Tense.* Cambridge: Cambridge University Press.

Corriente, Federico. 1977. *A Grammatical Sketch of the Spanish Arabic Dialect Bundle.* Madrid: Instituto Hispano-Arabe de Cultura.

Cowell, Mark. 1964. *A Reference Grammar of Syrian Arabic.* Washington DC: Georgetown University Press.

Croft, William. 1990. *Typology and Universals.* Cambridge Textbooks in Linguistics. Cambridge: Cambridge University Press.

Czapkiewicz, Andrzej. 1975. *The Verb in Modern Arabic Dialects as an Exponent of the Development Processes Occuring in them.* Wroclaw: Wydawnictwo Polskiej Akademii Nauk.

Denz, Adolf. 1971. *Die Verbalsyntax des neuarabischen Dialektes von Kwayris (Irak) mit einer einleitenden allgemeinen Tempus- und Aspektlehre. AKM* 40:1.

Diem, Werner. 1986. "Alienable und inalienable Possession im Semitischen." *ZDMG* 136 (2):227-91.

Downing, Pamela, and Michael Noonan, eds. 1995. *Word Order in Discourse.* Typological Studies in Language, 30. Amsterdam/Philadelphia: John Benjamins.

Eid, Mushira. 1983. "On the Communicative Function of Subject Pronouns in Arabic." *Journal of Linguistics* 19 (2):287-303.

_______. 1991. "Copula Pronouns in Arabic and Hebrew." *Perspectives on Arabic Linguistics III*, ed. Bernard Comrie and Mushira Eid, 31-61. Current Issues in Linguistic Theory, 80. Amsterdam/Philadelphia: John Benjamins.

_______. 1992. "Pronouns, Questions, and Agreement." *Perspectives on Arabic Linguistics IV*, ed. Ellen Broselow, Mushira Eid, and John McCarthy, 107-42. Current Issues in Linguistic Theory, 85. Amsterdam/ Philadelphia: John Benjamins.

_______. 1996. "Things are Not What They Seem: Pronoun Doubling in Bilinguial and Monolingual Grammars." *Perspectives on Arabic Linguistics VIII*, ed. Mushira Eid, 7-30. Current Issues in Linguistic Theory, 134. Amsterdam/Philadelphia: John Benjamins.

Eisele, John. 1988. "The Syntax and Semantics of Tense, Aspect and Time Reference in Cairene Arabic." Unpublished Ph.D. dissertation, University of Chicago.

_______. 1990a. "Time Reference, Tense, and Formal Aspect in Cairene Arabic." *Perspectives on Arabic Linguistics I,* ed. Mushira Eid, 173-212. Current Issues in Linguistic Theory, 63. Amsterdam/Philadelphia: John Benjamins.

_______. 1990b. "Aspectual Classification of Verbs in Cairene Arabic." *Perspectives on Arabic Linguistics II*, ed. Mushira Eid and John McCarthy, 192-233. Current Issues in Linguistic Theory, 72. Amsterdam/Philadelphia: John Benjamins.

_______ . 1992. "Egyptian Arabic Auxiliaries and the Category of AUX." *Perspectives on Arabic Linguistics IV*, ed. Ellen Broselow, Mushira Eid, and John McCarthy, 143-65. Current Issues in Linguistic Theory, 85. Amsterdam/Philadelphia: John Benjamins.

Ennaji, Moha. 1985. *Contrastive Syntax: English, Moroccan Arabic and Berber Complex Sentences.* Wuerzburg: Koenigshausen and Neumann.

Erwin, Wallace. 1963. *A Short Reference Grammar of Iraqi Arabic.* Washington DC: Georgetown University Press.

Fassi Fehri, Adbelkader. 1988. "Agreement in Arabic, Binding and Coherence." *Agreement in Natural Language: Approaches, Theories, Descriptions*, ed. Michael Barlow and Charles A. Ferguson, 107-58. Palo Alto: Center for the Study of Language and Information.

Feghali, Michel. 1928. *Syntaxe des parles arabes actuels du Liban.* Paris: Édouard Champion.

Ferguson, Charles A. 1959a. "The Arabic Koine." *Language* 35:4, 616-30.

_______ . 1959b. "Diglossia." *Word* 15:325-40.

Fischer, Wolfdietrich. 1959. *Die demonstrativen Bildungen der neuarabischen Dialekte: Ein Beitrag zur historischen Grammatik des Arabischen.* The Hague: Mouton.

_______ . 1995. "Zum Verhältnis der neuarabischen Dialekte zum Klassisch-Arabischen." *Dialectologia Arabica. A Collection of Articles in Honour of the Sixtieth Birthday of Professor Heikki Palva,* ed. Tapani Harviainen, Asko Parpola, and Harry Halén. Studia Orientalia 75. Helsinki: Finnish Oriental Society.

Fischer, Wolfdietrich, and Jastrow, Otto, eds. 1980. *Handbuch der arabischen Dialekte.* Wiesbaden: Otto Harrassowitz.

Fleisch, H. 1974. "Sur l'Aspect dans le Verbe en Arabe Classique." *Arabica* 22:11-19.

Givón, Talmy. 1979a. *On Understanding Grammar.* New York: Academic Press.

_______ , ed. 1979b. *Discourse and Syntax.* Syntax and Semantics, 12. New York: Academic Press.

Grand'henry, Jacques. 1976. *Les Parlers Arabes de la Region du Mzab.* Studies in Semitic Languages and Linguistics, V. Leiden: Brill.

Green, Georgia M., and Jerry L. Morgan. 1996. *Practical Guide to Syntactic Analysis.* CSLI Lecture Notes, No. 67. Stanford University: Center for the Study of Language and Information.

Greenberg, J., Ferguson, C. and Moravicsik, E., eds. 1978. *Universals of Human Language.* Stanford: Stanford University Press.

Grotzfeld, Heinz. 1965. *Syrisch-arabische Grammatik (Dialekt von Damaskus).* Porta Linguarum Orientalium 8. Wiesbaden: Otto Harrassowitz.

Haeri, Niloofar. 1996. *The Sociolinguistic Market of Cairo: Gender, Class, and Education.* Library of Arabic Linguistics, 13. London: Kegan Paul International.

Haiman, John. 1985. *Natural Syntax.* Cambridge: Cambridge University Press.

Harning, Kerstin Eskell. 1980. *The Analytical Genitive in the Modern Arabic Dialects.* Orientalia Gothoburgensia, 5. Stockholm.

Harrell, Richard. 1962. *A Short Reference Grammar of Moroccan Arabic.* Washington DC: Georgetown University Press.

Harris, John. 1984. "Syntactic Variation and Dialect Divergence." *Journal of Linguistics* 20: 303-27.

Hawkins, John A. 1994. *A Performance Theory of Order and Constituency.* Cambridge: Cambridge University Press.

_______ , ed. 1988. *Explaining Language Universals.* Oxford: Blackwell.

Holes, Clive. 1983. "Bahraini dialects: Sectarian Differences and the Sedentary/Nomadic Split." *ZAL* 10:7-38.

_______ . 1990. *Gulf Arabic.* London: Routledge.

_______ . 1991. "Kashkasha and the Fronting and Affrication of the Velar Stops Revisited: A Contribution to the Historical Phonology of the Peninsular Arabic Dialects." *Semitic Studies in Honor of Wold Leslau,* ed. Alan S. Kaye, i:652-78. Wiesbaden: Otto Harrassowitz.

_______ . 1995. *Modern Arabic: Structures, Functions, and Variations.* London: Longman.

Hopper, Paul J. 1979. "Aspect and Foregrounding in Discourse." *Discourse and Syntax*, ed. Talmy Givón, 213-42. New York: Academic Press.

_______, ed. 1982. *Tense-Aspect: Between Semantics and Pragmatics.* Amsterdam/Philadelphia: John Benjamins.

Hopper, Paul J., and Sandra Thompson. 1980. "The Transitivity Hypothesis." *Language* 56:251-99.

Ingham, Bruce. 1973. "Urban and Rural Arabic in Khuzistan." *BSOAS* 36:533-53.

_______. 1982. *North east Arabian Dialects.* Library of Arabic Linguistics, 3. London: Kegan Paul International.

_______. 1994. *Najdi Arabic: Central Arabian.* London Oriental and African Language Library, I. Amsterdam/Philadelphia: John Benjamins.

Isaksson, Bo. 1995. "Arabic Dialectology: The State of the Art." (Review of *Dialectologia Arabica. A Collection of Articles in Honour of the Sixtieth Birthday of Professor Heikki Palva,* ed. Tapani Harviainen, Asko Parpola, and Harry Halén. Studia Orientalia 75. Helsinki: The Finnish Oriental Society.) *Orientalia Suecana* 43-44 (1994-1995):115-32.

Janda, Laura A. 1999. "Whence Virility? The Rise of a New Gender Distinction in the History of Slavic." *Slavic Gender Linguistics*, ed. Margaret H. Mills, 201-28. Amsterdam/Philadelphia: John Benjamins.

Jastrow, Otto. 1978. *Die Mesopotamisch-Arabischen Qəltu-Dialekte.* 2 vols. *AKM* 45-46.

Jelinek, Eloise. 1983. "Person-Subject Marking in AUX in Egyptian Arabic." *Linguistic Categories: Auxiliaries and Related Puzzles*, ed. Frank Heny and Barry Richards, i:21-46. Dordrecht: D. Reidel Publishing Co.

Jiha, Michel. 1964. *Der arabische Dialekt von Bismizzin: Volkstumliche Texte aus einem libanesischen Dorf mit Grundzugen der Laut- und Formenlehre.* Beiruter Texte und Studien, 1. Wiesbaden: F. Steiner.

Johnstone, T.M. 1967. *Eastern Arabian Dialect Studies.* London Oriental Series 17. London: Oxford University Press.

Keenan, Edward L. and Bernard Comrie. 1977. "Noun Phrase Accessibility and Universal Grammar." *Linguistic Inquiry* 8:63-99.

Khalafallah, Abdelghany. 1969. *A Descriptive Grammar of Saʿīdi Egyptian Arabic.* The Hague: Mouton.

Khan, Geoffrey A. 1984. "Object Markers and Agreement Pronouns in Semitic Languages." *BSOAS* 47:468-500.

_______. 1988. *Studies in Semitic Syntax.* Oxford: Oxford University Press.

Kuno, Susumu. 1976. "Subject, Theme, and the Speaker's Empathy--A Reexamination of Relative Phenomena." *Subject and Topic*, ed. Charles N. Li, 417-44. New York: Academic Press.

Kurylowicz, J. 1973. "Verbal Aspect in Semitic." *Oriens* 42:114-20.

Lerchundi, Joseph. 1900. *Rudiments of the Arabic-Vulgar of Morocco.* Trans. James M. Macleod. Tangier: Spanish Catholic Mission Press.

Levin, Aryeh. 1987. "The Particle *la* as an Object Marker in Some Arabic Dialects of the Galilee." *ZAL* 17:31-40.

Lewin, Bernhard. 1966. *Arabische Texte im Dialekt von Hama.* Beiruter Texte und Studien, 2. Beirut: Orient-Institut der Deutschen Morgenländischen Gesellschaft.

Li, Charles N. 1997. "On Zero-Anaphora." *Essays on Language Function and Language Type,* ed. Joan Bybee, John Haiman, and Sandra A. Thompson, 275-300. Amsterdam/Philadeplphia: John Benjamins.

_______, ed. 1976. *Subject and Topic.* New York: Academic Press.

_______, ed. 1977. *Mechanisms of Syntactic Change* Austin: University of Texas Press.

Li, Charles N., and Sandra A. Thompson. 1976. "Subject and Topic: A New Typology of Language." *Subject and Topic,* ed. Charles N. Li, 457-89. New York: Academic Press.

_______. 1977. "A Mechanism for the Development of Copula Morphemes." *Mechanisms of Syntactic Change*, ed. Charles N. Li, 419-44. Austin: University of Texas Press.

_______. 1981. *Mandarin Chinese: A Functional Reference Grammar.* Berkeley, Los Angeles, London: University of California Press.

Li, Charles N., Sandra A. Thompson, and R. McMillan Thompson. 1982. "The Discourse Motivation for the Perfect Aspect: The Mandarin Particle *le*." *Tense-Aspect: Between Semantics and Pragmatics*, ed. Paul Hopper, 19-44. Amsterdam/Philadelphia: John Benjamins.

Longacre, Robert E. 1995. "Left Shifts in Strongly VSO Languages." *Word Order in Discourse*, ed. Pamela Downing and Michael Noonan, 331-54. Typological Studies in Language, 30. Amsterdam/Philadelphia: John Benjamins.

Lord, Carol, and Kathleen Dahlgren. 1997. "Participant and Event Anaphora in Newspaper Articles." *Essays on Language Function and Language Type*, ed. Joan Bybee, John Haiman, and Sandra A. Thompson, 323-56. Amsterdam/Philadeplphia: John Benjamins.

Lyons, John. 1977. *Semantics.* 2 vols. Cambridge: Cambridge University Press.

Mahdi, Muhsin, ed. 1984. *Alf Layla wa Layla.* 2 vols. Leiden: Brill.

Marçais, P. 1977. *Esquisse Grammatical de L'Arabe Maghrébin.* Paris: Librarie d'Amérique et d'Orient.

al-Maʿtūq, Šarīfa. 1986. *Lahjat ʿAjmān fī l-Kuwayt.* Kuwait: Markaz al-Turāṯ aš-Šaʿbī li-Duwal al-Xalīj al-ʿArabiyya.

McCarus, Ernest. 1976. "A Semantic Analysis of Arabic Verbs." *Michigan Studies in Honor of George C. Cameron*, ed. Louis Orlin, 3-28. Ann Arbor: Dept. of Near Eastern Studies, University of Michigan.

Mills, Margaret H., ed. 1999. *Slavic Gender Linguistics*. Pragmatics and Beyond, 61. Amsterdam/Philadelphia: John Benjamins.

Mitchell, T.F. 1952. "The Active Participle in an Arabic dialect of Cyrenaica." *BSOAS* 14:11-33.

_______ . 1956. *An Introduction to Egyptian Colloquial Arabic*. London: Oxford University Press.

_______ . 1973. "Aspects of Concord Revisited, with Special Reference to Sindhi and Cairene Arabic." *Archivum Linguisticum* 4 (new series):27-50.

_______ . 1978. "Educated Spoken Arabic in Egypt and the Levant, with Special Reference to Participle and Tense." *Journal of Linguistics* 14:227-58.

Mitchell, T. F., and S. A. El-Hassan. 1994. *Modality, Mood and Aspect in Spoken Arabic With Special Reference to Egypt and the Levant.* London: Kegan Paul International.

Moutaouakil, Ahmed. 1989. *Pragmatic Functions in a Functional Grammar of Arabic.* Drodrecht/Providence: Foris Publications.

al-Najjar, Balkees. 1984. "The Syntax and Semantics of Verbal Aspect in Kuwaiti Arabic." Unpublished Ph.D. dissertation, University of Utah.

Nelson, Gayle L., Mahmoud Al-Batal, and Erin Echols. 1996. "Arabic and English Compliment Responses: Potential for Pragmatic Failure." *Applied Linguistics* 17 (4):411-32.

Palmer, F. R. 1986. *Mood and Modality.* Cambridge: Cambridge University Press.

Palva, Heikke. 1977. "The Descriptive Imperative of Narrative Style in Spoken Arabic." *Folia Orientalia* 18:5-26.

_______ . 1991. "The form jāk in Bedouin narrative style." *Studia Orientalia* 67:55-64.

Parkinson, Dilworth. 1985. *Constructing the Social Context of Communication: Terms of Address in Egyptian Arabic.* Contributions to the Sociology of Language, 41. Berlin: Mouton.

Payne, Doris L. 1995. "Verb Initial Languages and Information Order." *Word Order in Discourse*, ed. Pamela Downing and Michael Noonan, 449-86. Typological Studies in Language, 30. Amsterdam/Philadelphia: John Benjamins.

Qafisheh, Hamdi A. 1975. *A Short Reference Grammar of Gulf Arabic.* Tucson: University of Arizona Press.

Reesnink, Pieter. 1984. "Similitudes Syntaxiques en Arabe et Berbère." *Current Progress in Afro-Asiatic Linguistics: Papers of the Third International Hamito-Semitic Congress*, ed. James Bynon, 327-54. Amsterdam: John Benjamins.

Retsö, Jan. 1983. *The Finite Passive Voice in Modern Arabic Dialects.* Stockholm: Göteborgs Universitat.

Rosenhouse, Judith. 1978. "Circumstantial Clauses in Some Arabic Dialects." *ZDMG* 128:227-36.

_______ . 1984a. *The Bedouin Arabic Dialects.* Wiesbaden: Otto Harrassowitz.

_______ . 1984b. "Remarks on the Uses of Various Patterns of Demonstrative Pronouns in Modern Arabic Dialects." *ZDMG* 134:250-56.

Sallam, A. M. 1979. "Concordial Relations within the Noun Phrase in Educated Spoken Arabic (ESA)." *Archivum Linguisticum* 10 (new series):20-56.

Shumaker, Linda. 1981. "Word Order and Case in Middle Arabic." Unpublished Ph.D. dissertation, Harvard University.

Spitaler, A. 1962. "Al-Ḥamdu Lillāhi llaḏi und Verwandtes. Ein Beitrag zur mittel- und neuarabischen Syntax." *Oriens* 15:97-114.

Spitta Bey, G. 1883. *Contes Arabes modernes.* Leiden and Paris: n.p..

Timberlake, Alan. 1977. "Reanalysis and Actualization in Syntactic Change." *Mechanisms of Syntactic Change*, ed. Charles N. Li. Austin: University of Texas Press.

Tomlin, Russell S. 1995. "Focal Attention, Voice, and Word Order: An Experimental, Cross-Linguistic Study." *Word Order in Discourse*, ed. Pamela Downing and Michael Noonan, 517-54. Typological Studies in Language, 30. Amsterdam/Philadelphia: John Benjamins.

el-Tonsi, Abbas. 1982. *Egyptian Colloquial Arabic: A Structure Review.* 2 vols. Cairo: American University in Cairo Press.

Traugott, Elizabeth C., and Ekkehard König. 1991. "The Semantics-Pragmatics of Grammaticalization Revisited." *Approaches to Grammaticalization*, ed. Elizabeth C. Traugott and Bernd Heine, 2 vols. Amsterdam/Philadelphia: John Benjamins.

al-Tūnjī, Muḥammad, and Rājī al-ʾAsmar. 1993. *al-Muʿjam al-Mufaṣṣal fī ʿUlūm il-Luġa (al-Alsuniyyāt).* Beirut: Dār al-Kutub al-ʿIlmiyya.

Versteegh, Cornelis. 1984. *Pidginization and Creolization: The Case of Arabic.* Current Issues in Linguistic Theory, 33. Amsterdam/Philadelphia: John Benjamins.

Wald, Benji. 1983. "Referents and Topic within and across Discourse Units: Observations from Current Vernacular English." *Discourse Perspectives on Syntax*, ed. Flora Klein-Andreu, 91-116. New York: Academic Press.

Walters, Keith. 1988. "Dialectology." *Language: The Socio-cultural Context*, ed. Frederick J. Newmeyer. Linguistics: The Cambridge Survey, IV. Cambridge: Cambridge University Press.

Wild, S. 1964. "Die resultative Funktion des aktiven Partizips in den syrisch-arabischen Dialekten des Arabischen." *ZDMG* 114:239-54.

Wise, Hilary. 1972. "Concord in Spoken Egyptian Arabic." *Archivum Linguisticum* 3 (new series):7-18.

Woidich, Manfred. 1968. *Negation und Negative Sätze im Ägyptisch-Arabischen.* Munich.

_______. 1975. "Zur Funktion des aktiven Partizips im Kairenisch-Arabischen." *ZDMG* 125:273-93.

_______. 1980a. "illi als Konjunktion im Kairenischen." *Studien aus Arabistik und Semitistik*, ed. Werner Diem and Stefan Wild, 224-38. Wiesbaden: Otto Harrassowitz.

_______. 1980b. "Zum Dialekt von il-ʿAwâmra in der östlichen šarqiyya (Ägypten). Teil II: Texte und Glossar." *ZAL* 4:31-60.

_______. 1989. *Bibliographie zum Ägyptisch-Arabischen.* I.M.N.O. Amsterdam: University of Amsterdam.

_______. 1991. "Die Formtypen des Zustandssatzes im Kaireischen." *ZAL* 23: 66-98.

Wright, William. 1898. *A Grammar of the Arabic Language.* 2 vols. London: Cambridge University Press.

Abbreviations:

AKM *Abhandlungen für die Kunde des Morgenlandes*
BSOAS *Bulletin of the School of Oriental and African Studies*
JAOS *Journal of the American Oriental Society*
ZAL *Zeitschrift für arabische Linguistik*
ZDMG *Zeitschrift der Deutsche Morgenländische Gesellschaft*

Subject Index

Author Index